time of the season:

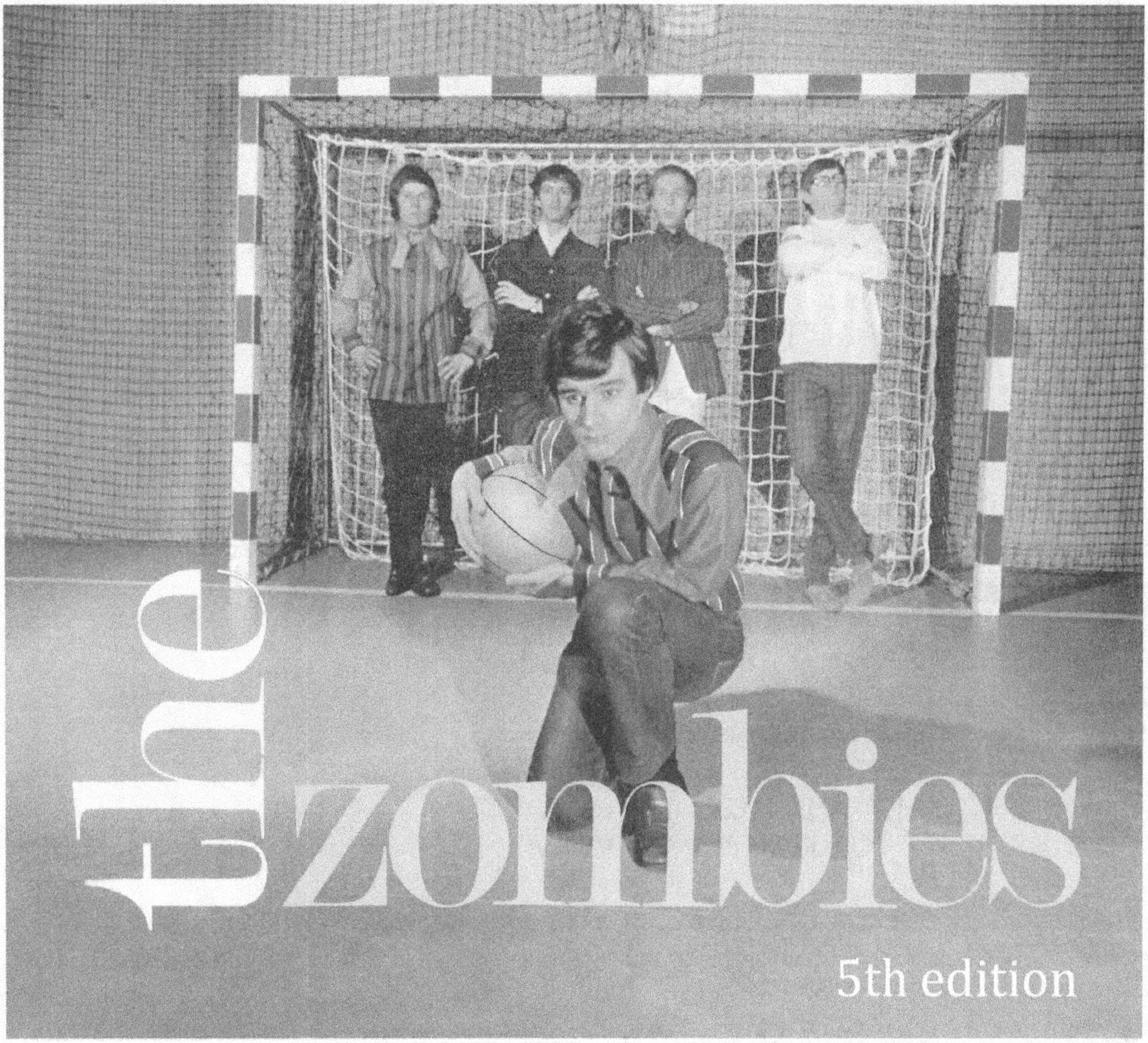

the zombies
5th edition

collector's guide
* * * *
greg russo

"Time Of The Season: The Zombies Collector's Guide" was completed March 30, 1999. The revised edition was completed on February 18, 2007, with additional revisions completed July 23, 2008. The 4th edition was completed on October 21, 2016. The 5th edition was completed on August 19, 2022.

First edition: May 1999. Revised editions: March 2007 and August 2008. 4th edition: November 2016. 5th edition - August 2022.

Copyright © 1999, 2007, 2008, 2016, 2022 Crossfire Publications.

All photos are from the collection of Greg Russo unless otherwise noted.

Special thanks: The Zombies, Carole Broughton, Mike Ober, Andy Barnes, Charles Patton, Priya Acharya, Frans de Graaff, Jerry Ramsey, Ron Furmanek, Paul Surratt, Phil Cohen, Doug Hinman, Don Pedini, Jean-Jacques Jonatowski, and Terry Hounsome.

All rights reserved. Printed in the US.

No part of this book may be used or reproduced in any manner whatsoever without written permission of Crossfire Publications.

The Chris White interview segments are courtesy of Mike Ober and originally appeared in his book "Then Play On."

MARQUIS ENTERPRISES LTD. is the worldwide owner of all Zombies master recordings. Please direct all inquiries to: CAROLE BROUGHTON, Director, Marquis Enterprises Ltd., 1 Wyndham Yard, Wyndham Place, London W1H 1AR, England. Phone: (0171) 402-7433, Fax: (0171) 402-2866.

Also available from Crossfire Publications are Greg Russo's other books:
YARDBIRDS: THE ULTIMATE RAVE-UP
MANNERISMS: THE FIVE PHASES OF MANFRED MANN
COSMIK DEBRIS: THE COLLECTED HISTORY & IMPROVISATIONS OF FRANK ZAPPA
ANCIENT ARMAMENTS: THE FRANK ZAPPA SINGLES PROJECT
FLYING COLOURS: THE JETHRO TULL REFERENCE MANUAL

For more details, please write to: Crossfire Publications, 54 Chester Avenue, Stewart Manor, New York 11530 USA.
Website: http://www.crossfirepublications.com   e-mail: crossfirepublications@gmail.com

The official Zombies website is located at: http://www.thezombiesmusic.com, and their YouTube page is located at: http://www.youtube.com/thezombies

The official Colin Blunstone website is located at: http://www.colinblunstone.co.uk

The official Rod Argent website is located at: http://www.rodargent.com

Please see the site for the late Sebastián Santa Maria: http://www.pianosantamaria.com

ISBN: 978-0-9791845-7-4

TABLE OF CONTENTS

	Page
Introduction	4
The History Of The Zombies	6
Origins	6
Putting It All Together	8
The Final Ingredient	8
Zombies Rise	9
The Herts Beat Competition	10
The First Recordings	12
"She's Not There"	13
Professional Zombies	14
Conquering America	16
The First Album And "Bunny Lake Is Missing"	21
Experimenting With The Past	23
"Begin Here"	24
Disappointment Sets In	27
The Philippine Debacle	31
"Odessey And Oracle" In The Making	31
The End And A New Beginning	35
"Time Of The Season" And The New Zombies	36
Zombies "R.I.P."	40
The Returns Of The Zombies	43
Reissues	50
The Zombies: 1999 To The Present	54
The BBC Recordings	68
Final Overview	68
What Have They Been Doing? – The Solo Years:	
Rod Argent	70
Colin Blunstone	80
Hugh Grundy	85
Paul Atkinson	85
Chris White	86
Zombies Discography	90
Decca/Parrot – Recorded Tracks	103
CBS/Date – Recorded Tracks	110
Various Labels – Recorded Tracks	113
Zombies Radio Appearances	118
Zombies Television, Film, and Video Appearances	120
Zombies Recording Placements in Television, Film, and Video	122
Zombies Recordings in Commercials	125
Samples/Remixes of Zombies Tracks	125
Zombies & Related Publications	125
The Zombies Concert Listing	126
The Solo Recordings of The Zombies (with radio, television, film, video appearances, and concert listings):	
Rod Argent	132
Colin Blunstone	157
Colin Blunstone Rod Argent The Zombies	173

INTRODUCTION

When I originally put a Zombies article together for the long-defunct Discoveries Magazine in 1993, I expected it to be printed within a few months. Little did I know that because of a change in Discoveries' ownership, it would finally come out as a book six years later! Since that time, of course, I have brought the information up-to-date.

Next to The Yardbirds, The Zombies are the most repackaged group ever. Thankfully, 1997's "Zombie Heaven" box set put nearly all of their recordings in one place. Combining that release with "Begin Here," "Odessey And Oracle," "The UK Singles As & Bs," "The DECCA Stereo Anthology," and "Into The Afterlife," a well-rounded and expansive Zombies audio presentation from the '60s has been realized. Tour dates for The Zombies, Rod Argent and Colin Blunstone are new to this edition.

In "Time Of The Season: The Zombies Collector's Guide," I look at the career of The Zombies from four different perspectives: as a musician, a collector, a music industry participant, and a fan. All of these perspectives are necessary to fully understand the legacy of The Zombies.

Writing on The Zombies without discussing the popular solo and band careers of Rod Argent and Colin Blunstone is to do both a great disservice. This book covers all of their solo recordings and sessions in great detail. Also covered is Colin and Rod's current (and top-notch) Zombies band and the original band's overwhelming success with their "Odessey And Oracle" concerts that debuted in March 2008. With this information, a fan can understand how Argent and Blunstone effectively employed their Zombies experiences in more contemporary musical surroundings. Not that Chris White, Hugh Grundy and Paul Atkinson were any less productive – far from it!

Thanks must go to all five Zombies for fielding all sorts of obscure questions about their backgrounds. Paul Atkinson, who helped coordinate the band's note, sadly passed away on April 1, 2004 and his great loss is still felt by fans worldwide. I must also thank Mike Ober for the use of his entertaining and informative Chris White interview. To all the others that have helped to verify information or contribute in any way, I greatly appreciate their efforts.

Now that the credits are behind us, it's the "Time Of The Season" to dive into the history of The Zombies!

below: Hugh Grundy, Colin Blunstone, Paul Atkinson, Chris White, Rod Argent.

When Greg Russo sent me the manuscript of this book, I was surprised at the amount of detail he'd managed to unearth. In fact, a couple of times I had to go back and listen to my copies of the original recording sessions only to discover that some of my recollections were incorrect and Greg was right! The discography is unbelievably detailed -- I'm astounded by the amount of research that must have gone into it.

Many thanks to Greg for putting this splendid Collector's Guide together and a special thanks to all of you who have kept our music alive and in your hearts for the last 35 years. The continuing interest in The Zombies' catalogue and history has meant a great deal to all of us. It is especially gratifying that younger people who come across The Zombies' music for the first time are finding it valid today. I suppose that if you always try to do what *feels* right, the music lasts.

Enjoy Greg Russo's book.

Best wishes.

Chris White

Chris White

Rod Argent

Colin Blunstone

Hugh Grundy

Paul Atkinson

THE HISTORY OF THE ZOMBIES

Since rock's inception, many of its artists have thrived on controversy. Whether it was The Beatles, The Rolling Stones, The Animals, The Who or any other British '60s group for that matter, the greater the number of media exposures, the more group members had to explain themselves. With these explanations, many unusual and controversial personal and professional practices were bared. These admissions fed the media's appetite and kept the groups in the public's eye. Yet, it was still possible for musicians to make it artistically and commercially without resorting to scandal. The Zombies were one such group.

By focusing on the intellectual nature of the band, The Zombies' music was immediately analyzed on a higher level than many of their contemporaries. As a result, The Zombies carried on without a hint of the controversial drug problems, massive egos and personnel changes that plagued many of their British counterparts.

While their debut single "She's Not There" was their only sizeable UK hit, that record plus "Tell Her No" and their swansong "Time Of The Season" have proven to be among the most durable and consistently enjoyed records in the US over the past four decades. The sheer long-lasting talent of the group after their late 1967 breakup was borne out by the ensuing record industry activity and success for vocalist Colin Blunstone, keyboardist/vocalist Rod Argent, Chris White (bass/vocals), guitarist Paul Atkinson, and Hugh Grundy (drums).

We "begin here"...

ORIGINS

The focal point of The Zombies is the southeastern British locale of St. Albans, Hertfordshire. St. Albans, 25 miles northwest of London, was not known for its artistic contributions during the late '50s and early '60s, but the crossover of traditional jazz to R&B and pop energized the youngest of its roughly 50,000 inhabitants to participate in creating the next trend in music. Rod Argent was certainly one brimming with this enthusiasm.

Rodney Terence Argent was born on June 14, 1945 in St. Albans. (Incidentally, "argent" is the French word for money.) Rod's father was a pianist in a long-running semi-professional dance band – The Les Argent Trio. This led to Rod's interest in the piano, as well as clarinet and violin. He attended St. Albans School, and spent several years developing his vocal skills with the St. Albans Cathedral Choir. However, Rod did not have the discipline for the two years of piano lessons he undertook starting at the age of 9. Despite being exposed to classical music masters like Johann Sebastian Bach, Ludwig van Beethoven, Peter Ilyich Tchaikovsky and Edvard Grieg in his piano lessons, Rod was not interested in practicing the instrument. However, the arrival of Elvis Presley on the pop music scene would work wonders. Argent's September 1956 discovery of the Elvis Presley rocking take on "Hound Dog" provided the motivation for Rod to really get into playing piano and, more importantly, rock and roll. Tracing "Hound Dog" back to its raw, original blues version by Willie Mae "Big Mama" Thornton (recorded August 13, 1952) proved to be a very instructive exercise and led to Argent making similar discoveries with other Presley covers like Arthur "Big Boy" Crudup's "That's All Right." These Elvis singles became the jewels of his record collection. Rod's first concert experience was also a very memorable one in 1956. Rod Argent's cousin Jim Rodford, born in St. Albans on July 7, 1941, nearly four years earlier than Rod, was playing stand-up bass with his band The Bluetones. Argent was so taken by this exciting experience that he had to form his own band. The local success of The Bluetones would, over the next few years, become the yardstick against which all St. Albans-area groups would be measured.

At the age of 11, Rod's interest in playing piano through "Hound Dog" resumed just as his lessons ended. What Argent lacked in pianistic discipline was more than compensated by his strong ability to play by ear. The first song that Rod learned by ear was Ted Heath's popular cover of The Moe Koffman Quartette's "The Swingin' Shepherd Blues." In the late '50s and early '60s, Rod started to listen to many different types of music, from classical to pop to jazz, and he examined the playing possibilities of all this music in a considerably more favorable perspective. On the jazz side, Rod would discover the magic of Charlie Parker, Miles Davis, and Bill Evans. The Miles Davis LP title track "Milestones" was heard by Argent for the first time in 1960, and he bought the EP, since that was all he could afford. Miles Davis' take of "On Green Dolphin Street" recorded on May 26, 1958 in New York City would prove to be an even more influential release for Argent. With Bill Evans now in Miles' band, Evans' piano solo on that Davis track impressed Argent immensely when he purchased this late 1960 EP (Fontana TFE 17320). What intrigued Argent most about Evans' unique solo was that it consisted of a succession of deft two-handed chord progressions instead of the usual keyboard pyrotechnics employed in jazz. Throughout the "Dolphin Street" solo five and a half minutes into the track, Argent discovered that Evans was expressive and expansive at the same time. These techniques would be duly noted by Argent for later use.

Rod purchased two other Miles Davis LPs ("Miles Ahead" and Kind Of Blue"). However, he had to make a large sacrifice: his Elvis Presley singles had to be traded in! This experience with Miles Davis led to Rod Argent seeking out Bill Evans' solo records, on which more inspired playing could be found. Miles Davis' "Porgy And Bess" album contained "Summertime," another track that had a strong impact on Rod. Classical made a return into the Argent consciousness, as he discovered more modern, experimental European composers like Bèla Bartòk, Igor Stravinsky, Maurice Ravel, and Benjamin Britten. With the onset of British R&B in the early '60s, Rod would take up harmonica as well. Combined with his love of blues greats John Lee Hooker and Muddy Waters, Rod Argent became a fan of Motown's fledgling Tamla label. Rod set out to write his first song – "Loneliness." Also known as "The Lonely One," Argent's song was recorded but not released by Rodford's group The Bluetones. The recording only exists on a demo disc. Despite this drawback, it was certainly a step in the right direction for Argent. It took Rod Argent five years from the time he first saw The Bluetones to his discovery of the right people to fulfill his dream of forming a band. The first piece of the puzzle was guitarist Paul Atkinson.

Paul Ashley Warren Atkinson was born March 19, 1946 in the Hertfordshire locale of Cuffley. The Atkinson family moved to St. Albans when Paul was about 9, and he was placed in the St. Albans School. Paul's musical path started on a recorder he received on his 10th birthday, and his mother purchased a violin and his required lessons two years later. Despite learning how to sight-read music, Paul's inability to play violin was personally frustrating. On Tuesday nights, the St. Albans school had a music club, and Paul put an end to his violin frustration by trading it for another club member's inexpensive guitar. Needless to say, Mrs. Atkinson was not happy about her son's actions, but Paul's great interest in the guitar led her to fund Paul's guitar lessons. Atkinson's greatest guitar hero was Chet Atkins, a discovery made when he was 13. Paul also got into folk and especially the blues of Leadbelly, Sonny Terry and Brownie McGhee, Etta James, and the highly regarded blues crossover master, Britain's own Alexis Korner. Atkinson would practice guitar prodigiously and regularly return to his school music club. One day in 1961, Paul Atkinson was playing guitar in the club and was spotted by Rod Argent. Rod was very impressed with Paul's playing and told him of his plans of forming a band. Atkinson was very interested in this prospect, and the search was on for the remaining members.

Hugh Birch Grundy was born in Winchester, Hampshire on March 6, 1945. Another St. Albans School student, Hugh became interested in the school army corps unit that met on Fridays. This unit did some role playing with non-functioning guns and the like, but Hugh was not happy with the aggressive behavior of the club. For refuge, Hugh sought out the bugle and drum corps of the club's marching band that met during the same time period. Grundy started out on bugle, but he soon realized that buglers were positioned in the back of the band during parades. To get up front, Hugh switched to side drum and played with the rest of the drummers. He immediately picked up drum sticks and started banging away on a drum that his father made for him. During drum practice one Friday in 1961, Grundy was spotted up front by Rod Argent. Rod noted that Grundy was the most accomplished of the school's army corps drummers, and he told Hugh of the band he was forming. For Grundy, this was the ideal way to express himself.

Argent, Atkinson and Grundy played in fall 1961 in an after-school music club. Grundy managed to make a drum or two disappear from the drum corps equipment stock each time the three met! Argent's enthusiasm was contagious, and he communicated his band intentions to his best friend from a rival St. Albans school, Paul Arnold. Saint Albans County Grammar School for Boys student Arnold took it upon himself to build a bass guitar, but he had never played the instrument. Argent wanted Paul Arnold to join his band despite his lack of experience, and introduced his bass trainee to Paul Atkinson. Arnold purchased the wood necessary to craft the bass, and it was soon arranged for the bass to be built at the workshop that Paul Atkinson's father had in their home. Meanwhile, Argent's music club trio practicing led to some informal performances in late 1961 and early 1962. At that point, Argent asked Arnold about the progress of his bass guitar. Paul Arnold told Rod that it would be ready soon and that upon its completion, he wanted a school friend of his who sang and played a little guitar to join them. That friend was Colin Blunstone.

Born June 24, 1945 in Hatfield, Hertfordshire, Colin Edward Michael Blunstone was an accomplished athlete specializing in track, basketball and rugby. In fact, Colin represented Hertfordshire at a national track competition. At 11, Paul Arnold, who sat in front of Colin in class at St. Albans County Grammar School for Boys, introduced himself. Colin soon became a student form (class captain) at the school, so perhaps it was better that Arnold immediately got on Colin's good side! With the increased lung power that his athleticism brought, Colin started working on his vocal talents. Blunstone was a big fan of '50s idols Elvis Presley, Chuck Berry and Little Richard, and without music lessons, he picked up what he could vocally and on guitar from his favorites. After leaving school, Colin would work in London as an insurance clerk. At this point, Paul Arnold asked Colin to join the band that Rod Argent was putting together. Besides Arnold and Grundy, Argent's original intent was to be the band's singer and pianist, with Blunstone on rhythm guitar accompanying Paul Atkinson.

PUTTING IT ALL TOGETHER

All five met on a Saturday morning outside the pub The Blacksmiths Arms. Argent's more experienced cousin Jim Rodford drove Rod to the get-together and picked up Colin Blunstone on the way. Blunstone was quite a sight, with a pair of black eyes and a broken nose from playing rugby! Equipment was a problem, so Rodford lent Argent & Co. some Bluetones gear for the occasion. In addition, this was the first time that Hugh Grundy had ever played a real drum kit. Again, Rodford helped out by showing Hugh how to keep a basic rock backbeat. Within an hour, Grundy had the required hand-foot coordination required to play drums – not an easy feat by any means.

The first real rehearsal took place at the Pioneer Youth Club in St. Albans in the spring of 1962, namely, on Easter Sunday (April 22, 1962). Colin Blunstone recalls that the band that morning played the instrumental standard "Malagueña." During a break, Rod was playing B. Bumble & The Stingers' hit "Nut Rocker," banging away on a piano that had seen much better days. For historical purposes, it is important to note that "Nut Rocker" was issued in the UK on March 30, 1962 and became a hit in late April, so this historic first band meeting could not have taken place any earlier. Not long after, they played The Shadows' #1 UK instrumental "Wonderful Land" (a March 1962 release). With Colin's numerous guitar playing mistakes on this song during rehearsal, it was agreed that Colin would be the lead singer instead of Rod, with the latter handling keyboard and alternate vocal duties. In Colin's opinion of Rod Argent, "Even then, I thought it was crazy not to use his talent in the band."

With Rod's band now in place, a name had to be developed. The first band name The Mustangs was too common, and The Sundowners became another temporary name. In the interim, joke names like Fred Grease And The Axles and Chatterley And The Gatekeepers were used. Paul Arnold then hit upon The Zombies, and all felt that no one else would use such an unusual name. (An unrelated group called The Zombies actually played on the same bill as The Beatles at Liverpool's Cavern Club on September 20, 1961, but they broke up shortly thereafter.) With the crossover from jazz to rhythm and blues in England, the band originally called themselves Zombies R&B. In their early days, Zombies R&B rehearsed the requisite hits of the day, like Johnny Kidd And The Pirates' "Shakin' All Over," and lesser-known Elvis Presley tunes. Mostly, however, they focused on instrumentals like "F.B.I." and "Nivram" by The Shadows, the latter an album cut released in September 1961, and The Ventures' "Perfidia." The songs they rehearsed were now ready for the live environment.

Colin Blunstone was able to arrange the first Zombies R&B group concert at his school. They functioned as the support band to a long-forgotten group on the local dance club circuit. The Zombies R&B also played at the Pioneer Youth Club, the site of their first rehearsal. Still, at this point, the band's repertoire mainly consisted of instrumentals. However, one thing was becoming clear: Paul Arnold's heart was not in the group. Songs like Buddy Holly's "Peggy Sue" in the key of A revealed Arnold's lazy tendency to play open strings with one hand in his pocket! Even after two or three gigs, Arnold had to be replaced, especially since he revealed his intentions to attend medical school (he later founded a successful Scottish medical practice). Paul Arnold's efforts in this regard were conflicting with the band, and the search was on for his replacement. In the interim, Jim Rodford would fill the slot until someone came along. (Two years later in November 1964, Rodford joined The Mike Cotton Sound – one of the premier backing bands of the '60s.) Chris White, a St. Albans Grammar School alumnus and current art school student, entered the picture.

THE FINAL INGREDIENT

Christopher Taylor White was born on March 7, 1943 in Barnet, Hertfordshire, and being two years older than most of the band, his experience would prove to be extremely valuable. Chris' father led something of a double life, inspecting buses during the day and playing bass in dance bands on occasion. When Chris was five, his family moved to Markyate, eight miles north of St. Albans, and Mr. White decided to open a Markyate grocery store. Chris learned double bass from his father, and it was on this instrument that he played in his school's orchestra. This group was with sax player/pianist Spider Robinson and accomplished guitarist Michael "Chas" Chaplin. Inspired by skiffle legends like Lonnie Donegan, White formed a skiffle group at 12. This group was known simply as Chris White's Skiffle Group and featured Chaplin with the New Zealand-born Duffy Coke. Ted White, Chris' uncle, was a Billy Ternant Orchestra arranger with some BBC television experience on his CV (for the benefit of Americans, a CV is a résumé!). Ted took his 14-year-old nephew to see the television broadcast of "Jack Good's 'Oh Boy!'" featuring pop singers Cliff Richard and Duffy Power (remember that name!). This show provided Chris with the enthusiasm of playing in a music group. Other music group experience followed, but Chris White really wanted to enter the pop field. Still, he enjoyed all types of jazz, from the traditional mode of Ken Colyer to modern practitioners like the upsurging Miles Davis. Switching to electric bass, White earned pocket money by playing with dance bands on an informal basis. While in the St. Albans Grammar School art department, White met Colin Blunstone (two years his junior) at a music session that Chris set up in his department. The conflict of school vs. music still remained, and Chris' overall goal was to become an art teacher after completing art school. Chris White had also met Rod Argent six months prior, when he asked Rod in 1961 to join a dance band he had at the time. The timing and the band's repertoire were not right for Rod, so he declined.

Through Blunstone's rugby club connections, Zombies R&B landed a dance gig at the Old Verulamians Club. At this dance, the band played for about 40 people during a 20-minute interval. Their success at the club led to another engagement a month later at which they played for twice as many people. Old Verulamians proved to be the band's first real stronghold and their fan base became so large over the next few months that a marquee had to be erected at the club to handle the vastly increased Zombies audience. By developing their repertoire at the club over the next year and half, the group elevated themselves to larger, more populated venues. This took place despite the fact that all of their sound was funneled through one Vox 30-watt amplifier! Also through Blunstone, Zombies R&B landed a gig at the St. Albans Girls Grammar School. At this show, Chris White's recommendation of playing "I'm Henery The Eighth, I Am" (with Rod's vocals) went over well, even though this was three years before the Herman's Hermits version! The song was written in 1910 and its most notable British version was by Harry Champion. Another Rod Argent-sung early favorite was Arthur Alexander's "You Better Move On."

The Zombies eclipsed the popularity of The Bluetones and became the biggest entertainment attraction in St. Albans. Musical advancement was still tempered by the band's view of their impending school plans. For The Zombies R&B, this was just a hobby to prepare them for their non-musical careers.

Much has been made of the band's school accomplishments, but the breakdown of their ordinary (O), advanced (A) and scholarship (S) levels is as follows:

	Blunstone	Atkinson	Argent	White	Grundy
36 O levels:	7	11	6	8	4
8 A levels:	2	3	2	1	0
2 S levels:	0	1	1	0	0
1 diploma:				1 National Diploma (Fine Art)	

Early rehearsals with Chris White took place at St. Ethelreda's in Hatfield, but the band soon made use of the upper room at the White grocery store at 68 High Street, Markyate on Sunday afternoons. After quickly discarding the overly whitebread Four Preps song "Big Man," more Top 20 hits were worked in, along with R&B standbys like "Road Runner," "I Got My Mojo Working," and "Just A Little Bit." In White's early days with the band, Hugh Grundy was somewhat of a mystery man to Chris, as he describes: "In fact, Hugh, our drummer, in our first rehearsals in Hatfield where we used to practice on Sundays, used to keep disappearing. So I hardly ever spoke to him, he didn't speak much. I found out later his girlfriend was the dean's daughter and he used to nip out every time to court her. After our third gig together, Hugh went up to Rod and said, 'What is the name of our bass player?' After a few years, the group became sort of local heroes, building up a reputation just playing for fun after college and after school at rugby clubs and things like that."

"I Got My Mojo Working" required a little bit extra from Rod Argent, as Chris White describes: "Rod used to sing that one! He learned to play harmonica for it and got up from the keyboards to sing it on stage. He also did 'I'm Your Hoochie Coochie Man.' All the groups did it and it used to go down well. We did loads of stuff, but of course in those days, you didn't do too many original things."

Chris White immediately knew that this band was a special group with a lot of growth potential: "Colin had this unusual voice and Rod was in fact still learning, and he's fanatical about music. Funnily enough, we all had this love of Miles Davis which influenced a lot of things. We picked up on a lot of American blues and played that music as well as the Mersey sound which was evolving. Songs were passed around by everyone and we used to rehearse two new songs each Sunday to put into the act."

ZOMBIES RISE

By late 1962, Zombies R&B elevated themselves to semi-professional status and simplified their name to The Zombies. To simplify their finances, Paul Atkinson handled all treasury issues. Their gigs in late 1962 leading into mid-1963 included the Liberal Club, the Free Church Youth Club and the high school in nearby Welwyn Garden City, and numerous St. Albans venues: the County Grammar School, St. Mary's Youth Club, Waverley Club, Mercer's, New Greens Hall, Cavalier Hall, Town Hall, and Co-Op Hall. They also made inroads to Hatfield (Hilltop, Parish Youth Club, and Memorial Hall), the Park Street Village

Hall and St. Andrew's Youth Club in Luton.

Early shows featured the Cliff Richard And The Shadows LP track "I'm Gonna Get You" (from the "Me And My Shadows" album in 1960) and Barrett Strong's smash "Money (That's What I Want)." The numerous instrumentals that made up half of The Zombies' set became a thing of the past with the ongoing Beat boom in the UK. Still, the band's formative influences remained as their repertoire changed. Chris White fills us in on who they looked up to most: "Buddy Holly definitely. As far as I'm concerned, he was simplicity itself. Eddie Cochran. Funnily enough, underrated innovators were The Everly Brothers. They started several new trends and shifted direction in music, for me personally. I mean, they really did push some boundaries out which people don't give them respect for. Also, a lot of blues people, Muddy Waters, all those sorts of things. Generally, pop music seemed to be very exciting in the early '60s. Basically, the guys in The Zombies had the same musical influences. We did a lot of Beatles stuff when they first came out with our own sort of edge on it. We did 'You've Really Got A Hold On Me' but we did the original (live) version (by The Miracles) with other songs inside it (like Sam Cooke's "Bring It On Home To Me" vocal duet with Lou Rawls) as well. The Beatles were what we aspired to."

Rod's uneventful year-long payroll clerk position at Ballito's Hosiery Mills in St. Albans led to the band's first high profile gig. In addition, an experience at the July 20, 1963 Ballito's Sports Ground gig would provide Rod Argent with a very valuable musical technique. The Zombies played with The Laurie Jay Combo, featuring future Animals guitarist Vic Briggs. Briggs recommended to Rod Argent that he could take a solo using the scale of a G minor 7 chord (G,Bb,D,F) while the band was on a C chord (C,E,G). These notes constitute a C 9th chord, expressed musically as C9. This discovery unlocked Argent's soloing capabilities and musical understanding, as much of the jazz he listened to employed similar chord techniques.

The Ballito's show would provide another first – the ability to hear Rod's playing! Argent's purchase of a Hohner electric pianet enabled everyone to hear his vital contributions, and the vast sound of the instrument easily differentiated The Zombies from the tremendous amount of guitar-based Beat groups. The pianet especially came in handy when The Zombies put together a jazzy version of the "Porgy And Bess" classic tune "Summertime" with an extensive Argent solo on his new instrument. George and Ira Gershwin's "Summertime" was given this type of arrangement by Miles Davis on his "Porgy And Bess" album (also with Bill Evans), and the entire band quickly latched onto the song's entrancing power on audiences. Chris White was already familiar with playing the song in this way, as he did it with Chas Chaplin using a 6/8 tempo.

Hugh Grundy was picking up a lot of musical techniques and sounds as well. Banging on tables and chairs at home while listening to Radio Luxembourg, Hugh nearly drove his mother crazy. On TV, the flashy (but prematurely bald!) Hollies drummer Bobby Elliott became Grundy's hero. When the members of The Zombies hit a Hatfield jazz club on an off-night, Hugh made sure he caught every move the club drummer made. These techniques were then incorporated into The Zombies' repertoire.

Ballito's opened up a whole new musical world for The Zombies, as the venue had just made the transition from jazz to R&B. At this gig, The Zombies played Lloyd Price's "Lawdy Miss Clawdy" and "What'd I Say" - the latter based on both the Ray Charles and Jerry Lee Lewis versions. This gig and the others throughout the summer of 1963 prepared the band for their first competition.

The Ovaltine Talent Competition, held in Kings Langley on September 20, 1963, was a very valuable experience for The Zombies even though they were not finalists. This exposure allowed the group to expand their concert base from St. Albans and Hatfield to London Colney, Hitchin, Ware, Luton, Watford, and Hemel Hempstead. After opening up with The Beatles' spirited arrangement of "Roll Over Beethoven," this period found the band playing songs like "One Fine Day" (Chiffons), "From Me To You" (Beatles), Major Lance's "The Monkey Time" and the Chris White-sung "Sweets For My Sweet" (The Drifters and The Searchers) to more upscale grammar school and college students. Chris White lets us in on what the early Zombies repertoire consisted of: "There was a lot more R&B, and of course, it was an exciting time because The Beatles were on the scene. Rod was into harmonies, which I liked, and we developed three-part harmonies which the band hadn't been able to do before. Rod was playing upright piano with the microphone hanging inside. He wasn't playing electric organ because they didn't exist at the time. In fact, the power generators at the places we used to play would go down and the tuning would go down and Rod's pianet would stop working, so we had to shout our heads off!"

THE HERTS BEAT COMPETITION

Early Zombies shows in 1964 carried the band through all their local haunts as well as their first engagement outside of the general St. Albans area on February 29. This gig at the Kingston-upon-Thames Coronation Hall also featured The Cheynes, a group featuring two musicians that would later find success: Pete Bardens (later of Camel and Keats, the latter with Colin

Blunstone) and Mick Fleetwood (co-founder of Fleetwood Mac). Despite their widespread popularity, The Zombies were still planning on breaking up when school started that September. As a last test of their abilities during their last few months together, Chris White suggested that The Zombies enter a songwriting competition called The Herts Beat Contest (pronounced "hearts beat" - get it?) in Watford.

The opening of The Herts Beat Contest took place at Watford Town Hall on April 5, 1964. This contest was organized by the Watford Borough Council with sponsorship by the London Evening News, and more than a dozen London theatrical agencies were vying for the groups. The winning group would earn £250 and the ability to record a demo for possible record contract consideration. Shane Fenton, at the end of his pop career with backup band The Fentones, was one of the judges along with local singer Sandra Barry. (Fenton later became Alvin Stardust in the glam '70s.) Groups from Watford (Eddie Falcon And The Fournotes, D. And The Vostocks, The Hully Gullys), Barnet (Peter And The Starliners), Hertford (Andy James And The Navaros) and Sawbridgeworth (The Dinos) were some of the acts that gave The Zombies strong competition during their concert rounds. Encouraging all of these groups was the sold-out crowd numbering around 1,200.

There were seven rounds, or heats, in the competition. Interestingly, The Bluetones entered the contest, but they were knocked out in the fifth heat by The Zombies. During heat #5, The Zombies played "Summertime," "I Got My Mojo Working" and two encores: "Bye Bye Johnny" and an unrehearsed "Boys" with judge Sandra Barry. (This heat of the competition, as well as all the others, was recorded unofficially, although no tape of The Zombies' performance has turned up yet.) Spurred on by their success in the early going, The Zombies started to write material for their upcoming appearance in the final round of The Herts Beat Contest that took place at 8PM on Sunday, May 10, 1964. This was the band's first real attempt at songwriting, and Rod Argent came up with "It's Alright" (aka "It's Alright With Me"). This song was the second in their set, following "I'm Goin' Home" and preceding "I Got My Mojo Working" and "Summertime."

According to Paul Atkinson, original Zombies manager Terry Arnold (Paul's brother) received a group offer for a Decca recording test by A&R (artist and repertoire) man Dick Rowe after they won their final heat performance at The Herts Beat Contest. Since Dick Rowe was aware that The Zombies were not yet old enough to sign contracts with Decca, he recommended that they get their parents' permission. The search was on for a professional band manager, especially since winning the contest enabled that group to appear May 24 with Billy J. Kramer And The Dakotas and The League Of Gentlemen at Watford Town Hall and St. Albans Market Hall on the 29th. In addition to these shows, other booking agencies were offering more widespread autumn tours of larger performance halls.

George Cooper, a well-established UK concert booker, was considered an unsuitable manager for the band. The same fate met the second (and long-forgotten) candidate they approached. Once again, Chris White, through his father's recommendation, came to the rescue: "Luckily, I had an uncle (Ted White) who was an arranger for the BBC and he recommended we see a fellow named Ken Jones of Marquis Enterprises for advice. So the whole group went along with these contracts to Ken and he went through them saying, 'That's a good clause, that's a bad one,' etc. and then we asked him what he could offer us. He initially said, 'I thought you were only coming for advice' and then said, 'We'll offer you the best of all these contracts.' The one thing they put in the contract was that we got 85% of everything that came in and that when the first 100,000 records sold, we'd have a joint publishing company. That's the thing that saved us. Everyone else in that era got ripped off, but that company is now run by the then secretary who later bought the company (Carole Broughton), and so we still get all our own royalties."

Prior to reviewing The Zombies' contracts, Ken Jones was already operating Marquis Enterprises as a partnership with well-respected publisher Joe Roncoroni. Jones had a wealth of experience as a television-oriented musician, writer and arranger for programs and series, along with notable commercial jingles for Tetley Tea and Murray Mints.

Rod Argent and Chris White, the main songwriters in The Zombies, had a publishing company name picked out for them – Verulam Music, reflecting the Roman name for the city of St. Albans. The Verulam title was in fact suggested by Joe Roncoroni just before its creation. Chris White was always writing songs, but none of them were appropriate for The Zombies. That would soon change.

Still, the potential demise of the group was a possibility. Colin Blunstone and Hugh Grundy were willing to give up their respective insurance and Barclays bank clerk positions and Hugh's mother created and ran their fan club, but the academic futures of Argent, White and Atkinson were still hanging in the balance. Argent's place to study English at Hull University was approved but Rod elected to delay his entrance for one year. Chris White was planning art teacher training in Sussex after he completed his studies at the St. Albans School Of Art, but he also chose to put off his studies. Paul Atkinson's situation proved to be more problematic.

Paul Atkinson's parents were the only ones not keen on having their son sign a Decca recording contract. Paul was still studying French and German while in the process of preparing for his 'A' level examinations at St. Albans School. Mr. and Mrs. Atkinson preferred that Paul continue his studies until he achieved three 'A' levels. At that point, he would be free to continue with the band. A very tenuous month went by when it looked as if Jim Rodford of The Bluetones would learn guitar to replace Paul Atkinson, but Ken Jones and Joe Roncoroni of Marquis Enterprises convinced the Atkinsons of the Decca contract's viability. More importantly, Paul passed his exams!

To get things off the ground, The Zombies set out to do some demo recordings. A band decision was also made to turn professional with the release of their first single. The confidence of the band was so high that they did not even consider the possibility of failure!

THE FIRST RECORDINGS

The Zombies arranged studio time on April 29, 1964 at Jackson's Studio in Rickmansworth. Owned by DJ Jack Jackson's sons John and Malcolm, this small 2-track studio was The Zombies' modest introduction to recording. Five demos were laid down that day: "Summertime," "Woman," "Kind Of Girl," "Leave Me Be," and "It's Alright With Me." All of these demos have now been released. The demo version of "Summertime" had the long pianet break of the live version, but with greater guitar and vocal presence. "Kind Of Girl" was heavier than its later commercial take with a different set of lyrics. Chris White's "Leave Me Be" was also harder-hitting than its later Decca version, but it lacked an introduction. The embryonic version of Rod Argent's "Woman" revealed a weak bridge section which was wisely omitted in its later re-recording. This flawed recording, more than any of their demos, showed the band's consistent attention to crafting a song worthy of release. The basic song structure was always there, but constant refinements over the next couple of months created a definitive Zombies track. These refinements included trimming the break between chorus and verse in half and perfecting the vocal harmonies. This demo session was first issued on the "Zombie Heaven" box set in 1997.

In the drawing to determine the order of groups to perform in the final Herts Beat round, The Zombies were in the lucky position to perform last. The other finalists were: The Trespassers (London Colney), The League Of Gentlemen and The Sapphires from Hitchin, The Beat Six (Hemel Hempstead), The Venders (Hoddesdon), The Dolphins (Barnet), The Vibratones (Radlett), and The Seminars (Waltham Cross).

"Summertime" proved to be the smash of the competition, as Rod Argent's overwhelming pianet solo was the deciding factor. First runner-up in the competition was The Beat Six, followed by The Trespassers and The Sapphires. As Chris White explains, euphoria was in the air: "We won the heats and then won the final. There were thousands of fans screaming for us. It was like we were The Beatles and it was one of the most moving moments of my life. Immediately we were approached by all sorts of people offering us contracts and we didn't know what to do." Paul adds, "Even my mom and dad had to agree that it was a great evening!"

The Zombies celebrating their Herts Beat win.

Meanwhile, The Zombies continued their concert rounds. On June 6, the group did the first of their arduous double concert dates, hitting Rickmansworth in the morning and their standby Old Verulamians at night. The extra stamina required to handle the increasing demands for their services would prove important.

With their demos and successful Herts Beat experience now behind them, The Zombies were ready to capitalize on their popularity. Discussions with Ken Jones had been going on during the weeks of the Herts Beat competition, but nothing was finalized until a crisis point was reached: Decca wanted to issue the Jackson Studio version of "Summertime" as the first Zombies single. Just after he completed a recording managerial arrangement with The Zombies, Ken Jones stepped in and prevented Decca from going any further. Jones arranged for a proper Zombies recording session at Decca's 4-track studio in West Hampstead. Ken Jones prepared the boys for the date by encouraging them to write a couple of songs to record. Along with their Herts Beat hit cover of "Summertime," Chris White contributed "You Make Me Feel Good," while Argent chimed in with the recent "It's Alright With Me" and his brand-new song "She's Not There." Rod Argent previewed the last song for Ken Jones at the Breaks Youth Club show in Hatfield (May 22), and Jones recommended that Rod add a second verse and an extra beat on the title line. These would prove to be the final elements that brought the entire song together. On June 12, 1964, The Zombies hit Decca Studio No. 2 and laid down these four songs.

"She's Not There" started out life as the second to fifth words of its first line – "No One Told Me," a John Lee Hooker track from his "The Big Soul Of John Lee Hooker" LP. Arranged in Chris White's Markyate bedroom, this Miles Davis-influenced song quickly took shape. The first part of the song simply alternated from A minor to D, and made an easy transition to its second section. Without being overly aware of musical mechanics, Rod Argent employed a modal chord sequence over this first section. (For all the musos out there, Rod used a Dorian mode!) In addition to his strikingly expressive modal changes, Argent used a bass note change for the F to F minor chords used in the second section ("it's too late to say you're sorry") which freed the chords from their F root bass notes. This idea was inspired by a similar section of the Brian Hyland hit "Sealed With A Kiss." The dual use of these techniques increased the dramatic tension and excitement of the song. When Rod's solo was uncoiled during the middle of the song, it led "She's Not There" toward an effective repeat of its second section and a driving conclusion. When "She's Not There" was all complete, Argent had created one of the rare pieces of music that was equally exciting to play as appreciating it from a listening standpoint. Rod's solo on "She's Not There" would prove to be a powerful influence for Byrds leader Jim (later Roger) McGuinn. The spiralling nature of Rod's solo empowered McGuinn to create the 12-string noodling that became an essential part of the Byrds classic "Eight Miles High."

"She's Not There" was not just an Argent accomplishment; all of The Zombies made fine contributions to the final product. As for who made the final arrangement decision, Chris White said: "Primarily Rod. Rod was the prime leader, he was the one we all looked up to. But we all put our ideas in. Rod was very open to everything." The backing track was recorded live and took seven takes; the lead and backing vocals were nailed on the first take! Starting off the song, Chris White's bass made a solid entrance which was maintained throughout the song. Equally important was Hugh Grundy's distinctive and hook-filled stop-start drum pattern, which later songs like The Youngbloods' "Get Together" would later use as an essential song element. Also interesting were Grundy's drum roll overdubs, which Ken Jones recorded directly into the mono mix. While drum overdubs are commonplace nowadays, they were practically unheard of in 1964. Paul Atkinson employed an electrified acoustic guitar on the session, and professionally filled in all the spaces that the keyboards, bass and drums left open. "She's Not There" marked the first Colin Blunstone "breathy" vocal on record. While much has been made of this quality over the years, very little has been said of its effect on the listener. On "She's Not There," Blunstone's voice effectively expressed the perfect amount of resignation and desperation that Rod Argent's chord changes dictated. Combined with harmonies from Rod and Chris, the vocal blend on the chorus created another irresistible hook. Another Zombies trademark also took place on "She's Not There" – it ended cold without any need for fading. This trait illustrated The Zombies' innate rehearsal ability, in that songs were recorded in the studio the same way they would be played live. Chris White explains what happened during the session: "In those days, people rehearsed thoroughly before they went into a studio, which we did. We recorded four numbers, 'Summertime,' 'She's Not There,' 'You Make Me Feel Good' and 'It's Alright With Me' on a four-track machine. The assistant tape operator was Gus Dudgeon, who later went on to produce Elton John. During the recording session, the engineer (Terry Johnson) was pissed out of his head as he had just come back from a wedding and had to be carried out. Gus Dudgeon had to take over (after being asked by Ken Jones). This was his first session ever. But we didn't know this!"

Dudgeon first worked on Chris White's "You Make Me Feel Good." This was the first of Chris' many consistently excellent songs. After a short keyboard run, Argent and Blunstone traded "call and response" vocals, making this catchy nugget the most Beatleish number they ever created. Again, Grundy added drum overdubs and the track was complete. As with all of their Decca recordings, The Zombies were not allowed to attend mixing sessions.

"Summertime" was a more subdued and stripped-down version than their prior demo or live performances, but it conveyed the song's mood with class. The vocal only required one take, and Grundy's snazzy light jazz beat was used to great effect. Rod Argent also placed a smoother pianet solo on this version. "It's Alright," later known as "It's Alright With Me" to avoid confusion with The Impressions' song of the same name, had an early Beatles feel and sported tumbling Grundy drums with a strong Atkinson guitar riff. This song's main selling point was the slowed down middle eight, which was used as a jumping off point for manic pianet and guitar solos in turn.

The songs were laid down, but a hard decision remained concerning the A-side of their first Decca single. Decca selected "She's Not There" and "You Make Me Feel Good" as the two songs for the single, but they could not agree on the top side. Ken Jones was so enamored with "She's Not There" that he decided that it was the A-side instead of their recent concert favorite "Summertime." By consensus, "You Make Me Feel Good" became the record's flipside. As part of the band's agreement, "She's Not There" was published by Marquis Enterprises. With the conclusion of the school year on July 18, The Zombies were completely devoted to their musical career.

The only problem was that of finding radio outlets for the record. Outside of new releases played on "Saturday Club" and other BBC offerings in "The Light Programme," there was no other official British radio programming that would play a record like "She's Not There." The power of television would soon prove to be another medium for airing new music.

On July 24, 1964, Decca released "She's Not There" and it was aired that day on British TV's "Juke Box Jury." To the band's surprise, guest panelist George Harrison of The Beatles raved about "She's Not There" during the program and set things in motion. Here's Chris White's reaction: "We had a TV program here (in the UK) called 'Juke Box Jury' in those days. George Harrison was on the show and he gave it a rave review when he heard it. Which was, to us, fantastic. Starf***ers basically! It got quite good reviews over here and got played quite a bit." Shortly after the single's release, The Zombies filmed TV appearances for "Ready, Steady, Go!," "Top Of The Pops," "The Cool Spot" and "3-Go-Round" between late July and mid-August.

With no respect for George Harrison's enthusiasm, sales for "She's Not There" started off slowly. The record took three weeks to appear on Record Retailer's singles chart and four weeks to be logged in on the New Musical Express (NME) listing. Over the ensuing weeks, the single only managed to reach #12 on Record Retailer's chart and a position lower on NME – a success, but a rather disappointing one considering the strength of the record. "She's Not There" still managed to sell over 100,000 copies and effect the reality of their Verulam Music publishing company.

PROFESSIONAL ZOMBIES

As planned, The Zombies turned fully professional and signed a management deal with The Tito Burns Organisation, the largest UK concert booking agent. As it turned out, bigger didn't mean better when Tito Burns was involved. The Tito Burns deal, as with most '60s arrangements, was only advantageous for the promoter. (To avoid UK stipulations that he could not act as both agent and promoter, Tito Burns used his wife in documents as agent. Burns also had a skimming racket going on at the same time, in which he would "sell" the services of the group to a mysterious middleman [agent] who would make deals with venues and get a higher kickback than just offering the group. As a result, Burns would charge £250 for a gig in which The Zombies were paid £100.) To start their management deal, The Zombies played their first gig as professionals at the Botwell Youth Club in Hayes on August 3. Terry Arnold (Paul's brother), remained as the band's first official road manager, despite the protests of his arch enemy, Colin Blunstone. Arnold received 10% of The Zombies' touring revenue.

Despite their first forays into songwriting, Zombies shows at this time still sported cover versions. The Impressions song "It's All Right," Searchers hits "Love Potion No. 9" and "Needles And Pins" (the latter with Chris White on vocals), The Beatles' "You Can't Do That" and the Elvis Presley hit "Ain't That Lovin' You Baby" kept the band musically current.

Along with current musical trends, The Zombies upgraded their equipment to accomodate larger halls. Paul Atkinson dabbled with a Gretsch on occasion, but he used a new Rickenbacker guitar on stage, while Rod Argent purchased a Vox Continental organ. Like fellow keyboard player Manfred Mann, he placed the pianet on top of the Vox for dual-voiced capabilities on stage. The old PA was scrapped, replaced by a Vox AC-100 amp and two T60 bass cabinets.

The full sound of The Zombies put them in a very elite class: one of the few groups around with a virtuoso keyboardist. Other than the most notable (Manfred himself and Animals organist Alan Price), keyboardists like Rod Argent were few and far between in standout British '60s pop groups. Certainly, the role of keyboards was almost non-existent during the '60s, but Rod notes that their inclusion in The Zombies was not premeditated: "I never really thought about it. I was so in love with music. The Beatles swung my head around. In 1962, it sounded fantastic to me. Even while I was so completely knocked out and saturated by what they were doing, I still loved buying and listening to Miles Davis' 'Kind Of Blue' and hearing Bill Evans for the first time. I saw no reason to listen to Stravinsky, Bartòk or other classical people at the time. In the end, I didn't try to introduce Miles Davis or Stravinsky into The Zombies' stuff – I didn't think of it like that – but in an very indirect way, those things sort of permeated and just came through my own keyboard playing without thinking about it. I wasn't really terribly conscious of the role of keyboards or the role of the guitar, I just thought we were doing something quite unusual. Our role was to push that in the sort of direction that excited us. That's the only way I looked at it."

In 1964, British groups had a stranglehold on both the UK and US markets. When The Beatles opened the doors for the worldwide sale of British music, US record companies were falling over themselves trying to locate British acts to cash in on this new trend. In the US, American subsidiaries of British labels had right of first refusal in terms of signing UK acts to US record contracts. Despite the British Invasion fever in the US, American record companies had a habit of initially turning down the most successful acts of the decade. This led to other companies, mostly smaller labels, licensing these releases and profiting tremendously. The most glaring example, of course, was Capitol Records' initial thumbs-down on The Beatles (on two occasions!). By licensing out Beatles recordings to other labels, Capitol lost out on nearly one year of enormous profits before they obtained an exclusive contract with the band. Not so with The Zombies. After some arm twisting by American publisher Al Gallico, the US counterpart of their Decca label in England, London Records, was convinced of the hit potential of this exciting new group and signed them up to their Parrot Records subsidiary.

If it wasn't for Al Gallico's connections and proven track record, The Zombies might never have been signed by Parrot at all. At his prior executive position with the Shapiro Bernstein publishing company, Gallico met Joe Roncoroni. Joe sent Al Gallico a copy of "She's Not There" and offered US rights if he liked it. Gallico flipped over "She's Not There" and phoned Walt McGuire at London Records to release this high-quality record as a favor. McGuire correctly noted that the single's UK performance did not immediately warrant a US release, but Gallico's salesmanship convinced him that a US single from this British group could outperform its UK counterpart.

As with early British reaction, the US release of "She's Not There" required some time before airplay and sales took place. In fact, "She's Not There" was not picked by Billboard Magazine to be a big hit – it was listed in their "recommended" section for records with a shot at making it between 61 and 100 on their Hot 100 singles chart. Even with very little promotion in America, it became a US smash. Incidentally, the American B-side was incorrectly billed as "You Make Me Feel So Good."

"She's Not There" was a worldwide smash, and the US statistics were very impressive: #1 in Cashbox and Music Business, and #2 in Billboard. The song even hit #1 in Australia, and successful Canadian and Japanese releases were put together as soon as the US record deal was finalized. "She's Not There" has been consistently played on American radio, and Rod Argent received a BMI award for 1 million US airplays in 1993. Four years later, a 2 million airplay award followed.

To prepare for their next release, The Zombies demoed four tracks at a Ryemuse studio on August 3: "Sometimes," "Woman," "Kind Of Girl," and "Leave Me Be." This studio time enabled them to lay down the backing tracks of the final versions at Decca's studios on the last day of the month along with the vocal tracks done on September 5. All of these demos debuted on the "Zombie Heaven" box in 1997.

Rod Argent's "Woman" was unusual in that it was a rocking number based on a Paul Atkinson guitar riff. Colin Blunstone's excited vocal alternated nicely with Vox Continental organ and guitar solos. Atkinson's noodling solo was typical of 1964 guitar work, and Chris White's bass links during the song filled in the gaps well. The group harmony of Rod's "Kind Of Girl" worked just as well, and Grundy's mono cymbal overdubs (another Ken Jones-inspired addition) completed this smartly arranged track. The "a capella" introduction of another Argent song, "Sometimes," was edited together with the band take. The reason for this editing was that the intro was a different take than the rest of the song, and the countoff between the two parts was eliminated. Another prime Atkinson solo was included here along with "call and response" vocals. In 1997, the "Zombies Heaven" box set included Colin's run-throughs of the intro as well as the final take.

The track from this session that received the most attention was the Chris White-penned tale of love lost, "Leave Me Be." White tells us what happened with the song: "The funny thing about that one was we were doing it on tour and rode all night on a train to record it in London the next morning and it was much better live than on record. We never got it quite right in the studio. Sonny And Cher did a lovely version of it." Why did it fall short? Well, producer Ken Jones insisted on repeating the hit formula of "She's Not There" – that is, emphasizing Colin Blunstone's breathiness. As a result, the vocals were not convincing enough since they conveyed the wrong mood. Jones' other misguided production touches on this track included a louder organ in the mix than was necessary, thereby burying Atkinson's guitar and leaving an unclear sounding bass response. These production errors would be repeated on nearly all future Decca singles. Even though the song had all of these negatives, it was still selected as the second Decca A-side for release on October 16 with "Woman" on its reverse.

The Zombies started out August in their local haunts, but they were heading north by the end of the month. A taped appearance on "Top Of The Pops" on August 26 led to three more TV appearances during September: "Ready, Steady, Go!" (taped on the 11th), "Dig This" on Scottish TV (the 27th), and "Saturday Club" (September 29). The band's schedule was very tight, sometimes too tight in fact. The "Ready, Steady, Go!" taping in London caused an embarrassing problem when the band missed a date in Erdington (near Birmingham) by arriving too late to perform. The audience let them know it by throwing bottles at them. This was the price to pay for expanding their horizons in all directions of the UK in October and November.

More TV and recordings were done in those two months than can be imagined. TV viewers were blitzed by Zombies appearances on "Five O'Clock Club," "Ready, Steady, Go!" and "Thank Your Lucky Stars" during this period. More demos were recorded at London's Regent Sound studio, but these unknown tracks have not turned up to this day.

Between October 17 and November 23, The Zombies participated in their first package tour, joining the likes of The Searchers, Dionne Warwick and The Isley Brothers as well as other itinerant passengers on the tour: Bobby Vee, Tony Jackson, Alan Elson And His Band, Tony Sheverton, and Syd & Eddie. The day after the tour ended, The Zombies' busy day included more Decca recordings. At the end of November, they even managed to tape a (unused) segment for "The Red Skelton Show."

The Zombies had been furiously writing songs over the past few months, and many were ready for studio treatments. Even so, the November 24 Decca session encompassed three covers: "I'm Goin' Home," "Road Runner," and "Sticks And Stones." The Bob Bain-written "I'm Goin' Home" was a UK-only single issued by Gene Vincent on the Capitol label. At #36, it proved to be Vincent's last hit. The Zombies' wild and slightly loose first take was first issued on "Zombie Heaven," while the second take was released erroneously through a tape mix-up in 1984 in place of "She's Coming Home" on the See For Miles "The Singles A's & B's" collection. It was also released by mistake on a budget US cassette the following year. Nevertheless, the song was pure, driving R&B with strong guitar by Atkinson and another impressive Argent solo.

CONQUERING AMERICA

The band's originals were saved for the next day's recording at Decca. On this expanded session, The Zombies laid down "Tell Her No," "What More Can I Do," "I Remember When I Loved Her," "I Want You Back Again" (its first version), "Walking In The Sun" (unissued until 1974), "I Don't Want To Know," and a failed attempt at "The Way I Feel Inside." With "She's Not There" selling extremely well in the US, the band received a very exciting phone call that day in the studio. Chris White explains: "We knew it ('She's Not There') was going up the charts in the States and during our second recording session in which we recorded and completed six songs from start to finish (plus starting 'The Way I Feel Inside'), beginning at midnight, our producer Ken Jones got a phone call, unknown to us, from our publisher (Al Gallico) saying it's number one in America (on Cashbox)."

The British "Leave Me Be" single (left) and the very rare US "Tell Her No" sleeve (right).

The excitement in the US was not matched in England, where "Leave Me Be" was a complete sales disaster. Decca in all likelihood figured that "Leave Me Be" would sell on the back of "She's Not There" and therefore promotion was nearly non-existent. "Woman" received some play, but not enough to produce any measurable sales. Parrot Records in the US was taking a "wait and see" attitude, and they passed on releasing any further Zombies product unless they produced something more accessible. Still, The Zombies signed with Universal Attractions for their debut US tour on Murray The K's Big Holiday Show (December 25 – January 3) at the Fox Theater in Brooklyn, New York. It was also a first for Universal Attractions – The Zombies were their first UK group booking! One can easily imagine who got the best of that deal.

The UK portion of the Searchers tour ended on November 23, but Scandinavia was up next for The Zombies. The first concert on this tour leg started on November 28 in Norway (3 days) and along with TV and radio in that country, appearances in Sweden (6 days), Finland (1 day) and Denmark (1 day) filled up their schedule before returning home on December 8. At Decca's offices in London, The Zombies were presented with Cashbox's "International Gold Award" on December 10. This award was given to the band for hitting #1 on the Cashbox singles chart. The same day, six songs were recorded at Decca: "Can't Nobody Love You," "I Can't Make Up My Mind," "I Got My Mojo Working," "The Way I Feel Inside," "Work 'N' Play," and "You've Really Got A Hold On Me." The same week, The Zombies played "Leave Me Be" on BBC Two's "Open House," and "Easy Beat" was broadcast. A 6-day tour of Poland was planned for the middle of December, but this was cancelled in favor of preparing for the upcoming Murray The K tour.

The original strategy was for "Leave Me Be" to be released as a follow-up US single to link with their tour. The failure of this record in the UK caused Parrot Records to change their plans. By auditioning the most recent Zombies tapes to locate a follow-up to "She's Not There," Parrot Records found something very accessible – "Tell Her No." Parrot made the unusual move of releasing "Tell Her No" before Decca, backed with the previous UK A-side "Leave Me Be." Similar to the UK publishing arrangement, Al Gallico created Mainstay Music, Inc. to handle new songs written by Argent and White. (Since "Leave Me Be" was an older song, Gallico published it through his company.) Decca would select "What More Can I Do" by Chris White as their B-side. In France, Decca would provide audiences with the first two UK A- and B-sides on an EP-only release (Decca 457.051).

The descending organ intro of "What More Can I Do" led to mouthfuls of increasingly frantic words that Blunstone was amazingly able to pull off convincingly with Grundy drum rolls breaking up each line. On top of this, Colin's vocal missives were divided by lunatic solos by Argent and Atkinson. The US single presentation of "Leave Me Be" used different overall equalization, leading some to incorrectly conclude that Colin Blunstone's vocal was re-recorded on this disc. There is no doubt that the US single's fidelity is inferior when compared to the UK 45. In Canada, the single was just like its US counterpart except that the B-side was mistakenly titled "You'd Better Leave Me Be."

By jumping the gun, Parrot scored a #6 hit with The Zombies' "Tell Her No." For once, the Billboard and Cashbox peak positions were in agreement. This Rod Argent song creation proved to be the most irresistible negative song since The Isley Brothers' "Nobody But Me." In its 2+ minutes, over 70 "no" backing vocals were featured as the song's hook, as well as Hugh Grundy's stuttered drums. With short, choppy major seventh and ninth chords, the song was clearly influenced by Burt Bacharach. "Tell Her No" was unusual in that it began with the word "and" – one of only a handful of songs in recent memory that start with this word (the most obvious ones are Paul Anka's "Puppy Love," "And I Love You So" by Don McLean and Argent's "Hold Your Head Up" – more on Argent later!). The use of "and" at the start gives the listener the feeling of coming into the middle of a conversation – a very interesting set-up for a song. Colin Blunstone's line following Argent's backing vocals was very emotive, and even his vocal mistake 55 seconds into the song only enhanced his emotional confusion! A guitar and keyboard link led right into the bridge, final verse and chorus, resolving the song nicely. "Tell Her No" earned Rod Argent another 1 million airplay award from BMI in 1995.

The UK release of "Tell Her No" proved extremely disappointing, producing a weak #42 response from Record Retailer and a slightly better #30 position in NME. With this poor showing, it became clear that The Zombies would do better by concentrating on their most successful market, namely the US.

In New York, all the Murray The K show preparations were in place. That is, except The Zombies' visas! In a rather childish backlash against the enormous US success of The Beatles and other British acts, the United States immigration office tried to limit the number of UK groups entering the country. If an American group could not do the job (that is, reproducing that UK group's act), an H-2 visa would then be awarded to that British band. Fanning the flames, a US immigration authority quoted that UK groups were "second-rate acts." The Zombies had to prove that their executed contracts for TV and concert dates in America required their presence in the country. Two or three days of hard bargaining with immigration authorities were necessary for The Zombies to gain limited US entry permission. Discussions concluded on Tuesday evening, December 15, just eight days before their planned flight to New York. It was a close call, but fellow Murray The K show performers The Nashville Teens and The Hullabaloos had to go through the same stressful ordeal in order to appear.

Upon arriving in New York on December 23, the band taped a "Shindig!" TV appearance for ABC-TV. The Zombies stayed in Brooklyn at The St. George Hotel on 51 Clark Street – a Brooklyn Heights hotel that had seen better days even in 1964! The next day was spent preparing for the Murray The K engagement and trying to understand the madness that is New York. Murray "The K" Kaufman had assembled a stellar lineup of mainly R&B acts, and Chris White talks about The Zombies' New York experience: "We played Murray The K's Brooklyn Fox. That was an education. It was like a magic land. The Brooklyn Fox was, to me, like walking into the television set of the series 'Naked City,' you know, 'There are 9 million stories out there...' To then hear the police sirens, the accents and the offhand New York attitude, it was magic! Except that we were playing many shows a day starting at 8 in the morning and ending at 11 at night. We had no time for leisure as you couldn't leave the building because in-between shows, they'd show the regularly scheduled movie and people were coming in and out of the place! And some of the other acts we played with were our heroes – Ben E. King, Dionne Warwick, The Shirelles, The Shangri-Las, Patti LaBelle And The Bluebelles. The Nashville Teens were there as well! We went out with The Nashville Teens on New Year's Eve to Times Square slightly pissed and someone was shot right in front of us! It was stunning seeing people like Dionne Warwick and The Shirelles singing harmonies in the wings of the dressing rooms which we shared. It drove hairs up your arms – it was so good! Murray The K would give continual lectures that the show wasn't good enough, it wasn't as good as last year! The fans were violent and they wanted to hack pieces off you. It was scary, to be quite honest."

Rod Argent provides his amusing thoughts on the St. George Hotel and the experience in general: "That was an extraordinary place. Obviously, at one time, it was quite a posh hotel but it was pretty seedy and run-down when we got there. There were lots of people in the foyer looking a bit strange. I remember waking at night to the sound of gunshots, which I thought was extraordinary and not knowing what's going on outside. Somebody was making money on us at that time! We had to travel home on the subway after midnight from the Brooklyn Fox to the St. George Hotel. The first day there, Colin and I were walking just outside the hotel. Walking down the street, we passed some coffee shop. This cop came up to us, and since we obviously looked very strange compared to how young American guys looked at that stage, he was very short and suspicious of us. As soon as he heard our English accents and what we were doing there, he said, 'Come on, I'll buy you coffee!'"

Colin Blunstone and Rod Argent on the streets of Brooklyn!
(photos: Barbara Campbell)

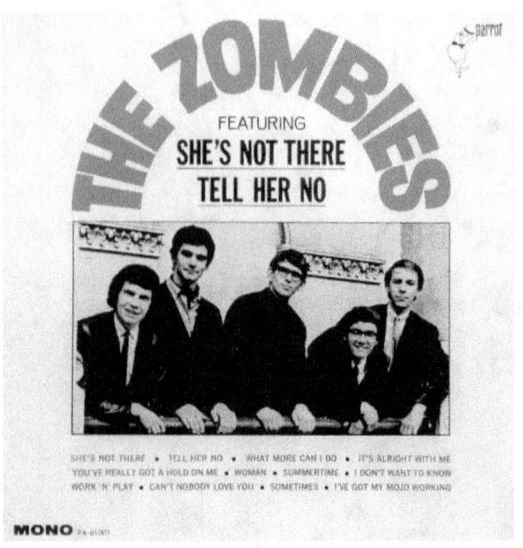

At left, the first US album (notice the reversed photo), and on the right, The Zombies' only British EP.

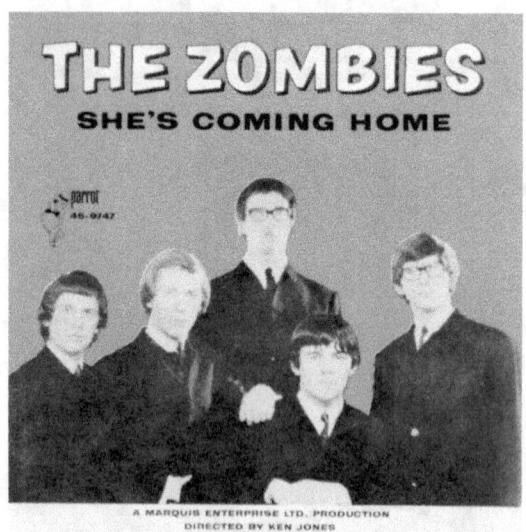

At left:
Dusty Springfield's US LP with Rod Argent's song "If It Don't Work Out."
At right:
The Parrot picture sleeve for "She's Coming Home."

It was clear that Chuck Jackson was the New York favorite based on the audible vocalizations of the crowd and show participants, but The Zombies did quite well. At these shows, The Zombies played two songs during five daily shows. On Sunday, there were six shows! With Murray The K out of the way, The Zombies spent January 4 and 5 at NBC's Rockefeller Center studios in New York City rehearsing for the first episode of "Hullabaloo." Their appearance was taped on the 6th and they flew home the next day. Radio and fan club meetings were also covered by the band at the end of their New York trip.

The Zombies simply did not have enough time to meet the demands of television and concert promoters. Ed Sullivan and Steve Allen offered the band TV appearances, and plans for The Zombies to go before the cameras in the film "Swinging Summer" (with The Searchers) were not finalized. On January 8, The Zombies had originally planned to play in New England for two more weeks (also mistakenly listed as a 4-week jaunt starting in Chicago), but their limited visas ran out. Plans to play South Africa in January with Dusty Springfield also broke down when Dusty was thrown out of the country.

With no other concerts on tap, January 1965 was something of a slow month for The Zombies. Their only EP was issued by Decca at the end of the month and featured three Argent originals ("Sometimes," "It's Alright" [aka "It's Alright With Me"] and "Kind Of Girl") and the cover of "Summertime." In late January and into February, appearances on the "Saturday Club," "Scene At 6.30," "Ready, Steady, Go!," "Easy Beat," "Thank Your Lucky Stars" and "Top Gear" programs were taped. Right on the back of this work, more UK gigs followed until the third week of April. At the "Thank Your Lucky Stars" taping, the late Dusty Springfield (born Mary O'Brien) asked Rod Argent if he could write a song for her. Rod worked on a song over a weekend and came up with "If It Don't Work Out." The song became one of the highlights on Dusty's "Ev'rything's Coming Up Dusty" #6 UK LP released that October, and just missed out on being released as a single.

THE FIRST ALBUM AND "BUNNY LAKE IS MISSING"

Parrot readied themselves for The Zombies' US tour by issuing the LP "The Zombies" in February 1965. Typical of most US LPs of British bands, "The Zombies" was a compilation of tracks from varied sources. Despite the "put together" nature of the record, a lot of thought went into Parrot's song selection. The album reflected a wide range of musical styles, from "Summertime" to the driving R&B standard "I Got My Mojo Working." Popularized by Muddy Waters, "Mojo" featured a rare, Argent lead vocal, his harmonica solo and Hugh's strong drumming. However, Ken Jones' confused and busy sounding mix obscured the bass frequencies. Therefore, this recording has proven to be among the least favorite tracks by Chris White and Paul Atkinson. Slower R&B came by way of "You've Really Got A Hold On Me" and "Can't Nobody Love You." "You've Really Got A Hold On Me" required only one take and was jointly sung by Blunstone and Argent. Seamlessly segueing into Sam Cooke's "Bring It On Home To Me," this medley was one of The Zombies' longest tracks at 3:37. It was Blunstone's recommendation that The Zombies cover "Can't Nobody Love You," the James Mitchell song brought to prominence by Solomon Burke. The Zombies don't disappoint here, using the simple backing of Colin's voice, Paul's first recorded use of his Burns 12-string guitar and Grundy's brushes, matched by strong Rod Argent backing vocals. Unlike many a Ken Jones-produced recording, Chris White is very audible here and deservedly so. The Ken Jones-written instrumental "Work 'N' Play" served two purposes: to give the producer some publishing royalties and to fill the gap in The Zombies' shortfall of original songs. Jones handled piano honors with Argent on harmonica. The idea for fading in the introduction was a tip of the hat to The Beatles' "Eight Days A Week." Still, Argent's harmonica solo and Grundy's spirited drumming throughout lifted the track above the average. The Chris White piece "I Don't Want To Know" illustrated his increasingly complex yet melodic writing style. Paul Atkinson had some difficulty in playing the ongoing 12-string guitar phrase on the recorded version, but he emerged successfully with more advanced playing skills that would be required on future recordings. Again, Hugh Grundy's drumming was solid, and the backing vocals of White and Argent gave Blunstone's lead voicing the proper buoyancy. Along with "It's Alright With Me," "Summertime," "Sometimes," "What More Can I Do" and the two US hit singles were here as well.

Parrot failed in getting a Zombies LP out by their US tour and it took a few weeks before sales returns were large enough to be listed on Billboard. The self-titled album reached an impressive #39 in its 17 chart weeks in 1965. Back in England, there were some standout Zombies shows. The now successful and transatlantic Zombies returned to St. Albans on February 20 for the first time since August 1, 1964. That was at the College For Further Education. An Empire Pool charity concert in Wembley for The Stars Organisation For Spastics took place on March 21 and also featured hitmakers Lulu, The Pretty Things, P.J. Proby, Sandie Shaw and The Merseybeats on the bill.

In the middle of this tour, The Zombies ventured to Decca and put down "I Must Move," "I Want You Back Again" (its second version), "Just Out Of Reach," "Remember You" (first version) and "She's Coming Home" on March 2. One week later, the band filmed a segment at the Tower Of London promoting the upcoming Dick Clark Caravan Of Stars tour. Michael Barclay, Decca A&R representative and soundtrack supervisor for the planned Otto Preminger-directed mystery film "Bunny Lake Is

Missing," was interested in including The Zombies in the film. Barclay recommended that Preminger attend an audition given by The Zombies on March 12 at the Cromwellian Club in order to determine their suitability. Preminger was visibly impressed, although he was no fan of pop music! With only a couple of weeks to assemble new songs for the film, Chris White (with two songs) and Colin Blunstone (one song – his first) ended up producing the goods.

Around this time, rehearsals also took place at the Argent home. Between Colin, Chris and Rod, arrangements would be hammered out, and the songwriter would have first say on vocal harmonies before Rod took a final crack at it. These rehearsals were important, as Rod and Chris did not write songs while on tour. All the songs by the band were getting more complex, and despite their inherent playing limitations, Rod Argent's enthusiasm pushed everyone (including himself) to a higher level.

The band's film involvement would cause some scheduling problems, since Tito Burns had them on tour from March 25 with Dusty Springfield, The Searchers, Tony Jackson And The Vibrations, Bobby Vee, Heinz And The Wild Boys, and occasional participants George Meaton and The Echoes. The tour was supposed to last through mid-April, but Otto Preminger's filming demands for "Bunny Lake Is Missing" forced The Zombies to miss two tour dates: March 31 and April 9. The Zombies used the first date to record other tracks used in the film and its trailer: "Come On Time," "Nothing's Changed," "Remember You" (first version), and a promo spot. Since March 31 was a travel day for the Tito Burns tour, no harm was done. However, missing the two April 9 Taunton Odeon gigs exacerbated rising tensions between the band and Tito Burns, as The Zombies were rehearsing for their movie debut to be filmed the next day. As a result, The Zombies had to leave the tour. Besides, they had better things to do by appearing on "Thank Your Lucky Stars," "Saturday Club," and "Top Of The Pops."

With all of the time and effort filming on the "Ready, Steady, Go!" set for "Bunny Lake Is Missing," The Zombies were hardly used in the finished film – they appeared on a television episode of "Ready, Steady, Go!" in a bar scene! The film's commercial trailer used a more extensive outtake of the band, but they could not help feeling used. Even more important, the film was not issued in America until October 3, 1965, and in the UK, February 10, 1966! This inevitably diluted the impact of their songs, which were quite old upon their eventual release. Here's Chris White's take on their film debut: "That was funny. It was directed by Otto Preminger and we were filmed for three days and got equal billing with Laurence Olivier and Keir Dullea and we wound up appearing for about two minutes in the movie inside a television in the background, performing! We made about £30 each! I wrote two songs – 'Remember You' and 'Nothing's Changed,' and Colin wrote 'Just Out Of Reach,' which was one of his first songs and he was ever so pleased he got it on the film."

Of the three songs recorded for the soundtrack, "Nothing's Changed" was the only one that had been previously released. It was on the UK charity album "14 (Benefit For The Lord's Taverners National Playing Fields Association)" which included new tracks by other Decca groups like The Rolling Stones, Lulu, and Tom Jones. In the US, the LP was more succinctly named "England's Greatest Hitmakers." "Nothing's Changed" from the pen of Chris White revealed another successful Zombies experiment: chorded half triplets by guitar, bass and pianet were played during its middle section over Hugh Grundy's 4/4 drum beat, reflecting excellent control. This unique musical passage was undoubtedly why this song required 16 takes to master, but the results were extremely worthwhile. An alternate backing track highlighting this section was first issued in 1997 on "Zombie Heaven" along with the final version.

The other two "Bunny" songs also required a lot of takes to perfect. "Just Out Of Reach" needed 18 attempts, but its more aggressive guitar sound led the way for another solid Argent organ solo and neat transition to its chorus and bridge. Hugh Grundy capped it off with a good drum roll ending. Noticing that Rod Argent and Chris White were doing well from their song royalties, Colin Blunstone decided to get into the act. "Just Out Of Reach" was the first of his two songs that The Zombies recorded. A short extract of the backing track was used in the song "Come On Time," an essential film trailer element specially recorded for the director. Otto Preminger wanted to make clear that latecomers would not be allowed to see the film, hence the song. A priceless part of the song is Rod Argent's exaggerated, Americanized pronunciation of the word "clock"! The revised lyrics were written with Harold Bunbrim and it was first issued on "Zombie Heaven." That box set also included a 1-minute "Come On Time" edit with a Laurence Olivier film excerpt as "'Bunny Lake Is Missing' Promo Spot." When the band later returned to record the single version of "Remember You" on August 27, 1965, twenty-one takes were required, while the soundtrack edition needed 17 passes for completion. Chris White tells us about the song's inspiration: "I think I got the idea for 'Remember You' from Winston Churchill's funeral when I heard bagpipes playing a melody which I liked and then used." The jazz waltz arrangement revealed another facet of the band's playing, using Rod Argent's short piano flourishes effectively. The soundtrack version of the song used a slower, slightly inferior arrangement.

EXPERIMENTING WITH THE PAST

Coinciding with their Taunton appearance (April 9) was Decca's release of the next Zombies single: "She's Coming Home." Its US release once again preceded Decca's issue due to The Zombies' stronger profile in the States. Originally known as "I Cry No More," "She's Coming Home" was a uniquely crafted and partitioned song developed from songs that Rod Argent sang in choir. For the chorus line of "She's Coming Home," Rod Argent used the chord sequence from Herbert Howells' "Nunc Dimittis," which Herbert wrote as the second half of a unified piece with "Magnificat." English composer Howells (1892-1983) wrote these two Anglican choral efforts in October 1954 for church services sung by the Choir of St. Paul's Cathedral in London. Both "Magnificat" and "Nunc Dimittis" were known as canticles, that is, liturgical songs based on Biblical source material. The former was the canticle of the Virgin Mary based on the book of Luke 1: 46-55, while the latter was Simeon's prayer based on Luke 2: 29-32. "Magnificat" was named by its first word, meaning "magnify," and "Nunc Dimittis" meant "now let you depart." While Rod Argent was not aware of it at the time, Howells freely used choral arrangements with 7th, 9th, 11th and 13th chords in both works. These sonoric chords would be very similar to the jazz structures that Rod was also taking in at the time. In fact, Argent's prior encounter with Vic Briggs of The Laurie Jay Combo reinforced his use of these chords in a more pop-related format.

On "She's Coming Home," Colin Blunstone's uplifting vocal was balanced nicely by good group harmonics and Rod Argent's piano presence. It was indeed unfortunate that the final, hollow mix lacked any clarity or power. Reflecting mostly midrange frequencies, the guitar and bass were not well-defined. Even Hugh Grundy's strong playing, the element that made their previous US hits stand out, was not presented properly in the mix. This was reflected in the record's lukewarm American response – a 48 peak in Cashbox, but only 58 in Billboard. The complete lack of interest in "She's Coming Home" by UK audiences was even more disappointing.

The single's experimental B-side, "I Must Move," was another Chris White song of great merit. Originally created as "I Believe In You," the song's original single mix featured a striking reverbed guitar. "I Must Move" was another down song, but one easily forgets about its tone when the band's harmony vocals carry things along. Most impressive about the song was Hugh Grundy's performance, in which he did not have to smash away to make his presence felt. French fans were able to enjoy this single pairing along with "Tell Her No" and "What More Can I Do" (the previous 45) on their unique EP (Decca 457.075).

Joining the already in-progress Dick Clark's Caravan Of Stars tour from April 24 to June 2, The Zombies' second US trek took the band into uncharted territory in the States and Canada. An ever-changing lineup of acts was featured, including Del Shannon, The Shangri-Las, The Velvelettes, Jewel Akens, Dee Dee Sharp, Mel Carter, Mike Clifford, The Ad Libs, Tommy Roe, The Executives (with Jim Guercio), The Larks, and Jimmy Soul. Despite the exposure, Chris White tells us this tour was not as glamorous as it may have seemed: "Of course, we didn't make any money from these things (tours) as we got ripped off by management. We did three tours of America and we travelled by bus. One was the Dick Clark Caravan Of Stars which we did 6 weeks playing every night, sleeping every other night on the bus with 16 other acts and we got £500 each, which was the only money we ever made off America without getting ripped off. Del Shannon was on this tour and used to come up and play with us live. In England, when we toured he'd come along to our gigs and come up and sing and play 'Runaway' and 'Tell Her No' and it would go down a storm. I really liked Del, he was great fun. He had this incredible collection of condoms of all different colors that he used to show us! We were the only English band on the tour. Also on the tour were The Shangri-Las, The Larks, The Ad Libs, and Dee Dee Sharp, who allegedly was thrown off the tour for pulling a gun on Mel Carter – they hated each other, Tommy Roe, and The Executives, who later evolved into Chicago! We were playing in Cornwall before the start of the tour, drove the whole night to London airport where we slept, got on a plane and flew to New York, got on another plane, got off the plane and drove off to join the tour which was already in progress, got to the dressing room and changed and went on stage doing 'She's Not There'! Everyone thought Colin's voice was something concocted in the recording studio and we felt we had to prove something, so there Colin went in front of the microphone and when they heard him sing they were knocked out. Then we got on the bus which drove 500 miles to the next gig and we hadn't slept anywhere for two days. All the black acts were singing gospel music all through the night on the bus in great harmony and they said, 'Come on you limeys, white boys, sing something' and Rod and Colin sang one of The Beatles' songs unaccompanied and it went down a storm. From that moment, we were accepted by everyone on the tour, and one of The Velvelettes, a black female group, who I sat next to the whole tour, said, 'You're the only English guy I've slept next to and enjoyed it!' It was a time when sometimes we couldn't get things to eat in the Southern states because restaurants wouldn't serve us because of the black acts. We didn't understand all this prejudice as we weren't exposed to it in England and it was something out of a horror film, actually." After years of playing "Tell Her No" live, Del Shannon finally issued the song as a single in 1975.

The grueling nature of the tour led to one major breakdown. After arriving at New York's La Guardia airport on April 24, a

30-hour traveling odyssey through Evansville, Indiana eventually brought them to Nashville, Tennessee in time for the next day's show. Hugh Grundy found himself in an Odessa, Texas hospital suffering from food poisoning on May 12, and The Crickets' drummer Jerry Allison was called in to take over that night. Zombies fans had another chance to catch the band, as another "Shindig!" appearance a week after Hugh's illness was on tap. The last day of the tour was a changeover point, as The Zombies joined the bill with Herman's Hermits and idols Little Anthony And The Imperials.

"BEGIN HERE"

At the end of April, Decca released the LP that The Zombies had been assembling for some time: "Begin Here." This project provided the incentive and proper outlet for their latest songs, according to Chris White: "We played around with doing original material, but people didn't want to hear it and you had to please your audience. When it came time to doing an album though, we had to do original material so we were writing all the time and throwing ideas off each other."

The 14-track "Begin Here" LP substituted "Sticks And Stones," "Road Runner," "The Way I Feel Inside," "I Can't Make Up My Mind" and "I Remember When I Loved Her" for "Tell Her No," "Sometimes" and "It's Alright With Me" on the US album. Despite these changes, the quality level of the album remained the same. The band's recent British chart failures did not motivate fans to purchase this LP either.

"Sticks And Stones" and "Road Runner" were covers of R&B workhorses that bands had to do at the time. Titus Turner's "Sticks And Stones" was a US Top 40 hit by Ray Charles in 1960, while the Ellas McDaniel (Bo Diddley) composition "Road Runner" earned its success through numerous cover versions. Overall, Chris White, most of the band (and even most fans) agree that these two tracks along with "I Got My Mojo Working" are the three weakest recordings in their career. Part of the reason for this is the poor mixing involved on the songs.

For "Sticks And Stones," the backing track is driving enough, but the drums are mixed up too high at the expense of the guitar and keyboard parts. Chris White's bass contributions are similarly buried, and as a result, Colin Blunstone did not sound gritty enough to rise above the muddled mix. Saving graces of the recording are a sweeping organ solo along with Paul Atkinson's guitar run. "Road Runner"'s mix sounded too busy as the guitar riff and organ unnecessarily dominated the proceedings. Grundy's banging works well here, although one wishes for a more "earthy" vocal and possibly a harmonica break. Again, Atkinson and Argent's solos save the day.

"I Can't Make Up My Mind" was another Chris White song of indecision, on which Paul Atkinson's 12-string guitar proved difficult for soloing and tuning. From its distinctive opening to the firm, massively echoed Blunstone lead, it gradually soared to exciting heights. Just for fun, notice the gap in the guitar track needed for Atkinson to prepare for his brief solo! Also unique about the song was that it faded, a rarity in the Zombies canon. Rod's "I Remember When I Loved Her" used his organ break to float above the eerie minor-keyed proceedings, and his vocal along with Colin's matched the mood appropriately. Ken Jones put in another guest appearance, supplying tambourine.

Of the album's new songs, Argent's "The Way I Feel Inside" revealed the highest level of advancement in their abilities through a very short, simple arrangement. Colin Blunstone exhibited exacting control by singing the first half of the song "a capella" and maintaining pitch and timing when Argent's organ quietly intruded. Not bad for a song that Rod wrote on the toilet while on their Isley Bros. tour! Ken Jones' idea of adding the sound of a coin dropping at the song's end added a brilliant, professional touch. However, the song was not as well defined in its earliest incarnation. The original version released on "Zombie Heaven" revealed studio chat and a rejected band version similar in feel to that of an early version of "I Wanna Be Free" by The Monkees recorded later in 1965.

Along with publisher Al Gallico, Parrot Records wanted unique single product to cash in on the Dick Clark tour, so "I Want You Back Again" b/w "I Remember When I Loved Her" formed a US-only release in late May 1965. Incorrectly labelled "Somebody Help Me" on its tape box, the A-side's somewhat inaccessible jazz waltz proved difficult to program on radio. For the first time (and far from the last), The Zombies were musically ahead of the more pop-oriented market. A good Hugh Grundy drum performance was the song's hook, along with a spiralling pianet solo and more prominent bass. Cashbox reflected a #92 peak position with Billboard coming in three positions lower. Other than the US, Australia was the only other country participating in this single's release (Decca 7239). An alternate version of "I Want You Back Again" made its first appearance on the 1969 US compilation "Early Days," although it was not quite as efficient as the single take. Parrot mistakenly credited the A-side as "Remember When I Loved Her."

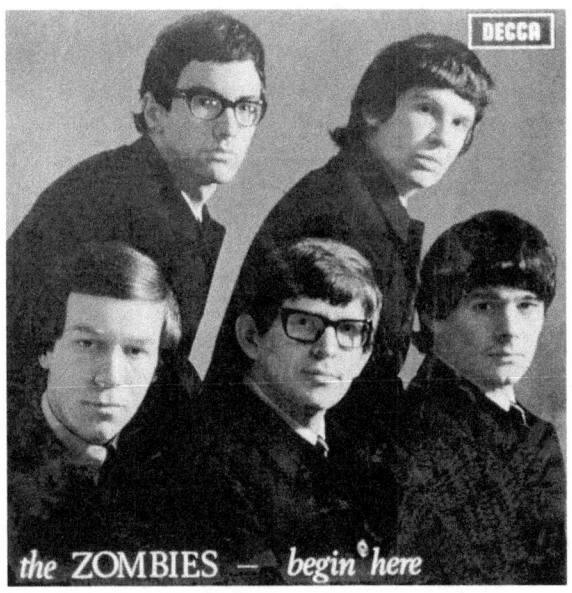

At left: the "Begin Here" album, the UK "Whenever You're Ready" 45, and the US version of the "14" LP: "England's Greatest Hitmakers."

Above is the US-only single "I Remember When I Loved Her" (with its slightly altered title), and below, the band is shown with producer Ken Jones.

25

Upon their return to the UK, The Zombies were found demoing their latest creations. Sometime in June (also shown as April, but this is unlikely due to their schedule), they went to Jackson's Studio and worked out "I Know She Will," "I'll Keep Trying," "Whenever You're Ready," and "You'll Go From Me." All of these first appeared on the "Zombie Heaven" box set in 1997. Of these songs, all but "I Know She Will" were recorded for Decca on June 24. "I Know She Will" was laid down at Decca on July 8 with "Don't Cry For Me," "How We Were Before," "I Love You," and "If It Don't Work Out." An unusual two-day engagement at Paris' La Locomotif fell in between on June 27 and 28, preparing The Zombies for their third (and what proved to be their last) US tour. Before they left, The Zombies filmed at Rediffusion's Wembley Studios for another "Ready, Steady, Go!" TV appearance.

Between July 15 and August 15, The Zombies played with The Searchers in an unusual cross-country US tour covering about 18,000 miles. Tito Burns managed both groups and coordinated this rather hasty trip with the William Morris Agency in the US. Again, some of the shows were extremely memorable, especially since both groups were in the unique position of playing 45 minutes apiece. An extravaganza at the Montgomery, Alabama Coliseum on July 23 had The Zombies playing to nearly 20,000 people with The Beach Boys, Del Shannon, and other bands. Tom Jones and Peter And Gordon were also on hand in Norfolk, Virginia (August 6), and The Zombies joined Johnny Rivers between August 16 and 19 at his official residence – the Whisky A Go-Go in L.A. Conveniently, another Zombies appearance on "Shindig!" coincided with their L.A. stint. The Zombies were back in St. Albans on the 20th, and they did another local gig there ten days later. At this time, The Zombies were playing Sam Cooke's "A Change Is Gonna Come," the B-side of "Shake." August 27 also marked the second (single) recording of "Remember You."

The Zombies originally felt that their touring should be directed to their strongest markets in America, Sweden, and the Philippines. However, it became clear that their US efforts were not achieving the desired sales effect, and their already ailing UK profile was becoming nearly invisible. Decca had sensed this, and their promo budget for Zombies releases was drastically cut for coverage in NME and Melody Maker.

The day after their last US tour ended, Parrot once again got the first crack at the next Zombies single: "Whenever You're Ready" b/w "I Love You." Both sides of the single have been universally praised as having the most overall hit potential of any record in their career. Still, the fact that it could only manage a #110 position in Billboard was a crushing blow to the band. Decca would release the single about two and a half weeks later with little interest. "Whenever You're Ready" employed Grundy's cymbal as a hook on verses with syncopated piano chords and vocals forming the song's emphasis. With well defined bass, it was the band's best sounding Decca single to date, using a descending chorus and good harmony. The embryonic demo version debuting on "Zombie Heaven" had a different solo structure and a more restrained Blunstone vocal, but this structure was essential in creating the final version.

"I Love You" took another White song structure and made a strong B-side statement. Using an EMI-like recording procedure, a guitar introduction was edited onto a later take of the body of the song. Besides "Sometimes," it was the only other Zombies song pieced together in this way. Blunstone's soaring vocals and group harmony overpower the listener and capture the moment at every turn. The swirling keyboard solo used "She's Not There"-like backing to work its magic, and Hugh Grundy's detached drum pattern was yet another hook in this multi-faceted song. It was just a shame that White's driving bass was not quite loud enough in the mix to deliver the over-the-top power that the band's performance outlined. Still, other groups looked beyond this and covered the song with great success. The Carnabeats had a Japanese language hit with the song (their debut single) in July 1967, and the next year, San Jose, California group People hit #14 in the US with an expanded take on the tune.

In September 1965, Rod Argent won two BMI (Broadcast Music Inc. of America) "citation of achievement" awards for "She's Not There" and "Tell Her No." Ironically, after all their previous immigration problems, these awards led to unrestricted US appearance visas for the band. The Zombies were requested to attend the US premiere of "Bunny Lake Is Missing" that October, but they turned it down to concentrate on England. They would never test their US visas again.

"Whenever You're Ready" was aired on TV on both sides of the Atlantic. "Ready, Steady, Go!," "Gadzooks!," and "Thank Your Lucky Stars Summerspin" covered England, while "Shindig!" was the US contribution. "Gadzooks!" was also unique in that The Zombies joined fellow Decca stablemates Lulu and The Small Faces on the inspirational "I'm On My Way, Great God." "Easy Beat," "Saturday Club" and the northern regional "The Beat Show" program kept The Zombies on the airwaves.

The "Bunny Lake Is Missing" soundtrack was finally released in October 1965, but it did not score since the film was not an overwhelming success. By the time it debuted at the Odeon Leicester Square on February 10, 1966, the Zombies songs in the film had no relevance to what they were currently doing. On the back of this album, another America-debuting single surfaced: "Just Out Of Reach" b/w "Remember You." The B-side was an alternate version of the song on the soundtrack, and this managed a miserable #113 Billboard placing. In January 1966, Decca flipped over the single and promoted "Remember You" to no avail. Once again, France had a unique issue: a "Bunny Lake A Disparu" ("Bunny Lake Is Missing") EP with the three Zombies soundtrack songs and Paul Glass' "Samantha's Waltz" (RCA Victor 86.507). A contest by British publication Record Mirror provided winners with a personalized message on an acetate with "Remember You." Only one copy of this unique acetate is known to exist today. It was included on "The Singles Collection: As & Bs 1964-1969" in March 2000.

An unusual one-song session at Decca on November 10 produced another Rod Argent gem: "Is This The Dream." Sixteen days later, it would be quickly released as their next UK A-side and the last recorded at Decca's studios. Quite unusual for an Argent song to rely on guitar, "Is This The Dream" sported its Motown influences well in a driving harmony number. Still, The Zombies were unhappy that the final mix did not capture the power of the raw tape. Grundy's work and White's looping bass runs were fine matches for Blunstone's strong vocal, but this time, the keyboard solo got lost in the shuffle. Incidentally, the backing vocals were directly recorded into the mono mix, so the stereo mix appearing on later versions does not have this essential song element. Since "Just Out Of Reach" was already in release in the US, the Parrot single was delayed until the end of February 1966 to give it proper attention. It also failed in the marketplace, this time without charting.

The B-side of "Is This The Dream" was yet another intelligent three-part Chris White number: "Don't Go Away." It started its life as "You'll Go From Me," a moody, differently arranged demo that first appeared on "Zombie Heaven" in 1997. Also guitar-based, "Don't Go Away" was another wistful observation on a failed relationship. Another French EP (Decca 457.100) captured all four tracks from this record and the previous single for fans.

The Zombies spent six days on a Swedish tour in mid-November. A proposed 3-day jaunt to Iceland, of all places, was planned but cancelled according to Chris White. At this time, The Zombies worked in two recent hits: "Since I Lost My Baby" by The Temptations and "Tracks Of My Tears" (The Miracles). Their TV schedule for 1965 was completed by an appearance on "Five O'Clock Club."

Rod Argent also had time to contribute the instrumental "Shadows" for the Jackson brothers' studio-bound project The Second City Sound. "Shadows" was recorded by Malcolm and John Jackson at their Rickmansworth studio as the B-side of the "Tchaikovsky One" single. Demo copies were originally pressed on their Jackson label, but it was released by Decca at the tail end of 1965. "Shadows," a fine melodic piece, sported one of the earliest uses of a mellotron. Although it did not sell enough to make the NME chart, "Tchaikovsky One" reached #22 on the Record Retailer listing. This small measure of success earned the record a US release on London Records.

DISAPPOINTMENT SETS IN

The year 1966 was very difficult for The Zombies, as success was elusive for the entire twelve-month period. January was filled with appearances on "Easy Beat," the "Pop Profile" interview series, and two Colin Blunstone guest spots on "Juke Box Jury" (with Tito Burns as guest judge) and "Dateline London" (a transcription service interview). A potentially ominous sign was present in February when Blunstone and the band in turn were notified of Ken Jones and Joe Roncoroni's discussions of making a Colin Blunstone solo single. This plan was similar to Yardbirds producer Giorgio Gomelsky's solo single plans for vocalist Keith Relf, but Blunstone had no intention of putting his name before the others. More importantly, Colin was tiring of the pop lifestyle, especially its diminishing returns.

Live shows continued with The Miracles' "Going To A Go-Go" now in the set. The Temptations' "My Girl" was enjoyed so much by The Zombies that they recorded a now-lost demo in the spring. With Otis Redding's big UK hit with the song, a Zombies version would be superfluous. On May 4, The Zombies entered Lansdowne Studios for the first time. The band was beginning to doubt their hit songwriting skills with the devastating failures of their recent self-penned A-sides. Despite feeling strongly about their previous records, The Zombies thought about doing some covers. They only attacked one cover in this four-song session – "Gotta Get A Hold On Myself" by Clint Ballard, Jr. and Angela Riela. Ballard had written a number of UK hits, including "You're No Good" (The Swinging Blue Jeans), The Hollies' "I'm Alive" and Wayne Fontana & The Mindbenders' "The Game Of Love," so he was a proven commodity. Along with this song, Rod contributed "Indication" and "She Does Everything For Me," and Chris White chipped in "I'll Call You Mine."

"Indication" and "How We Were Before" were rushed out by Decca on June 17 and met with immediate disinterest. "Indication" was even more powerful than usual for a Zombies A-side – in fact, it was their most aggressive and progressive single to date. However, what was lacking was commerciality in the singles market. A strong Blunstone/Argent joint vocal

Clockwise from top left are the rare US stock copy of "Is This The Dream," the American single B-side "Shadows" written by Rod Argent for The Second City Sound, and an advance copy of "Gotta Get A Hold On Myself."

made the most of the pulsating 4/4 backing track, as Hugh Grundy drilled his performance. The song's unique feature was its rave-up section lasting from the middle to its unusual pianet ending. This section was developed from their live version of Jimmy Reed's "Baby What You Want Me To Do." Using an old jazz technique, Argent sang along with the pianet riff that accompanied Paul Atkinson's playing. One could only imagine how the response would have been if Ken Jones properly harnessed their group power in the final mix. Parrot Records thought the rave-up was completely unnecessary and faded the three-minute track to a 2:07 length. It comes as no surprise that Atkinson for one considered "Indication" a wasted opportunity as he was brought up too far in the muddled mix. Colin Blunstone's "How We Were Before," recorded all the way back in July 1965, was the B-side – a nice acoustic song with the tasty accompaniment of Grundy's brushes.

On July 6, 1966, The Zombies played their most notable show from this period. The Brighton Box Club featured The Zombies with powerhouse group The Who. Keith Moon's twisted sense of humor was unleashed on The Zombies in the form of a tear gas bomb dropped in their dressing room – minutes before showtime! Chris White recalls, "I had purchased a starting pistol for a laugh on stage and we were sharing a dressing room with The Who. I thought Keith might appreciate the joke, so I fired it! Keith then had a big grin all over his face as he pulled his pistol out and fired it, and the rest of The Who suddenly rushed out of the room, leaving us wondering what was going on – and then the tear gas hit us!" Despite this "excitement," very few shows of this magnitude would come their way in the future.

The band's St. Albans friend Mick Trounce gave them Dee Dee Warwick's US single of "Gotta Get A Hold On Myself." In The Zombies' version, Argent took on a ghostly organ sound and White's sprightly bass runs joined a progressively soaring Blunstone vocal into potent Rod and Chris vocal harmonies. It would become their next Decca single in September 1966, but another hollow-sounding mix did them in. Parrot had had enough of The Zombies' failures, and they passed on this record when it flopped in the UK. Even though they had enough recorded material, Decca used "The Way I Feel Inside" from the "Begin Here" LP as this single's B-side. This move indicated Decca's lack of confidence in their output. "Gotta Get A Hold On Myself" was used on the TV program "Hippodrome" on July 12, 1966, although the single was not released to American audiences. It is the only existing color footage of the band, and it featured them singing and playing on top of the backing track.

Chris White started to rely on home demos to express his more involved songs, and "I Don't Want To Worry" was one of his first attempts. It featured Colin with harmony vocals, but unusually, Hugh Grundy was not present at its recording. The song was never officially recorded, initially appearing on the "Zombie Heaven" box set. The same fate befell the demos that followed: "A Love That Never Was" and "One Day I'll Say Goodbye." The former was a Rod Argent guitar song with minor keyboard input that had Grundy using "She's Not There"-type drum fills. White's "One Day I'll Say Goodbye" would later evolve into "Maybe After He's Gone" on the "Odessey And Oracle" LP.

After completing a live spot on "The Joe Loss Show," The Zombies found themselves under increasing pressure by Decca and promoter Tito Burns to turn out another hit. They were forced to search for another outside song to cover and went after "Goin' Out Of My Head," having adored Little Anthony And The Imperials' US hit version. Dodie West had just breached the British Top 40 with the song in 1965, but The Zombies felt that they would not be going after the same audience by covering the song in their style. Unfortunately, Ken Jones made his last recording mistake by recording horns and vibes on Colin Blunstone's vocal track, thereby obliterating his stellar performance. The song was originally recorded at Kingsway Studio on October 23, but Colin had to double-track his vocal at Advision Studios in November in an attempt to salvage the record. Despite his efforts, Decca issued the single-tracked vocal version, and The Zombies were furious. At this point, Ken Jones was respectfully told that Argent and White would be producing themselves on an upcoming LP they planned with the group. "She Does Everything For Me" was the B-side of "Goin' Out Of My Head," and could have been an A-side in its own right. A driving guitar rocker with handclaps and prime keyboard playing, the song debuted double-tracked harmonies. These choir-like harmonies worked well with Colin Blunstone's uplifting lead vocal. Paul Atkinson's droning guitar used sitar-like effects, and Chris White and Hugh Grundy carried the background along in good measure. Again, what was needed was more lower-end response in the mix. This deficiency would not take place again.

In late October to mid-November, The Zombies found themselves in some wide-ranging places. After doing a show in Belgium, The Zombies were in Paris on October 29, 1966 appearing on the Emperor Rosko TV show "Dents De Lait, Dents De Loup" with Sylvie Vartan and Marianne Faithfull. The show's title means "First Set, Second Set," a musical play on the word "set" taken from its literal translation of "Baby Teeth, Wolf's Teeth" – the first and second set of teeth. That performance was significant because the band performed "This Old Heart Of Mine" and "Going To A Go-Go," the latter of which was a rare Zombies performance of the song. This program was followed up by their usual "Saturday Club" stint in early November. Between the 8th and 20th of November, The Zombies toured Scandinavia and ran into Bluesology keyboard player Reg Dwight (you know him better as Elton John). These shows would feature songs like The Four Tops' "Loving You Is Sweeter Than Ever."

More home demos followed upon their return, such as "This Will Be Our Year," "Out Of The Day," and "Call Of The Night." All of these were written by Chris White and were first issued on "Zombie Heaven." The first song was later redone on "Odessey And Oracle," and "Out Of The Day" used backing vocal styles that would be employed later on that LP although the song was not tackled again. Unusually constructed, it had a striking guitar introduction, Grundy cymbal accents and a Chris White vocal with a brief jazzy middle section. "Call Of The Night" would evolve into the later tune "Girl Help Me," and with "Out Of The Day," it is conceivable that White may have written these two as a linked pair of songs. The fade-in on "Call Of The Night" also provided a unique touch. Concluding 1966, Decca in Sweden provided Zombies fans with a unique LP drawn from their prior Decca LP and singles. It was issued as Decca LK 4843.

Financial concerns were starting to become very obvious within the band. Paul Atkinson and Hugh Grundy were not earning publishing royalties since they were not songwriters, and Colin Blunstone's two songs ("Just Out Of Reach" and "How We Were Before") were not on hit records. Their touring income was also in decline, especially since they were unwittingly being taken advantage of by Tito Burns. It became obvious to all five members that unless they scored a massive hit, it would soon be all over.

Despite Ken Jones' recent errors, The Zombies still relied on Jones and Joe Roncoroni for advice on their next move. (In fact, The Zombies' working relationship with Jones and Roncoroni always remained strong, even after the breakup of the group.) Clearly, their days with Decca were about to end and preparing a self-produced album proposal with another record company was their goal. Joe Roncoroni arranged a meeting with CBS A&R representative Derek Everett, and Joe and Ken's collectively excellent reputations not only helped get The Zombies a CBS contract, but recording arrangements with EMI's landmark Abbey Road Studios. CBS gave The Zombies £1,000 to produce some product without any time constraints. This Argent/White-produced Zombies LP would be the first independent (i.e. non-EMI) project at the four-track studio complex, and they had the good fortune to obtain the services of seasoned engineer Peter Vince.

Through week-long rehearsals at a Wheathampstead village hall, the band started to work on their CBS album early in 1967. Rod Argent did a demo of one of his songs from this project, "I Want Her She Wants Me," for The Mindbenders in late 1966. Their version came out at the tail end of '66, and even earned a US release in early 1967. Unfortunately, neither edition sold, but that group's somewhat one-dimensional take on the song did not detract from Argent and White's use of it for CBS. In the unique position of not having any record company pressure, The Zombies hibernated for about three months and chose to clear any outstanding gigs off their schedule to fully devote their time to this LP. One of the gigs they turned down was at The Queens College in Oxford on March 10, 1967.

The obscure US release of The Mindbenders' take on Rod Argent's "I Want Her She Wants Me."

The Zombies' last original Decca single – "Goin' Out Of My Head."

THE PHILIPPINE DEBACLE

One touring exception was made in late February, when Tito Burns arranged a weeklong Zombies tour of the Philippines. Chris White explains that the tour offer was too good to be true: "One day our manager Tito Burns said, 'I've got the gig for you in the Philippines – it's 10 days, they pay all your travel costs, all your food, all your keep, everything, £75 a night between you.' This was just after The Beatles had been thrown out of there for insulting Marcos. I was into travel and The Searchers had just played there and I said, 'Let's do it.' So we travel to the Philippines, ideas in our heads because we had been writing songs and thinking about 'Odessey And Oracle.' After a 30-hour flight, we arrived in Manila at 3:00 in the morning and were met by about 3,000 kids at the airport, not realizing three things: 1) the Philippines was the third biggest English speaking nation in the world, 2) we had three records in the Top 20 there, and 3) we were playing at the biggest stadium in the world after the Houston Astrodome. For £75 a night split amongst the group we were playing to 30,000 people a day. The whole show was built around us with dancers choreographed by a Hollywood producer. We were prisoners. We had signed a deal saying that all social and outside activities had to be okayed by the promoter. We were told that Manila was a dangerous place and they didn't want to lose their investment. They had their own private army and wouldn't let us out. The head of our record company in the Philippines, who loved The Zombies' music, a Chinese guy (S.Y. Cheng), actually told us we were being screwed. He said to ask for more money when they asked to extend the concert dates because by playing our previous gigs we had apparently made up the debt for 2 1/2 years of previous losses at the Stadium. The promoters literally held our passports and when we asked for more money, they said, 'No, you're finished – get out' but didn't give us our passports back. It was a scene like 'Danger Man,' and as the oldest, I was elected by the group to take charge. We had to go to the airport carrying our suitcases with all these screaming kids charging us and there were two big, burly guys with our passports. Trembling, I asked them for the passports saying that we were going to China and then home but would be coming back. With hands shaking, I got them and the burly guys said, '(promoter) Mister Araneta's not going to be happy.'"

What happened was that on February 28, 1967, the band left England and arrived in Manila the next day to follow Sam The Sham And The Pharoahs' ten-date Araneta Coliseum stint. The original Zombies tour was to last from March 3 to 9, but the engagement was then extended three days with a side trip to Hong Kong. The Zombies played to crowds consistently numbering around 30,000 at Araneta Coliseum in Cubao, Quezon City, run by promoter Jorge Araneta. During one of their 40-minute show-ending sets, The Zombies found themselves playing for 46,000 people. Araneta had inadvertently licensed the services of The Zombies through a third party that originally bought the group's performance rights from Tito Burns. Sian Yola Cheng, the head of their Philippine record label Super Record Company, tipped The Zombies off about this corruption and offered the band gigs in Hong Kong for additional income. Cheng was also the one that notified the band that the royalties from their "hit" singles were also among the missing. (While it is possible that Zombies singles could have been in Manila's local Top 10, official national charts sent to Billboard's Philippine office reveal no Zombies Top 10 hits.) On March 12, the band went to Hong Kong and returned to Manila on the 15th. Through Cheng, The Zombies tried to obtain two more weeks of shows at Manila's suburban nightspots, but only the dates at The Plaza Restaurant, The Nile Club (the 18th) and the El Dorado Club (18th and 19th) took place. The El Dorado show also included appearances by The Crystals and The Dyna Souls. Meanwhile, Jorge Araneta held their passports and told Philippine authorities that they were violating their temporary visa status by playing these club dates instead of the gigs he thought they were contracted for. The Zombies requested an additional £1,000 for their appearances and Araneta was incensed. At this point, Araneta revealed that he was in effect overpaying for The Zombies through his roundabout deal with a Tito Burns "fence." With this revealed and The Zombies surviving their passport ordeal, Paul Atkinson called Burns in London and fired him.

Upon their return to England, The Zombies and Decca officially parted ways. Also at this time, The Hollies and even John Lennon had offered to produce the band, but Rod Argent and Chris White had the whole in-house album project mapped out and respectfully declined their services.

"ODESSEY AND ORACLE" IN THE MAKING

The Beatles had finished the main recording on their landmark "Sgt. Pepper's Lonely Hearts Club Band" LP on April 3, 1967 and The Zombies would be following in their footsteps on the first day of June. That day, The Zombies completed "Friends Of Mine" and the backing track to "A Rose For Emily." "This Will Be Our Year" (minus horn overdubs) was completed the next day. The Zombies were busy preparing material, so they passed on appearing at what seemed to be a fascinating June 18 concert at the Saville Theatre in London with The Yardbirds, Manfred Mann, The New Vaudeville Band, Unit 4+2, The Settlers, and a long-forgotten opening band. After this, gigs remained thin on the ground and The Zombies concentrated on pre-production recording for the rest of their songs. One of the songs that The Zombies worked into their act at this point was a cover of the Turtles hit "Happy Together."

Back in the studio, "A Rose For Emily" was completed on July 10 and "Hung Up On A Dream" was started on the 11th. Abbey Road was being used for the rest of the month, so The Zombies went to Olympic Studios to record "Beechwood Park," "Maybe After He's Gone," "I Want Her She Wants Me," and finishing work for the master of "Hung Up On A Dream." "Butcher's Tale (Western Front 1914)" was attacked successfully on July 20, and "Time Of The Season" was laid down in mid-August. The brass overdubs for "This Will Be Our Year" were placed on a mono mixdown created on August 15, and the next two days were spent on "Brief Candles" and "Care Of Cell 44." The last track recorded for the album, "Changes," was done on November 7, 1967. Chris White explains the differences in their mixing involvement: "In those (Decca) days, we weren't involved in mixing, but then later when we weren't doing so well and Decca dropped us and we signed with CBS, we were. Rod and I wanted to produce our next album because we wanted to be there and we talked the record company into letting us do it. We booked Abbey Road, and in those days you used to do sessions there from either 10 to 1, 2 to 5, or 7 to 10. They were 3-hour sessions, it was like a factory; it still is. Everyone finished in those hours. In three hours you used to do three numbers, backing and vocals!"

Abbey Road still had only 4-track capability, but The Zombies circumvented this deficiency and maximized the capabilities of the studio. The songs that Argent and White brought into the studio covered a wide range of topics, remembrances and styles, and their personal and musical maturity was clearly reflected in every highly developed musical and lyrical song element used on the 12-song album project. This high degree of Argent/White song production clarity was also revealed in the full frequency response and in obtaining the best performances from themselves and their bandmates. Even though some of the tracks were recorded at Olympic, it is to Rod and Chris' tremendous credit that they were able to obtain homogeneous results comparable with their Abbey Road recordings. The immediate bass presence of Chris White along with Hugh Grundy's well-recorded drum tracks provided a firm foundation upon which the contributions of Colin, Rod and Paul could be clearly used to maximum effect. White was able to achieve these results through the substitution of a more expressive Fender Precision bass instead of a Gibson, and Rod liberally made use of numerous keyboard instruments throughout the sessions. Most importantly, White and Argent carefully crafted their songs to avoid excessive psychedelic imagery and production tricks that were de rigeur in 1967. In this way, their recordings would work on their own merits without being tailored for any current musical trends. Chris White described the album this way: "It's very lyrical and wistful in a way. Our hearts poured into the album and we really believed in it. Everything that was written for this album was recorded and used on the album. There were no unrecorded or unused songs for it."

In the months before their final session, The Zombies played colleges, universities and BBC radio: "The David Symonds Show," "The Pete Brady Show" (one self-titled program and the other with the subtitle "Swingalong"), "The Jimmy Young Show," "Monday, Monday," and "Pop North." Most of their college appearances were at teacher training institutions, prime locations for educators to catch up-and-coming groups. One of these late shows included the rising blues-based rock band Ten Years After. Denny Laine's 1967 hit "Say You Don't Mind" became the final song The Zombies played live at these latter-day gigs.

Eight months after signing with CBS, The Zombies finally delivered their first single for release on October 23: "Friends Of Mine" b/w "Beechwood Park." Unusually, both sides were written by Chris White. The A-side played off Colin's airy vocal using choirlike backing vocals in spots, and Atkinson's guitar riff with Argent's descending piano during the break worked well. The song's upbeat topic was about the band's closest supporters, as White tells us: "The weird thing about that is we actually used real people's names on it. It was a song about couples and most of them have split up over the years or are unfortunately dead! The only ones that didn't were Jim and Jean, who were in fact Jim Rodford, later of Argent and The Kinks, and his wife Jean." The very end of "Friends Of Mine" catches Colin Blunstone making an apparent mistake, but White again fills us in on what happened: "Colin just caught his breath and we left it on the record! It's always accidents that happen when you're recording on a high. They're the best things really. I believe in accidents in recording." The flipside "Beechwood Park" was like a mini- "A Whiter Shade Of Pale" without being overly pompous or loud. In fact, the song's drum patterns and rolls are reflective of the Procol Harum hit. White started writing it in 1966, but it was not finalized until album pre-production commenced. Chris tells us how this setting near Markyate formed the basis for the song: "I had this image of a little village where I lived where there was this private girls' school. This was actually the place where they filmed the movie 'The Dirty Dozen.' It was right in the wilds of the country which I loved. 'Beechwood Park' was actually an evocation of the lovely heat at the time in England. 'Do you remember summer days, after summer rain?' – that was really just the implication of that." Paul Atkinson played his guitar through a Leslie speaker cabinet, achieving a tremelo effect also used on the vocal at one point before the repeated introduction and suspended ending. Last but not least, short organ links held this British-sounding track together. Their efforts would not be successful with singles buyers, and its failure did not lead to a US release.

In fact, "Friends Of Mine" met with such disinterest that CBS followed up the single just one month later with the next coupling – "Care Of Cell 44" and its B-side "Maybe After He's Gone." Rod Argent supplied "Care Of Cell 44," originally known as "Prison Song" and then "Care Of Cell 69." The latter was vetoed by US publisher Al Gallico when he notified the group of that number's sexual connotations! From an outside perspective, Rod captured the emotional turmoil experienced by a man waiting for his woman's return home from prison – an interesting role reversal. At 3:53, it was one of the group's longest recordings, but it efficiently used time to explain its involved story. Rod Argent used a driving tack piano and humming backing vocals, and humming was also used to burst into overpowering Blunstone vocals during the "feel so good you're coming home soon" sections. The mix was an artful production through the use of vocal and mellotron elements floating in and out of the song. Chris White's bass played a strong role here along with tastefully employed double-tracked vocals. The song's bridge was similar to Fontana-era Manfred Mann in its use of a mellotron and high-end vocals, and the massed chorale at the song's end was another highlight. "Care Of Cell 44" was edited for single release, but it did not score with fans. For real fans, the long mono single mix of this song first turned up on the 1998 CD edition of the album.

"Maybe After He's Gone" was Chris White's fleshed-out version of his 1966 home demo "One Day I'll Say Goodbye." Paul Atkinson's more technically advanced guitar playing was especially obvious on this track. The chorus of "Maybe After He's Gone" combined multi-level vocals with Argent's tinkling piano. Another striking production touch was the treatment of Grundy's drums. During verses, echo was placed on drum rolls before the vocal bridge. Finally, choruses with and without drums perfectly set up overlapping "a cappella" vocals at the song's end. Again, the single was a UK failure, but "Care Of Cell 44" merited a US release the same week on Columbia. Very few commercial copies of the American single exist, and a copy of the A-side label is shown here. Interestingly, this record and all the other single releases from these sessions credit Marquis Enterprises as producer instead of Argent and White!

The band's US publisher, Al Gallico, was able to sell their album idea to two Columbia Records executives, Jack Gold and Bill Gallagher. Subsequent to the sabotaged Columbia release of "Care Of Cell 44," Clive Davis became the label's new vice president and Columbia decided to pass on the album. After receiving copies of the album masters in early 1968, the tapes remained in Jack Gold's office for months, at which point Gallico notified Gold of his intention of finding a new home for the album.

Press articles at the time of "Care Of Cell 44" indicated that The Zombies would break up if that record did not achieve a more positive sales result. With this dark prospect hanging above them, the balance of the songs on the still-unnamed album proved to be the most difficult to make. The difficulties were in the complexity of the songs and in the higher playing abilities required to perform and record them. The final contributions to the album were either story-based, purely original British psychedelia, or straight pop.

Rod Argent had read noted author William Cuthbert Faulkner's short story "A Rose For Emily," and put together an unrelated story of a spinster using the same title. The Rolling Stones and The Beatles had covered the same thematic ground with their respective tunes "Lady Jane" and "Eleanor Rigby," but the topic still had room for further development. Argent wrote this piano-based ballad of an aging and forgotten woman at his parents' house. Colin and Rod supplied equal vocals on this pretty number. The chorus melody of "A Rose For Emily" merges into the next verse – a finely crafted touch equal to the song's suspension to major chord keyboard ending. Two aborted prototype stereo mixes reflected the contributions of a session cello player and another with a cello and a mellotron-generated flute effect. Both of these mixes were rejected because the extra parts were unnecessary and conflicted with the serious, real-life story depicted in the song. One of these extant mixes was on "Zombie Heaven" and the other debuted on the 1998 CD edition of the album.

Chris White briefly tells us about how he created "Brief Candles": "That was the lovely title of a book by Aldous Huxley using different stories about different people. The candles are burning and going out." The song was a double-tracked extravaganza, with verses sung by Argent, White and Blunstone in that order. Rod Argent's piano played a very strong role along with the mellotron-drenched bridge and the concluding piano fade after Colin's vocal chorus. It was easily one of the LP's highlights.

By far the most serious song on the album was another White creation: "Butcher's Tale (Western Front 1914)." Based on Chris White's fascination with World War I, the song presented a soldier's viewpoint of a battle that took place in 1916 (a typographical error listed the year as 1914). The serious tone of the song was influenced by The Bee Gees' "New York Mining Disaster 1941 (Have You Seen My Wife, Mr. Jones)," and it was mastered in only one take. White used a reversed and sped up Pierre Boulez LP extract as the proper musique concrète bed to develop the song's serious overtones of war. White had Blunstone in mind to do the vocals, but he tells us how it developed into his own vocal showcase: "That was the only Zombies track I ever sang lead on with the exception of one verse of 'Brief Candles.' I got emotionally involved reading about the history of the First World War, which was what this was about. I had an old pedal harmonium-type American (reed) organ and we actually carried it into Abbey Road Studios to record, and Rod said 'You've got to sing this because your wavery, nervous voice is fine for it.' It was such a weird track." The stark arrangement of "Butcher's Tale" lacked guitar or drums (it was only Rod and Chris) and the eerie echo placed on certain words added an aura that could not be matched by the Bee Gees song that provided its inspiration.

Touching on the fringes of 1967 psychedelia were "Hung Up On A Dream" and "Changes." The former was a trippy Rod Argent tune featuring his lead vocal and massive mellotron usage throughout. Throughout the album, that was John Lennon's mellotron that Rod was using! According to Chris White, "We really believed in the flower power movement at the time and that's the one that sounds a bit like Spinal Tap, actually!" Strings and flute were emulated by the mellotron, which rose and fell artfully with the guitar in the mix. Peter Vince assisted Argent in obtaining the synthesizer-type effect on the link featuring lead guitar, piano, and mellotron. Choirlike vocals again came into play all throughout the song, and the end backing vocals on the last verse accompanied a piano coda with mellotron. White's "Changes" (originally known as "Changes Etc."), also employed massed vocals with even Paul Atkinson and Hugh Grundy providing bass harmonies to Rod, Chris and Colin's live vocals due to the 4-track recording limitations. An unexpected sound effect also hit the tape at this time, according to Chris White: "Paul and Hugh were singing the bass lines double-tracked while the time was up at our session at Abbey Road. The door opened and the fellows in the white coats were removing the piano while we were recording it. That's actually on the album!" "Changes" was probably the most British sounding track on the album, although Indian-influenced percussion backing formed the foundation for mellotron flourishes and strong multi-level vocal choruses. Also striking was Rod's piano with the doubled Blunstone vocal – completely different than anything done in 1967. Top-notch production bounced the piano from channel to channel with Blunstone's descending vocal before two choruses and a mellotron coda of the chorus concluded the recording. Advanced studio techniques matching their advanced performance on tape had an impressive effect on the listener.

The Zombies take of "I Want Her She Wants Me" perfected this pop-filled Argent gem. The Mindbenders' single version the previous year was a rigid 4/4 guitar-based take that eliminated any of the catchy aspects of the song. Atkinson's guitar played 4/4, but Chris White's playful up and down bass line joined Argent playing the Olympic Studios harpsichord along with his lead vocal. Another of only a handful of Zombies songs with a fadeout ending, the chorus was repeated 12 times before it completely disappeared! The stereo mix included backing vocals that are not audible on the mono edition.

White also supplied "This Will Be Our Year," first demoed with Argent's vocals and different phrasing and melody as "Took A Long Time To Come." With Colin Blunstone on mainly doubled-tracked vocals this time, Argent's simple piano backing cleared the way for an effective pop song. Ken Jones supplied the arrangement for the overdubbed trumpet and other brass played by sessioners. These overdubs were recorded during the mono mixdown, and the demo and stereo mix (lacking the brass) debuted on "Zombie Heaven."

The song that created the most band turmoil was the Rod Argent masterpiece "Time Of The Season." Rod had erroneously heard "it's the close of the season, it's easy to trace the tracks of my tears" as the title line lyrics to The Miracles' "Tracks Of My Tears" instead of "if you look close, it's easy..." Another interesting parallel can be drawn between "Time Of The Season" and their previous recording of Gershwin's "Summertime": one line in "Summertime" is "your daddy's rich...," while a similar line in "Time Of The Season" goes "who's your daddy, is he rich like me?" Colin Blunstone did not want to sing on "Time Of The Season" at all, as Chris White lays out: "I remember when we were doing 'Time Of The Season' and Rod was trying to get Colin to sing it and Colin was going, 'I can't do this f***ing song, you sing it!' Rod was going, 'No, no, try it again.' And Colin tried it again and said, 'Oh f*** it, I hate this song!' He always remembers that now as he thought it was an awful song and he still doesn't have any trust in his ability to pick songs. He just thought that it would never be a hit, you know." With a little persuasion and coaching, Rod was able to get the performance from Colin that he felt the song required. And how right Rod was!

On the surface, "Time Of The Season" appeared to be a deceptively simple song, especially since it was quickly written and recorded. However, it was more involved than any listener could imagine. Based on a classic 1-flatted 3rd-4 bass riff, it was similar to Rod's very early Zombies writing. In fact, the signature handclapped percussion and vocal effect were extensions of the sound used at the end of "Tell Her No." This time, Rod did the "ah"s, and Peter Vince helped Rod and Chris obtain the exact duplicate on tape of what was in their heads. Colin Blunstone's vocal and the echo used on that vocal were highly distinctive and evoked the time perfectly. The "call and response" Colin and Rod vocals on the verses were laid over yet another distinctive Hugh Grundy drum pattern. During mixing, it was decided that the drums were to be pulled out at the end of each verse to create "a cappella" choruses. This decision proved to be the wisest one made in the production of the album.

In contrast to the direct rock track, Rod Argent used a jazzy organ sound. By mistake, two organ solo tracks at the end of the song were played on top of each other and it was another of those happy accidents that worked well enough to leave in the final master. Another nice touch was that the song faded to a cold ending as one organ solo ended in a very convenient place! An alternate mono mix with Grundy's drums playing all the way through is on the 1998 CD edition. The single went on to sell almost two million copies in 1969. Although not a hit in the UK, "Time Of The Season" was included on the hit British CBS sampler "The Rock Machine Turns You On." A multi-colored vinyl single of "Time Of The Season" was originally released in Germany and is illustrated on this book's back cover. "Time Of The Season" has proven to be the band's most popular song on radio, earning three separate awards in 1989, 1994 and on November 3, 1998, celebrating one, two and three million US airplays respectively. Rod Argent is still amazed by the success of the song: "When I went to the BMI ceremony, I realized that getting to 3 million (US airplays) with one of only 32 British songs ever to reach that level in America is pretty amazing. And I think it was 'Eleanor Rigby' that got an award for 3 million on the same day as 'Time Of The Season,' and I thought, 'Well, this is great company to be with!'"

THE END AND A NEW BEGINNING

With a lot of their time wrapped up in recording and not performing, Blunstone, Atkinson and Grundy stated that they were having difficulty surviving on the small income that the band was earning at this time. Of the three, Grundy was the only one still interested in soldiering on past this album. A few more college dates took place in December, concluding with their final live show near Hereford on December 20, 1967. This concert was the last day that all five members worked together. After The Zombies played a Christmas Show at Keele University on December 12 at which Princess Margaret was in attendance, dates at Worthing Assembly Hall (December 14) and the next day's Ashton-Under-Lyne College Of Further Education gig were scrubbed. Rod Argent was unable to take a mellotron on the road, so he elected to use a weighty Hammond B-3 organ. Without a mellotron, the less expressive organ limited the new songs that the band could play in front of audiences. Of their newly recorded songs, only "Friends Of Mine" and "A Rose For Emily" made the transition to live stages. They were not well received. Road manager Dave Blaylock refused to carry the Hammond up and down stairs, and quit the tour with a few gigs to go. Colin Blunstone and Paul Atkinson took it upon themselves to carry the touring equipment burden until its conclusion.

With two failed British singles, CBS did not hold The Zombies in very high regard. However, they did expect to put out the long-promised album that they paid for. The Zombies completed mixing the most involved song on the album, "Time Of the Season," on December 27, 1967 and finished the mono LP master the next day. However, CBS also wanted an individually mixed stereo counterpart rather than a rechanneled stereo edition. CBS was not forthcoming with funding for the stereo mix, especially since they were not overwhelmed with both failed singles and the remainder of the songs on the mono edition. Rod Argent and Chris White dipped into their songwriting royalties to the tune of £200 each and completed a stereo LP master on New Year's Day 1968. Chris White was more involved with the stereo mix than Rod Argent, but the final result was a collaborative effort. The only thing outstanding was a name for the album.

Contrary to popular belief, Chris White says the resulting CBS album title "Odessey And Oracle" was not based on any overriding theme: "It was a collection of songs that wasn't planned to be a concept. My best friend, Terry Quirk, who was an art teacher at the time, did the cover. It's called 'Odessey And Oracle' because we were just telling stories and Terry misspelled 'odyssey' when he designed the cover and we didn't realize this until it was too late! We really enjoyed making that album and really thought we'd hit our peak. We were well rehearsed and recorded three songs in three hours at a time at Abbey Road. The album was recorded in about 8 days. I remember when it first came out on CD, Rod called me up and said some of it sounds really great but a lot of it sounds like Spinal Tap!" In part, Terry Quirk's album artwork was influenced by Klaus Voormann's cover for The Bee Gees' "1st" LP.

The band's dilemma was expressed by Chris White: "We didn't know we were going to break up when we started doing the album. We really loved doing 'Odessey And Oracle,' but when it didn't get a good reaction from the record company, the others lost heart. That was the last straw. Basically, the record company didn't like it and wasn't planning on putting it out. It was actually after the recording of the album that Hugh, Colin and Paul basically said that they couldn't survive on what the group was making, it wasn't enough. 'How do we eat?' Rod and I didn't lose heart and wanted to continue in the record business."

With the decision to break up firmly in their minds, the March 30, 1968 edition of Disc and Music Echo reported Rod Argent's comment: "We felt we were becoming stale. We didn't think we were progressing musically as a group. We are ending our career with recordings we wrote and produced ourselves for the CBS label. We have made up our minds not to reform even if the records are big hits." This decision was confirmed by Rod and Chris' appearance on Kenny Everett's BBC radio program. Colin Blunstone, Hugh Grundy and Paul Atkinson all left the music business for more stable lines of work. In early 1968, Blunstone started his one-year stint as a clerk at Sun Alliance Insurance Company near London's Piccadilly area, while Hugh Grundy worked in various capacities, including car sales. Paul Atkinson was a computer programmer trainee for Computers In Business. Paul was also offered a lot of guitar sessions at Lansdowne and Mayfair Studios, but he turned them down as he felt sessions were soulless work. With the unpredictable events that would unfold in 1969, all three re-entered the music business full-time. Blunstone signed with Decca as the solo artist Neil MacArthur, and Grundy and Atkinson joined CBS as A&R men in succession.

In the US, a great deal of effort was required for The Zombies to obtain any further American releases of their material. By luck, American CBS A&R man and session keyboard player Al Kooper had heard "Odessey And Oracle" at a recent London party and raved about the tracks "Butcher's Tale (Western Front 1914)," "Care Of Cell 44," "A Rose For Emily," "Beechwood Park," and "This Will Be Our Year." Kooper spotted the tapes in Jack Gold's office and in one of his rare altruistic exhibitions, convinced Gold to release the album. The album was exiled to CBS' distant label cousin, Date Records, a label started in January 1966 for mainly underground pop and rock acts.

"TIME OF THE SEASON" AND THE NEW ZOMBIES

On both sides of the Atlantic, it was agreed that another single would be required to accompany the release of "Odessey And Oracle." The pairing was "Time Of The Season" b/w "I'll Call You Mine." UK CBS released it on April 5, with Date following the next month. Chris White had supplied the now two-year-old B-side, which was recorded at Lansdowne Studio with tracks like "Indication" and "Gotta Get A Hold On Myself." Instead of the usual guitar-based White song treatment, "I'll Call You Mine" was a driving piano-fuelled number with strong vocals from Colin and Rod. The single met with total indifference everywhere, and the US edition became an extremely hard record to find. The British release of "Odessey And Oracle" trailed the single by two weeks. Again, sales were dreadful. In the US, Al Kooper recommended that Date release "Butcher's Tale (Western Front 1914)" b/w "This Will Be Our Year" as the next single in June 1968 – not a very commercial prospect. Compounding this questionable decision, Date mistakenly thought that the song was an anti-Vietnam treatise! To no one's surprise, this single failed and the album also bombed upon issue in mid-July.

In the middle of this madness, something strange happened: the American group People had a US #14 hit with Chris White's 1965 Zombies song "I Love You." Decca decided to shamelessly cash in on the American success of the song by issuing "I Love You" as a single in mid-June. Once again, "The Way I Feel Inside" was called upon as a B-side. Decca's plan backfired.

Al Gallico was always convinced that "Time Of The Season" was a great song, and he convinced Jack Gold to give the song another lease on life as a single. Just before 1968 ended, the song backed by the first UK CBS A-side "Friends Of Mine" was issued again by Date Records. Things started slowly with one US radio station in Boise, Idaho, but radio stations across the country picked up on the song the second time around. A typically silly US radio spot first issued on the "Zombie Heaven" box illustrates how that commercial helped in a small way to make the record a success. In early 1969, "Time Of The Season" became a tremendous hit. It reached #1 in Cashbox and #3 in Billboard, earning The Zombies their only gold single for sales over 1 million as mentioned in the April 26, 1969 Billboard issue. The only problem was that the band was out of business for about a year! "Odessey And Oracle" sold enough copies on the back of the single to reach #95 on Billboard's album chart. A revised front cover for the album was created for the new US edition

Top row: the UK promo single of "Time Of The Season" and another rare US sleeve – "Butcher's Tale (Western Front 1914)."

At left is Decca's failed attempt at cashing in on the US success of People's hit version of the Chris White song "I Love You."

Below are the original British and revised American covers of the "Odessey And Oracle" album.

which played up "Time Of The Season." Seemingly out of nowhere, interest in The Zombies had reached fever pitch again and demands for more records and live appearances poured in. However, The Zombies' CBS contract ran out when "Time Of The Season" was at its apex.

Once again, Al Gallico tried to come to the rescue. After Clive Davis of Columbia failed in getting Rod Argent to re-sign with the label, Gallico ventured to the UK to no avail. In the year since The Zombies announced their breakup in late March 1968, Argent and White formalized their partnership in the shape of the Nexus Productions company and their joint manager was Mel Collins. The other item in the partnership was the creation of a new group to record the songs that they were writing. This group, which simply became known as Argent, had already recorded a good deal of tracks. With the ammunition of a big hit single and successful album, Mel Collins worked out a production/recording arrangement with Clive Davis. Through the arrangement reported in the April 12, 1969 issue of Billboard, this Argent/White product would be exclusively released worldwide on the CBS label. Argent and White also agreed at this point that all of their songs would have joint writing credits regardless of actual writing contributions. Here is Chris White's view of the deal: "After Rod and I paid for the stereo mix of the 'Odessey And Oracle' album out of our own pockets and put the group Argent together, Rod said, 'Why don't we put our joint names on every song we write whether we write it jointly or not like Lennon or McCartney, because one hit can make all the difference?' This was totally magnanimous of Rod as he had written the two big Zombies hits (up until then). I think we only wrote one song actually together, 'Like Honey,' which Argent recorded for the first album. I wrote one bit and he wrote the other and we worked on putting them together. Oh yeah, we also wrote one other song together called 'Kingdom,' which was on an Argent B-side. We'd throw and exchange ideas to each other."

Al Gallico's efforts had to come to a conclusion, because imitation Zombies groups were popping up left and right. One group even had the nerve to claim that Colin Blunstone died in a car accident. The imitators had to explain why they sounded different than the recorded band, and plenty of tour promoters and fans were victimized financially. The real Zombies were offered £20,000 to reform, but they were already in the next stages of their careers. Instead of reforming, Rod Argent and Chris White used the opportunity to release some of their Argent recordings under the Zombies name to make it clear who the real group was. Tracking down any of these fast-moving phony groups proved to be impossible, and fake Zombies groups continued to make the rounds throughout 1969 and into 1970. Another '60s group that fell prey to the same exploitation was The Animals, broken up by Eric Burdon in 1968. In fact, bogus Animals and Zombies groups played at the same show.

As early as the tail end of 1967, Argent and White had been planning their next group. In March 1968, Rod Argent and Chris White assembled a prototype group to work on the stockpile of their more progressively oriented songs. With rock music getting harder edged and requiring ever increasing levels of musicianship, an absolutely top-notch group of musicians was necessary. The first lineup of this still-unnamed group featured Rod, Hugh Grundy, and Chris White. Only one recording was released by this lineup in the '60s – "Conversation Off Floral Street," originally known as "Bonnie & Clyde." It was the first song done as part of the Argent/White joint songwriting partnership. Recorded at Central Sound in London, this piece was originally designed as a dance number for Rod's girlfriend (and future wife) Cathy, who danced with Paul's first wife Molly. Percussion would later be added at Morgan Studios that December. For all future recording, however, Chris White wanted a non-playing role that involved writing, producing, and backing vocals. Rod's cousin Jim Rodford came in on bass and backing vocals at this point. After The Bluetones ran their course, Rodford joined The Mike Cotton Sound in November 1964. This group broke up in 1968 even though the horn section kept the group name for hired session work.

Joining Argent, Grundy, White and Rodford was folk guitarist Rick Birkett (formerly of the psychedelic group The Accent), who was referred to Rod and Chris by recording engineer Gus Dudgeon. Three different blocks of demo sessions at Central Sound were done over the next few months, and Birkett's inability to gel musically with the band did not enable him to get past the initial sessions. The first session block consisted of the Birkett-featured "To Julia (For When She Smiles)" and "Telescope (Mr. Galileo), the latter of which sported guitar work by Chris' school friend and former Donovan guitarist Mac MacLeod. Rod Argent and Chris White wrote "Tick Tock Man" for MacLeod, and this recording first appeared in 2003 on the MacLeod compilation "The Incredible Musical Odyssey Of The Original Hurdy Gurdy Man." Incidentally, overdubs on "To Julia" were done at Morgan Studios in December 1968, but this version apparently does not exist. "Telescope" was recorded in German as "Mr. Galilei" by Dave Colman and an orchestra directed by the omnipresent Mark Wirtz. It was released in late April 1968.

The second session block included the tracks "It Never Fails To Please Me," "She Loves The Way They Love Her," and "I Could Spend The Day." At this point, no one remembers who played guitar on these tracks, but it is possible that Birkett and/or MacLeod were involved. The third and final session for this lineup involved the recording of "Unhappy Girl." There is also an unreleased acetate of "Girl Help Me" ("Call Of The Night" with different lyrics) with Mac MacLeod on guitar. At this point, Argent and White had to make some personnel and repertoire changes to realize their initial band vision.

Robert Henrit then replaced Hugh Grundy, now in his A&R role at CBS. While a member of The Roulettes, Henrit did the same TV show as The Zombies and really impressed Rod Argent. Rod in turn made a mental note of Henrit's skills. Rod had to act fast, because John Mayall offered Henrit a job in his band. The search was on for a lead vocalist and guitarist. Russ Ballard met both of these criteria. Ballard and Henrit were planning on leaving the band Unit 4+2, and both were highly seasoned players. The lineup of Argent, Rodford, Ballard and Henrit became the solid, final group that Rod and Chris were seeking.

Interestingly, the histories of Russ Ballard and Robert Henrit always seemed to be intertwined. Russ Ballard was born on October 31, 1945 in Waltham Cross, while Robert Henrit was born in Broxbourne on May 2, 1944. As a thirteen-year-old, Ballard formed Rick Nicol & The Rebels before the 1961 formation of Buster Meikle & The Daybreakers. This group featured Russ and his brother Roy, along with David "Buster" Meikle, Bernie Benson, and Robert Henrit. They recorded an unreleased single, and at this time, Russ wrote an instrumental called "The Lost City" for The Shadows. (It was recorded over four years later in 1966 as "Atlantis" because they already had a hit called "The Lost City"!) The Daybreakers quit in 1962, with Henrit joining The Hunters and Meikle teaming with Tommy Moeller, Brian Parker and Peter Moules as the group Unit 4+2. With Henrit on board, The Hunters released their third single "The Storm" and their second LP. Henrit then joined bassist John Rogers, Peter Thorpe (guitar) and Alan "Honk" Jones (sax) to form pop singer Adam Faith's backing band The Roulettes. When Jones was replaced by Henry Stracey (ex-Hunters), they released an English language single of "La Bamba" on Pye. In May 1963, John Rogers of The Roulettes died in a car accident and John Rogan replaced him. Along with this change, Russ Ballard initially joined The Roulettes on keyboards to replace Henry Stracey before moving over to lead vocals and second lead guitar. Now with Ballard and Henrit, The Roulettes recorded for Parlophone (just like Adam Faith) and played on most of Unit 4+2's recordings starting with their major hit "Concrete And Clay." After a few UK hits on Decca, Unit 4+2's fortunes declined and they ended up on Fontana. At the end of 1967, Henrit and Ballard joined Unit 4+2 and were featured on their last Fontana recordings. The most notable of these was their take on Bob Dylan's "You Ain't Goin' Nowhere," produced by Manfred Mann. When Unit 4+2 finally broke up in 1968, Russ and Robert joined the Argent/White team.

The story of how Rod Argent and Chris White met Russ Ballard and Robert Henrit to create Argent has never been documented before, but Rod can now enlighten us with the details: "I really wanted Jim Rodford to be in the new group, so the two of us said, 'Who else are we going to use?' Initially, Hugh Grundy was going to be playing drums and we got another guitarist named Rick Birkett, and we did a couple of demos. Some of the demos that we did were done with Rick Birkett and Hugh Grundy, some of the demos were done with Hugh Grundy without Rick Birkett – a bit of a melting pot, really – and then Jim mentioned these two guys that he'd seen playing with The Roulettes. That was Russ Ballard and Bob Henrit, and Jim said they were great. We found out they were playing at a local youth club, not local to us – it was about a hundred miles away! Chris and I went along and we walked in the door. It was a little church club, and both were playing in Unit 4+2 at the time. There may have been ten people in the entire place, and I'm thinking, 'My God, this must be a laugh to meet the guys in the band,' because we knew Unit 4+2. They came up to us and said, 'Hi, what are you doing here?' We said, 'We were just passing and we thought we'd walk in and see you!' They had just gotten a new manager – Russ and Bob hadn't told the manager or the rest of the group that they were thinking of joining me. We went backstage afterwards and got a bit drunk, and the manager said, 'I can tell you in three words what's wrong with this group – 'Stop drinking!'' We saw them and we were really taken with Russ' voice and musicianship and Bob's drumming, and then we sort of moved out of that interim phase with Hugh Grundy and Rick Birkett into what was to become the final phase."

Argent and White later found out that Ballard was a proficient songwriter, a talent that they soon drew upon. The earliest evidence of the new lineup with Ballard and Henrit was "Girl Help Me," a song derived from White's 1966 "Call Of The Night" demo. This time, it was credited jointly to Argent and White. "Girl Help Me" was recorded at Morgan Studios, their first experience in an 8-track recording environment. A stop at Trident Studios on December 16, 1968 produced "She Loves The Way They Love Her," and another Morgan trip on the 19th resulted in "I Could Spend The Day," "Imagine The Swan," and "Smokey Day." Rod Argent sang on all of these tracks, and the timing of the tracks was perfect as "Time Of The Season" took off in the US in early 1969.

ZOMBIES "R.I.P."

Having renegotiated a deal with CBS, White and Argent agreed to supply additional material under the Zombies name before they could officially put the Zombies name to rest. The appropriately named "R.I.P." album, a compilation of unreleased and touched-up Zombies masters from various points in their career, was proposed and assembled with the help of engineer Gus Dudgeon. With 8-track capability, Argent and White could take existing 4-track Zombies recordings and add as many as four overdub tracks to create fresh sounding productions that did not reveal the true age of the original sources. Through the inclusion of some newly recorded tracks, "R.I.P." would also serve as a transition

The two posthumous Zombies 45 releases – "Imagine The Swan" and "If It Don't Work Out."

 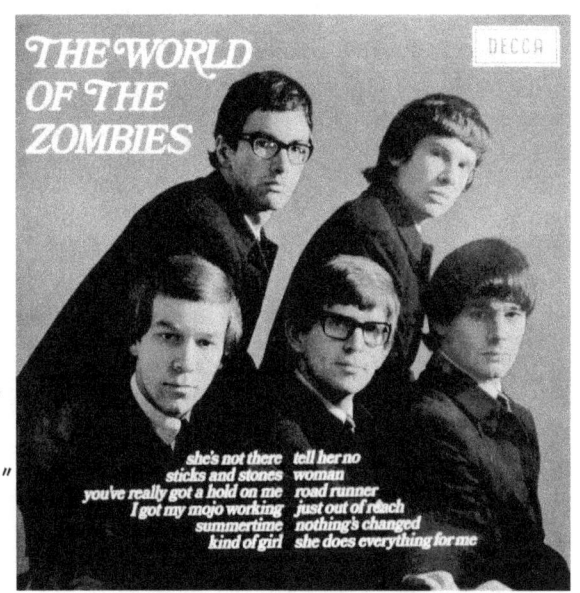

London and Decca made sure to catch the interest of Zombies fans with their respective LPs "Early Days" and "The World Of The Zombies."

Ignore these imposters below!
(John, Terry, Eddie, Gary, and Howie)

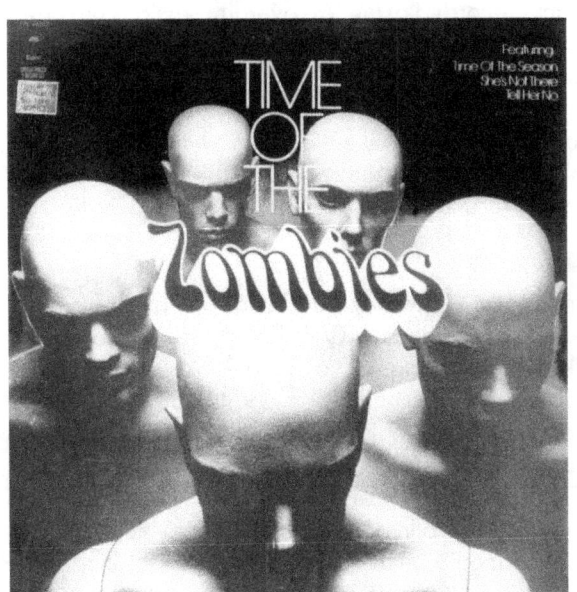 

In 1974, "Time Of The Zombies" offered the first solid overview of the band's career. At right, we have some of the phony Zombies that toured during 1969-1970.

to the start of Rod and Chris' still-unnamed group. With the fact that their new recordings were going to be released as The Zombies, Rod Argent was careful to retain as much of The Zombies' sound as possible by handling nearly all lead and backing vocals himself even though Russ Ballard was fully capable of assisting him. On occasion, Chris White provided backing vocals on the tracks.

As a taster, an initial Zombies single was prepared for spring release in the US: "Imagine The Swan" b/w "Conversation Off Floral Street." Cleverly, both the new and old groups were represented. Since the disc was the follow-up to "Time Of The Season," it was released in the US before Europe (but not in the UK). At the very least, large residual sales were expected. It was a tremendous sales disappointment, only peaking at #77 in Cashbox and a dismal #109 in Billboard.

While the song quality was definitely there, interest in The Zombies, regardless of the lineup, was as fleeting as ever. "Imagine The Swan" had all the hallmarks of the classic Zombies sound: wall to wall vocals (Rod [lead], Chris White and Colin Blunstone [backing vocals]), nice keyboard work on harpsichord and organ, and a full-bodied production and sound. If anything, the lyrics of the song proved to be a little complicated for a US market interested more in the mindless fun of bubblegum pop. Also interesting was the ear-splitting organ feedback at the end of the song that was mercifully faded on the single, but revealed in all its excruciating detail on the 1987 Rhino CD version of "Odessey And Oracle"! Other mixes of the song with incomplete vocal overdubs have also appeared on CDs over the years. On original mixes, "Imagine The Swan" was designed to crossfade into "Smokey Day" on "R.I.P.," and it was only issued this way on the "Time Of The Zombies" collection. The crossfade involved panning the last sustained organ chord of "Imagine The Swan" across the channels into the first chord of "Smokey Day." "Conversation Off Floral Street" was a classy jazz keyboard showcase for Rod on organ and piano, leading to impressive counterpoints throughout. Hugh Grundy gave his last excellent '60s drum performance, and Chris White contributed his usual solid bass. When released in the US, the song was incorrectly credited as "Conversation Of Floral Street" – quite another thing entirely!

Date Records decided to give it another go by taking "If It Don't Work Out" coupled with "Don't Cry For Me" as the next single. Disappointingly, CBS in England would have no part of this release or any other. This time, both songs were 1965 recordings dressed up with late 1968 overdubs – another uncommercial prospect. There was talk of re-doing "If It Don't Work Out" as it was rehearsed with the new lineup, but it was decided to add backing vocals (including Colin Blunstone) to the original. However, what really made the song stand out was the orchestration by former Manfred Mann guitarist/sax player Mike Vickers. Chris White's "Don't Cry For Me" included massive backing vocals and another piano track to the driving guitar and piano tracks already on the 1965 master. Hence, the difference between the Ken Jones-produced original and the revised production was enormous. The original, undubbed versions of both tracks first appeared on "Zombie Heaven." Unfortunately, sales were not large enough to register on any charts. After some deliberation, Argent and White told CBS that their new group would be called Argent. This news combined with the failure of both neo-Zombies singles caused the cancellation of the "R.I.P." album.

Along with all four tracks from these singles, other tracks that would have been included on "R.I.P." are worth mentioning as their untreated states all originally appeared on "Zombie Heaven." That is, with one exception: "I'll Call You Mine," the flipside of the first issue of "Time Of The Season." Two additional piano tracks recorded at the '68 overdub sessions provided fascinating counterpoints to the original piano track. The overdubbed edition was sneakily included on the 1974 UK Epic reissue single of "Time Of The Season" before its inclusion on a Japanese box set and "Zombie Heaven."

"I Know She Will" was an unreleased Chris White number from 1965 that also received Mike Vickers' early 1969 string and horn embellishments. These additional arrangements added another dimension to this unusually chorded song. As with all of the Vickers contributions, White worked on the arrangements at Mike's home. With the cancellation of "R.I.P.," the overdubbed version first turned up on the 1974 "Time Of The Zombies" 2LP collection.

Three other intended "R.I.P." tracks were first released in 1974: "Walking In The Sun," "Smokey Day," and "She Loves The Way They Love Her." "Walking In The Sun" was a 1964 Rod Argent composition with a brand new Colin Blunstone lead vocal and Vickers orchestration. The reason for re-recording the vocal was most likely that the original vocal track was recorded with far too much echo. The original was first issued on "Zombie Heaven." Still, it was originally submitted to Parrot for release at that time. Similar to the way the Vickers work was done, vocal overdub plans were discussed and transcribed at a flat that White shared with Argent at the time. Rod provided the backing vocal, and Chris White's moving bass lines were firmly expressed in the mix. White tells us who developed the vocalizations: "To be quite honest, it was primarily Rod who did the vocal arrangements. We did a lot of three-part harmony between Rod, myself and Colin and got that magical blend. Since, Rod was in the St. Albans Choir, he had a more rudimentary knowledge of harmonies. I always thought Rod was incredible because he had an unusual mind. He was a perfectionist but with great enthusiasm. I think enthusiasm is the key. If you do things cold-bloodedly just so that they will sell, it won't work."

The 1968 tracks "Smokey Day" and "She Loves The Way They Love Her" used many interesting structures. The former relied on suspension chords during its bridge with expressive Argent harpsichord throughout. "Smokey Day" featured Rod and Chris singing together in harmony, and Mike Vickers supplied a beautiful flute accompaniment to complete the picture. "She Loves The Way They Love Her" bookended audience tape segments to create a fictional tale of adulation. Jim Rodford's running bass line worked well here, along with the descending guitar hook. Another rare Zombies song featuring a faded ending, an alternate mono mix of the track did not feature the crowd tape.

A very unlikely source was the first home of the final three proposed "R.I.P." album tracks – the US budget album "The Best And The Rest Of The Zombies" on the tiny Backtrac label in 1984. "I'll Keep Trying" was the first of these cuts. A 1965 Argent direct pop song with fresh backing vocals, it employed a simple but completely efficient piano solo. Its "naked" version was first on "Zombie Heaven." "Girl Help Me" and "I Could Spend The Day" were of very recent vintage. Based on the Blunstone-sung original Zombies demo "Call Of The Night," "Girl Help Me" used a new lyric set, a restrained piano and Argent lead and backing vocals. It is important to note that the original LP mix differs from the "Zombie Heaven" CD mix in that the guitar crosses over from channel to channel while the CD version guitar part remains on one channel. After a unique combination of jazz trills within its classical piano progression intro, a similar vocal treatment was used on "I Could Spend The Day." Russ Ballard's muscular guitar riffs used on the choruses became a frequent motif in later Argent recordings. The song's bridge takes a rising vocal section into an impressive double-tracked piano solo utilizing jazz and classical stylings in the key of G major. The classical flourishes were inspired by, but not directly taken from, Beethoven's "Sonata For Piano" series.

THE RETURNS OF THE ZOMBIES

Just after Argent broke up in June 1976, The Zombies received an offer from the Key Seven company to re-record their hits. In 1977, all of the Zombies except for Paul Atkinson re-recorded "She's Not There" and "Time Of The Season" for this company. Although "Tell Her No" could have been re-recorded, Key Seven's song logs do not confirm its existence. The tracks were done in England and Atkinson was busy working in the States, so Tim Renwick filled in for him on this session. The reunion recording of "Time Of The Season" was the first to be released. Key Seven licensed the track to the Vancouver, Canada-based Total Records label, who in turn offered it to the Rebound label as a B-side for an early 1979 single. The A-side was a re-recording of Paul & Paula's "Hey Paula." Following this, Key Seven licensed both completed reunion recordings to another Canadian label, Ruby Records, for release on two extremely cheap various artist re-recorded hits LPs in 1981 and 1982. The infamous K-Tel label also got their hands on the recordings and issued them over and over. After "Time Of The Season" was issued by K-Tel in the US in 1983, K-Tel issued both tracks on more than a dozen other packages. Other than this Key Seven project, no other attempt in the '70s was made to reunite the band.

Inadvertently, a revival of "Odessey And Oracle" caused the next reformation of The Zombies. In 1987, Los Angeles-based Rhino Records head Harold Bronson asked Paul Atkinson about obtaining the rights to re-releasing "Odessey And Oracle" on LP and the upsurging CD format. This release was extremely successful and remained in print for many years. The packaging included the LP's color back cover which was previously issued Stateside in black and white. However, no one knew what trouble would be caused in the following months.

On July 3, 1988, Florida rock fan Randy Haynes paid $10 along with about 600 others to see The Zombies at Miami's China Club. Haynes was so appalled by what he saw and heard by this obvious group of imposters that he demanded his money back. After he was refused a refund, Randy Haynes set out to expose this fraudulent group. Randy called a Miami newspaper reporter that led to Tracy Hill of Rhino Records getting involved. Tracy told Paul Atkinson, also based in L.A., of her concerns that people seeing this fake group would not want to buy the new version of "Odessey And Oracle." Not only were these concerts continuing to go on, some radio stations promoting the concerts falsely claimed that this Zombies group had Colin Blunstone and Rod Argent in their ranks. (And we all thought the last round of imposters said Colin was dead!) This particular group featured someone called Ronald Hugh Grundy that was passed off as the original Zombies drummer. Atkinson was understandably furious and called the real Hugh Grundy in England, as well as booking agents in Virginia and Boca Raton. The Boca Raton call was to booking agent Steve Green's company Artists International Management. Green said that a London promoter was offering a Zombies group for a one-month tour and convinced him that at least one original member (Grundy) was involved. This tour involved East coast clubs of various sizes, and the band's lead singer and promoter was Brian Gannon. Steve Green should have realized that something was wrong when it took him two months to finalize such a short-term deal. Green's representative David Jenkins faxed the band's certificate of incorporation and

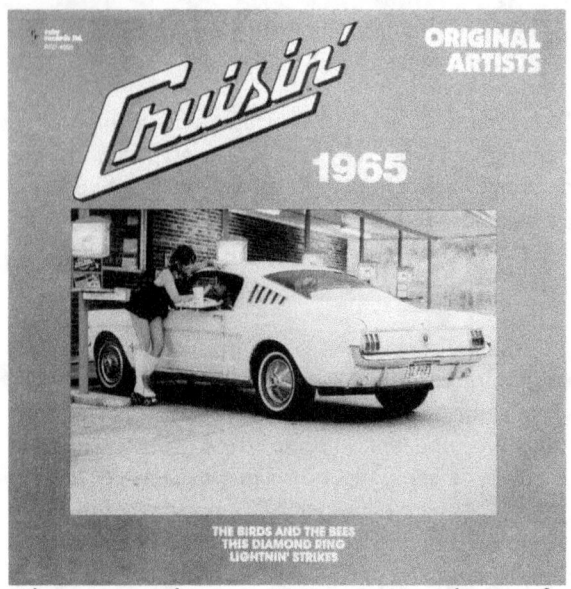

Above are the two "Cruisin'" volumes from Canada that respectively included the 1977 re-recordings of "She's Not There" and "Time Of The Season." The latter was a hit in 1969, but "She's Not There" is definitely on the wrong volume!

The Canadian single at right is the first release (1979) of the "Time Of The Season" re-recording.

Below is the very difficult 1974 stock copy reissue of "Time Of The Season" that accompanied the release of "Time Of The Zombies" and the budget collection "The Best And The Rest Of The Zombies." This album featured three unreleased tracks: "I Could Spend The Day," "Girl Help Me," and "I'll Keep Trying."

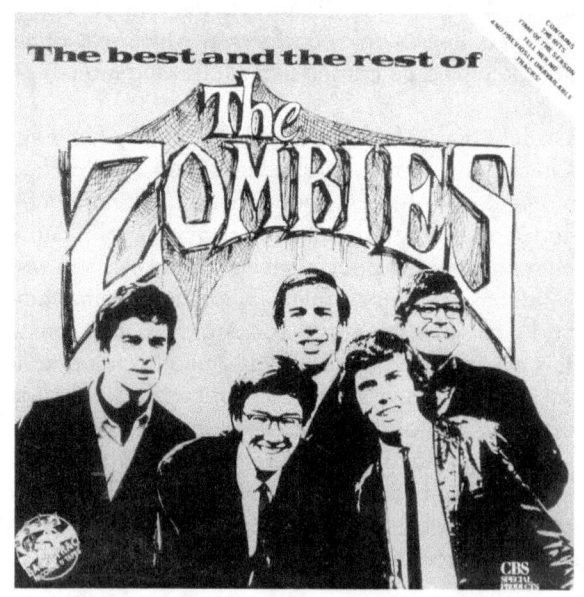

Dear Mr Chern,

I have just received a copy of your letter and tape that you sent to Paul Atkinson, and, whilst I had already found out about this bogus group, I must admit to being dumbfounded by the sheer effrontery of the man purporting to be me. It certainly came as quite a shock.

I think that as a result of your exposure and other evidence collected, we can put a stop to this group by exposing this group for what they are.

As the discerning American public have found out for themselves, this group are completely bogus.

Thank you for your interest in the music of the 60's and in particular our group, the original 'Zombies'. Maybe we'll get to meet someday

Yours faithfully
Hugh Grundy
H B GRUNDY

Letters from Hugh Grundy and Colin Blunstone to Florida DJ Evan Chern explaining their concern over the 1988 bogus Zombies group.

2nd August 1988.

Dear Evan,

Paul Atkinson has sent me a copy of your interview with the so called Zombies. I didn't know whether to laugh or cry they sound so unconvincing, but I would hate to think people are being conned into paying to see this bunch of imposters. We're doing all we can over here to put a stop to their pathetic game, and I just wanted to write and thank you for your interest and concern.

Perhaps I should take this opportunity to confirm that no members of the original Zombies (including Hugh Grundy) have anything to do with this strange bunch of people who recently toured America claiming to be the Zombies.

Must go now just off to form "the Beatles Ltd" and book Shea Stadium you don't know anyone called Ringo do you?

Thanks again
All the best
Colin Blunstone.

visa petition to the reporter that Randy Haynes called. Upon receiving these documents, Paul Atkinson immediately called Green in Boca Raton. In turn, Tracy Hill of Rhino told Billboard to report this story quickly, and their July 23 issue reported that a fake Zombies group claiming participation of at least two original members had been touring the Eastern coast of the US. This group actually played only three Zombies numbers ("She's Not There," "Tell Her No" and "Time Of The Season") and padded out their set with songs like "Everlasting Love," "Pinball Wizard," "For Your Love," a "Sgt. Pepper" medley, "Please Please Me," and "Nights In White Satin." Rhino Records very clearly stated that no original Zombies were involved.

Randy Haynes had gone to the China Club that night with friend Evan Chern, a WDNA-FM disc jockey and '60s music aficionado. To set up a trap, Evan Chern set up an interview with "Hugh Grundy" that aired on July 20, 1988. Unsurprisingly, this Grundy didn't have much knowledge about the real Hugh Grundy, and his refusal to record a promotional spot for WDNA-FM reeked of controversy. In this interview, "Hugh Grundy" said that he was playing bass instead of drums because as the only original member, the others wanted him up front! Grundy also had the audacity to bring his passport to prove who he was. Chern knew that this Grundy was a fraud and notified the real members about this fake group. Paul Atkinson received a tape of this interview as further proof. Letters from Hugh Grundy and Colin Blunstone to Evan Chern appear for the first time here. Legally, the real Zombies could not stop this group since the rights to their corporate name had lapsed in 1985. Paul Atkinson and Rod Argent were looking into legal action with their British attorneys, and there was even some discussion of having the ersatz Zombies bill themselves as "The Zombies, Ltd." In true political mode, Steve Green continued to state that he was an innocent victim and never admitted to his participation in this fraud. Green tried to smooth things over by ridiculously offering to have interested original members join the band on tour, and he was even discussing the recording of an album! Therefore, recording a reunion album served as the motivation for the real Zombies to legally reclaim their name. To reinforce the fact that this was a complete Zombies group effort, Chris White did not want to produce the project alone.

There were two hurdles that the real Zombies had to overcome. Rod Argent was very busy doing sessions and also did not want to be involved with a potentially regressive project, despite its absolute necessity. As head of A&R for the RCA label in L.A., Paul Atkinson was unable to devote extended periods of time in England for any Zombies reunion. While in Switzerland, Chris White came across Chilean keyboard player Sebastián Santa Maria (born September 24, 1959), who had a fair approximation of the Argent style and enthusiasm. Santa Maria and White had previously collaborated on projects that Chris had produced in that country, and Sebastián played guitar and sang as well. Replacing Atkinson involved using a revolving door of guitarists, including Tim Renwick again, along with John Wooloff, Laurie Wisefield, and Duncan Browne.

Chris White, Colin Blunstone, Hugh Grundy and Sebastián Santa Maria rehearsed their best material together and were ready for recording in 1989. Obtaining a one-off deal with RCA in Germany, the album title became out of necessity "The Return Of The Zombies." The band had difficulty getting a record deal because record companies were looking for a known producer to work with them; they did not want the band to produce themselves. Chris White tells us that quite a lot of politics are involved: "Unless you use a name studio or a name engineer, the record company won't give it any credit at all. For the Zombies reunion album we worked with Dave Richards who's worked with Queen in Montreux, because without those names on it, the record companies won't even listen. The A&R people don't judge music for what it is or what they feel; their basic idea is that they tried it in the best studio with the best engineer and the best producer, so they did their bit and they don't care if it's a failure. That way, they keep their jobs! They did their best! If they accept something which is done for a minimal amount of money in a small studio, that says something frightening about them!"

The Zombies took on manager John Sherry, head of John Sherry Enterprises (JSE), and they were all set to go. Using Dave Richards as co-producer, "The Return Of The Zombies" took the band to The Point Studios (London) and the more exotic Prisme Studios (Lausanne) and Mountain Studios in Montreux. Mixing also took place at Mountain.

Starting the album off, Chris White and nephew Andy Nye's "New World" captured the vocal magic of the original Zombies while maintaining a modern feel. This was most likely due to the fact that Andy Nye was born in 1959! Paul Atkinson played guitar on this track, his only contribution to the album on a visit to London. Hugh Grundy surprised everyone by sounding modern and fresh, not only on this track, but on the entire album. This anthemic song was released as a CD single a month before the album was released in February 1990 and should have been a hit by all rights. Disappointingly, it did not sell. The song would be later billed and remixed as "New World (My America)" on the retitled "New World" UK edition of the album in 1991. Although Rod Argent was not on the original album, "New World" was his favorite track. The "New World" single included two other tracks: "Moonday Morning Dance" and "Alone In Paradise." Santa Maria wrote the lively keyboard-propelled first track, and "Alone In Paradise" was another excellent uptempo Blunstone/Nye song with Claude Nobs on harmonica. This track would later be added to the 1991 album on the JSE/Castle Communications label.

"I Can't Be Wrong" was also remixed when repeated on the 1991 version. Along with "Blue" and "Moonday Morning Dance," these were Sebastián Santa Maria's only self-written song contributions to the album. The chorus of "I Can't Be Wrong" was its strongest selling point, as was Colin's vocal on "Blue." "Nights On Fire" was another successful Blunstone/Santa Maria song collaboration, and it was parallel to the softer music that Blunstone issued on his own. Colin was also unhappy with two other songs he wrote for the album, as they both came out softer than he originally intended. "Losing You" was written with Phil Dennys and proved to be a solid effort regardless, but it was recast with new lyrics for Colin's 1998 album

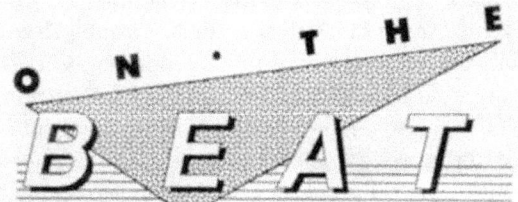

"The Light Inside." Colin's own "Knowing You" had some imprecise overlapped vocals, and the fact that it had no drums diluted its impact somewhat. Colin also re-cut this song with much greater success in 1998.

White and Nye came through again with the strong chorus of "Heaven's Gate," on which Hugh Grundy used a modern update of the "She's Not There" drum pattern. White's only solo song, "Lula Lula," became the album's second single in April 1990. It was coupled with "I Can't Be Wrong" and "Nights On Fire."

By far, the most surprising disappointment on "The Return Of The Zombies" was "Time Of The Season." Its stark, truncated arrangement was very disturbing and unsettling, especially since Hugh Grundy was not involved. An "a cappella" vocal with mainly piano backing led into fuller vocals on the chorus, but one could not help but notice that overlapping vocals at the song's end did not work well at all. It was certainly a missed opportunity, and it only appeared on the RCA version of the album. With this in mind, "Time Of The Season" was redone at The Point in London in 1990. This time, Rod Argent and latter-day Argent guitarist John Verity were on hand to give the song the most appropriate Zombies treatment. The deepening of Colin Blunstone's voice gave the song a different but interesting vocal blend with Rod and Chris. Rod Argent's organ solo was longer on this occasion, and only one solo was used.

"New World" was supposed to be released by JSE in the US along with the British release, but John Sherry's firm was not financially solvent. These plans were scrapped, but not before JSE's recommendation to record some more material to make it more accessible and modern to US audiences. "When Love Breaks Down" and "Love Conquers All" were done at Livingstone Studios in London. The first was a Prefab Sprout song written by the band's vocalist/guitarist Patrick "Paddy" McAloon that took three UK single releases to finally hit #25 in 1985. Blunstone supplied "Love Conquers All" and it ended the CD on a strong note. Along with the non-album track "Alone In Paradise," these two tracks and the new version of "Time Of The Season" were featured on the JSE "New World" album. The album was reissued in 1994 on Castle Communications. Other tracks that did not make the album were songs by Duncan Browne ("High Windows") and a cover of The Association's "Never My Love." Coincidentally, independent American producer Mike Ober asked Colin Blunstone to record a duet version of the recent outtake "Never My Love" with original Renaissance vocalist Jane Relf for a Relf solo album in 1991. This project did not get off the ground after Colin showed little interest in recording the track again.

The 1990 "Time Of The Season" Point session had another carry-over effect. Along with that track, further retakes of "She's Not There" and "Tell Her No" with Argent and guitarist John Verity were included on the "Colin Blunstone Sings His Greatest Hits" 1991 CD of re-recordings. Chris White was the producer and these tracks were recorded and mixed at that studio. Colin attacked old favorites like "Say You Don't Mind," "Caroline Goodbye," "Andorra," "I Don't Believe In Miracles," "What Becomes Of The Broken Hearted," "Tracks Of My Tears" (in its original Jimmy Ruffin arrangement), his Alan Parsons Project vocal classic "Old And Wise," and two new songs ("Still Burning Bright" and "Don't Feel No Pain No More"). The latter was written with Sebastián Santa Maria, and was most likely rehearsed by The Zombies for their reunion. Chris White contributed further by singing backing vocals on "She's Not There" and "Time Of The Season." Colin's album suffered the same fate as the reunion disc, but it was reissued by Castle Communications in 1993. To promote his album, Colin did a January 30, 1991 BBC session with Rod Argent, Hugh Grundy, Jim Rodford and John Verity on which he performed "She's Not There," "Time Of The Season," "Andorra," and "Caroline Goodbye."

In Germany, The Zombies appeared on some television programs, but it made no sense to tour the US without product. Even if they were able to release a CD in the US, Rod Argent would still not commit to the project, as Chris White relates: "Rod doesn't like going backwards; he thinks that what's then shouldn't be recreated today, but he actually loved some things from the new album, especially 'New World,' which I think is the closest thing to The Zombies of old. Since the album, he's played with the rest of The Zombies on Colin's solo album of greatest hits and loved doing that. In actuality, Rod arranged the vocal parts of my original version of 'Lula Lula' on the album. Rod did play on 'Time Of The Season' on the revised 'New World' album. There was no tour on line with Rod. The record was supposed to have been released in the USA but the company it was supposed to go out on went bankrupt and it's not worth touring without a record to support. We didn't have a guitarist as such because Paul Atkinson wasn't available, although he did play guitar on the album title track, so people like Tim Renwick and John Verity played guitar. The album originally came out in Germany, and the American record company, which was still solvent at the time, wanted us to add 'When Love Breaks Down,' a Prefab Sprout song and a couple of other tracks to give it a contemporary feel. The album only took a short time to record but the mixing and coming and going took a long, long time. The first five tracks we recorded were done in ten days. It was a group effort between Colin, Hugh Grundy, who's still a good drummer with that '60s feel, Sebastián and myself. My favorite songs on the album, other than my own, are 'I Can't Be Wrong,' which Colin sings great, and 'When Love Breaks Down.'" Sadly, Sebastián Santa Maria passed away on October 20, 1996 at the very young age of 37 of adrenoleukodystrophy (ALD) in Lausanne, Switzerland.

The two singles released from the reunion album – "New World" and "Lula Lula."

The original German "The Return Of The Zombies" album, and "New World," its more solemn-covered British counterpart.

At right:

Chris White and his wife Vivienne Boucherat (first and second from left) received a first prize award for their song "Let The Flame Be Strong." Presenting this award in November 1998 were third place songwriters Roger Webb and Norman Newell (center and second from right) and British Academy of Songwriters and Composers and Authors (BASCA) chairman Guy Fletcher (far right).

Another Zombies reunion, albeit unofficial, took place in London in 1992 when the band recorded "Tell Her No" for a Scope mouthwash commercial. Again, Chris White has the story: "Scope wanted to use 'Tell Her No' for a commercial. Our publisher said they'd have to compensate the boys or they wouldn't get sound licenses. So, he said, 'Why don't you get them to play it?' So we agreed and Rod, myself, Colin and Hugh went to the studio. Our guitarist Paul Atkinson was head of A&R at MCA in the USA and he couldn't make it, so we got another guitarist in (Clem Clempson). It was a 30-second commercial and we did the track in 2 hours complete! You get a feel going you don't forget. It's like a bicycle or sex, really!" This was really funny because 24 hours of studio time was booked.

At Chris White's marriage to Vivienne Boucherat in the summer of 1996, Colin, Chris and Hugh played "She's Not There." Rod and Paul were unable to attend. White and Boucherat started writing songs together from the first night they met, and in November 1998, they both won the first Festival Organisations for Peace and Friendship International Song Contest with their song "Let The Flame Be Strong." The prize was $5,000 US, and a compact disc of the contest's top 10 songs was released at the MIDEM convention in Cannes, France during January 24-28, 1999.

REISSUES

Numerous reissues of Zombies material have proliferated over the years, starting with the American cash-in collection on Parrot entitled "Early Days." This album had first-time stereo mixes of many popular Zombies songs, but the initial mono impact of some tracks could not be duplicated in stereo. Rod Argent, Chris White and engineer Peter Vince were in charge of preparing these unique stereo offerings. Two stereo mixes prepared but not included on "Early Days" were for "I'm Goin' Home" and "Tell Her No." The latter was inexplicably presented in rechanneled stereo on the LP, but the stereo mix was finally issued on the second pressing of an American back-to-back hits 45 in 1970. In the UK, Decca's "The World Of The Zombies" employed a different recording selection to continue the legacy of The Zombies.

Interest in The Zombies continued to grow, and the unavailability of "Odessey And Oracle" with Date's demise in the early '70s led to a pent-up demand for an album re-release. Once again, CBS, through their Epic Records label, asked Rod Argent and Chris White to assemble a double LP with this album and a disc of single sides and unreleased material. Argent and White complied with "Time Of The Zombies" in 1974, an album that was in print until CDs dictated the discontinuance of vinyl LPs a decade later. Numerous Decca repackages like "Rock Roots" and "She's Not There" carried on the Zombies tradition until Decca lost their ability to release Zombies recordings in 1981. When compact discs entered the scene, Edsel Records mentioned that they were planning to issue "Odessey And Oracle" in 1986, but their announcement was premature. The Rock Machine label (a division of Razor Records) ended up obtaining the proper licensing and issued the album on LP (1986) and CD (1988) with completely different packaging. A different type of marketing was used to promote Grolsch beer, as a Patio Music label CD single using "Time Of The Season" and "She's Not There" was issued. This promotion involved four different Grolsch beer brands – one for each season, hence it's the "Time Of The Season" to purchase Grolsch beer! American house music act The Ladbroke Groovers sampled "Time Of The Season" for their "Seasons Of Time" 12" single in May 1997.

An onslaught of mainly unnecessary Zombies reissues have followed to this day, but the 1997 4CD box "Zombie Heaven" endeavored to collect nearly everything in one place. Compiled by Zombies fan Alec Palao through Ace Records' Big Beat label in England, "Zombie Heaven" gave fans everything they needed to know about the '60s activities of The Zombies. Out of the 119 tracks on this universally praised box set, 42 were previously unreleased.

Promotion for "Zombie Heaven" was extensive. A promotional CD with tracks and interviews from all five members timing out at 80:01 (!) was released in early November to prepare fans for the original November 17 release date. Although not a US release, copies were freely exported for American fans. Unfortunately, a slight defect on the first disc of the set caused a delay and a December 8 availability date.

Undeterred, a significant Zombies reunion took place at the Jazz Café in London's Camden Town area on November 25, 1997. All five Zombies were in attendance at this Ace Records "Zombie Heaven" release party, and they decided beforehand that they would play if they felt the time was right to follow Colin Blunstone's own 9:30 set. Colin played "Wonderful," "Old And Wise," "What Becomes Of The Broken Hearted," "Andorra," "Misty Roses," "Tell Her No," "This Will Be Our Year," "A Rose For Emily," "Indication," "Caroline Goodbye," "Levi Stubbs Tears" and "Say You Don't Mind" before The Zombies played "She's Not There" and "Time Of The Season" without any rehearsal. Paul Atkinson forgot the chords to the latter song, so Rod Argent filled him in just before they played it! The crowd at this invitation-only affair mainly consisted of jaded music journalists, and even they were screaming for more!

Colin Blunstone on tour in the Netherlands in 1997.
(photo: Frans de Graaff)

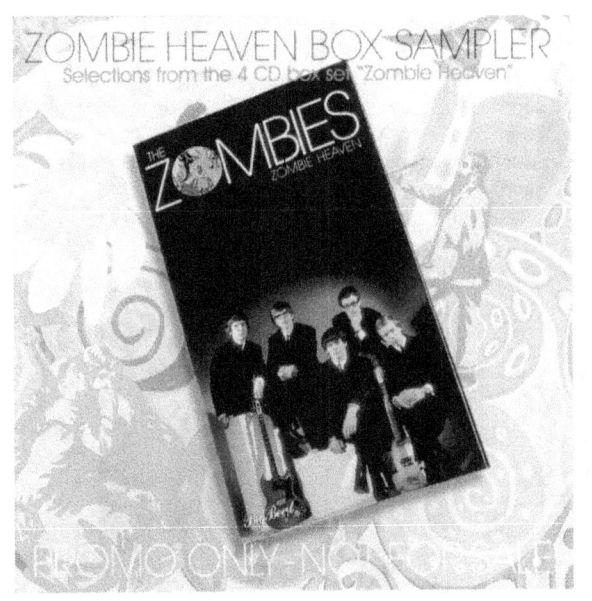

At left is the "Zombie Heaven" box set and the promotional sampler for the 4CD set. This disc includes otherwise unavailable interview segments with all five Zombies.

Jazz Café memories:

Above, Chris White enjoys the moment while Rod Argent gets the job done. Below, Rod is showing Paul Atkinson the chords of "Time Of The Season" while Colin looks on, and Paul gets back into the groove.
At right, the group shot.

All photos except for the group shot are courtesy of Frans de Graaff.

Zombies songs have always been in the spotlight. Santana's searing version of "She's Not There" is Rod Argent's favorite cover version, and Juice Newton's techno-pop version of "Tell Her No" became her last US Top 40 hit (at #27) in 1983. In fact, "She's Not There" was Santana's biggest UK hit at #11 and it also made #27 in the States. Many TV shows such as "Friends" and "Beverly Hills, 90210" have included Zombies hits in their episodes. Films have been no exception to the Zombies magic. "She's Not There" was included in 1979's "More American Graffiti," and "Time Of The Season" was used in the films "1969" and "Good Morning, Vietnam" (both released 1988), and "Awakenings" (1991). Randy Newman provided the soundtrack for the latter film, and "Time Of The Season" formed the lead track of a CD single released to tie-in with the movie. The Zombies entered the MTV/ VH-1 age through a new video for "She's Not There" that was prepared for the 1985 television program "Deja View" hosted by The Lovin' Spoonful's John Sebastian. Even though The Zombies did not appear in the video, their music was being appreciated by a new generation of fans in a relatively new medium. "She's Not There" plus some other videos from the series were issued as a home video later on. The indie band The Chrysanthemums went so far as recording the entire "Odessey And Oracle" album plus other Zombies covers on a dual LP/CD release in 1990. On December 5, 1994, a Zombies tribute CD entitled "The World Of The Zombies" was issued by the PopLlama label (PLCD-85). The front and back covers spoofed the like-titled UK LP and "Begin Here" respectively, and the album had its share of interesting cover versions by a wide range of lesser-known bands from the Seattle area. It was produced by Zombies fans The Posies. "Time Of The Season" was also featured in the popular US late-night animation series "South Park."

From February 13th to 15th, 1998, a series of Zombies tribute concerts took place at The Fez, located in the basement of the Time Café in New York's Greenwich Village. These shows, part of the club's "Loser's Lounge" series, were organized by noted session man Joe McGinty and featured The Kustard Kings as backup band to numerous guest vocalists. The first part of these shows consisted of a recreation of the entire "Odessey And Oracle" album, followed by popular Colin Blunstone and Zombies songs in the second part. The concluding section covered other Zombies, pre-Argent, and Argent favorites. The most notable participants at these shows were hit songwriter Jules Shear (singing "Care Of Cell 44"), They Might Be Giants ("Butcher's Tale [Western Front 1914]"), and J. Mascis of Dinosaur Jr. ("Imagine The Swan"). The popularity of these dates and the informal tapes made at the venue had an impact on Colin Blunstone, who immensely enjoyed tape copies sent to him. The excitement on those tapes persuaded Colin Blunstone to book three shows at the same club almost exactly one year later – February 12-14, 1999. Colin's appearance, his first in New York in over 20 years, was subsidized by Sony Records, owner of his '70s solo material on the Epic label. Blunstone's storming 20-song set covered all of his solo and Zombies hits, and his outstanding voice did not compromise one note in the entire program. On the more delicately arranged tracks like "Misty Roses" and "Say You Don't Mind" from Colin's "One Year" album, a string quartet led by classically trained cellist Jane Scarpantoni provided excellent accompaniment. The rest of the songs featured Loser's Lounge guitarist Kris Woolsey as musical director of a top-notch 7-piece band. The performance on February 13 was by invitation only, but the other two shows were open to the public and received extremely positive reviews.

In April 1998, the 79:56 packed edition of "Odessey And Oracle" was released by Ace's Big Beat label. For those who thought "Zombie Heaven" was all they needed, hard-core fans were not happy about buying this album again for what seemed like the tenth time! The saving grace of the CD was its inclusion of the album's mono and stereo mixes (some of which are markedly different) and three alternate versions. In April 1999, Ace's "Begin Here" CD offered bonus demos of "I Know She Will" and "I'll Keep Trying" as well as alternate takes of "Sticks And Stones" and "It's Alright With Me." Ace followed up this disc with "The Singles A's & B's" in March 2000. This collection supplied mono single masters of every UK single plus the very rare "Remember You" Record Mirror contest winner message. "The DECCA Stereo Anthology" took things further in November 2002 by presenting all-new stereo mixes of nearly all the Decca tracks, three unreleased alternate backing tracks ("Leave Me Be," "Just Out Of Reach" and "Whenever You're Ready"), and a false start/ alternate take combination of "Work 'N' Play." A self-titled US CD in June 2004 included the differently equalized US single version of "Leave Me Be," and Ace's long-awaited "Into The Afterlife" in July 2007 presented four Zombies tracks (orchestral mixes of "Walking In The Sun," "I Know She Will" and "If It Don't Work Out" along with the French TV version of "Going To A Go-Go"), nine Colin Blunstone tracks as Neil MacArthur (one unreleased and four in stereo), six Rod Argent and Chris White pre-Argent demos, and a late 1970 track with Chris White and the band Argent. (The Neil MacArthur and Argent/White tracks are discussed elsewhere!) This just leaves the first stereo mix of "Girl Help Me" and its earlier, unreleased acetate version as the only recordings not to appear in digital form. Reissues just keep on flowing!

THE ZOMBIES: 1999 TO THE PRESENT

When this book was first published, Colin Blunstone and Rod Argent had started recording together for the first time in decades. A lot has happened to them since, and it's all good! With their first album still in production, Colin and Rod put together a band to see how things would work out. Joining them were Rod's cousin and Argent bassist Jim Rodford, Jim's son Steve on drums, and Australian guitarist Mark Johns. Six British trial gigs were done in May 1999 and they went over extremely well. While Rod worked on their album, Colin did 40 UK dates with The Manfreds, Chris Farlowe and Alan Price (of The Animals) from October to December 1999.

In addition to recording during the early part of 2000, Colin Blunstone and Rod Argent did some UK dates in May accompanied by an official Blunstone/Argent recording partnership announcement and news of their first UK tour. Rod and Colin kicked off more live shows on June 1 at the Bournemouth Pavilion, with a wider-scale UK tour starting on September 8 at The Robin 2 in Bilston. British dates in September, November, and December followed. Also in September, Colin squeezed in some solo shows in the Netherlands. The week before Christmas 2000, a 500-copy limited edition vinyl EP of Zombies cover versions entitled "Wake Up Your Windows, Let's Do The Zombies" was issued by the Norwegian label Zapruder Groove. I had the pleasure of writing the liner notes, and the EP sold out quickly. The tracks were performed by The Tables (Oslo, Norway), Photon Band (Philadelphia, Pennsylvania), The Dipsomaniacs (Trondheim, Norway), Green Pajamas (Seattle, Washington), and Pontius Sky Pilot (Seattle, Washington).

At the beginning of 2001, a US tour offer came in for The Zombies to play a series of gigs with Manfred Mann's Earth Band in June and November of that year. No paperwork was signed. Now that Argent and Blunstone were back in the groove playing live, a UK and Dutch tour followed in March and April 2001. These shows were in support of the album "Out Of The Shadows," which was issued on Rod's own Red House label in late March. Most of the songs on the album were previously recorded by Rod, but all were very suitable for Colin's voice. US fans were absolutely thrilled to find all five Zombies at the four shows that took place at The Village Underground in New York City from May 24-27. Chris White, Paul Atkinson and Hugh Grundy did not perform, but they were very conspicuous in the crowd. Fans were thrilled by how approachable all five Zombies were before, during, and after the concerts. More UK dates took place in November, and they featured the brilliant new Rod Argent song "I Want To Fly." Perfectly crafted to Colin's voice, "I Want To Fly" showed how far Colin Blunstone and Rod Argent had come in just a short time back together.

Mark Johns left the band at this point and was replaced by Keith Airey, brother of Rod's keyboard contemporary Don Airey. Keith Airey came on board in time for three gigs in Japan (two in Tokyo and one in Osaka) that took place in late January and early February 2002. More shows followed in England, the Netherlands and Belgium throughout March and April, and then Colin went off on his own to do The Manfreds' "Maximum R&B Tour" with Chris Farlowe and the late Long John Baldry spanning April to June. Colin and Rod made another US trip in September, and two shows were opened by Al Stewart. In between all of this, Rod Argent had Hugh Grundy come to his Red House Studio on August 14, 2002 to overdub some parts on old Zombies recordings for the Big Beat 2CD collection "The DECCA Stereo Anthology." Hugh recorded drum overdubs on "She's Not There," and he added tambourine to "Is This The Dream." BMI awarded Rod Argent a 4 million performance award for "Time Of The Season" on October 24, 2002.

In terms of their sound, performance ability and the songs that Rod was in the process of writing and recording, Colin and Rod's band started to feel more and more like The Zombies. With full respect to the original band, they started billing themselves as Colin Blunstone & Rod Argent – The Zombies. The Netherlands and Belgium got another taste of the latest Zombies incarnation during the last week of January 2003. More American dates followed during August, and Colin did another Manfreds tour – this time in the fall and winter. "Out Of The Shadows" was belatedly released in the US in 2003 by Koch, who did absolutely nothing to generate sales. Not surprisingly, the CD was deleted from Koch's catalog and was unavailable in the US. The Big Beat label also issued the "New World" album in 2003 with two demos from 1978 that Chris White recorded at a four-track studio with Colin Blunstone and Rod Argent. "Hold My Hand" was an early version of the song that was later titled "Lula Lula," and "When My Boat Comes In" was another brilliant White composition.

Sadly, Paul Atkinson was in the final stages of his life, and he needed assistance to deal with the enormity of his medical bills. Hosted by Shadoe Stevens, a "Time Of The Season Concert" at the L.A. House Of Blues was set for January 27, 2004 to recognize Paul's courage and music industry accomplishments, and to assist Paul and his family in covering medical expenses. Colin Blunstone, Rod Argent, Chris White and Hugh Grundy flew to L.A. to perform with Paul at this show – the last ever Zombies performance. They all rehearsed a day before the show, and they performed "Time Of The Season" and "She's Not There" after Colin and Rod performed Rod's inspirational song "I Want To Fly" for Paul. In addition to the appearances of artists that Paul signed (like Bruce Hornsby, Micky Thomas of Starship, Patty Smyth of Scandal, Michael Penn, and Richard Page of Mr. Mister), former Beach Boy Brian Wilson and his band performed one of Atkinson's favorite songs: "Don't Worry Baby."

Paul Atkinson was presented with the Recording Academy's President's Merit Award at the event, and an auction of items donated by the concert's participants and B.B. King, Bob Dylan, Tom Hanks and Matchbox Twenty took place to raise funds for The Atkinson Family Trust, The Gift Of Life Foundation, and The United Network For Organ Sharing. Paul Atkinson passed away on April 1, 2004, and he will be sorely missed by everyone.

A month-long US tour in February 2004 was followed by a six-week British tour ending April 30 at The Bloomsbury Theatre in London. A concert at that London theater on June 7, 2003 was filmed and recorded for a double CD and DVD UK release on February 3, 2005. The British DVD was called "As Far As I Can See...", while the US double CD and edited DVD were titled "Live At The Bloomsbury Theatre, London" upon their belated release in April 2007.

The year 2004 continued to be a very busy one for Colin, Rod and company, with British dates in March and April, and a trio of German shows in May. Their next studio album, "As Far As I Can See...," was launched at the first date on March 4. "As Far As I Can See..." contained ten fresh Rod Argent originals plus a new recording of "I Don't Believe In Miracles." The sound was more expansive this time, with a 21-piece orchestra appearing on seven tracks. Chris White chipped in backing vocals on three tracks as well. A remix of "I Want To Fly" was planned for release as a Dutch single, but it never materialized. The soundtrack of the film "Kill Bill: Volume 2" included Malcolm McLaren's "About Her." It used a slowed-down sample of "She's Not There" as its basis.

The US album release on Rhino coincided with a US tour with the late Arthur Lee & Love from September 28 to October 16. Having completely won over Dutch audiences, a thorough 25-date Netherlands theater tour took place from November 2 to December 3. It should be noted at this point that string quartets have been featured at dozens of shows throughout the years, and these players have contributed an exciting additional dimension to the overall concert experience. Meanwhile, Rod Argent received a 3 million performance award for "She's Not There" on October 4, 2004.

"A Tribute To Mike Smith" was hosted by David Letterman's bandleader Paul Shaffer to raise funds for former Dave Clark Five vocalist Mike Smith, who terribly damaged his spinal cord and became paralyzed in September 2003 after a fall outside his home in Spain. Colin and Rod were definitely interested in appearing at both B.B. King's shows in New York on August 2, 2005. The other main participants were Denny Laine, Billy J. Kramer, The Fab Faux, and Peter And Gordon, the latter reuniting for the first time since 1968. The format of the show was very interesting in that each act would play a small set of their own material plus one Dave Clark Five song that Mike Smith sang. As expected, Argent and Blunstone did The Zombies' three big US hits plus "I Love You" and "Sticks And Stones," but their DC5 surprise was "Can't You See That She's Mine." They also joined the cast to play "Bits And Pieces" and "Glad All Over."

Nearly four decades about their touring debacle in the Philippines, the band returned there in February 2006. One of the dates, February 13 to be exact, was performed at the Araneta Coliseum. Rod Argent joined Ringo Starr's All Starr Band for a series of high-profile summer gigs with additional guests Sheila E., Edgar Winter, and Billy Squier. Rod had little time to recover for shows planned with Colin in Canada between August 30 and September 5. The Zombies closed out the year by taking part in Miami Steve Van Zandt's "Little Steven's Underground Garage" tour.

Zombies songs were used in more TV commercials, especially "Time Of The Season," which was used in 2006 for Crest toothpaste and Fidelity Investments. "This Will Be Our Year" was placed in a Nike TV commercial during June 2006 in a retrospective of golfer Tiger Woods and his late father. The timeless quality of The Zombies' songs will ensure that their impressive output will be heard by future generations. Proof of that point was illustrated by yet another BMI award for "Time Of The Season," which was cited for 5 million performances on October 3, 2006.

Colin Blunstone and Rod Argent continued to record with Jim Rodford, Steve Rodford and Keith Airey. The demand for their live performances remained very strong. The Zombies hit Canada in March 2007, and lots of European and North American dates continued into 2008, along with special trips to new touring territories such as the Ukraine.

For years, fans asked Rod Argent and Colin Blunstone to play "Odessey And Oracle" in its entirety as part of a concert. On February 20, 2007, the four surviving Zombies met to discuss a proposal to perform "Odessey And Oracle" 40th anniversary shows at Shepherd's Bush Empire in London. They agreed to do two shows, which became three shows (March 7-9, 2008) shortly after tickets went on sale May 1, 2007 – ten months before the concerts! The game plan was to play a two-part show, with a nine-song first set (including three Colin Blunstone songs with a string quintet) and the complete "Odessey And Oracle" for the second part. For the "Odessey And Oracle" portion, fan favorite Keith Airey reproduced the guitar parts of the late Paul Atkinson, Darian Sahanaja (from Brian Wilson's band) reproduced Rod's original Mellotron overdubs, and The Shotgun Horns played on "This Will Be Our Year." Rod had a Victorian pedal organ brought in for just one song: Chris White's "Butcher's Tale (Western Front 1914)." Jim Rodford and Chris White's wife Vivienne Boucherat provided backing vocals, and Steve and Jim Rodford added percussion.

In the meantime, Ace's Big Beat label worked the band's catalog. A CD single pairing "Time Of The Season" and "This Will Be Our Year" was used for a Magners Irish Cider TV commercial. Released on May 14, 2007, the single was followed on June 26 by a cardboard "mini-LP" CD edition of "Odessey And Oracle" and the aforementioned "Into The Afterlife" on July 2.

The band prepared for their Shepherd's Bush Empire shows and then launched into some warmup appearances in early 2008. They did a couple of songs for a February 24, 2008 charity show at Her Majesty's Theatre in Haymarket to commemorate the life and work of Ian Adam, a world-renowned singing coach that influenced Colin and Rod. The concert was called "I'd Like To Teach The World To Sing" and more than 50 actors and recording artists appeared. The Stables in Wavendon held two Zombies practice "Odessey And Oracle" shows on March 2 and 3. The band worked out everything by the time they hit Shepherd's Bush Empire on March 7, and the pre-concert press coverage was solid. Every Zombies fan knew that this was a big event!

Al Kooper introduced The Zombies, who launched into "I Love You," "Sticks And Stones," "Can't Nobody Love You," "What Becomes Of The Broken Hearted," "Misty Roses," "Her Song," "Say You Don't Mind" (the previous three songs with a string quintet), "Keep On Rollin'," and "Hold Your Head Up." Audiences were thrilled with these offerings and the anticipated excitement of the upcoming second set centerpiece, "Odessey And Oracle." Upon The Zombies' completion of "Time Of The Season," fans were ecstatic. They had just experienced a magic recreation of a landmark album that they never thought was possible. The Zombies completed the shows with "Tell Her No" and "She's Not There." The performances of all the original Zombies were outstanding, as were those of their accompanists. Chris White brought the house down every night after completing "Butcher's Tale (Western Front 1914)," and fans were rocking with Hugh Grundy's energetic drumming. In addition, the rich vocal harmonies were completely perfect. Press coverage posted universal raves, as did attendees Robert Plant (Led Zeppelin), Tim Rice, Paul Weller (The Jam, The Style Council), DJ Mark Lamarr, Robyn Hitchcock, Gary Lightbody and Nathan Connolly (both from Snow Patrol), and Duke Erickson (Garbage). Paul Weller was so dedicated that he caught every note of all three shows! The March 8 show was recorded for CD and DVD release, and the CD entitled "Odessey & Oracle {Revisited}" was released on June 30, 2008. The DVD followed almost ten months later.

High off this triumph, the current Zombies did a couple tunes at the Childline Rocks charity concert on March 13 at IndigO2 in London. Russ Ballard joined The Zombies on stage, and the concert also featured Lulu, Roger Daltrey,

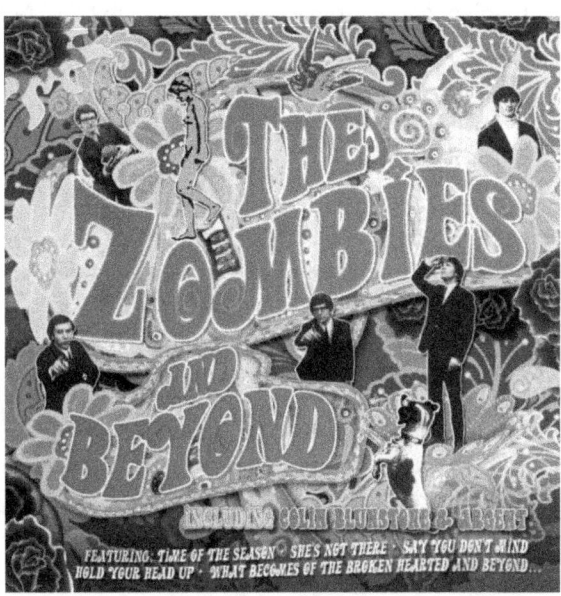

Fish (doing an acoustic Marillion set), Glenn Hughes And Thunder, and Brian Bennett of The Shadows. Another Zombies accomplishment was their first tour with The Yardbirds, and it was about time they played together! The tour covered UK theaters from May 14 to June 27, 2008. Meanwhile, Universal's TV marketing division issued a first-ever collection of essential Zombies, Argent and Colin Blunstone tracks entitled "The Zombies And Beyond." Released on May 26, 2008, it hit #43 on the UK album chart – the band's first chart appearance in decades. Also interesting was VileEvils' set of remixes for "The Way I Feel Inside." The quiet song was placed within six unquiet surroundings!

The Zombies' summer 2008 North American tour featured two new songs: Colin's "Any Other Other Way" and Rod's "I Do Believe." Since both went over very well with audiences, Argent wished to record the next batch of songs by playing live in the studio instead of employing numerous overdubs. The recording of the next Blunstone/Argent album with the touring Zombies band would have to wait until Colin Blunstone finished his ninth solo collection: "The Ghost Of You And Me." It was his first solo project since "The Light Inside" in 1998. "Ghost" heavily featured Chris Gunning's string quintet charts. Colin had hoped to finish the album in time for a Christmas 2008 release, but it finally materialized on March 9, 2009. Before 2008 was over, Colin and Rod filmed a "Face To Face" interview with Rod's keyboard contemporary Rick Wakeman. It was visible on rockondigital.com. In the meantime, Colin promoted "The Ghost Of You And Me" with 12 dates in England during February 2009. At the end of that month, Canadian R&B vocalist Melanie Fiona released the track "Give It To Me Right." The mid-sized hit used "Time Of The Season" as its main component.

North American fans were clamoring for their own "Odessey And Oracle" concerts, and fan pressure started the discussions

for a concert run. It would take more than two years until the wishes of fans were finally met in the fall of 2011. Accompanying the DVD of "Odessey & Oracle {Revisited}" was a brief four-date run of UK dates from April 21-25, 2009 to perform the album in its entirety with Chris White and Hugh Grundy on board. The last show was the biggest – the Hammersmith Apollo. Rod Argent wanted to make it clear that the entire album would not be performed live again, but he later softened that position. The album was the subject of a "Mojo Classic Award" given to the band on June 11, 2009 (at right). About two weeks later, the band was on the road as part of the "Rock Royalty Live!" package tour with The Yardbirds and The Spencer Davis Group. They also did three Canadian dates in mid-July at the end of that tour. The year was completed by another Colin and Rod interview with Rick Wakeman (first broadcast October 8) and a tour of Belgium and the Netherlands taking up all of November.

Colin Blunstone did a brief solo tour in February 2010 with Keith Airey (guitar), Pete Billington (keyboards), Pat Illingworth (drums), and Chris Childs (bass). After the tour, Colin and Rod turned up on BBC One television's "The One Show." As usual, they spoke about "She's Not There" and "Odessey And Oracle"!

Keith Airey informed the band that he wanted to end his Zombies tenure. Chris Childs recommended guitarist Christian Phillips for a Dutch tour starting on April 22 which would continue on to Bahrain and the UK. Phillips could not commit long-term, so Colin brought in Tom Toomey as the new Zombies lead guitarist. Tom has been with the band ever since. Toomey had already played on Colin's "Echo Bridge" and "The Ghost Of You And Me," so he knew what was required from his playing in a Zombies context. This guitar changeover forced the band to cancel May dates in Bulgaria.

The Rod Argent/Russ Ballard/Jim Rodford/Robert Henrit original lineup of Argent reunited on July 25, 2010 for the High Voltage Festival in Victoria Park, London. The concert was released as a double CD that October. November dates in Spain by The Zombies led into five Argent reunion concerts in England in December. By the way, if you were watching yet another Fidelity Investments or Magners Cider commercial at this time, you unmistakably heard "Time Of The Season"!

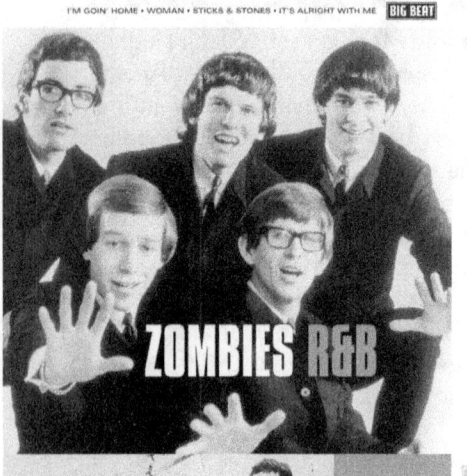

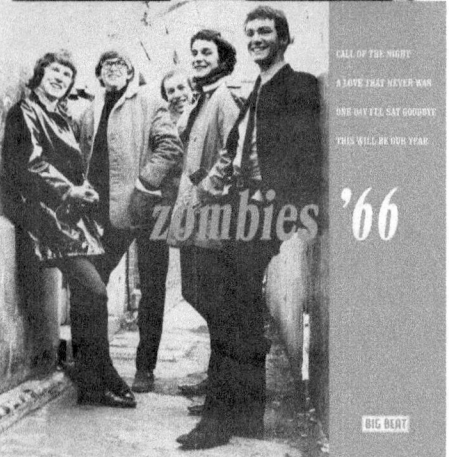

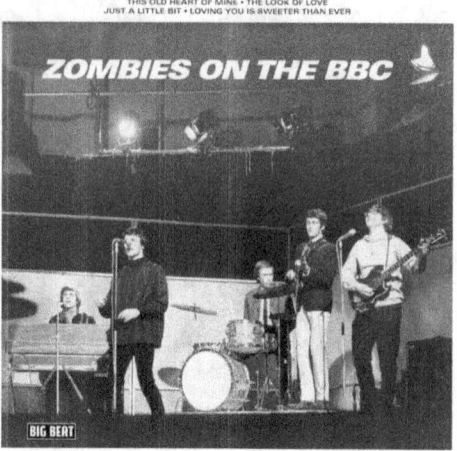

Behind the scenes, the Ace label was working on a six-volume series of 7" vinyl EPs for release in October and November. Every track in the series made its vinyl debut. More importantly, many tracks were available for the first time anywhere. It seems that when October rolls around, Rod Argent seems to receive another BMI "Million-Air" award! This time, Rod was awarded a 6 million performance award for "Time Of The Season" on October 5, 2010.

At left is the initial Metropolis Studios DVD, and at right is the subsequent CD/DVD combo release.

Solid ticket sales meant that The Zombies' tour lineup of Argent, Blunstone, Toomey and the Rodfords had a packed schedule for 2011. They began the year recording and filming a live album at Metropolis Studios in London. The show was initially just a DVD before it became a special CD and DVD package the next year. While Colin Blunstone recorded an appearance on the radio special "Men @ Work" and toured solo with his own band, the final touches were put on the next group album.

Still called "The Zombies Featuring Colin Blunstone & Rod Argent," the band unleashed the studio album "Breathe Out, Breathe In" on May 9, 2011. Blunstone's song "Any Other Way," which was cut in a string arrangement for "Ghost," was given a rock treatment on "Breathe Out, Breathe In." As the song was a clear standout on the new album, a video was made to promote it. The video was the first one that The Zombies have ever made. "Breathe Out, Breathe In" also sported two Argent remakes: the popular "Christmas For The Free" (first recorded for the LP "In Deep") and the lesser-known "Shine On Sunshine" (a cut from "Circus"). Also, "A Moment In Time" was promoted as a single on iTunes that August.

Just five days after "Breathe Out, Breathe In" was released, The Zombies celebrated the 50th anniversary of the first seed planted in the eventual formation of the band (May 14, 1961). Live dates in England and Germany were fortified by summer appearances in France, Japan (Tokyo and Osaka), Greece, and Tel Aviv, Israel. The May 27 date at Shepherd's Bush Empire in London featured Chris White and Hugh Grundy as special guests. During the month-long North American leg of the tour that started in Canada, The Zombies appeared on "Late Night With Jimmy Fallon" (September 11). Dutch fans caught the band in early November, and more British concerts took the band until early December. In the middle of all this activity, Rod had time to do a joint interview with Russ Ballard and host Bob Harris about the 40th anniversary of "The Old Grey Whistle Test." In Japan, "Time Of The Season" could be heard in a Nissan commercial. "She's Not There" reached the 4 million performance mark, and Rod was given another BMI award on October 4, 2011.

Another honor for The Zombies came in the shape of a Blue Plaque at The Blacksmiths Arms in St. Albans, where they had their first rehearsal (the date shown should have been 1962!). The April 27, 2012 plaque unveiling ceremony hosted by English Heritage included the four surviving Zombies. Budget cuts at English Heritage just four months later severely limited further plaque issuances. So, The Zombies received their plaque just in time!

Live recordings during British dates in 2012 were first made available on the American CD "Extended Versions" in November. The British release (titled "Live In The UK") would not come until the end of April 2013, but it had far superior packaging.

These were the first albums that simply billed the group as The Zombies. Both Colin and Rod felt that the musical progression and familial atmosphere of the Zombies touring band had reached a point where they felt that what they were doing was a modern continuation of what the original Zombies would have done if they had stayed together. Therefore, performing with the sole billing as The Zombies was fully justified.

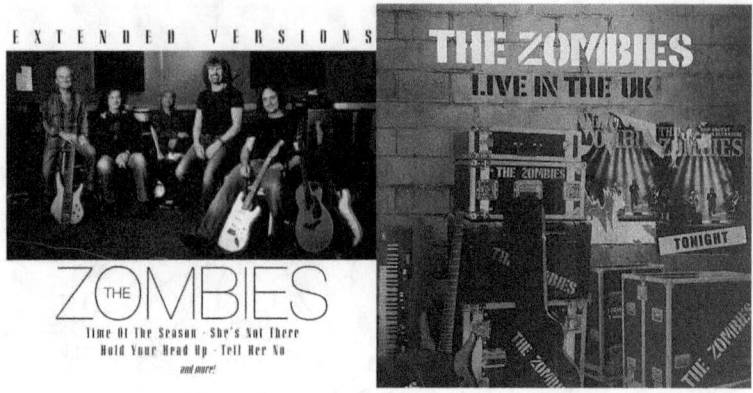

Above: the "Extended Versions" CD and its better dressed relative "Live In The UK."

Below: The Blue Plaque is on the left, and Frans de Graaff is standing in front of The Blacksmiths Arms, where the plaque is located. (Thanks to Frans for both photos.)

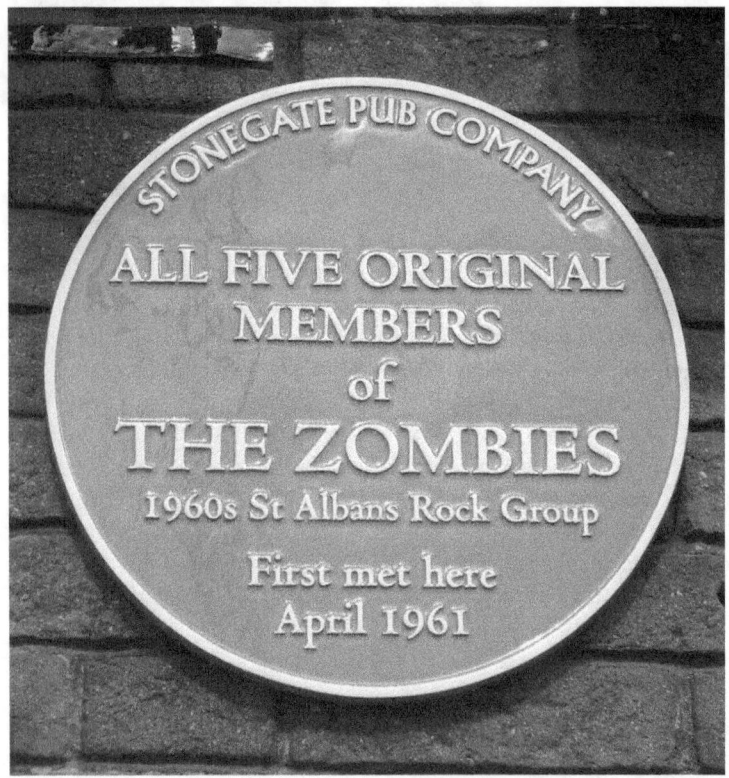

Rod Argent had some time to do some outside sessions. He appeared on the track "School" for the CD "Songs Of The Century: An All-Star Tribute To Supertramp," and he played on a cover version of The Doors' "Riders On The Storm" for Nektar's "A Spoonful Of Time" album. Both of those were issued in 2012. The next year, Rod Argent and Steve Hillage recorded "Rock'n Me" for the CD "Fly Like An Eagle: An All-Star Tribute To Steve Miller Band."

Colin Blunstone's next solo album, "On The Air Tonight," was released in the middle of October 2012. Unfortunately, Colin was stricken by a nasty virus which made the rounds worldwide. He had to cancel a series of November "On The Air Tonight" dates in England and the Netherlands, but he was able to reschedule them during January and February of the following year. To close out 2012, Colin Blunstone, Rod Argent and Chris White recorded an "Odessey And Oracle"-themed interview for BBC Radio 4's "Mastertapes."

After being eligible since 1990, The Zombies received their first Rock & Roll Hall Of Fame nomination in October 2013. However, their vote total was inadequate for entry into that elite group at the time. Meanwhile, rap master Eminem used "Time Of The Season" for his track "Rhyme Or Reason." It was part of his November 2013 collection "The Marshall Mathers LP 2." A British package tour with The Yardbirds, The Animals & Friends, Maggie Bell and Dave Berry took the band from January 21 to March 7, 2014. Dave Berry replaced Spencer Davis, who was ill from a blood clot at the time.

A recent marketing development in the music industry is the release of "Record Store Day" limited edition vinyl records to promote independent record stores. These releases take place on a Saturday in the middle of April each year, and this ritual has been taking place since 2007. The first of many Zombies vinyl releases on Record Store Day took place on April 20, 2013 with Varèse Sarabande's reissue of the first US Zombies album. Only 1,000 copies were made of this record. Varèse produced two further Record Store Day vinyl LPs in April 2014: "Odessey And Oracle" and "The Zombies" – the latter a reissue of the Swedish LP from late 1966.

Another marketing angle to promote legacy (older) recording artists and performers involves special "rock and roll royalty"-styled cruises. The Moody Blues held their second annual Moody Blues Cruise in the Bahamas from April 2-7, 2014 with The Zombies on the MSC Ship Divina. The Zombies went from this cruise to their own American tour, which included some festival action. After the tour was completed, Colin Blunstone did a week of dates from May 8-15. Crowds were very small, but that was not important. Colin clearly enjoyed the intimacy of the moment and spoke directly to his most devoted fans. The band accompanying Blunstone consisted of current Zombies members Tom Toomey and Steve Rodford, along with keyboardist Pete Billington and bassist Elliot Mason.

Also of interest for Colin Blunstone fans was the Dutch triple-disc set "Collected." In addition to including four Zombies tracks, "Collected" featured an excellent selection of tracks spanning Blunstone's solo and vocal session career. The package was completed by Colin's informative commentary about each track.

Another recent online development in the realization of projects is crowdfunding. Colin Blunstone and Rod Argent decided on a new approach in August 2014 for their next Zombies album. While they could have easily paid for the recording and production of that album out of their own pockets, Colin Blunstone and Rod Argent decided to further the connection to their fanbase by offering contributors exclusive pre-release video and audio of the tracks in progress and the ability to obtain Zombies merchandise and rare items from their collections. The site that they used was PledgeMusic, and 10% of the funds raised were set aside for the music education charity Music Unites. A total of 958 contributors helped Blunstone and Argent raise 143% of their desired funding level. With the funding part out of the way, it was time for Colin and Rod to get down to the business of creating the album. The finished project was entitled "Still Got That Hunger."

Fans were treated to two more Record Store Day releases in 2015: a green vinyl British 7" ("She's Not There"/ "You Make Me Feel Good") with an art sleeve from a French EP dating back to December 1964, and a US vinyl LP of "R.I.P." from Varèse Sarabande. Varèse also came through with a vinyl edition of "Odessey And Oracle" a few months later. Also on the archival front, an undubbed mono mix of "Don't Cry For Me" was used as part of an Ace 40th anniversary box set of seven vinyl 45s.

The Zombies had a double-barreled surprise for fans in the fall. Not only would the crowdfunded album "Still Got That Hunger" be released on October 9, but an 18-date American tour would be devoted to performing "Odessey And Oracle" in its entirety with Chris White, Hugh Grundy, Darian Sahanaja and Vivian Boucherat reprising their previous roles from the 2008-2009 dates. All of the major markets throughout America would experience the joy of this presentation. The tour started at the Majestic Theatre in Dallas, Texas on September 30. "Still Got That Hunger" was released on the same day as the show at the New York Society For Ethical Culture Concert Hall in New York City. When the tour hit The Saban Theatre in Beverly Hills, California, Bangles vocalist Susanna Hoffs sang "This Will Be Our Year" during The Zombies' sound check. Tom Petty and many other musical luminaries were in the audience. The tour ended at The Fillmore in San Francisco, California on October 27. Three days later, The Zombies appeared on "The Late Show With Stephen Colbert." The complete coverage of The Zombies was also highlighted by a 7 million performance award of "Time Of The Season" from BMI on October 18.

And now for the album..."Still Got That Hunger" would be a completely different Zombies album than its predecessors. For starters, an outside producer, Chris Potter, was brought in for a fresh production technique. In a sense, it was as if The Zombies were beginning again with Ken Jones producing. With three exceptions, "Still Got That Hunger" was filled with brand new Rod Argent compositions. One exception was "And We Were Young Again," which Rod wrote with his wife Cathy. The Colin Blunstone tune "Now I Know I'll Never Get Over You" (originally orchestrated on "The Ghost Of You And Me") was recrafted in a more Zombies styling. Colin and Rod were well aware that Tom Petty had been performing The Zombies' "I Want You Back Again" live for many years, so The Zombies created a jazzier update for "Still Got That Hunger." Among the many fine songs on the album was "New York," which depicted Rod's love for the city which has always remained a bountiful source of Zombies fandom.

The Cherry Red label issued the UK edition of "Still Got That Hunger." On the US side of things, The End Records handled the album. "Still Got That Hunger" hit Billboard's album chart at #100 for the week of October 30, 2015. The same week in Billboard, the Varèse Sarabande reissue of "Odessey And Oracle" re-entered the Top LP Vinyl Albums chart at #24. Colin and Rod were ecstatic with the amazing showings of these albums!

Varèse Sarabande wasn't done yet. Former Rhino Records reissue producer Andrew Sandoval had been diligently researching Zombies BBC recordings for Varèse. Sandoval felt that there were other BBC recordings somewhere out there. He was right, as a couple of interviews and some alternate versions were located. The final results of Sandoval's research became "The BBC Radio Sessions," a two-LP release on Black Friday (the day after Thanksgiving). An expanded edition of the album on two CDs was issued in May 2016.

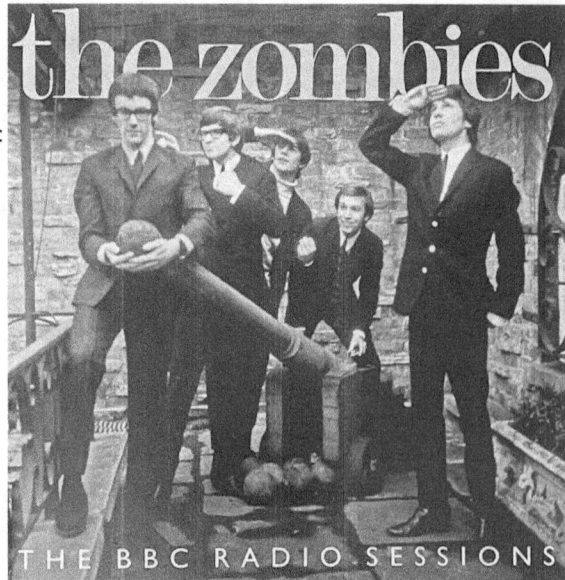

Beginning 2016, "Now I Know I'll Never Get Over You" was promoted as a single from "Still Got That Hunger." The album was issued on vinyl, as promised on the PledgeMusic site. The original single mix of "She's Not There" made its stereo debut on the CD "Hard To Find Jukebox Classics 1960-1964: 30 Amazing Stereo Hits" on February 19. A British reissue of the Swedish self-titled Zombies album became the next Record Store Day release on standard and clear vinyl.

At right: the promo single drawn from "Still Got That Hunger": "Now I Know I'll Never Get Over You."

(from left to right: Jim Rodford, Rod Argent, Steve Rodford, Colin Blunstone, Tom Toomey)

With a US tour in September 2016, The Zombies announced that they would honor the 50th anniversary of "Odessey And Oracle" by one final tour in 2017. (Rod and Colin made it <u>really</u> final in 2019!) They also mentioned writing a book about the recording of the album. That book ended up being "The Odessey: The Zombies In Words And Images," and it was released on March 30, 2017. Tom Petty wrote the book's foreward. A month after the tour announcement, The Zombies received their second Rock & Roll Hall Of Fame nomination. Once again, they did not receive enough votes to get in.

The Flower Power Cruise was how The Zombies kicked off 2017. The Celebrity Summit ship left from Fort Lauderdale, Florida on February 27, and the voyage ended on March 4. Tour host Micky Dolenz of The Monkees was accompanied by The Yardbirds, Eric Burdon And The Animals, The 5th Dimension, The Family Stone, The Lovin' Spoonful, Rare Earth, Three Dog Night, Vanilla Fudge, and British contemporaries Peter Asher (from Peter And Gordon) and Spencer Davis.

Starting on March 10, 2017 and continuing for the next two months, all four original Zombies played "Odessey And Oracle" for North American audiences. It was the 50th anniversary of the album's recording. Little did the band know that Brian Reed, host of the podcast "S-Town," liked playing "A Rose For Emily." Before they knew it, The Zombies ended up on Conan O'Brien's program that May. Before that happened, three Record Store Day 7" singles were released – two official releases, and one from the illegal side of town.

Below: all three Record Store Day 7" single releases for 2017.

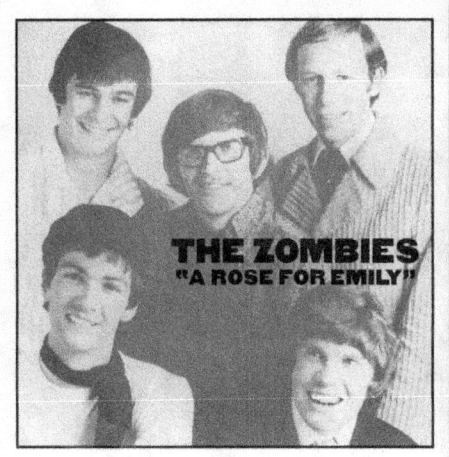
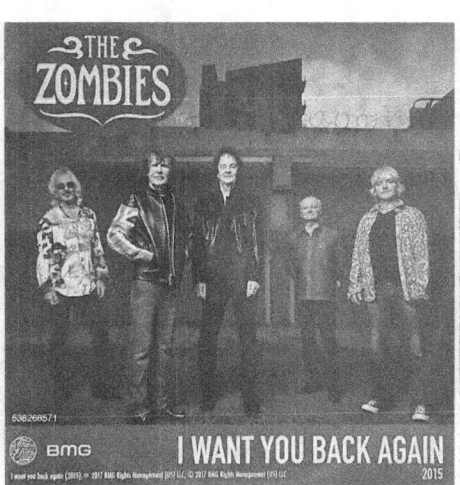
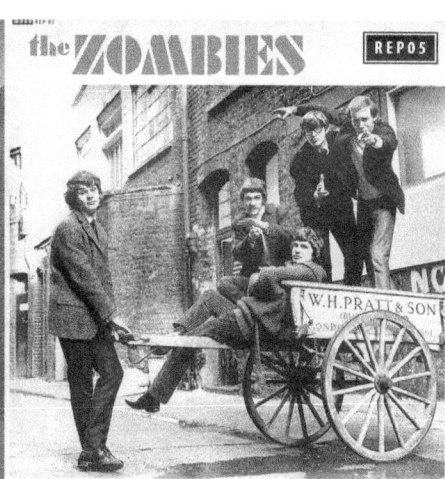

The first legitimate Record Store Day release was from "Still Got That Hunger." It was half archival, half new: a pairing of the current (2015) version of "I Want You Back Again" with the 1965 version. The other single fully came from the archives: "A Rose For Emily" b/w "This Will Be Our Year." Pressed on translucent rose vinyl, the disc's A-side was the outtake stereo version with cello accompaniment with the standard mono mix of the flipside.

Fans might not want to admit it, but the unlicensed EP "Broadcast '66" was just as interesting as the other two Record Store Day offerings. One side was related to The Zombies' appearance on the TV show "Hippodrome" – namely, their performance of "Gotta Get A Hold On Myself" and the announcer introduction. Of course it should have been presented the other way around, but this was not a legit product! The other side of the disc was a pair of live tracks from the French TV program "Dents De Lait, Dents De Loup": "This Old Heart Of Mine" and "Going To A Go-Go." Only the latter has been officially released.

Near the end of 2017, a third Rock & Roll Hall Of Fame nomination came and went with the same disappointing outcome. Undeterred, The Zombies completed the nearly two-week "Odessey And Oracle 50th Anniversary Finale Tour" on January 14, 2018 with the 30A Songwriter's Festival in Miramar Beach, Florida and returned home to England. Just six days later, on January 20, Jim Rodford perished from a fall at home in St. Albans. He was 76.

With the "Edge Of The Rainbow" tour to commence at City Winery in New York on February 27, 2018, a new bassist had to be located. Danish bassist Søren Koch (born November 10, 1970 in Copenhagen, Denmark), was a Scandinavian music veteran whose most recent band was The Beatophonics.

Led Zeppelin and The Zombies are usually not mentioned in the same conversation, but a most unusual concert appearance for Rod Argent and Colin Blunstone took place at Carnegie Hall's Isaac Stern Auditorium in New York on March 7, 2018. Their piano and voice arrangement of Led Zeppelin's "Thank You" not only honored that band, but it served as a fitting tribute to Rod's cousin Jim Rodford.

At the end of another rigorous year of touring, The Zombies received their fourth Hall nomination in December 2018. This time, more than 300,000 votes led to their induction into The Rock & Roll Hall Of Fame on March 29, 2019! The event took place at Barclays Center in Brooklyn, New York – the borough in which they had spent much of their time when they first visited the US. The other Rock & Roll Hall Of Fame inductees were The Cure, Radiohead, Stevie Nicks, Janet Jackson, Def Leppard, and Roxy Music. Susanna Hoffs of The Bangles gave the induction speech. The four Zombies played "Time Of The Season," "Tell Her No" and "She's Not There," and at the end of Def Leppard's set, Ian Hunter led guest guitarist Brian May, Roxy Music's Phil Manzanera, Steve Van Zandt, Susanna Hoffs, as well as Rod on keyboards and Colin on vocals to finish the evening with "All The Young Dudes." That performance, and Def Leppard's entire set, was later released as a Record Store Day 12" single on August 29, 2020. It was mentioned in the run-up to the event that it was the 50th anniversary of the March 29, 1969 issue of Cashbox in which "Time Of The Season" was #1, but that was coincidental, as that issue was prepared and published the week before. On either side of the Atlantic, 5LP sets of Zombies studio tracks were issued by Demon and Varèse on the same day (February 22, 2019), with the Demon set featuring colored vinyl.

Photos from The Zombies' brief set at the Rock & Roll Hall Of Fame ceremony in Brooklyn:

Previous page (left to right): Rod Argent, Chris White, Colin Blunstone, Tom Toomey.

Top of this page (left to right): Chris White and Colin Blunstone.

Bottom of this page (left to right): Hugh Grundy and Chris White.

Next page (top): Rod Argent.

Next page (middle – left to right): Tom Toomey, Steve Rodford.

Next page (bottom): Hugh Grundy.

The Zombies were supposed tobe involved with the "Woodstock 50" three-day festival, but the financial bigwigs involved pulled out. In May 2019, they announced the "Something Great From '68" tour at which they would co-headline with Brian Wilson, Al Jardine, and Blondie Chaplin while playing "Odessey And Oracle" for was what really the final time.

Meanwhile, Chris White tasked his sons Jamie and Matthew with going through his cache of tapes for remastering purposes. Many surprises were found, but none as important as the demo tapes that Colin Blunstone recorded prior to his debut album "One Year." Those demos would accompany Sundazed's reissue of the album in late 2021. The B-side "I Hope I Didn't Say Too Much Last Night" was not included, but its demo (titled "Too Much Too Soon Last Night") was. Chris White went through the other tapes and ended up creating a series called "The Chris White Experience." The releases were distributed in 2019 and 2020. A collection of tracks by the little-known '70s group Sparrow formed a separate release in the series. The first three volumes and the Sparrow album were available on CD and as digital downloads, while the other two volumes were only issued as downloads. Colin Blunstone and Rod Argent contributed to tracks on all five volumes.

Colin and Rod started out the year 2020 in a strong way by telling Rolling Stone magazine in their February 14 issue that they had just finished the first three tracks of their next album a couple days before. They were planning to do the Flower Power Cruise in March and headline the On The Blue Cruise in April before hitting the southern US and back up to Canada.

At right: a promotional card for the ill-fated On The Blue Cruise for 2020.

From left to right: Steve Rodford, Tom Toomey, Søren Koch, Rod Argent, Colin Blunstone.

COVID-19 hit, and touring plans for 2020 and then 2021 were halted. There may not have been any gigs, but Colin and Rod did lots of radio and podcast appearances to make up for it. To get around the frustration of not being able to perform anywhere, Blunstone and Argent jointly announced on May 18, 2021 that they would create a September 18 "World Tour In One Night" livestream event at Abbey Road's Studio Two (the recording home for most of "Odessey And Oracle") at 8PM Greenwich Mean Time (3PM US Eastern Standard Time). Similar to an in-person concert, tickets to access the concert to be streamed at veeps.com were sold at thezombies.veeps.com. The concert tied in nicely with the 90th anniversary of Abbey Road. Concurrently, "Time Of The Season" was used to promote Chelsea Football Club gear, namely, their new shirt, and a "Chelsea FC & Harvey Gunn" remix of the track was made available in June 2021.

At the Abbey Road livestream, new songs such as "Different Game," "You Could Be My Love," "Merry Go Round" and "Runaway" were performed, and some song arrangements featured the quartet Q Strings. The concert was recorded and filmed, and a question and answer session with Colin and Rod took place afterward with American music journalist David Fricke as the moderator. Argent and Blunstone were thrilled to reach places like Australia and South America with this livestream, as they had never played on either continent. The CD/DVD "Live From Studio Two" was eventually released at their gigs at the start of April 2022.

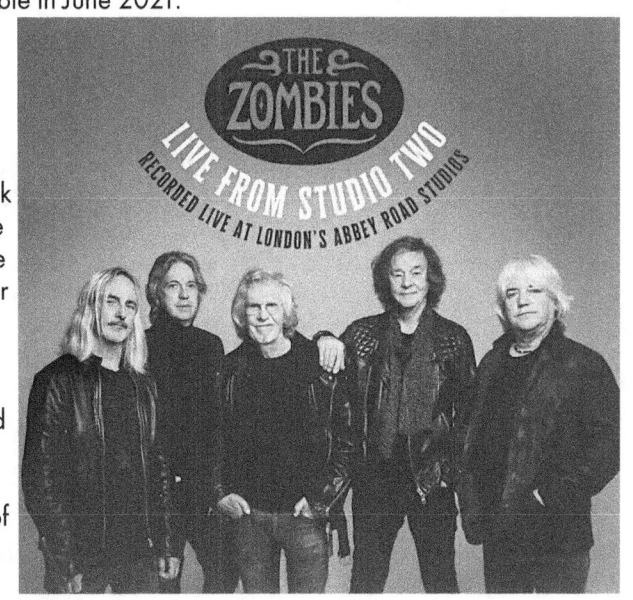

With 2022 plans underway for gigs in the UK, North America and Europe starting in February and ending in September, it became obvious in January that the UK was not quite ready and that tour leg was put off until 2023. The "Life Is A Merry-Go-Round" tour of the US began after the Flower Power Cruise in late March 2022. When that part of the tour was done, the band returned home.

In late May 2022, Colin and Rod both tested positive for COVID-19, and Rod was still testing positive just before their flight from London to Toronto, Canada. Despite their mild cases, they elected to postpone a concert in San Francisco, California and two in Canada (in the Ontario locations of Belleville and Mississauga). The tour was resumed at Penn's Peak in Jim Thorpe, Pennsylvania on June 24.

As for those postponed UK dates, "The Invaders Return Tour" has been scheduled for 2023. Catch it!

THE BBC RECORDINGS

Performing for the BBC, whether on television or radio, gave The Zombies a dual opportunity to promote their latest record and display cover versions of their favorite songs. Quite a number of these performances have been lost to time, but the ones released on "Zombies At The BBC" and "Zombie Heaven" proved that the band's likes were wide-ranging and interesting. Many R&B cover versions made their only appearances on BBC airwaves. Little Richard's hits "Early One Morning" and "Rip It Up" got the Zombies treatment, including a jazzy intro on the latter. James Brown's "Showtime" album was the source for The Zombies' BBC rendition of "For You My Love," while Aretha Franklin's R&B hit "Soulville" was discovered in New York by Paul Atkinson during their first US trip. "When The Lovelight Starts Shining Through Her Eyes" was the male counterpart of the Holland/Dozier/Holland song that provided The Supremes their initial US chart success. Two Curtis Mayfield songs done with The Impressions ("It's All Right" and "You Must Believe Me") and the Shirelles hit "Will You Love Me Tomorrow" marked more soulful excursions for the band. Also in this vein was The Isley Bros.' "This Old Heart Of Mine." The rollicking Dave Berry arrangement of Rosco Gordon's "Just A Little Bit" discovered by Colin Blunstone revealed the other extreme of the group's capabilities. Billy Stewart's "Sitting In The Park" would have been a good single contender during their 1966 chart slump, but Georgie Fame scored a large early 1967 UK hit with the song. The arrangement of Dusty Springfield's Bacharach/David hit from that year, "The Look Of Love," was adopted by The Zombies for their brilliant late '67 BBC version. Although never played live, Rod's song for Dusty, "If It Don't Work Out," was aired for BBC audiences.

Rod Argent gives his opinion of the early days of the BBC: "I was always really worried about live sessions because sometimes the sound that one got was appalling, but you could be lucky and it could be good." This was apparent when the band's own songs were presented differently on occasion. "She's Not There" used Rod's Vox Continental organ instead of his pianet to create a less powerful but interesting variation. Another keyboard subsitution took place on one version of "Tell Her No" when an acoustic piano was used as the pianet was being repaired. A more pounding "What More Can I Do" sported longer Argent and Atkinson solos, and their "I'm Goin' Home" cover used an arrangement that differered substantially from its recorded version.

"Odessey And Oracle" was given every promotional opportunity by The Zombies on the BBC. "Friends Of Mine" was recorded at their last BBC session in late 1967, and Rod and Chris' appearance on Kenny Everett's spring 1968 show had them playing the album cuts "Time Of The Season," "A Rose For Emily," and "This Will Be Our Year." In between, a very humorous Rod/Chris choral jingle for the departing host was aired. It has been archived on "Zombie Heaven." A 2010 BBC EP and "The BBC Radio Sessions" have turned up even more interviews and alternates.

FINAL OVERVIEW

While much has been said about The Zombies, why do they still appeal today? One main reason is Rod Argent – an amazingly talented catalyst. His choral background, awareness of each instrument's accompaniment possibilities and capabilities, and ability to obtain the best from each Zombies member without dominating the group were tremendous accomplishments. Chris White still marvels about Argent's songwriting: "I think Rod is one of the best songwriters I've ever come across because he has a vision and he has a beautiful sense of melody and lyrics. The difference between Rod's songs and mine was that Rod's were primarily keyboard-based and mine were guitar-based, although I wrote on keyboards later. We had a great respect for each other and we'd try to do unusual things musically, which I think we learned from The Beatles. A lot of Rod's songwriting and musicianship rubbed off on me and vice versa in regards to the songwriting. There was no competition or jealousy with each other. We appreciated what each other did. We had and still have a lot of respect for each other. Even now, I write with a lot of different people, but Rod at his best was one of the best songwriters ever. We didn't do many demos in those days but actually played our songs live to the band, and Rod and I would mainly work the ideas out. The whole group would have to like a song for us to record it."

Through The Zombies made great listening music, their music was also extremely complex. Chord patterns and vocal phrasings, although mainly downcast in minor keys, used jazzy major 9th or 13th chords for their powerful transitional upsurges to more positive terrain. Here's White's take on this topic: "Melodies and rhythms in our minds were our basic interests. I think there's a link between 'She's Not There' and 'Time Of The Season.' They both used bass and drum riffs with unusual chords and Colin's soaring vocals. We used that a lot. I think the combination of Rod's pianet playing and Colin's voice and some of the unusual chord structures we did made us different, and there was no pressure from the record companies to sound like someone else. There are certain formulas, but you can't recreate them."

Like all musicians that have been affected by today's fast-moving music industry, Rod Argent explains how difficult it is to make it today: "There is a problem with radio everywhere, really. Everything is categorized so strictly that sometimes when you do something a bit more imaginative, which crosses a few boundaries, you can't get it airtime, and yet you know that the record companies are extremely willing to have much more open ears than that, but the difficulty is getting past those categories."

For most groups, the failure of songs that they strongly believe in would be a devastating blow. To The Zombies' credit, they accepted failure with a more positive outlook and made musical impacts in different environments. As Rod Argent sincerely feels, "The Zombies broke up at exactly the right time, at the right point in the natural cycle of things. It's wonderful that our music has transcended the decades and still sounds good." In his parting comment, Chris White gives his view of the band's up and down career: "It was all the luck of the draw. I think we had thirteen singles out and the first and last got to number 1 in America according to Cashbox, and 'Time Of The Season' sold over a million copies. You can call it a failure or success sandwich depending on how you want to look at it. The bread on either side of it was a success but the middle was a little dip! We were just happy to have records coming out, basically. It was a great period, I had a great deal of fun and I wouldn't change anything. I would have liked to have made a lot more money, but I don't think that would have changed my life and I'm happy, so are the others, actually. They enjoy their lives and when we get together socially and play today it's great fun. I think a lot of the fun's gone out of the business. It's become a business with a capital 'B' and the fun element's definitely gone. The nice thing is we're still all friends. You went through the hard times together and you'll never ever lose that feeling. I think what you have to do basically, and what we did, is do what you feel like. If you really believe in the music and have fun, the money will come along." Yearly sales of over 100,000 Zombies CDs (and their download equivalent) are proof of that.

It is indeed heartening to see that The Zombies' recorded dedication to their craft has enabled decades of fans, new and old, to continually marvel at their creativity and musicality.

"The Odessey: The Zombies In Words And Images"

WHAT HAVE THEY BEEN DOING? – THE SOLO YEARS

Rod Argent

Rod Argent has been extremely productive in the music industry over the past five decades since the demise of The Zombies, yet his contributions have been practically invisible! Why is that, you may ask? After the breakup of his group Argent in 1976, Rod Argent chose record production and sessions as his means of contributing to music. However, this phase of his life started in 1968 after The Zombies ceased to exist. While putting the Zombies name to rest in 1969, Rod Argent and Chris White intended to create a stable, self-contained group that did not overlap with the legacy of The Zombies. That group became Argent. In order to accomplish this goal, manager Mel Collins worked out a CBS Records deal that enabled White and Argent to record and produce new recording artists through their newly created Nexus Productions company. The first acts that Argent and White produced for Nexus were Free Ferry (two singles) and Sykes & Medina (one disc). Duffy Power (remember him?) was then recorded by the pair on their revised arrangement of the Robert Johnson blues "Hellhound" (also known as "Hell Hound On My Trail"). The B-side was a gospel-influenced Leon Russell tune called "Hummingbird." Originally released on CBS, it was reissued on Epic with its sides reversed. Different combinations of Argent members also recorded most of an album with Duffy Power, and nearly all of those tracks were included on Duffy's CD "Just Stay Blue" in 1995.

The story of how his band was simply named Argent has never been told, so Rod was good enough to fill us in: "First of all, we were looking for some sort of play on words on my name and then the meaning of my name (money), and the drummer Bob Henrit came up with the idea of 'Silver Surfer.' It was then decided we couldn't use that name because there were trade restrictions on the use of the name, but the connection between Argent and silver (as in coins) was there. In fact, when my name was called out at school for the (attendance) register, I didn't like the sound of it! It was Russ (Ballard) that said we should call the band 'Argent,' and I said, 'Oh no, we can't call it that – I don't feel comfortable with it!' In the end, the other guys felt strongly that it should be called Argent. That wasn't my suggestion at all; I would have been quite happy with a name that had no reference to me. The name Argent was considered short and to the point. At the time, I don't think people were doing that – calling a group by a surname."

To prepare for their upcoming career as Argent, the group warmed up through German and Italian club gigs in 1969. Of these, their Munich residency at The PN Hit House was the most successful. A small 8-track Chelsea studio, Sound Techniques Studio, was the recording spot for their self-titled debut LP. Their first outpouring was a US single, "Liar," written by Russ Ballard. It was the last record that Argent and White created for the Date label, and all future Nexus-produced releases would be handled by Epic in America. (This changeover to Epic would not take place in the UK until after the "Celebration" single in 1971, when they moved from CBS.) The record's B-side was "Schoolgirl," a more advanced pop number. The American "Argent" LP came out in November 1969, two months before its UK debut. Response was muted, but American pop group Three Dog Night latched onto "Liar" and had a big US hit with the song in 1971. The Argent debut album extended the Zombies pop format with a more aggressive band approach and Rod's more intricate keyboard work. Chris White felt the same impact: "I thought we had it there. There were three great songwriters involved in Argent: Rod, Russ Ballard, who also had a great voice, and myself. Rod didn't want the group to be called Argent, there were all sorts of names bandied about, but Bob Henrit basically got the group to call themselves that. The record company, of course, wanted the group to call themselves The Zombies. I thought Argent was one of the best things I'd ever been involved in. I wasn't playing, but my God, did I really feel it! I oversaw Argent, did some of the sound at shows, produced the albums, and then produced Colin Blunstone's first solo album (with Rod), which was done after the first Argent album. The first Argent album was basically a crossover and transition from The Zombies. It was my favorite Argent album. It was recorded on 8-track. 'Liar' was one of my favorites, 'Schoolgirl' had a lovely melody and was a great song. I think 'Freefall' was the first thing we actually recorded as Argent. 'Stepping Stone' was fantastic live. The only Zombies song Argent played live was 'Time Of The Season' and perhaps, I'm not sure, 'She's Not There,' as Rod wanted to remove the group from The Zombies." After completing their album, the Argent group contributed backing tracks to Colin Blunstone's debut LP "One Year," also on Epic. "One Year" became Blunstone's most highly respected album.

Colin Blunstone had a bad experience singing under the name Neil MacArthur for Deram Records, but he was unsure as to his next move. Blunstone was not meant to be included in Argent, but getting the group together was an incentive for Colin to obtain his Epic label contract, as Chris White explains: "He (Colin) was out of the business, loved Argent, went to some of the rehearsals and thought it was great and wanted to do an album again. So we did an album with him ('One Year') which Rod and I produced right after the first Argent album. Originally we wanted it to be just his voice and strings, but the record company didn't know how to market something like that and we used Argent on some tracks as well as doing some string things like 'Say You Don't Mind,' which was a hit in the UK."

MEET ARGENT, SON OF ZOMBIE.

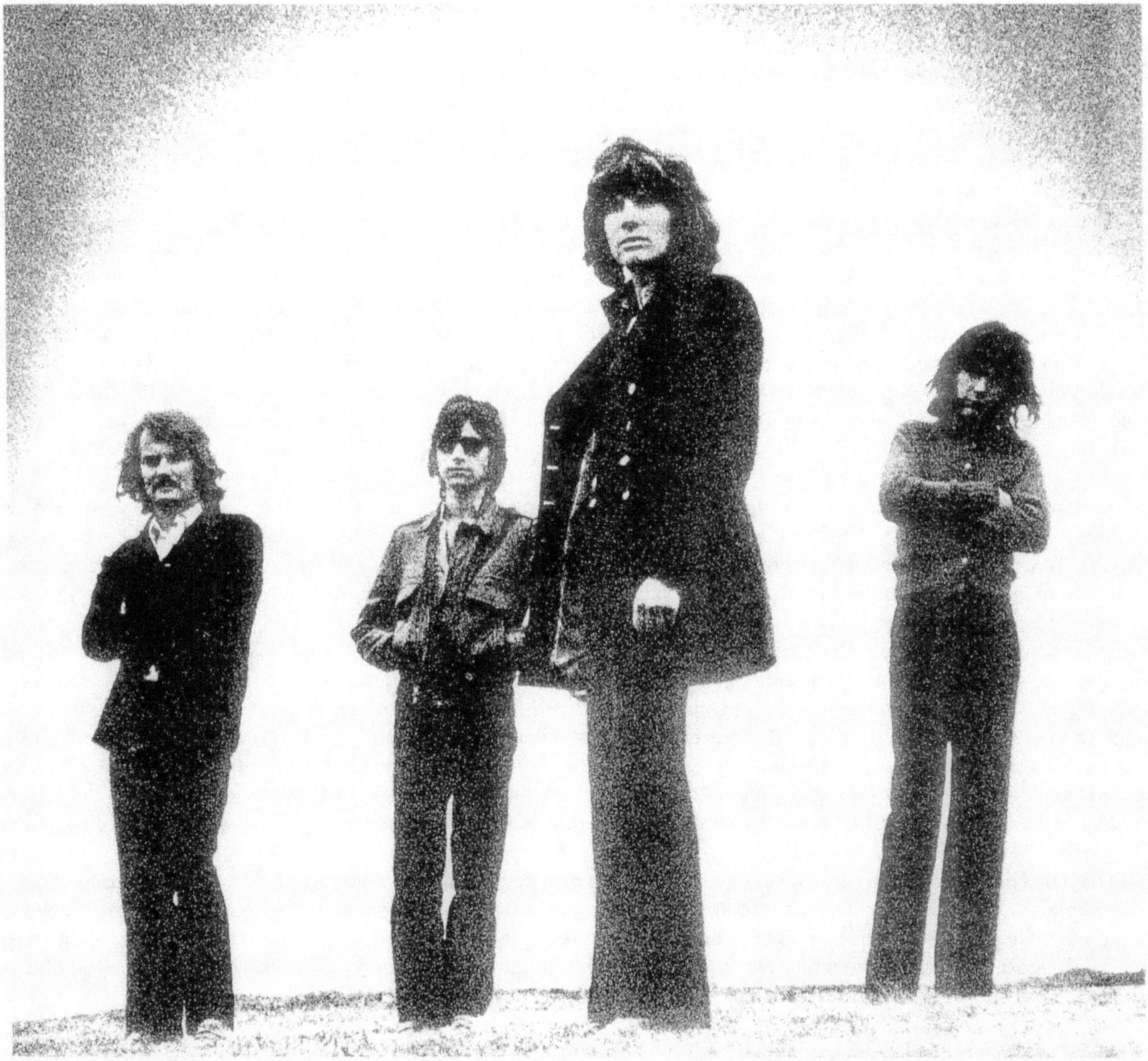

Remember "Tell Her No" and "She's Not There"? Two very big hits by the Zombies. And then they disappeared for a while and everybody thought they'd had it. Until not too long ago when they re-emerged with "Time of the Season," a two-million selling single that proved the Zombies were still very much alive musically. Now again it's been a long time since we've heard from them and the rumors are starting again: "Have the Zombies permanently gone under?" "Is it true that the only good Zombie is a dead Zombie?" Well, sorry to say, they have—although not entirely. Rod Argent, former chief Zombie, has put together a new group, ARGENT. And Chris White (another "dead" Zombie) has co-produced the group's first album with Rod. The album displays Rod's known talents as a singer, songwriter and keyboardist supreme.

Les Zombies sont morts.
Vive L'ARGENT!

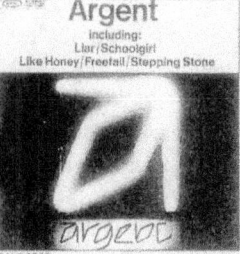

argent
Argent
including:
Liar/Schoolgirl
Like Honey/Freefall/Stepping Stone
argent

BN 26525

®"EPIC", Marca Reg. T.M. PRINTED IN U.S.A.

EPIC

There was still some residual interest in anything related to The Zombies, so a first US tour for Argent was in order. This tour was to last the better part of a month. At the Boston Tea Party, Argent opened for Mother Earth from March 12-14, 1970. Argent also played three nights at the Fillmore East in New York (March 19-21), opening for Lee Michaels and The Moody Blues. The experience was far from successful, according to Chris White: "Rod and I formed Argent and one of the first shows we played was at the Fillmore East. It was stunning. It was the best venue in rock and roll. The sound system was good, incredibly professional stage management, backstage projection and back lights. I was doing the sound and suddenly the staff there found out I was one of The Zombies and they kept saying, 'You should be touring. The Zombies are one of the best acts ever.' We lost money on that Argent tour while at the same time, there were three phony groups going around America calling themselves The Zombies and cleaning up! People kept on calling us about this and we kept calling the promoters up to put a stop to it, saying that we are the original Zombies, and they didn't believe us! They'd tell us back that 'The original singer Colin Blunstone was killed in a car crash' and this other fellow has taken over with the original Zombies! We took legal action but it didn't do much good. Eric Burdon And The Animals had the same problem. Whenever we'd catch up to one of these phony bands, they'd have already played the gigs, made their money and split. They even played the Whisky A Go-Go in L.A. and The Move, who were fans of ours, were in the audience and they actually threw beer cans at the stage yelling, 'F*** off, you're not the real Zombies!' The imposter bands were making $7,000 a night and that's what we each personally lost on that tour with Argent. That's $7,000 in 1969 dollars! What we should have done is gone out on the road with The Zombies and introduced Argent as a second act, but we had spent a lot of time and a lot of our own money putting Argent together and we thought at the time that emphasizing The Zombies in front of Argent would be going backwards. If I could do things over, that's what I would have done in retrospect. Rod might still have done the same thing as he doesn't believe in going backwards." The Zombies and Argent on the same bill? The possibilties would have been endless. . .

Argent entered Sound Techniques Studio again to record their "Ring Of Hands" album in 1970. Two singles were taken from it - "Celebration" and "Sweet Mary." "Celebration" was an uplifting rock song, and its song lyric formed the basis for the album title. It was released as a UK single first, but in the US, it followed up "Sweet Mary." US and German fans were the only ones to receive its rare B-side "Kingdom," while in England, the flipside was "Where Are We Going Wrong." Chris White tells us what he thinks of the song: "One of my favorite tracks of Argent was 'Celebration.' Rod gave me the idea of using the word 'invitation' to follow-up on the word 'celebration,' so I worked on that. It usually roughly worked out that we had equal songs involved except in the later stages of Argent, when I was a little disillusioned as the music had become too esoteric and wandering in its presentation. My songwriting input dropped and Russ Ballard, who is a great songwriter, had more songs placed on the Argent albums as a result." "Sweet Mary" just missed the Billboard Top 100 at #102, thanks to the overall mistaken radio station perception that the song had subtle drug references. "Ring Of Hands" did not sell well either, but it revealed that Argent's audience was growing substantially. The album was the band's last collection of pure pop-based songs, and as such, Rod Argent and Chris White agree that their favorite Argent material was on the first two albums they created.

Argent as a unit really started to gel, especially as the writing and singing of Russ Ballard and Rod Argent became more and more complementary. Touring continued and Rod and Russ prepared songs for their next release. The only problem was that they did not have enough material for an LP at that point. Agreeing that they could not tour on a single, UK Epic and Argent agreed on releasing an EP. More than anything, Rod Argent did not want his band to be strictly known for hit singles – he and Chris White had just gone through that and had no interest in repeating the exercise.

Argent ventured into a much more impressive studio – Abbey Road – to maximize the impact of their newest material. Prior to their tour, the band completed the 1972 EP A-side "Hold Your Head Up" and the two songs on its reverse: "Keep On Rollin'" and "Closer To Heaven." The 6+ minute "Hold Your Head Up" was a quantum leap in the band's development and featured Rod's 3-minute organ solo. Alan "Fluff" Freeman was the primary British DJ that championed this release and played "Hold Your Head Up" weekly despite its length. The record was not selling, but the band went on tour anyway. Since Chris White was in the convenient position of not touring with the group, he was asked by Epic to provide an edited version of "Hold Your Head Up" that was more suitable for airplay. Rod's solo was excised and the 3-minute version was re-released as a standard single with "Closer To Heaven" on its flip. This edit finally cracked Britain's Top 50 and made #5. This led to a TV appearance on "Top Of The Pops." The US first received "Hold Your Head Up" along with the edited UK release and it entered the June 17, 1972 Billboard chart at #82. The record also hit #5 on Billboard and Cashbox in America, but it took two edits to do the trick! A 2:52 edit was prepared for radio, but the 3:15 edit was the one that worked best on the airwaves. Chris White says this about the music industry and how "Hold Your Head Up" came about: "The business has changed. It's changed a lot. But most of all, it's luck. I mean, I've written songs over the years which I thought were great but didn't have commercial success, and my biggest selling hit was 'Hold Your Head Up' for Argent. Even though both my name and Rod's were on it as part of our songwriting partnership, I actually wrote it. I got the idea of 'Hold Your Head Up' from a riff off 'Time Of The Season.' When it was put out originally, the record company said they thought it was a potential hit but it was 6

At left, the first record released as Argent. It was their only output on Date – later US releases were handled by Epic. At right, the UK EP featuring "Hold Your Head Up."

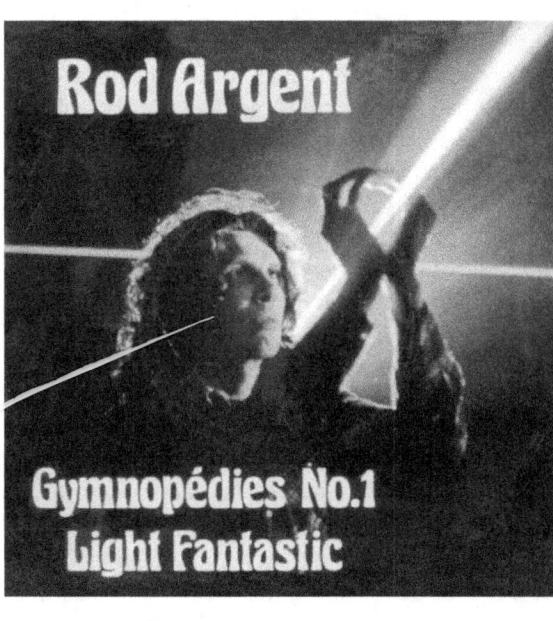 

Two of Rod Argent's more obscure items – "Gymnopédies No. 1" and his "Metro" LP with John Dankworth.

Rod Argent's three greatest production successes: Tanita Tikaram, Joshua Kadison, and Soraya.

minutes long – could I edit it down? So, I edited it down to 3 minutes by cutting the long organ solo, and after 3 months when we had a new single about to be released, suddenly this re-edited single takes off. No one pushed it; it was selling on its own accord. It was the biggest selling thing I've ever been involved in." The biggest misconception people have about "Hold Your Head Up" is the chorus, in which the line "Hold your head up, woman" is sung. Most people think the band is singing "Hold your head up, whoa"! And yes, "Hold Your Head Up" starts with the word "and" – another conversation in progress! The most recent and artistically successful cover version of "Hold Your Head Up" was recorded by British hard rock band Uriah Heep as the single from their 1989 album "Raging Silence." It is also quite conceivable that the "hold your head up" section in the Eurythmics hit "Sweet Dreams (Are Made Of This)" was derived from this Argent song.

After their tour was over, Argent completed the "All Together Now" album. It became a #23 Billboard hit in the US. With the success of the LP, Rod Argent took the group into a more progressive direction. The follow-up single "Tragedy" could not duplicate the success of "Hold Your Head Up," reaching #34 in the UK. American response was even more negative, with peaks of #81 (Cashbox) and #106 (Billboard). The pressure of having to come up with an increasing amount of songs proved too much for Russ Ballard to handle, and he broke down after the album was recorded. He recovered for a short time and was able to resume his work with the band. In the interim, Rod Argent was able to contribute to albums by Trapeze and Barclay James Harvest member John Lees. Toward the end of the recording for "All Together Now," Rod and Chris White gave their 1968 demo "Telescope (Mr. Galileo)" another shot with Chris doing a rare vocal accompanied by the entire Argent lineup. That demo was first released on "Into The Afterlife." Also attempted was Colin Blunstone's vocal on the 1968 Argent/White demo "Unhappy Girl," but the song was too high for Colin's voice and was shelved.

In 1973, Russ Ballard rebounded with his strongest song yet: "God Gave Rock And Roll To You." The song appeared on the equally impressive "In Deep" LP. Russ' song hit #18 in England, while it could only manage a #114 Billboard placing. Unusual about the single was its B-side, "Christmas For The Free" – a Christmas song released in March! American fans bought the album instead for a #90 peak position. The follow-up single "It's Only Money Pt. 2," borrowing heavily from "Money (That's What I Want)," received more in the way of airplay than sales. Still, Kiss revived "God Gave Rock And Roll To You" successfully in 1992, and Argent's version was the 2,000,000th song played on New York's WNEW-FM in the mid-'90s. "In Deep" was recorded and released in both quad and stereo formats. The band was still performing on Colin Blunstone albums, but their participation decreased as their popularity spread. Argent also did a Pepsi radio commercial in 1973, on which New York DJ Scott Muni introduced "The heads-up sound of Argent" singing the jingle "The Pepsi Generation."

"Nexus" was the next Argent album, but Chris White was having trouble relating to the more progressive direction of the band. Groups like Emerson, Lake & Palmer and Yes were getting ripped by the press for following this same direction, but Rod Argent felt that he was following the right path. This involved ending his songwriting (but not production) arrangement with Chris White. Chris explains his dilemma: "I didn't write anything that made it to this album as my compositions weren't applicable at the time. I enjoyed watching them play but I began to think, 'Where are the songs?' The music was getting more orchestral like Pink Floyd. I personally wasn't identifying with its direction so much. Rod and I decided to amicably end our songwriting partnership as our songs were getting far too different. Russ wanted to leave and pursue his own thing and it didn't come as a shock to me when he left. He couldn't pursue a solo career and stay in the group during that period in music, as music was a 24-hour thing then, total dedication, not like today. I think Russ as a songwriter liked simple songs and I think he was getting fed up with long, long keyboard-based solos. He wrote some great stuff. Rod and Russ' songwriting styles were totally different. Russ was under a lot of pressure from things and left."

As a celestial-themed album, "Nexus" included very strong singles in the shape of "Thunder And Lightning" and the low-key "Man For All Reasons." Audiences were getting fed up with this direction, and sales dropped off markedly – a #149 apex in Billboard. The band went on tour to promote "Nexus" and Russ Ballard announced prior to the tour that he was going off on his own at its conclusion. Once again, Chris White gives his opinion of these problems: "What happened in the later days of Argent as far as I'm concerned, and I'll say this quite clearly, was that Rod got too conscious about musicianship and it got boring – long solos which were musically good but took away from the song. Rod was a musician – I'm not a musician, I'm a songwriter – and as a musician he wanted to stretch himself, that I understand, but it doesn't sell records. I remember what The Isley Brothers said when I was talking about jazz and Miles Davis. They said it was 'starvation music.' Rod is purist. He has to really believe in what he's doing. Otherwise, he wouldn't do it. He refuses to go back to old times. He thinks what was done then was done then. He still does write good songs." Also at this time, the remaining Argent band members played on Michael Fennelly's "Lane Changer" album. Fennelly was previously in the bands Millenium and Crabby Appleton, the latter of which scored in the US with "Go Back."

The farewell tour with Ballard became the double "Encore" album, and it was cross-promoted in England by a single featuring an alternate studio version of "Keep On Rollin'" backed with a live LP take of "I Am The Dance Of Ages." Rod tells us why "Keep On Rollin'" was redone: "On the original version, we slowed it slightly to make it a bit funkier. When we got a new manager after Russ left, he heard the track and loved it, but felt it should be a bit faster. We took it at least up to its normal speed, sped it slightly, remixed it and overdubbed it to make it a bit more dynamic and it was then released as a single."

While at Abbey Road, Rod and Chris mixed "Encore" entirely on headphones because the studio's monitors were being fixed and Epic wanted the album on time. It only made #151 in the US. Although none of Russ Ballard's solo records were hits, many of his compositions have been hits for others: "Liar" (Three Dog Night), "I Don't Believe In Miracles" (Colin Blunstone), "So You Win Again" (Hot Chocolate), "Since You Been Gone" (Rainbow and Head East), "New York Groove" (Hello and Ace Frehley), "I Know There's Something Going On" (Frida), "You Can Do Magic" (America), and "Can't Shake Loose" (Agnetha). Among others, Russ also produced Leo Sayer's "Moonlighting" album. At the time, Russ Ballard expressed his frustration: "Sometimes onstage it would get to be ridiculous. I'd be backing Rod, plunking on chords, and he'd go into a solo for about ten minutes on one chord. I used to be bored; I don't know how the audience felt."

Aware of Russ Ballard's departure, the progressive group Yes asked Rod Argent to replace the departing Rick Wakeman in 1974, as Rod reveals: "I was approached by Yes and invited to a blow, with a view to joining them, but I preferred to stay with Argent." Yes ended up replacing Wakeman with Patrick Moraz, who appeared on one Yes studio album ("Relayer") prior to that band's first extended period of inactivity.

Finding one person to replace Russ Ballard's guitar, vocals and songwriting talents proved to be impossible. With hindsight, Rod Argent today feels that the band should have packed it in. However, at the time, he and the band still felt that they had something to say. In May 1974, John Verity and John Grimaldi were drafted to replace Ballard. Verity was born on July 3, 1949 and was a talented guitarist/songwriter with considerable solo and group recording experience. The considerably younger John Grimaldi was born on May 25, 1955, but his playing was phenomenal for his age. The two LPs that this lineup respectively released in 1975 and 1976 ("Circus" and "Counterpoints") were somewhat scattershot in terms of quality, and Russ Ballard's consistency was sorely missed. "Circus" only managed to reach a dismal #171. The failure of this album and tour, both of which were heavily invested in, was devastating, according to Chris White: "They did an album called 'Circus' and then did a special concert that was recorded and filmed at the Roundhouse with trapeze acts, clowns, tightrope walkers, human cannonballs, everything. The whole thing was based on a circus. It was magic. The place was packed wall-to-wall and the atmosphere was electric. It was a magic concert. One of the best things I've ever seen. That week, the reviews came out and slagged it to smithereens. A year later, Bob Henrit, Argent's drummer, was in a pub when someone came up to him and introduced himself as a writer and apologized for the review. Bob said, 'You had to say what you thought and I understand. The fact that it finished the group had nothing to do with it.' The writer then looked at Bob and owned up. Apparently what had happened was that the place was so packed that the fans took over a section that was meant for the press to sit, and when the press came and couldn't get to their seats, they went to the nearby pub, got sloshed and being pissed off, decided to slag the group without seeing the show. The reviews of that show totally destroyed the band. They just thought, 'What's the point of going on? We think this is great, but no one seems to like it.'"

Argent and White employed the services of co-producer Tony Visconti for "Counterpoints," their only album for RCA (UK) and United Artists (US). Visconti's services could not save the album and it quickly became a bargain bin special. Robert Henrit contracted hepatitis and was unable to record for a few weeks, so Genesis drummer Phil Collins took the drum stool for a few tracks on the album.

After an American tour, Grimaldi quit the band in June 1976. Rod Argent decided that his band was over. Grimaldi soon fell ill with multiple sclerosis (MS) and died shortly thereafter (December 12, 1983). Jim Rodford, John Verity and Robert Henrit became the band Phoenix and released an absolutely dreadful album for CBS in late 1976. With this failure, Verity went back to his solo career and Rod would do some sessions on two of Verity's '80s albums. Jim Rodford became The Kinks' bassist on April 20, 1978. Rodford had met The Kinks on the same day he joined The Mike Cotton Sound's tour in November 1964. He renewed his relationship with the Davies brothers when Argent was the opening act for The Kinks in 1972 and 1973. After Phoenix, Rodford played for short time with the band Limey right before joining The Kinks. Ironically, Jim turned out to be the band's longest serving bass player and lasted until the final Kinks show on June 15, 1996 at an Oslo, Norway festival. Rodford had a side band with Robert Henrit called The GB Blues Band that also included Derek Griffiths (former Artwoods guitarist) and some former members of The Mike Cotton Sound. Along with playing with The Animals II, Rodford and Argent were on the concept CD "The Doomsday Clock." Jim was also on former Jethro Tull drummer Clive Bunker's "Awakening" album in 1998.

Robert Henrit would also end up in The Kinks, although his path was more involved. Henrit played with the group Charlie and his sessions with The Who's Roger Daltrey and the entire Dave Davies' "Glamour" and "Chosen People" LPs (1981 and 1983, respectively) complemented occasional work with The GB Blues Band. He also did sessions with Ian Matthews and Russ Ballard's Barnet Dogs. In July 1984, Henrit replaced long-term Kinks drummer Mick Avory (who retired) and lasted until their final show in 1996.

After the breakup of Argent, Chris White did more independent production and compositional work for various labels. Rod Argent elected to take himself out of the spotlight to concentrate on other musical avenues. He opened a central London shop on Denmark Street called Rod Argent's Keyboards and ventured into various recording sessions. These session experiences would provide Rod with the background to work with any kind of musician, regardless of the medium. In 1976 and 1977, he played on albums by The Hollies, Easy Street, Dirty Tricks, and the Intergalactic Touring Band project. Two of Rod's solo piano pieces, "The Prince" and "Five Finger Blues," were released on a US-only Vee Jay album in 1977. Also in 1977, Argent was commissioned to provide original music for the Royal Academy's Laser Exhibition. Rod supplied the instrumental "Light Fantastic," which became the B-side of his first single for MCA. The A-side was "Gymnopédies No. 1," a version of the Erik Satie classical piece. He also joined Colin Blunstone on Mae McKenna's "Walk On Water" LP and made his presence known on albums by Roger Daltrey, Gary Boyle, and Chris Rea.

Throughout 1978, Rod Argent recorded his first solo LP "Moving Home" with drummer Phil Collins among others. Touring in St. Albans and London for this album involved the creation of a top-notch group of musicians: bassist Alphonzo Johnson, Peter Robinson and Robin Lumley (keyboards), Chester Thompson (drums), John Goodsall (guitar), Morris Pert on percussion, and a Gary Barnacle-led horn section. A few live tracks from their shows were released on the 1995 Zombies compilation "1964-67." Among others, Lumley and Collins joined Argent on Jack Lancaster's "Skinningrove Bay" concept album, which has been reissued many times over the years under this title and "Wild Connections." More sessions followed, including the title track of The Who's "Who Are You" LP. The second Phoenix LP "In Full View" featured Rod's playing, as well as albums by Matthew Fisher, Marti Webb, and Lea Nicholson.

The most successful sessions that Argent did at this time were with Andrew Lloyd Webber, who approached Rod after hearing "Light Fantastic." Rod felt he was not able to play Webber's written music charts because he thought he was not a good sight reader at the time, so he took the better part of the year after his band's demise to improve his sight reading. Webber's "Variations" LP was the start of many fruitful relationships for Rod, who would play with an orchestra for the first time. This album was based on Paganini's "A Minor Caprice" and featured other musicians like Gary Moore, sax player Barbara Thompson, drummer John Mole and Clem Clempson. "Variations 1-4" from the album served as the theme for the London Weekend Television (LWT) program "The South Bank Show." Along with jazz player John Dankworth, Argent, Thompson, Mole and Clempson played on a few LPs in different permutations. Argent's album with Dankworth, "Metro," is the most overlooked release in his career, as most people are unaware of its existence. Rod's duet album with Barbara Thompson was called "Ghosts," and both were key members of the group Shadowshow.

Andrew Lloyd Webber scored heavily with his productions "Cats" and "The Phantom Of The Opera," and Argent was on both massively popular UK cast albums. Among others, Rod indeed plays piano on the original London "Cats" cast version of the classic song "Memory," sung by Elaine Paige. For the first five weeks of the show, Rod Argent played first piano with the orchestra. Argent also did work on Webber's "Starlight Express" but was not credited on the live cast album. In fact, Rod laid the groundwork for "Starlight Express" at Andrew Lloyd Webber's house on mobile equipment. The mobile was taken to live shows, and three shows were recorded. Argent again supplied first piano along with the orchestration for the first five weeks of "Starlight Express." At that show in 1984, Rod Argent met Peter Van Hooke, who was supplying electronic percussion for the ensemble. In his career, Van Hooke has also played drums for Van Morrison and Mike & The Mechanics. They would soon form a production team that would take them in many unusual musical directions.

Rod was also on the San José single "Argentine Melody (Canción de Argentina)" under the hilarious name Rodriguez Argentina (just remove some letters from both names!). It was a #14 hit in England. Argent has a funny story about that one: "That World Cup Theme was written by Andrew Lloyd Webber. I had done a lot of work with Andrew at that time and he asked me to play on it. He put me in dark glasses on 'Top Of The Pops' with two other players! First of all, he was going to call us Los Rodos Argentinos! He then said, 'No, we can't do that,' so he ended up calling it 'San José featuring Rodriguez Argentina.' That was his sort of idea of humor!" Rod also provided "Baby Don't You Cry No More" for Abba vocalist Frida's 1982 album "Something's Going On," and he produced and played on the Cleo Laine/John Williams version of the tune the next year. The late Sweet vocalist Brian Connolly utilized Rod Argent's services in early 1982 during sessions at Livingstone Recording Studios. Originally, an album was planned, but the single "Hypnotised" b/w "Fade Away" was the only released product from their efforts. Joining Connolly and Argent for these dates were former Argent members John Verity and Robert

Henrit, along with Brian Willoughby (guitar) and Dave Wintour (bass).

In 1981, Argent wrote the music for a stage adaptation of Kit Williams' book "Masquerade." Frank Dunlop directed the production of this play, which was staged at the Young Vic Theatre in London. This work was the bridge that led Rod into film and television scoring in 1985. Rod's first work with Peter Van Hooke involved remixing the self-titled album by The Electric Bluebirds, along with adding keyboards to one track. This experience was a complete failure, as the group was so unhappy with Rod and Peter's work that they didn't bother to fully convey their displeasure. When the album was re-released on CD in 1996, the band went out of their way to only include the original album mixes that producer Will Birch made! The band felt that Will Birch, drummer and songwriter of Kursaal Flyers, had more of the pub band feel for their material than the arena-experienced Rod Argent and Van Hooke.

In 1988, another Rod Argent solo album followed, "Red House." Named after his studio, it revealed Rod to be in prime new age form. The album featured the song "A 4th Gymnopédie," again inspired by Erik Satie's beautiful classical piece. Rod's version of the song he gave to Frida appeared here as "Baby Don't You Cry." "Red House" bass player Mo Foster became another musician with which Argent would work frequently, and Rod played on Foster's "Bel Assis" album the same year. Rod Argent sold his keyboard shop in the mid-'80s, enabling him to concentrate full-time on his productions with Van Hooke. Their joint work included many private UK music library albums.

When Peter Van Hooke met singer/songwriter Tanita Tikaram at London's Mean Fiddler club through her manager Peter Charles, Van Hooke knew he had the ideal artist that he and Rod could work with. Even at her first appearance, Tikaram was a natural and innovative songwriter and performer. Argent and Van Hooke produced and played on Tanita's first three albums between 1988 and 1990: "Ancient Heart," "The Sweet Keeper," and "Everybody's Angel." "Ancient Heart" sold over 4.5 million copies worldwide, and "The Sweet Keeper" passed the 1.5 million mark.

Meanwhile, Rod Argent scored music for various programs and events, mainly soccer themes. In 1985, Argent and Peter Van Hooke came up with "Goal Crazy," a 1985 theme for the ITV program "The Match." Although not issued at the time, it was used as the program's theme throughout the rest of the '80s. Cover versions by Stanley Black and The London Symphony Orchestra and also by the dubiously named Power Pack Orchestra held soccer fans over until the original 1985 theme was used on another popular soccer program – "Saint & Greavsie." During this period, Rod and Peter also produced a theme for a television program by UK entertainer Jimmy Tarbuck.

Using the name Silsoe (the Bedfordshire location of his home and Red House Studio), Rod provided "Aztec Gold" as the #48 hit ITV theme to the 1986 World Cup soccer finals. The B-side was a Mort Shuman song "On Wings Of The Wind." Rod would later work on what turned out to be Mort Shuman's last album "Distant Drum" before his death in 1991. At the Mort Shuman memorial service, Rod Argent sang "Little Sister," an Elvis Presley hit written by Shuman and frequent collaborator Doc Pomus. The Silsoe pseudonym would also be used on the LWT TV series theme single "The Two Of Us" for the Sierra label (Colin Blunstone was on Sierra at the same time!). Two singles for the LWT series "Not With A Bang" and "The Piglet Files" formed another single, and Rod created "Tutti Al Mondo" as ITV's official sport theme for the 1990 World Cup finals. The flip was "Hot Foot," another ITV theme for the program "Athletics." The popularity of "Saint & Greavsie" gave rise to a CD entitled "Favourite TV Themes" that used three out of the four Argent/Van Hooke soccer themes ("Goal Crazy," "Tutti Al Mondo," and "Hot Foot").

For films, Rod struck up another writing/production partnership with Royal Academy Of Music graduate Robert Howes. They provided scores for some Paul Berriff films. Berriff's Scottish Television documentary "Rescue," airing January 22, 1990 on UK television, featured Argent, Howes, guitarist Tim Renwick, and Peter Van Hooke on drums. Argent and Howes also did incidental music for The Children's Company production of "The Adventures Of Roger And The Rottentrolls." Another area that Rod got into was an instructional video entitled "A Keyboard Approach." This 1992 video, written and presented by Rod, revealed how his keyboard experimentation produced his most popular songs, and it also featured an otherwise unavailable solo piece called "Blues In Bb." Back in 1988, Rod wrote, sang and played on his tune "Living In The Real World" with the group The Brakes for the Mickey Rourke film "Homeboy."

The Argent/Van Hooke production of Nanci Griffith's "Late Night Grande Hotel" (1991) brought her to greater pop and country audiences while retaining her original fan base. US songwriter/pianist Joshua Kadison was another production success story for the duo. Kadison's 1993 album "Painted Desert Serenade" (mostly produced by Argent and Van Hooke) scored extremely well, netting pop and adult contemporary hits with the songs "Jessie" and "Beautiful In My Eyes." Rod and Peter's next project was not successful, as Jule Shear's excellent "Healing Bones" album in 1994 was quickly deleted.

The last artist that Rod and Peter worked with was the late Colombian singer Soraya. Her first English album, "On Nights Like These," and its Spanish counterpart ("En Esta Noche") sold 800,000 copies in the pop, adult contemporary, and Latin markets. The most popular song from the album, "Suddenly" ("De Repente" in Spanish), did well in all of these categories. Needless to say, Argent and Van Hooke learned a lot about recording Soraya the first time, especially since they didn't know Spanish! Soraya did many live dates, including sharing a Mexico City bill with Alanis Morissette in 1996. The next year, Soraya rejoined Argent and Van Hooke to work on another English and Spanish album, and this time, both albums used different backing tracks to reflect the softer nature of the Spanish release and the funky feel (à la Alanis) of the English edition. To Argent's disappointment, this incorrect decision was made by Soraya's management, and the anemic sales results proved it. The Spanish edition entitled "Torre De Marfil" ("Ivory Tower") emerged first Stateside in October 1997, with the differently packaged "Wall Of Smiles" following in the summer of 1998. Like her previous album, "Wall Of Smiles" used the same songs, except that "Es Un Amor" was replaced by "Manhattan In The Sand" for the English collection. Despite Soraya's US success and the issuance of "Torre De Marfil," "Wall Of Smiles" was released everywhere but America! Sales for "Wall Of Smiles" were unable to match its predecessor, and its German chart peak (#63) fell well below expectations.

Rod played on Paul Carrack's album "Blue Views," released in 1996 in the UK and the following year in the US. A potential 1996 collaboration between massively popular Greek vocalist George Dalares and the Argent/Van Hooke production team would have been an interesting project, but it fell through despite Rod and Peter's trip to Greece to visit the singer. The album would have been produced in London.

Starting in 1996, Rod immersed himself completely in classical piano with a view to create a solo piano CD. Argent found his already brilliant piano skills reaching even higher levels. The resulting CD issued in 1998 was "Classically Speaking" and was available through Argent's own website (shown on page 2) and many online retailers. "Classically Speaking" contains classical staples from Bach and Chopin along with later composers like Ravel, Elgar and Grieg. Argent contributed three of his own fine originals to the mix.

BBC Radio 2's "Maestro" series hosted by Richard Stilgoe included a visit by Rod Argent in May and June 1996, and he answered musical questions of a serious nature with Kate Robbins. In 1997, Rod Argent surprised everyone by reuniting the original Argent lineup for some limited visibility charity events, namely for Philippine children. The band relished the experience and their playing remained at the same high level. By late 1997, Russ Ballard and Rod Argent wrote songs together for the first time in years. Recording and touring plans for 1998 did not take place.

More sessions with Rod Argent took place in 1997 and 1998. UK musician Mark Law's concept album "The Doomsday Clock" was a very enjoyable CD with numerous Argent organ contributions. Also on this album were Mick Abrahams and Clive Bunker from the original Jethro Tull lineup, along with Robin Lumley (keyboards), Jim Rodford, and Moody Blues drummer Graeme Edge. Rod also played and arranged quite a bit of Luka Bloom's "Salty Heaven" CD from 1998, and other outside sessions followed (shown in the solo discography).

The most positive recording session that Rod Argent was involved with in 1998 dealt with Zombies compadres Colin Blunstone and Chris White. Rod first came by the studio to catch Colin recording in April. In early August, White's son Matthew remixed Blunstone's song "Walking In The Rain" for a CD single, and one of the bonus tracks was yet another version of "She's Not There." Argent and White provided backing vocals for this Matthew White-engineered version at Rod's Red House Studio. The session proved to be very productive, with Blunstone supplying vocals to the Rod Argent songs "Danger Zone" and "Helpless." The aim of the collaboration was for Colin to sing an entire album of Rod's songs, and Rod and Colin were extremely enthusiastic about the results. In fact, Colin Blunstone's manager took three of their completed tracks with him for presentation at the MIDEM convention in Cannes, France in late January 1999 to look for a record label deal. Combined with Chris White's award winning song ("Let The Flame Be Strong"), 3/5 of The Zombies were presented at MIDEM!

In December 1998, Rod appeared at a Bedfordshire village concert with actress Jennie Linden (star of "Women In Love"). This show was intended to help raise funds for the local church's restoration. In between poetry and prose readings by Jennie Linden, Argent gave a solo piano recital of his compositions as well as those of Bach, Ravel, Debussy, Chopin, and Duke Ellington. The concert was sold out in a matter of weeks.

Argent's next performance required a tremendous amount of preparation and discipline. The Stables Theatre in Wavendon, Milton Keynes, England, run by highly respected recording artists John Dankworth and Cleo Laine, also required restorative funding. On January 17, 1999, Rod Argent put together an eclectic three-part show spanning three disparate musical genres. Similar to the previous month's show, the first half of the Stables Theatre program consisted of solo piano performances of

Argent, Ravel, Chopin and Debussy pieces along with Bach's keyboard concerto in G minor (BWV 1058). Rod tells us what inspired this show: "I got the idea for doing the concert from the very first classical thing I did in public a couple of years ago at a Christmas concert for John Dankworth and Cleo Laine in Wavendon, Milton Keynes. They have had a theater there for about 27 years (at the time) and they've got concerts almost every night of the week. They have everything from Chick Corea to (conductor Vladimir) Ashkenazy to The Blues Band with Paul Jones – it's really across the board – a lot of jazz as well. Their daughter's group Field Of Blue would play, and then Cleo would do a bit, there would be a Bach violin sonata and a bit of jazz, and the audience had no problem at all in dealing with it. It was that idea that made me think it would be great to put together an evening of doing music that I loved and also had interest in, and to try to stretch myself in a jazz direction and try to bring some classical playing to fruition. That's what I did, and it went down an absolute storm! I don't think any other rock musician has ever crossed over from the rock side to do pure classical music. You have a lot of hybrids like Keith Emerson and Rick Wakeman, etc., although Ian Anderson of Jethro Tull did an album of classically themed pieces. What I've done is unique, really."

The Conspirito String Quartet accompanied Argent on the three-part Bach concerto, originally written in 1744 as "Harpsichord Concerto No. 7 in G minor." The next part of the program was Rod's participation in a jazz trio set, playing half an hour of Miles Davis and Duke Ellington music. The trio consisted of Rod, Jim Rodford on bass, and Bobby Graham on drums. Graham's appearance was especially interesting as he is more known as the real studio drummer on The Kinks' "You Really Got Me" and "All Day And All Of The Night," and most of The Dave Clark Five's hits (sorry to disappoint those that didn't know this!). Topping off the evening was a reunion set by all four members of the band Argent. During the Argent set, Colin Blunstone, seated a short distance away from Chris White, came on stage to sing "She's Not There." A good time was had by all, and Rod Argent's extensive preparation was evident in his consistently strong performance throughout the evening. The concert raised over £3,000 for the Stables Theatre and was privately videotaped for Argent's personal collection.

Rod Argent moved away from lucrative productions in order to stretch and develop his own talents and material into directions involving jazz and classical music. Working regularly with Colin was the first step in that direction.

When he's not working with Colin Blunstone, Rod Argent stays fresh by outside sessions and the occasional guest spot. Rod was part of Ringo Starr's All Starr Band in 2006, and performances for that tour were issued on CD and DVD two years later. The original Argent lineup got back together on July 25, 2010 for the High Voltage Festival in Victoria Park, London. Their performance was released on a double CD a few months later. Five further reunion shows followed that December, and five more took place in January and February 2012. An Aylesbury, England benefit concert on June 2, 2013 was Argent's final reunion appearance. Rod Argent's most recent sessions were with Matthew Sweet in 2017, Paul Weller in 2018, and the track "Shine On You Crazy Diamond (Parts 6-9)" on the 2021 album "Still Wish You Were Here: A Tribute To Pink Floyd."

Argent reissues of note involve the stereo/quad edition of "In Deep. "Nexus" and "Ring Of Hands" on the Vocalion label and the excellent 2LP/single CD "Hold Your Head Up – The Best Of Argent" by Demon/Edsel.

Through his keyboard and arrangement skills, Rod Argent continues to be a very influential musician. Certainly, more of today's musicians will be taken to higher playing levels through their exposure to his accomplishments.

At right: Rod Argent's instructional video "A Keyboard Approach."

Colin Blunstone

Colin Blunstone had no idea that he would be getting back into the music business after he became a clerk for Sun Alliance in early 1968. Later that year, he was talked back into recording by producer Mike Hurst, who convinced Colin that changing his name would get around any association with The Zombies. There was also that pesky problem of phony Zombies groups! The record deal was with the psychedelic-leaning Deram label and covered Europe and both sides of the Atlantic. Mike Hurst originally recommended that Colin be billed as James MacArthur. Deram's US distributor, London Records, sent a very urgent telegram notifying all concerned that James MacArthur was an actor on the extremely popular "Hawaii Five-O" US TV program – the famous Danno! So, Colin became Neil MacArthur and squeezed in his recording sessions after work. The first single for Deram was a drastic Hurst reworking of "She's Not There" that hit #34 in England. With this promising start, Colin quit his job. Colin also recorded an Italian version of "She's Not There," entitled "Ma Non É Giusto." The B-side supplied by Hurst, "World Of Glass," was also unique, but Colin did not not write any of his material at this time. Two more singles followed: Billy Vera's "Don't Try To Explain" (with its "A Whiter Shade Of Pale"-influenced organ) coupled with Colin's nice take on Harry Nilsson's "Without Her," and Barry Mann/Cynthia Weil's "It's Not Easy" backed by "12.29" (by Peter Lee Stirling, aka Daniel Boone). Unfortunately, no further attention was given to Colin's work. Two other unreleased covers from the time were The Association's "Never My Love" and Buffalo Springfield's "Hung Upside Down," the latter of which was a stunning version. All of Colin's output as Neil MacArthur was released on "Into The Afterlife," and four of the tracks were newly mixed in stereo: both sides of the first single, "Without Her," and "Hung Upside Down."

Soon after his Deram contract lapsed, Colin got a ride from London to his Hatfield flat from Chris White. They discussed working together, especially since Nexus Productions was already up and operating. Rod and Chris obtained an Epic Records deal for Colin and discussions for his debut album took place right after. The album was called "One Year" because the album took one year to record – an eternity by early '70s standards.

Colin's contract with Epic immediately started out on the wrong foot. Tim Rice invited Colin to sing on the musical he just wrote with Andrew Lloyd Webber, "Jesus Christ Superstar." It was to be released on the MCA label. Epic immediately told Blunstone that he could not record for another company first since he just signed with them! Although Colin does not remember whether he was to portray Jesus or Judas, it is most likely that he was to sing Judas' part based on the material. Mike d'Abo, fresh from the breakup of Manfred Mann, sang on "King Herod's Song" instead. d'Abo would supply the song that became Colin's first Epic single, "Mary Won't You Warm My Bed." This song and its follow-up "Caroline Goodbye" featured Argent as session musicians and preceded the "One Year" album. The Argent group was also on the Rod-arranged album track "She Loves The Way They Love Her" (a new take of the unreleased "R.I.P." cut).

Argent and White's production touches were all over "One Year," and to great effect. Although mainly softer rock, the material resonated strongly. Another "R.I.P." castoff, "Smokey Day," was included here with session player involvement. Rod and Chris contributed the exclusive piece "Her Song," and Rod and Tony Visconti arranged "She Loves The Way They Love Her," "Mary Won't You Warm My Bed," and "Caroline Goodbye."

The album's final single was a cover of Denny Laine's hit "Say You Don't Mind," the latter-day Zombies finale. According to Colin Blunstone, the Argent band did not play on the song's rejected original version. The original take was arranged by John Fiddy and entirely featured outside session players. Rod and Chris suggested string quartet backing, and the song became a #15 British hit. Chris Gunning's arrangement on the song proved to be the keeper. Colin toured on the strength of this hit with a 4-piece band and string quintet, and he opened up for The Electric Light Orchestra (ELO). Blunstone wanted Argent's group to back him up on records, but the band's popularity with "Hold Your Head Up" made this an impossibility. In its place, Rod Argent tried to contribute as much as he could in the production department with Chris White.

Now located in the Knightsbridge section of London, Colin Blunstone was sharing a flat in Ennismore Gardens with the singer/songwriter Duncan Browne and Duncan's manager. Drawing upon this location, "Ennismore" became Colin's second Epic album, released in October 1972. It was promoted by the British hit single "I Don't Believe In Miracles," written by Russ Ballard. The single hit #31 on the UK chart, but Colin, Rod and Chris were expecting more from the song, as Chris White reflects: "Russ wrote a great song for the album called 'I Don't Believe In Miracles' that should have been a hit. Russ thought that it should have been titled 'I Do Believe In Miracles' – he thought the negativity of it stopped it from being more successful. One of the things that hurt this song in England was that Colin played it live with his touring band for the first time on a radio show, and radio stations kept playing that version instead of the studio version because there was a limitation on how many records you could play on the radio. The live version was totally different from the record, which is why it never sold. In concert, Colin was actually quite good. He performed the Zombies hits along with his solo stuff. I did most of the production work on Colin's

album as Rod was on the road touring most of the time. Rod came along and added his weight, though."

"How Could We Dare To Be Wrong" was a #45 UK single, and songs like "Andorra" and "I Want Some More" were taken as Dutch and US-only singles from the album in 1973. None of them succeeded to any degree. Chris White had other plans for "Andorra": "'Andorra' was originally written for Argent, and in fact, Argent played on the backing of that." The Argent version was originally known as "Siempre La Misma," which is Spanish for "Always The Same," but it was decided that Colin's voice was better suited for the song.

After "Ennismore" was released, Epic placed a lot of pressure on Colin to find a manager with some international clout. Unbelievably, Colin had no manager at this point! Blunstone signed a 3-year deal with Cat Stevens' manager Barry Krost, who made a large dent into the US market with Cat's music. No matter what Krost did over the next few years, Blunstone could not break through in America. Colin toured the US in March 1973 with a new band featuring Derek Griffiths (ex-Mike Cotton Sound and Artwoods guitarist) and Derek's keyboard collaborator Pete Wingfield. Half of their 18-song set consisted of songs from Colin's past. It proved to be his last full US tour in many years.

The next album "Journey" was produced just by Chris White, due to Argent's extensive live commitments. The material on this LP was considerably weaker, especially the songs by Pete Wingfield. Using the beat of "Hold Your Head Up," Rod and Chris provided the album's main single "Wonderful." The duo also provided "Beware," a track that was replaced on the US edition by two Russ Ballard-written and produced songs: "It's Magical" (a non-album UK single) and the US-only "You Who Are Lonely." The album highlight came from The King's Singers, who sang on the first LP side song suite beginning with "Wonderful."

At this time, Colin started a writing partnership with Richard Kerr, writer of "Brandy" – later covered by Barry Manilow as "Mandy." A song that Blunstone and Kerr wrote in 1973 was "Ain't It Funny," which first appeared on a publisher's sampler LP of Kerr's work along with two other collaborations. Colin's other new writing partner was poet David Jones, a Hatfield doctor's son unrelated to either the Monkees member or David Bowie.

Colin was experiencing increasing friction with Epic Records and felt the need to get out of his contract. An overly cute 1976 single "When You Close Your Eyes" was not a good choice of material for Blunstone, and was not included on any album. This single was the first in an interim period in which Colin's product was issued on different labels. Manager Barry Krost wanted Colin to move to Rocket Records, especially since they were able to revive Neil Sedaka's career and they achieved elusive US success for Cliff Richard and Kiki Dee. A three-album deal was negotiated with Rocket, although Epic retained the rights to Colin's recordings in the UK and the Netherlands. When the Rocket deal ended, Epic asked for two more albums without any studio cost funding on their part. The matter between Blunstone and Epic Records bubbled under the surface for years until it was settled two weeks before it went before the High Court in England. Alan Parsons' partner, Eric Woolfson, took the head of CBS out to a magnificent lunch and the settlement was worked out!

A cover of Elton John's "Planes" was the kickoff single from the album of the same name. The album was produced by "She's Not There"'s engineer Gus Dudgeon and was surprising by its lack of original Colin material. Instead, Blunstone covered Neil Sedaka's "Beautiful You" (another A-side), Buddy Holly's "Tell Me How," and even The Zombies' own "Care Of Cell 44." "Planes" did feature the 1973 Blunstone/Kerr song "Ain't It Funny." The album did poorly, and Rocket passed on releasing the LP Stateside. Roger Daltrey covered Colin's song "Single Man's Dilemma" for his "One Of The Boys" album issued on both sides of the Atlantic. Colin and Rod Argent also turned up on the aforementioned Mae McKenna LP "Walk On Water."

Blunstone had met young engineer Alan Parsons at Abbey Road while The Zombies were recording "Odessey And Oracle." Years later, Parsons still had Colin in mind when he created his unique, studio-only Alan Parsons Project. Alan had asked Colin to sing on his "I Robot" album in 1977, but Colin's commitments prevented his performance on that project. The next year, Blunstone sang on the Project album "Pyramid." Colin would also sing on the later Parsons albums "Eye In The Sky," "Ammonia Avenue," and "Vulture Culture." Of these tracks, "Old And Wise" from "Eye In The Sky" was the most successful artistically and commercially (a #74 UK single). The tracks that Blunstone sang on each album were usually the standout tracks. Colin's success with Alan Parsons opened up a whole new world of session work, ranging from concept pieces by Mike Batt and Mitchell-Coe Mysteries to charity records with The Crowd and his own "Every Living Moment" for leukemia research in 1992.

Rocket and Epic were still due product, so Colin put together the "Never Even Thought" album in 1978. This time, it was released in the US. The reason this took place was that Rocket star Elton John recommended that Colin record the album in Los Angeles with his guitarist Davey Johnstone and the city's top session players. On paper, the idea must have sounded good, but the execution was far from satisfactory. Producer Bill Schnee was more suited to California-based pop acts like Pablo

Cruise, and his work with Blunstone led to an extremely bland and unexciting album. Colin's voice was not well suited for the arrangements, and the album sank as a result, regardless of Rod Argent's additional vocal contributions. "Ain't It Funny" was recorded for the second straight album, indicating a lack of material and interest in providing a top-notch product for both unsatisfied record labels. The album was delayed to such an extent that it found itself being released into a dance-oriented market. Colin sought to rectify this on his next album.

The Rod Argent-produced "Late Nights In Soho" LP was issued in late 1979, but only Dutch and Australian audiences had easy access to it. A customer at Rod's keyboard shop, former Hatfield And The North and National Health musician Dave Stewart (unrelated to the Tourists and Eurythmics member), wanted to use Colin as vocalist on his revival of Jimmy Ruffin's "What Becomes Of The Broken Hearted." Stewart's occasional partner Barbara Gaskin recommended Colin for the job, and it didn't hurt that her older sister Jennifer was in Colin's primary school class! After Colin notified Stewart about a possible lawsuit if Epic found out about this project, Colin recommended that the record have the billing "Dave Stewart, guest vocals: Colin Blunstone." The single was Colin's biggest UK hit at #13 in 1981, and it was a #8 success in Belgium. A cover of another R&B hit, "Tracks Of My Tears," scored more chart action for Blunstone (#60) and was his first single for PRT. Its B-side was the Colin original "The Last Goodbye." In 1983, he recorded former Camel member Pete Bardens' song "Touch" as his other PRT single, but it did not carry on his recent sales pattern. He recorded Argent's debut LP track "Freefall" for PRT, but this remains unreleased.

The next project for Colin was a group effort called Keats. The band members came from the core members of the Alan Parsons Project. Again a studio-based unit, Keats included drummer Stuart Elliott and Pete Bardens. Colin sang lead on nearly every track. Keats recorded one self-titled album for EMI, and their recording schedule for Parsons and others prevented them from recording another LP. Only one unreleased backing track is still in the vaults. Blunstone discovered that Elliott was a fine songwriting partner. Two singles for the Sierra label (including another "She's Not There"!) followed in 1986 before the minor hit "Cry An Ocean" was released on IRS in 1988. After this, Colin did other sessions with Karel Fialka and Nadieh. He also married his wife Suzy, and their daughter become a doctor in 2016.

In the middle of recording the Keats LP, Blunstone received a call from the South West Electricity Board (SWEB) to do a commercial jingle. Colin sang "That's the SWEB shopping surprise!" and another door was opened for his career. A 1990 British Telecom commercial used a new Blunstone voicing of "She's Not There," and commercials followed for Midlands Gas, Quick-Brew Tea, and Noxzema face cream. For Noxzema, Colin recorded "Time Of The Season" in a New York studio with an American accent!

In the mid-'80s, Colin formed a band called Camino with Duncan Browne and Sebastian Graham-Jones that created some demos. Three of their songs were recorded by the late Browne on his album "Songs Of Love And War" in 1994: "Misunderstood," "Love Leads You," and "I Fall Again." Other mid-'80s demos were covers of hits: Dave Berry's "The Crying Game" and Harry Nilsson's "Without You." The ensuing success of these songs by Boy George and Mariah Carey made Blunstone's versions redundant.

Another Alan Parsons Project session fell apart in 1987 as Eric Woolfson sang "Inside Looking Out" instead of Colin for the "Gaudi" album. Colin rebounded by singing on keyboardist Don Airey's "K2: Tales Of Triumph And Tragedy" later that year. His appearance on this album named after the famous mountain led to numerous projects with Airey. Don Airey then assembled a charity concert and got Colin to play a six or seven song set live for the first time in what seemed like an eternity. Colin called upon Airey when he wanted to record again. After signing with JSE/Castle Communications, the 1991 album "Colin Blunstone Sings His Greatest Hits" was supposed to have all new material. Things didn't turn out that way, but Airey appeared on some non-Zombies re-recordings. Blunstone used Rod Argent, Hugh Grundy, John Verity and Jim Rodford to promote the LP for a January 30, 1991 BBC session.

Colin did more sessions with The Bolland Project and Timecode 64, the latter consisting of yet another version of "She's Not There." The same song was played with a harder-edged, Santana-type arrangement at the "Night Of The Proms '93" concert. In 1992, producer John Sweet sent Colin some of his demos. The "Echo Bridge" album developed from these demos in 1995, but the Permanent Records label folded due to financial difficulties a few weeks after the album was released. Early in 1996, Colin sang "Triangular chocolate – that's Toblerone!" for the popular chocolate brand. In February 1997, Airey and Blunstone teamed up again for another tour, including a November stint at London's Café Royal. Before "Zombie Heaven" was released, Airey and Blunstone were on the road again. British disc jockey Mike Read employed Colin's vocals on "Peggy" and "In Memory" for his Sir John Betjeman "Words And Music" poetry-based music project. A master tape defect delayed its release, but it was issued in June 1998. Donovan and Gene Pitney are also featured on the collection. In between, Blunstone sang on Steve Hackett's "Genesis Revisited" CD and Mike Batt's soundtrack for the film "Keep The Aspidistra Flying" (US title: "A Merry War"). In addition to appearing in that film and the 2001 BBC TV series "The Savages" (a cover of The Kinks' "Days"), Colin did his version of the Yes hit "Owner Of A Lonely Heart" for Batt, issued in early 1999.

Stuart Elliott and Colin Blunstone were still busy writing, and their "You Make Love So Good" was one of the many highlights on Colin's album "The Light Inside." Released at the beginning of June 1998 on Mystic Records, it revealed perhaps the strongest Blunstone material yet. The album was mainly done live with a band, without programming, and Colin wrote 75% of the Don Airey-produced album. Besides new versions of "Losing You" and "Knowing You" from the 1989 Zombies reunion album, Nik Kershaw's "Your Love Is Like The Sun" was another highlight. "Losing You" was dedicated to late drummer Cozy Powell, who played on this and other tracks on "The Light Inside" as his final recordings. The first single "Walking In The Rain" was written by Colin Blunstone and Jess Bailey, and featured remixing treatment by Chris White's son Matthew during the summer. One of the single's additional tracks was a new take of "She's Not There" with Rod Argent and Chris White on backing vocals. After recording this version, Colin says this about "She's Not There": "I vow I will never record this wonderful old song again!" You've read it here first! With Colin singing on Rod Argent's songs "Danger Zone" and "Helpless" at an early August 1998 session, another exciting chapter of Colin's career started. "The Ghost Of You And Me" (2009) and "On The Air Tonight" (2012) are Colin's most recent solo studio albums, but he has also recently appeared on Emile Haynie's 2015 album "We Fall" and all five volumes of "The Chris White Experience."

Above is the rare UK picture sleeve of Colin's hit "Say You Don't Mind" and his 1991 album of re-recordings. Below, Colin (center) is shown with the short-lived studio band Keats in 1984.

While Hugh Grundy, Paul Atkinson and Chris White did not make any solo recordings, all three have been very involved in the music industry:

Hugh Grundy

Hugh Grundy left his CBS A&R position and started running his own horse transport operation in England. Hugh later became a pub landlord and concert booker in Aston, England. On occasion, Grundy sat in with the bands he booked. Hugh used to run The Vine Pub in Buckden, Cambridgeshire, where Rod Argent and Jim Rodford played on occasion. Other musicians used The Vine Pub as a staging area to prepare for northern UK gigs. While with CBS in England, Hugh was involved with some LPs and singles:

THE LOVE AFFAIR: Speak Of Peace, Sing Of Joy/ Brings My Whole World Tumbling Down (UK CBS 5017) (released 05/22/70; producer: Hugh Grundy, executive producer: Mike Smith)
THE LOVE AFFAIR (billed as L.A.): "New Day" LP (UK CBS 64109) (released 09/04/70; producer: Hugh Grundy, executive producer: Mike Smith)
WORTH: Shoot 'Em Up Baby/ Take The World In Your Hands (UK CBS 5309) (released 11/20/70; produced by Mike Smith and Hugh Grundy)
TITANIC: Sing Fool Sing/ Sultana (UK CBS 5365) (released 02/19/71; although Hugh Grundy and Martin Clarke were listed as producers, the single was actually produced by Jean-Jacques Souplet at CBE Recording Studios in Paris, France. Since it was recorded outside the UK, Hugh Grundy most certainly was the UK CBS A&R man for this release. Incidentally, the record was flipped on 05/14/71 and became a #5 UK hit and a #5 Norwegian hit. The record was originally released on 01/15/71 in other countries with "Sultana" as the A-side, using the same catalog number. It was first issued in the US on 12/13/71 as Epic 5-10810.)
ALAN HAVEN: "St. Elmo's Fire" LP (UK CBS S 63900) (released 02/19/71; Grundy is shown as the coordinator of the LP)
TITANIC: Santa Fe/ Half Breed (UK CBS S 7278) (released 03/10/72; produced by Martin Clarke and Hugh Grundy)
WORTH: Shoot 'Em Up Baby/ Take The World In Your Hands (US Epic 5-10886) (released 08/13/72; produced by Mike Smith and Hugh Grundy – a belated US release of the above UK single)
JACKIE FLAVELLE: "Admission Free" LP (UK York FYK 408) (released 08/18/72; Grundy played drums on the tracks "Spectrum," "Belfast Town," and "Spring Morning")
LEA NIXON: A New Kind Of Feeling/ Off To Find A New Land (UK Epic EPC 1673) (released 08/17/73; produced by Hugh Grundy)
SILK: Sing Me A Song/ Freewheelin' (UK CBS S EPC 1721) (released 08/31/73; Hugh produced the B-side with the band)

As you well know, Hugh performed at all of the Zombies reunion and "Odessey And Oracle" shows! He has recently driven for the Royal Air Force (RAF).

Hugh has also been represented on these recent releases:

THE GECKOS: I'd Do It All Over Again - Rock Star (5" CD single; Spanish The Geckos B06XCP4 5TD) (released 03/11/17; played drums on both tracks)
THE CHRIS WHITE EXPERIENCE: "Volume One" CD/download (Sunfish CWE001CD) (released 03/29/19; Hugh played drums on Colin Blunstone's track "Taking The Wings From Butterflies")

Paul Atkinson

After The Zombies' breakup, Paul spent a year as a computer programmer, which oddly enough he quite enjoyed. But, the music business soon called him back, and after managing several struggling bands, he went into the music business proper in 1969, working for the legendary Dick James, publisher of The Beatles and Elton John. As a talent scout alongside Elton and Bernie Taupin (a long-time friend), Paul discovered a budding songwriter/singer named Joan Armatrading in the London cast of "Hair." When Dick refused to sign her, Paul quit and in 1972 he joined CBS Records UK. Very soon, he scored a huge success by signing ABBA from Sweden when they were unknown, for a very low advance of $1,000. They went on to gross over $75 million for CBS UK in the next few years. He also launched the Philadelphia International label in England and oversaw the Bruce Springsteen campaign in Britain in 1975. With his first wife Molly, Paul had a son Matt.

In 1976, he was promoted to a newly-created position at CBS Records International in New York, in charge of all A&R activities worldwide. During this period, CBS' international sales and profits eclipsed those of the US division for the first time. He was soon promoted again, to Columbia Records, to take charge of a large portion of their artist roster, including Paul McCartney, Pink Floyd and Aerosmith, among others. "Working on 'The Wall' with Bob Ezrin and Roger Waters was an amazing experience," says Paul. "Also, walking back into Abbey Road after 11 years to meet Paul and Linda McCartney and hear a playback of his new album was truly thrilling. I felt that I had the most incredible job in the world!"

After a decade with CBS/Columbia, he was hired by RCA Records in Los Angeles as senior vice president A&R to revive the somnolent company. Within three years, he had signed and executive-produced Grammy winner Bruce Hornsby's platinum debut album, and developed a total of five #1 hits in a single eighteen-month period. He oversaw the success of many foreign artists, such as Eurthymics, for whom he organized collaborations with Aretha Franklin and Stevie Wonder for their platinum "Be Yourself Tonight" album. Paul was a judge on the January 6, 1985 edition of TV's "Star Search." He was interviewed for the home video "Guitar" that was a VHS tape release (Warner Reprise Video 3-38251) on September 16, 1991.

In addition to dozens of A&R credits, Paul Atkinson did a small amount of production work over the years:

SLIGHT ACHE: For this Dutch group in 1970, Atkinson produced the tracks "White Stocking" and "Lieutenant O'Brennan" in London for the Imperial label. These tracks were not released until March 13, 2018, when a related group, Neerlands Hoop In Bange Dagen, issued a large box set consisting of 9 DVDs, 3 CDs, and one 10" vinyl record: "Neerlands Hoop In Bange Dagen Compleet" (Dutch Roje Hel Rubinstein ISBN 9789047624318).
LEONARD RUSK: Nobody Needs You More/ I've Got My Pride (UK DJM DJS 253) (released 09/17/71; Paul Atkinson produced both sides)
MARTI JONES: "Any Kind Of Lie" LP (UK RCA PL/PD 90478; US RCA 2040-1/2-R) (released 05/15/90; Paul played acoustic guitar on "I've Got Second Sight" and "Old Friend")

In 1990, Paul joined MCA Records as executive vice president A&R. Here, he was responsible for guiding the careers of many notable artists, including Lyle Lovett, B.B. King, Meatloaf, Elton John, and Tom Petty. Later, he left to co-found a new multimedia production company and interactive record label, and he then took charge of the creative management of the entire Capitol/EMI Records catalog, which included The Beatles, Pink Floyd, Frank Sinatra, The Beach Boys, and many more. Paul and his second wife, Helen, became dual American/British citizens and lived in Los Angeles with their two children James and Lucy. Atkinson had been ill for 10 years, during which time he had two liver transplants. His kidneys had failed and he was also suffering from biliary cancer. Paul had hoped to work with Warner Music Group, but that was not meant to be. Paul Atkinson passed away on April 1, 2004 at the UCLA Santa Monica Medical Center of liver and kidney disease.

Chris White

So many musicians wanted the Chris White production touch that he couldn't take them all on. After Argent broke up in 1976, White furthered his independent production accomplishments, and he ended up working with Dire Straits before their big breakthrough in 1978: "I turned down a lot of people like Al Stewart and Murray Head because I was totally involved in Argent – very altruistic but poverty making! I produced the demos for the first Dire Straits album, which Mark Knopfler preferred to the finished album! I thought Dire Straits was great but they couldn't get a deal at the time. In regards to the Michael Fennelly album 'Lane Changer,' Jim Rodford and Robert Henrit played on it as well as Jeff Beck. After Jeff's session work, he called me up and said he wasn't happy with his playing and didn't charge a fee and we just put a pseudonym ('mystery singer') for him on the album. Jeff is a great guitarist and lovely to work with, but he's very picky about his own playing. He didn't think he played up to par." Thanks to Chris White's groundbreaking work, Dire Straits landed a contract with Vertigo (UK) and Warner Bros. (North America). In the late '70s and early '80s, White worked in Spain and produced some local talent. He also worked on a musical and wrote songs for others. White came back to England to produce Matthew Fisher's early '80s albums, and he's been based in England ever since. Recently, Chris has been recording music for soundtracks and satellite radio. Along with his wife Vivienne Boucherat, Chris has been productively writing songs. The first fruits of a very promising songwriting partnership began in late 1992, when White and Boucherat became the prime movers behind The Beacon Europe Singers. They put together a single to celebrate the European Union (EU), which was undone by the UK "Brexit" vote in late 2016. As previously mentioned, Chris and Vivienne's award-winning song "Let The Flame Be Strong" in 1998 took their talents worldwide. Let's not forget his "Odessey And Oracle" live appearances!

Chris White and Vivienne Boucherat continue to write, produce and perform. Along with Chris' youngest son Matthew, Chris and Vivienne recorded as the group White Circle. They released the album "The Key" in 2007. The same year, Chris co-produced and played bass on an album by another one of his sons, Jamie, who performs as JJ White. JJ's album was called "Featherhead." Most recently, Chris and Vivienne wrote the song "Would You" and sang backing vocals for John Verity's album "My Religion." It was released in March 2016.

With a wealth of outside studio work to his credit, Chris White did not have a remastered catalog to draw upon. His sons Matthew and Jamie went through all of their father's session tapes to remaster them, and they found a goldmine. The Whites not only found many fascinating, long-forgotten sessions, they also located Colin Blunstone's demos for the album "One Year"! Those 14 demos, subtitled "That Same Year," were incorporated into the late 2021 reissue of the album issued by Sundazed.

The main output of these Chris White tape discoveries was a series of albums called "The Chris White Experience." To date, there are five volumes in the main series, and a collection of tracks by the group Sparrow formed a sixth release. The first three volumes and the Sparrow album were issued on CD and as digital downloads. The fourth and fifth volumes were download-only releases. All of these releases offer unique cross-sections of Chris' work with different artists over the years. To promote his album series, Chris White conducted a lot of Facebook Live events.

In addition to his compositions and productions for Colin Blunstone and Argent (please see their solo sections), Chris has produced and/or written for many others. The following Chris White discography covers the original releases of all his productions. If Chris White made additional contributions, those are noted below:

SINGLES

TITLES	UK & FOREIGN LABEL/NO.	RELEASE DATE	US & CANADA LABEL/NO.	RELEASE DATE
DAVE COLMAN UND DAS ORCHESTER MARK WIRTZ - Mister Galilei/ Alaska Quinn (the A-side with the original title "Mister Galileo" was written by Rod Argent, Chris White, and translated into German by Fleming, and the B-side was a German version of "Mighty Quinn")	German Columbia C 23 755	04/26/68		
METAL - Mike (Like Honey)/ Dix Ans Ont Passé (Liar) (A-side written by Chris White and Rod Argent, with lyrics translated into French by Michèle Senlis, and the B-side written by Russ Ballard with French translation by Senlis, translates to "Ten Years Have Passed")	French Disques Meys 10.039	08/ <</72		
MOONSTONE - The World's Too Good For You/ When The Moon Has Lost Its Stare	Epic S EPC 1426	04/13/73		
MOONSTONE - A Place To Hide/ Drinking Song	Epic S EPC 1961	11/30/73		
MICHAEL FENNELLY - Lane Changer/ Over My Dead Body	Epic S EPC 2242	04/19/74		
MICHAEL FENNELLY - Shine A Light/ Easy To Love			Epic 5-11133	05/27/74
LIFE - Woman/ Bless My Soul	Polydor 2058 500	08/02/74		
MICHAEL FENNELLY - Touch My Soul/ Flyer			Epic 8-50019	09/23/74
A BAND CALLED O - Rock And Roll Clown/ Red Light Mama Red Hot	German Epic EPC S 2677	09/24/74		
SPARROW - Oh Doctor/ Eli's Coming (produced both sides)	CBS S CBS 3527	08/08/75	Columbia 3-10234	10/27/75
TIGER TIM - Merry Christmas, Mr. Christmas/ Moving On	President PT 445	12/05/75		
SPARROW - Celebration/ Burning Bridges (produced both sides)	CBS S CBS 3819	01/09/76		
WATER - The Last Seagull/ (What Has Happened To) Your Dreams (produced both sides)	Dutch Vertigo 6012 952	02/06/76		
WATER - Damburst/ It's Over (produced both sides)	Dutch Vertigo 6012 954	02/06/76		
SPARROW - House Of Swing/ Catch Sorrow (produced B-side)	Bronze BRO 24	04/02/76		
LIMEY - Both In Love With You/ National Health Kid	RCA 2758	10/29/76		
LIMEY - Silver Eagle/ Spanish Picture	RCA PB 5014	03/04/77		
SPARROW - Half Of My Life/ It's Alright Now (produced B-side)	Bronze BRO 38	04/08/77		
WATER - On We Rode/ Up The Ladder	Dutch Vertigo 6012 955	<</ <</77		
MARTI CAINE - Woman In Your Arms/ Let Go (produced both)	Pye 7N 45704	07/08/77		
ELAINE SIMMONS - Never Together (But Close Sometimes)/ Singer Of The Song (produced B-side)	Polydor 2058 927	10/08/77		
LAZY RACER - Keep On Running Away/ Every Other Day (wrote the A-side with Tim Renwick)	A&M AMS 7614	07/13/79	A&M 2152-S	06/01/79
MATTHEW FISHER - Can't You Feel My Love/ Only A Game (produced, written and engineered by Chris White and Matthew Fisher)	Dutch Mercury 6000 415	03/28/80	A&M 2226	03/17/80
MATTHEW FISHER - Why'd I Have To Fall In Love With You/ Just How Blind (produced both tracks with Matthew Fisher)	Vertigo 6000 455	07/04/80	A&M 2257-S	08/28/80
MATTHEW FISHER - Give It A Try/ Running From Your Love (produced both tracks with Matthew Fisher)	German Mercury 6000 486	08/16/80		
FRANCIE CONWAY - Do You Want To Make Love?/ Up Against The Wall Again (in addition to producing both sides, Chris White wrote the B-side with Conway)	RCA 139	09/18/81		
MATTHEW FISHER - Living In A Dream/ She Makes Me Feel (produced, written and engineered by Chris White and Matthew Fisher)	German Mercury 6000 687	10/16/81		
DUNE - Dancin' Heatwave/ Lovers Run Away! (produced and wrote both sides)	Ultra ULT 1002	07/16/82		

FRANCIE CONWAY - Something I Heard/ One Night Love	Irish WEA CON 1	<</ <</83
FRANCIE CONWAY - To The Edge Of Time/ The City's Going Down (produced with John Woolloff)	Irish WEA CON 2	<</ <</84
FRANCIE CONWAY - To The Edge Of Time/ The City's Going Down (produced with John Woolloff)	Lamborghini LMG 15	<</ <</84
FRANCIE CONWAY - Somebody Stole My Girl/ Now That You're Gone (produced the B-side with John Woolloff)	Irish Round Tower RTMS 25	<</ <</90
FRANCIE CONWAY - New York Skyline (Where Do We Go From Here)/ Fly With The Night (produced the B-side with with John Woolloff)	Irish Round Tower RTMS 27	<</ <</90
THE BEACON EUROPE SINGERS - Drumfire/Feu De Joie (Unity Version) - Drumfire (Beacon Europe) (7"; Chris White produced this single for the European Unity celebration on 12/31/92. The A-side was written by White/Boucherat/Williams, and the B-side was written by White/Boucherat.)	Polydor PO 249	12/07/92
THE BEACON EUROPE SINGERS - Drumfire/Feu De Joie (Unity Version) - Drumfire (Beacon Europe) - Feu De Joie (Beacon Europe) - Drumfire (A Cappella Version) (cassette single/CD5; tracks 1 and 3 were written by White/Boucherat/Williams, and tracks 2 and 4 were written by White/Boucherat)	Polydor POCS/ PZCD 249	12/07/92

ALBUMS

TITLES	UK & FOREIGN LABEL/NO.	RELEASE DATE	US & CANADA LABEL/NO.	RELEASE DATE
DORIS TROY AND THE GOSPEL TRUTH - The Rainbow Testamant (supervised recording of the album)	Mojo 2956 001	09/01/72		
MICHAEL FENNELLY - Lane Changer	Epic EPC 80230	07/26/74	Epic KE 32703	02/25/74
A BAND CALLED O - A Band Called O	Epic EPC 80120	06/07/74		
LIFE - Life After Death	Polydor 2383 295	09/06/74		
WATER - Damburst	Dutch Vertigo 9286 575	<</ <</76		
ELAINE SIMMONS - The Singer Of The Song	Polydor 2383 402	09/17/76		
LIMEY - Silver Eagle	RCA PL 25032	02/04/77		
LAZY RACER - Lazy Racer (co-wrote "Keep On Running Away" with Tim Renwick)	A&M AMLH 64768	07/13/79	A&M SP-4768	06/15/79
MATTHEW FISHER - Matthew Fisher (produced with Fisher)	Vertigo 9198 652	02/15/80	A&M SP-4801	02/25/80
MATTHEW FISHER - Strange Days (produced with Fisher; White and Fisher wrote "Something I Should Have Known," "Without You," "Living In A Dream," "Why Can't You Lie To Me," "Only Yourself To Blame," "She Makes Me Feel," "Take Me For A Ride" and "Strange Days.")	German Mercury 6302 108	04/10/81		
FRANCIE CONWAY - I Know (produced the album with John Woolloff)	Irish WEA FC LP 1/ German Lamborghini 6.25995	08/<</84		
SEBASTIÁN SANTA MARIA - Latino (CD; produced by Chris, Philippe Mercier and Sebastián Santa Maria)	no label or #	<</ <</94		
DUFFY POWER - Just Stay Blue (CD; contains unreleased tracks recorded with the Argent lineup and produced by Rod Argent and Chris White)	Retro 802	06/05/95		
MATTHEW FISHER - Matthew Fisher/ Strange Days (CD; reissue)	BGO BGOCD 308	03/20/96		
DUFFY POWER - Vampers & Champers (2CD; includes tracks recorded with the band Argent, produced by Argent/White)	RPM RPM 320	09/25/06		
SEBASTIÁN SANTA MARIA - Corpus (CD; Chris White was credited for additional production)	Swiss SMS 690102	<</ <</97		
VARIOUS ARTISTS - MIDEM Awards 1999 (CD; promo-only release with Chris White and Vivienne Boucherat's "Let The Flame Be Strong")	MIDEM no #	01/24/99		
MAC MAC LEOD - The Incredible Musical Odyssey Of The Original Hurdy Gurdy Man (CD; with a demo of Rod Argent and Chris White's "Telescope" performed with the early version of Argent that he was briefly in. Also included is "Tick Tock Man," written by Argent and White.)	RPM RPM 258	05/11/03		
WHITE CIRCLE - The Key (CD; produced by Chris White, Vivienne Boucherat and Matthew White, and Chris wrote and performed – also featuring vocalist Bianca Kinane)	Songscape Ltd. SNGS CD001	<</<</07		

JJ WHITE - Featherhead (CD; co-production and bass)	JJW CD001	07/02/07
JOHN VERITY - My Religion (2LP/CD; Chris White and Vivienne Boucherat wrote "Would You" and provided backing vocals – the double LP has 4 extra tracks)	VaVoom VVMR01V/ VVRM01	03/19/16
ET TU BRUCÉ - Et Tu Brucé (CD; Chris and Vivienne Boucherat backing vocals on "The Flood")	Worldwide ETB003CD	07/22/16
MATTHEW FISHER - Matthew Fisher/ Strange Days (CD; reissue)	Angel Air SJPCD510	02/09/18

THE CHRIS WHITE EXPERIENCE - Volume One (CD/download)   Sunfish CWE001CD   03/29/19
Tracks: COLIN BLUNSTONE - Why Can't You Lie To Me; STEVIE LANGE - Power Over Me; SCOTT BENNETT - A Trick Of Starlight; JOHN VERITY - I'm Coming Home; TIM RENWICK - Good For You Darlin'; NICO RAMSDEN - My Love Tonight; CHRIS WHITE - When My Boat Comes In; FRANCIE CONWAY - Something I Heard; STEVE GOULD - She Makes Me Feel; COLIN BLUNSTONE - Taking The Wings From Butterflies; MAGGIE RYDER - Like A Shotgun; JOHN VERITY - Ride On The Wind; BIANCA KINANE - I Danced The Dance

THE CHRIS WHITE EXPERIENCE - Volume Two (CD/download)   Sunfish CWE002CD   08/31/19
Tracks: KEVIN FINN: Good Good Morning; JOHN VERITY - Heard Your Song; COLIN BLUNSTONE - Don't Go Looking; BIANCA KINANE - How I Miss You; KEVIN FINN - Teddybears; CHRIS WHITE - Hold My Hand (Lula Lula); TIM RENWICK - Make The Lady Smile; COLIN BLUNSTONE - Normal Heart; BIANCA KINANE - Eyes; JJ WHITE - Killing Rose; TIM RENWICK - Is There Anyone Out There; KEVIN FINN - Got To Be Now; STEVE GOULD - Waiting For The Night To End

THE CHRIS WHITE EXPERIENCE - Volume Three (CD/download)   Sunfish CWE003CD   12/18/19
Tracks: SPARROW - Celebration; ELVIS CHAMBERS - Out Through The Stars; ET TU BRUCÉ - Can't Seem To Fall In Love; MAGGIE RYDER - Your Heart Is Mine; TIM RENWICK - To Live A Dream; KEVIN FINN - Loving You; FRANCIE CONWAY - Up Against The Wall Again; JOE LEE WILSON - Man Go Find A Woman; JOHN VERITY - Hold On To Me; COLIN BLUNSTONE - Unhappy Girl; CHRIS WHITE - Today More Than Ever; BIANCA KINANE - Would You; KEVIN FINN - Let's Have A Party

MATTHEW FISHER - Matthew Fisher/ Strange Days (CD; reissue)   Japanese Wasabi WSBAC-0130   03/25/20

THE CHRIS WHITE EXPERIENCE - Volume Four (download-only)   Sunfish (no #)   07/03/20
Tracks: FRANCIE CONWAY - Do You Want To Make Love?; MARTI CAINE - Woman In Your Arms; CHRIS WHITE - Mr. Galileo; SPARROW - Oh Doctor; DUNE - Dancin' Heatwave; SEBASTIÁN SANTA MARIA - Latino; DUFFY POWER - Hummingbird (B-side); ARGENT - Alexis, You're A Circus; DIANA DORS - I've Seen And Done It All; LIFE - Ball And Chain; JJ WHITE - Clockwork; COLIN BLUNSTONE - New World

THE CHRIS WHITE EXPERIENCE - Volume Five (download-only)   Sunfish (no #)   12/25/20
Tracks: MICHAEL FENNELLY - Death Of A Rock 'n' Roll Star; PETE BROWN - Friends From A Distance; KEVIN FINN - Sharing Your Life; BRIAN CULLMAN - Safety; BIANCA KINANE - Rain; COLIN BLUNSTONE - When I Was All Alone; SPARROW - Take It Easy; DUFFY POWER - Love Song; DIANA DORS - Security; FREE FERRY - Magic Carpet Ride; JOHN VERITY - Chocolate Cake; MOONSTONE - Take Me Another Way Home

SPARROW - The Chris White Experience Presents: Sparrow (CD; all of the tracks that Chris White produced are included)   Sunfish CWP001CD   09/24/21

Chris also provided backing vocals on Colin and Rod's album "As Far As I Can See...," and he appeared at all of the reunion and "Odessey And Oracle" concerts. He's still writing and playing.

Please note that there was another Chris White that made some excellent music for the Charisma label. Sadly, he passed away on December 23, 2014.

ZOMBIES DISCOGRAPHY

SINGLES

TITLES	UK & FOREIGN LABEL/NO.	RELEASE DATE	US & CANADA LABEL/NO.	RELEASE DATE
She's Not There/ You Make Me Feel Good	Decca F.11940	07/24/64	Parrot 45-PAR 9695	09/07/64
Leave Me Be/ Woman	Decca F.12004	10/16/64		
Woman/ You'd Better Leave Me Be (sic)			Can. Parrot 45-PAR 9713	11/16/64
Tell Her No/ Leave Me Be			Parrot 45-PAR 9723	12/28/64
Tell Her No/ What More Can I Do	Decca F.12072	01/29/65		
She's Coming Home/ I Must Move	Decca F.12125	04/09/65	Parrot 45 PAR 9747	03/27/65
I Want You Back Again/ I Remember When I Loved Her			Parrot 45-PAR 9769	05/31/65
Whenever You're Ready/ I Love You	Decca F.12225	09/03/65	Parrot 45 PAR 9786	08/16/65
Just Out Of Reach/ Remember You			Parrot 45 PAR-9797	10/25/65
Is This The Dream/ Don't Go Away	Decca F.12296	11/26/65	Parrot 45 PAR 9821	02/28/66
Remember You/ Just Out Of Reach	Decca F.12322	01/21/66		
Indication/ How We Were Before	Decca F.12426	06/17/66		
Indication (edit)/ How We Were Before			Parrot 45-3004	07/15/66
Gotta Get A Hold On Myself/ The Way I Feel Inside	Decca F.12495	09/23/66		
Goin' Out Of My Head/ She Does Everything For Me	Decca F.12584	03/17/67		
Friends Of Mine/ Beechwood Park	CBS 2960	10/23/67		
Care Of Cell 44/ Maybe After He's Gone	CBS 3087	11/24/67	Columbia 4-44363	11/20/67
Time Of The Season/ I'll Call You Mine	CBS 3380	04/05/68	Date 2-1604	05/06/68
Butcher's Tale (Western Front 1914)/ This Will Be Our Year			Date 2-1612	06/10/68
I Love You/ The Way I Feel Inside	Decca F.12798	06/14/68		
Time Of The Season/ Friends Of Mine			Date 2-1628	12/30/68
Imagine The Swan/ Conversation Off Floral Street	German CBS 4242	05/30/69	Date 2-1644	04/29/69
If It Don't Work Out/ Don't Cry For Me			Date 2-1648	06/18/69
She's Not There/ Tell Her No			London Grt. Hits 5N-59029	01/30/70
Time Of The Season/ Imagine The Swan			Date Hall Of Fame 2-1203	04/17/70
She's Not There/ Road Runner			Canadian Parrot 9695DEX	09/18/70
She's Not There/ You Make Me Feel Good			Parrot 45-9695	08/06/73
Time Of The Season/ I'll Call You Mine	Epic S EPC 3380	09/07/73		
Care Of Cell 44/ Maybe After He's Gone	Epic S EPC 2220	03/29/74		
Time Of The Season/ Imagine The Swan			Epic 5-11145	06/19/74
Hey Paula (re-recording by Paul & Paula)/ Time Of The Season (1977 re-recording)			Canadian Rebound RB 256	01/29/79
She's Not There/ You Make Me Feel Good	Decca F.11940	03/26/82		
Time Of The Season/ Rock 'N' Roll Hoochie Koo (by Rick Derringer)			Eric 4018	07/18/83
She's Not There/ Tell Her No	Old Gold OG 9346	10/14/83		
Tell Her No/ She's Not There			Collectables 3556	06/11/84
Time Of The Season/ She's Coming Home			Collectables 3557	06/11/84
Time Of The Season/ Imagine The Swan			Rhino R7 4513	10/20/87
She's Not There - Time Of The Season - Tell Her No - I Got My Mojo Working (CD3)	Special Ed./ Castle Comm. CD3-12	08/15/88		
She's Not There - Go Now (by The Moody Blues) - Friday On My Mind (by The Easybeats) (CD5)	Old Gold OG 6123	03/28/89		
She's Not There/ Tell Her No			Eric 314	11/27/89
Time Of The Season/ She's Coming Home			Eric 315	11/27/89
New World - Moonday Morning Dance - Alone In Paradise (CD5)	German RCA PD 43428	01/15/90		
Lula Lula - I Can't Be Wrong - Nights On Fire (CD5)	German RCA PD 43672	04/16/90		
Time Of The Season/ Dexter's Tune (by Randy Newman) (7")	Reprise W 0022	03/18/91		
Time Of The Season/ Dexter's Tune - Leonard (12"; both B-sides by Randy Newman)	Reprise W 0022T	03/18/91		
Time Of The Season - Dexter's Tune - Leonard (CD5/cassette single; last two tracks by Randy Newman)	Reprise W 0022CD/ W 0022C	03/18/91		
She's Not There - Leave Me Be (CD5)	Old Gold OG 6305	08/01/95		
Time Of The Season - Tell Her No (CD5)	Old Gold 12623 63262	09/25/95		
She's Not There/ You Make Me Feel Good (7"; part of a quintuple 7" set entitled "1960's Rock & Roll" – this single has the release number 72438-77747-7-3, and the other singles are by Manfred Mann, Ike & Tina Turner, The Turtles, and The Beach Boys)			Restoration Hardware Sound/ Rock River/ EMI Music Special Markets RH-9172	02/26/02

Time Of The Season - This Will Be Our Year (CD5; promotion for Magners Irish Cider TV ad)	Big Beat ZOMBIE 001	05/14/07
The Zombies And Beyond: Album Sampler (promo CD-R; with "Time Of The Season," "She's Not There" and tracks by Argent, Colin Blunstone, and Dave Stewart Featuring Colin Blunstone)	Universal no #	05/26/08
She's Not There/ You Make Me Feel Good (green vinyl; Record Store Day release with art sleeve)	Not Bad BAD7005	04/18/15
Don't Cry For Me (mono undubbed mix)/ Keys To Your Heart (by The 101'ers) (part of a 7-disc box set of 7" singles: "Ace Records 40th Anniversary Single Box Set")	Ace ACE 40	11/27/15
A Rose For Emily (alternative version 2)/ This Will Be Our Year (mono mix) (Record Store Day 7"; translucent rose vinyl)	Varèse Vintage 302 063 206 1	04/22/17
I Want You Back Again (2015) (by the touring Zombies group)/ I Want You Back Again (1965) (Record Store Day 7")	The End 538268571	04/22/17

NOTE #1: A "Remember You" UK acetate with a personalized message from The Zombies was issued as a Record Mirror prize in 1966. Only one copy is known to exist. This message was released as part of album **UK63**.

NOTE #2: The "Broadcast '66" EP (UK Rhythm & Blues REP 05) was another Record Store Day release for 04/22/17. While not authorized, it contains some interesting tracks: Gotta Get A Hold On Myself ("Hippodrome" TV performance – live vocal and instrumentation over a pre-recorded backing track); An Introduction To The Zombies (the introduction from "Hippodrome");/ This Old Heart Of Mine (live); Going To A Go-Go (live) (both from "Dents De Lait, Dents De Loup").

EPs

UK & FOREIGN:

UKEP1 - "The Zombies"   Decca DFE 8598   01/29/65
Kind Of Girl; Sometimes;/ It's Alright With Me; Summertime

UKEP2 - "Zombies R&B" (7")   Big Beat LTDEP 003   10/04/10
I'm Goin' Home (Take 2); Woman (Demo);/ Sticks And Stones (Alternate Take); It's Alright With Me (Demo)

UKEP3 - "Zombies à go go" (7")   Big Beat LTDEP 004   10/04/10
If It Don't Work Out (Undubbed); Come On Time;/ I'll Keep Trying (Undubbed); Going To A Go-Go (Live)

UKEP4 - "at work (n' play)" (7")   Big Beat LTDEP 005   10/04/10
Walking In The Sun (Undubbed); Sometimes (Demo);/ Work 'N Play (Alternate Take); The Way I Feel Inside (Rehearsal)

UKEP5 - "Zombies '66" (7"; 33 1/3 rpm)   Big Beat LTDEP 006   11/01/10
Call Of The Night; A Love That Never Was;/ One Day I'll Say Goodbye; This Will Be Our Year (Demo)

UKEP6 - "Time Of The Season" (7"; 33 1/3 rpm)   Big Beat LTDEP 007   11/01/10
Time Of The Season (Original Mono Mix); A Rose For Emily (Original Mono Mix With Cello);/ Care Of Cell 44 (New Stereo Mix); Hung Up On A Dream (New Stereo Mix)

UKEP7 - "Zombies On The BBC" (7")   Big Beat LTDEP 008   11/01/10
This Old Heart Of Mine (#1); The Look Of Love;/ Just A Little Bit (#1); Loving You Is Sweeter Than Ever (#1) - all tracks recorded live on the BBC

ALBUMS

UK & FOREIGN:

UK1 - "Begin Here" Decca LK 4697 04/30/65
Road Runner; Summertime; I Can't Make Up My Mind; The Way I Feel Inside; Work 'N' Play; You've Really Got A Hold On Me; She's Not There;/ Sticks And Stones; Can't Nobody Love You; Woman; I Don't Want To Know; I Remember When I Loved Her; What More Can I Do; I Got My Mojo Working

UK2 - "14 (Benefit For The Lord's Taverners National Decca LK 4695 05/21/65
Playing Fields Association)"
Nothing's Changed; plus tracks by other artists

UK3 - "Bunny Lake Is Missing" (Original Soundtrack) RCA RD 7791 04/22/66
(mono)
Nothing's Changed; Just Out Of Reach; Remember You; plus other tracks by Paul Glass

UK4 - "The Zombies" Swedish Decca 12/09/66
LK 4843
The Way I Feel Inside; How We Were Before; Is This The Dream; Whenever You're Ready; Woman; You Make Me Feel Good;/ Gotta Get A Hold Of Myself; Indication; Don't Go Away; I Love You; Leave Me Be; She's Not There

UK5 - "Odessey And Oracle" (mono) CBS 63280 04/19/68
Care Of Cell 44; A Rose For Emily; Maybe After He's Gone; Beechwood Park; Brief Candles; Hung Up On A Dream;/ Changes; I Want Her She Wants Me; This Will Be Our Year; Butcher's Tale (Western Front 1914); Friends Of Mine; Time Of The Season

UK6 - "Odessey And Oracle" (stereo) CBS S63280 04/19/68
same tracks as **UK5**

UK7 - "The World Of The Zombies" (mono) Decca PA 85 09/18/70
She's Not There; Sticks And Stones; You've Really Got A Hold On Me; I Got My Mojo Working; Summertime; Kind Of Girl;/ Tell Her No; Woman; Road Runner; Just Out Of Reach; Nothing's Changed; She Does Everything For Me

UK8 - "The World Of The Zombies" (stereo) Decca SPA 85 09/18/70
same tracks as **UK7**

UK9 - "Time Of The Zombies" (2LP) Epic EPC 68262 11/23/73
She's Not There; Tell Her No; Whenever You're Ready; Is This The Dream; Summertime; I Love You; You Make Me Feel Good; She's Coming Home;/ She Loves The Way They Love Her; Imagine The Swan; Smokey Day; If It Don't Work Out; I Know She Will; Don't Cry For Me; Walking In The Sun; Conversation Off Floral Street;// disc two same tracks as **UK5**

UK10 - "Rock Roots" Decca ROOTS 2 05/21/76
She's Not There; You Make Me Feel Good; Leave Me Be; Indication; How We Were Before; I Remember When I Loved Her; Is This The Dream; Woman;/ Tell Her No; Whenever You're Ready; I Love You; Summertime; I Can't Make Up My Mind; Remember You; Gotta Get A Hold Of Myself; Goin' Out Of My Head

UK11 - "She's Not There" Decca TAB 34 01/15/82
She's Not There; How We Were Before; Indication; The Way I Feel Inside; Whenever You're Ready; Leave Me Be; Tell Her No;/ Goin' Out Of My Head; You Make Me Feel Good; Woman; I Remember When I Loved Her; Gotta Get A Hold On Myself; Remember You; What More Can I Do

UK12 - "Begin Here" Decca DOA 4 10/12/84
same tracks as **UK1**

UK13 - "The Zombies" See For Miles SEE 30 11/03/84
She's Not There; Leave Me Be; Tell Her No; I'm Goin' Home (incorrectly listed as "She's Coming Home"); I Want You Back Again; Whenever You're Ready; Is This The Dream; Remember You; Indication; Gotta Get A Hold On Myself; Goin' Out Of My Head;/ You Make Me Feel Good; Woman; What More Can I Do; I Must Move; I Remember When I Loved Her; I Love You; Don't Go Away; Just Out Of Reach; How We Were Before; The Way I Feel Inside; She Does Everything For Me

UK14 - "The Zombies" (revised edition) See For Miles SEE 30 01/18/85
She's Not There; Leave Me Be; Tell Her No; She's Coming Home; I Want You Back Again; Whenever You're Ready; Is This The Dream; Remember You; Indication; Gotta Get A Hold On Myself; Goin' Out Of My Head;/ You Make Me Feel Good; Woman; What More Can I Do; I Must Move; I Remember When I Loved Her; I Love You; Don't Go Away; Just Out Of Reach; How We Were Before; The Way I Feel Inside; She Does Everything For Me

UK15 - "Odessey And Oracle" (LP) Rock Machine 12/12/86
same tracks as **UK6** MACH 6

UK16 -	"Odessey And Oracle" (CD) same tracks as **UK6**	Rock Machine MACD 6	03/28/88
UK17 -	"Meet The Zombies" (LP)	Razor RAZ 34	06/13/88

Conversation Off Floral Street; Don't Cry For Me; She's Not There; Imagine The Swan; She Loves The Way They Love Her; Walking In The Sun; If It Don't Work Out; I Could Spend The Day;/ Girl Help Me; Time Of The Season; I Know She Will; Hung Up On A Dream; A Rose For Emily; This Will Be Our Year; Tell Her No

UK18 -	"Meet The Zombies" (CD) same tracks as **UK17**	Razor RAZ CD 34	06/13/88
UK19 -	"The Collection" (2LP)	Castle Commun. CCSLP 196	08/15/88

Goin' Out Of My Head; Leave Me Be; Gotta Get A Hold On Myself; Kind Of Girl; Sticks And Stones; I Can't Make Up My Mind;/ Summertime; Woman; I Got My Mojo Working; Road Runner; You've Really Got A Hold On Me; Nothing's Changed;// You Make Me Feel Good; She's Not There; Don't Go Away; How We Were Before; Tell Her No; Whenever You're Ready;/ Just Out Of Reach; Remember You; Indication; She Does Everything For Me; Time Of The Season; I Love You

UK20 -	"The Collection" (CD) same tracks as **UK19**	Castle Commun. CCSCD 196	08/15/88
UK21 -	"The Collection" (CD)	Castle Commun. CACD 2005	08/15/88

Tell Her No; She's Not There; Time Of The Season; Sticks And Stones; You've Really Got A Hold On Me; Road Runner; You Make Me Feel Good; I Got My Mojo Working; What More Can I Do; Goin' Out Of My Head

UK22 -	"The Singles A's & B's" (CD) same tracks as **UK14** plus: I'm Goin' Home	See For Miles SEECD 30	09/19/88
UK23 -	"Collection Vol. 1" (CD)	German Impact/Line IMCD 9.00692 O	04/17/89

She's Not There; You Make Me Feel Good; Leave Me Be; Woman; Tell Her No; What More Can I Do; I'm Goin' Home (incorrectly listed as "She's Coming Home"); I Must Move; Kind Of Girl; Sometimes; It's Alright With Me; Summertime; Road Runner; I Can't Make Up My Mind; The Way I Feel Inside; Work 'N' Play; You've Really Got A Hold On Me; Sticks And Stones; Can't Nobody Love You; I Don't Want To Know; I Remember When I Loved Her; I Got My Mojo Working; Whenever You're Ready; I Love You

UK24 -	"Collection Vol. 2" (CD)	German Impact/Line IMCD 9.00693 O	04/17/89

Is This The Dream; Don't Go Away; Just Out Of Reach; Remember You; Nothing's Changed; Indication; How We Were Before; Gotta Get A Hold Of Myself; Goin' Out Of My Head; She Does Everything For Me; I Want You Back Again; Time Of The Season; Conversation Off Floral Street; Don't Cry For Me; Imagine The Swan; She Loves The Way They Love Her; Walking In The Sun; If It Don't Work Out; I Could Spend The Day; Girl Help Me; I Know She Will; Hung Up On A Dream; A Rose For Emily; This Will Be Our Year

UK25 -	"Five Live Zombies" (LP) same tracks as **US18**	Razor RAZM 41	05/29/89
UK26 -	"Five Live Zombies" (CD) same tracks as **US18**	Razor RAZM CD 41	05/29/89
UK27 -	"Begin Here" (CD) same tracks as **UK1**	German Beatline/Line BACD 9.00837 L	07/17/89
UK28 -	"Love & Peace – 16 Greats From The Flower Power Era" (CD) She's Not There (1977 re-recording); plus tracks by other artists	K-Tel ONCD 3440	10/25/89
UK29 -	"Back To The 60's" (CD) She's Not There (1977 re-recording); plus tracks by other artists	K-Tel ONCD 3442	10/25/89
UK30 -	"Collection Vol. 1" (CD) (corrected version)	German Impact/Line IMCD 9.00692 O	01/22/90

She's Not There; You Make Me Feel Good; Leave Me Be; Woman; Tell Her No; What More Can I Do; She's Coming Home; I Must Move; Kind Of Girl; Sometimes; It's Alright With Me; Summertime; Road Runner; I Can't Make Up My Mind; The Way I Feel Inside; Work 'N' Play; You've Really Got A Hold On Me; Sticks And Stones; Can't Nobody Love You; I Don't Want To Know; I Remember When I Loved Her; I Got My Mojo Working; Whenever You're Ready; I Love You

UK31 - "The Return Of The Zombies" (LP) Germ. RCA PL 74505 02/19/90
New World; I Can't Be Wrong; Moonday Morning Dance; Lula Lula; Heaven's Gate;/ Blue; Nights On Fire; Losing You; Time Of The Season (1989 re-recording); Knowing You

UK32 - "The Return Of The Zombies" (CD) Germ. RCA PD 74505 02/19/90
same tracks as **UK31**

UK33 - "Night Riding" (CD) Knight KNCD 10015 10/01/90
She's Not There; It's Alright With Me; I'm Goin' Home (incorrectly listed as "She's Coming Home"); Is This The Dream; Summertime; Work 'N' Play; You've Really Got A Hold On Me; I Got My Mojo Working; I Don't Want To Know; You Make Me Feel Good; Sometimes; Tell Her No; Can't Nobody Love You; Sticks And Stones

UK34 - "The Best Of The Zombies" (CD) Music Club 02/25/91
  MCCD 002
She's Not There; Time Of The Season; I Must Move; I Got My Mojo Working; I Remember When I Loved Her; Summertime; What More Can I Do; Can't Nobody Love You; I Can't Make Up My Mind; Tell Her No; I Don't Want To Know; I Love You; You've Really Got A Hold On Me; Whenever You're Ready; Sticks And Stones; The Way I Feel Inside; You Make Me Feel Good; Road Runner

UK35 - "Colin Blunstone Sings His Greatest Hits" JSE ESSLP 139 04/01/91
by COLIN BLUNSTONE (LP)
She's Not There (Autumn 1990 re-recording); Tell Her No (Autumn 1990 re-recording); Time Of The Season (Autumn 1990 re-recording); plus other Colin Blunstone tracks

UK36 - "Colin Blunstone Sings His Greatest Hits" JSE ESSCD 139 04/01/91
by COLIN BLUNSTONE (CD)
same tracks as **UK35**

UK37 - "New World" (LP) JSE ESSLP 131 05/07/91
New World; When Love Breaks Down; I Can't Be Wrong; Lula Lula; Heaven's Gate; Time Of The Season (Autumn 1990 re-recording); Moonday Morning Dance;/ Blue; Nights On Fire; Losing You; Alone In Paradise; Knowing You; Love Conquers All

UK38 - "New World" (CD) JSE ESSCD 131 05/07/91
same tracks as **UK37**

UK39 - "The Zombies" (3CD) Razor RAZCDBOX 1 07/01/91
same tracks as **UK16**, **UK18**, and **UK26**

UK40 - "Begin Here" (CD) German Repertoire 09/14/92
  REP 4215-WZ
same as **UK1** plus: You Make Me Feel Good; Leave Me Be; Tell Her No; She's Coming Home; I Must Move; Kind Of Girl; It's Alright With Me; Sometimes; Whenever You're Ready; I Love You; Is This The Dream; Don't Go Away; Remember You; Just Out Of Reach; Indication; How We Were Before; I'm Goin' Home

UK41 - "Odessey And Oracle" (CD) German Repertoire 09/14/92
  REP 4214-WZ
same tracks as **UK6** plus: I'll Call You Mine; She Loves The Way They Love Her; Imagine The Swan; Smokey Day; If It Don't Work Out; I Know She Will; Don't Cry For Me; Walking In The Sun; Conversation Off Floral Street; I Want You Back Again; Gotta Get A Hold On Myself; Goin' Out Of My Head; She Does Everything For Me; Nothing's Changed; I Could Spend The Day; Girl Help Me

UK42 - "The EP Collection" (CD) See For Miles 10/12/92
  SEECD 358
She's Not There (mono version); Nothing's Changed; Leave Me Be; Summertime; Sometimes; Woman; It's Alright With Me; I'm Goin' Home; Kind Of Girl; Is This The Dream; What More Can I Do; Tell Her No; She's Coming Home; Just Out Of Reach; Whenever You're Ready; I Must Move; Remember You; I Love You; I Want You Back Again; You Make Me Feel Good; It's Alright (live); Time Of The Season; Brief Candles; I'll Call You Mine; She Loves The Way They Love Her; She's Not There (stereo version)

UK43 - "Zombies Box Set" (3CD) Razor RZCDB 1 11/02/92
same tracks as **UK16**, **UK18,** and **UK26**

UK44 - "Time Of The Season" (3CD box) Japanese Century 02/19/93
  CECC 00500
Road Runner; Summertime; I Can't Make Up My Mind; The Way I Feel Inside; Work 'N' Play; You've Really Got A Hold On Me; She's Not There; Sticks And Stones; Can't Nobody Love You; Woman; I Don't Want To Know; I Remember When I Loved Her; What More Can I Do; I Got My Mojo Working; Kind Of Girl; Sometimes; It's Alright With Me; Nothing's Changed; I'll Call You Mine; I'm Goin' Home;/ You Make Me Feel Good; Leave Me Be; Tell Her No; She's Coming Home; I Must Move; Whenever You're Ready; I Love You; Is This The Dream; Don't Go Away; Remember You; Just Out Of Reach; Indication; How We Were Before; Gotta Get A Hold On Myself; Goin' Out Of My Head; She Does Everything For Me; I Want You Back Again; I'll Call You Mine (with overdubbed second piano); Imagine The Swan; Conversation Off Floral Street;/ Care Of Cell 44; A Rose For Emily; Maybe After He's Gone; Beechwood

Park; Brief Candles; Hung Up On A Dream; Changes; I Want Her She Wants Me; This Will Be Our Year; Butcher's Tale (Western Front 1914); Friends Of Mine; Time Of The Season; I Could Spend The Day; Girl Help Me; She Loves The Way They Love Her; Smokey Day; If It Don't Work Out; I Know She Will; Don't Cry For Me; Walking In The Sun

UK45 -	"Colin Blunstone Sings His Greatest Hits" by COLIN BLUNSTONE (CD) same tracks as **UK35**	Castle Commun. CLACD 351	08/16/93

UK46 -	"Uncovered (18 Classic Tracks By Their Original Artists)" (CD)	K-Tel ECD 3017	11/09/93

She's Not There (1977 re-recording); plus tracks by other artists

UK47 -	"Back To The 60's - Volume 1" (CD)	K-Tel ECD 3046	11/09/93

She's Not There (1977 re-recording); plus tracks by other artists

UK48 -	"Hits Revival" (CD)	K-Tel ECD 3050	11/09/93

She's Not There (1977 re-recording); plus tracks by other artists

UK49 -	"New World" (CD) same tracks as **UK37**	Castle Commun. CLACD 348	05/09/94

UK50 -	"Memories (18 Love Songs Of The Sixites)" (CD)	K-Tel ECD 3078	11/04/94

She's Not There (1977 re-recording); plus tracks by other artists

UK51 -	"1964-67" (CD)	More Music MOCD 3009	01/30/95

She's Not There; A Rose For Emily; I Can't Make Up My Mind; You Make Me Feel Good; Tell Her No; Kind Of Girl; Leave Me Be; Sometimes; It's Alright With Me; I Don't Want To Know; I Love You; Indication; Nothing's Changed; Hung Up On A Dream; Whenever You're Ready; Time Of The Season; plus four live tracks by Argent

UK52 -	"Days Of Flower Power" (CD)	K-Tel ECD 3124	08/02/96

She's Not There (1977 re-recording); plus tracks by other artists

UK53 -	"Bands Of Gold" (CD)	K-Tel ECD 3050	11/05/96

She's Not There (1977 re-recording); plus tracks by other artists

UK54 -	"Zombie Heaven Box Sampler" (CD)	Big Beat ZOMPROM 1	11/03/97

She's Not There; Tell Her No; I Love You; She Does Everything For Me; Time Of The Season; Care Of Cell 44; Friends Of Mine; If It Don't Work Out; Summertime (demo); Nothing's Changed; I'll Keep Trying (undubbed); One Day I'll Say Goodbye (home demo); 10 interview tracks with Zombies members

UK55 -	"Zombie Heaven" (4CD box)	Big Beat ZOMBOX 7	12/08/97

She's Not There (Take 1 announced as "No One Told Me" – this track can only be played by playing Track 1 and holding the rewind key down until its start); She's Not There; You Make Me Feel Good; Leave Me Be; Woman; Tell Her No; What More Can I Do; Road Runner; Summertime; I Can't Make Up My Mind; The Way I Feel Inside; Work 'N' Play; You've Really Got A Hold On Me; Sticks And Stones; Can't Nobody Love You; I Don't Want To Know; I Remember When I Loved Her; I Got My Mojo Working; She's Coming Home; I Must Move; I Want You Back Again; Whenever You're Ready; I Love You; Is This The Dream; Don't Go Away; Remember You; Just Out Of Reach; Indication; How We Were Before; Gotta Get A Hold On Myself; Goin' Out Of My Head; She Does Everything For Me;/ Care Of Cell 44; A Rose For Emily; Maybe After He's Gone; Beechwood Park; Brief Candles; Hung Up On A Dream; Changes; I Want Her She Wants Me; This Will Be Our Year; Butcher's Tale (Western Front 1914); Friends Of Mine; Time Of The Season; I'll Call You Mine (single version); Imagine The Swan; Conversation Off Floral Street; If It Don't Work Out (overdubbed); Don't Cry For Me (overdubbed); I Know She Will (overdubbed); Walking In The Sun (overdubbed); I'll Keep Trying (overdubbed); I'll Call You Mine (overdubbed); Smokey Day; She Loves The Way They Love Her; Girl Help Me; I Could Spend The Day; A Rose For Emily (alternative version); This Will Be Our Year (stereo remix); Time Of The Season (US radio spot);/ Summertime (demo); Woman (demo); Kind Of Girl (demo); Leave Me Be (demo); I'm Goin' Home (Takes 1 & 2); I'm Goin' Home; Sometimes (Intro takes 1,2,4,5,6); Sometimes; It's Alright With Me; Kind Of Girl; Walking In The Sun (undubbed); (Studio Chat) - The Way I Feel Inside (false start); The Way I Feel Inside (rehearsal); I Want You Back Again (alternative version); Nothing's Changed (backing track); Nothing's Changed; Remember You (soundtrack version); Come On Time; I'll Keep Trying (undubbed); Whenever You're Ready (demo); You'll Go From Me aka Don't Go Away (demo); I Know She Will (undubbed); Don't Cry For Me (undubbed); If It Don't Work Out (undubbed); One Day I'll Say Goodbye (home demo); I Don't Want To Worry (home demo); A Love That Never Was (demo); Call Of The Night aka Girl Help Me (demo); Out Of The Day (demo); This Will Be Our Year (demo); Bunny Lake Promo Spot to music of "Come On Time";/ Road Runner*; You Make Me Feel Good*; Wee Baby Blues (incorrectly titled Early One Morning)*; She's Not There*; Tell Her No (#1)*; What More Can I Do*; I'm Goin' Home (#2)*; For You My Love*; Tell Her No (#2; acoustic piano version)*; Soulville*; Rip It Up*; Can't Nobody Love You*; You Must Believe Me (#1)*; She's Coming Home*; I Must Move*; Just Out Of Reach*; If It Don't Work Out*; Whenever You're Ready (#2)*; It's All Right*; Will You Love Me Tomorrow*; When The Lovelight Starts Shining Through Her Eyes*;

Just A Little Bit (#2)*; Sitting In The Park (#1)*; Gotta Get A Hold On Myself (#3)*; Goin' Out Of My Head (#3)*; This Old Heart Of Mine (Is Weak For You) (#2)*; Friends Of Mine*; The Look Of Love*; Kenny Everett Interview & Jingle Medley: Time Of The Season - A Rose For Emily - Jingle - This Will Be Our Year* (* = live on the BBC)

UK56 - "Cool Britannia" by THE YARDBIRDS/ Summit Deluxe 04/23/98
THE SMALL FACES/ THE ZOMBIES (3CD) SDCDBX 3659
same tracks as **UK51**; plus tracks by The Yardbirds and The Small Faces

UK57 - "Odessey And Oracle" (LP) Big Beat WIKD 181 04/27/98
same tracks as **UK6**; "This Will Be Our Year" is mono instead of the inferior rechanneled version on the original LP

UK58 - "Odessey And Oracle" (CD) Big Beat CDWIKD 181 04/27/98
same tracks as **UK5 and UK6** plus A Rose For Emily (alternate version 2); Time Of The Season (alternate mix); Prison Song aka Care Of Cell 44 (backing track) – the rechanneled version of "This Will Be Our Year" was replaced by a stereo remix

UK59 - "Heartbeats: 100 Romantic Sounds From The 60's" K-Tel ECD 3465 08/02/98
(CD)
She's Not There (1977 re-recording); plus tracks by other artists

UK60 - "Begin Here" (CD) Big Beat CDWIKD 191 04/26/99
same tracks as **UK1** plus It's Alright With Me; Sometimes; Kind Of Girl; Tell Her No; Sticks And Stones (Alternate Take); It's Alright With Me (Alternate Take); I Know She Will (Demo); I'll Keep Trying (Demo)

UK61 - "Love Grows: 25 Romantic Classics" (CD) K-Tel ECD 3536 08/02/99
She's Not There (1977 re-recording); plus tracks by other artists

UK62 - "Greatest Hits" by COLIN BLUNSTONE (CD) Mystic MYS CD 138 12/06/99
She's Not There (Autumn 1990 re-recording); Tell Her No (Autumn 1990 re-recording); Time Of The Season (Autumn 1990 re-recording); plus other Colin Blunstone tracks

UK63 - "The Singles Collection: As & Bs 1964-1969" (CD) Big Beat CDWIKD 200 03/14/00
She's Not There; You Make Me Feel Good; Leave Me Be; Woman; Tell Her No; What More Can I Do; She's Coming Home; I Must Move; Whenever You're Ready; I Love You; Is This The Dream; Don't Go Away; Remember You (with special Record Mirror contest winner message); Just Out Of Reach; Indication; How We Were Before; Gotta Get A Hold On Myself; The Way I Feel Inside; Goin' Out Of My Head; She Does Everything For Me; Friends Of Mine; Beechwood Park; Care Of Cell 44 (single edit); Maybe After He's Gone; Time Of The Season; I'll Call You Mine; Imagine The Swan; Conversation Off Floral Street

UK64 - "The Best Ever Sixties Revival – Volume 1" (CD) K-Tel ECD 3593 10/09/00
She's Not There (1977 re-recording); plus tracks by other artists

UK65 - "The Best Ever Sixties Revival – Volumes 1, 2 & 3" K-Tel ECD 3593/ 10/09/00
(CD) 3594/3595
She's Not There (1977 re-recording); plus tracks by other artists

UK66 - "Say You Don't Mind" Armoury ARMCD 029 11/13/00
by COLIN BLUNSTONE (CD)
She's Not There (Autumn 1990 re-recording); Tell Her No (Autumn 1990 re-recording); Time Of The Season (Autumn 1990 re-recording); plus other Colin Blunstone tracks

UK67 - "Anthology" by COLIN BLUNSTONE (CD) Brilliant Classics 02/02/02
BT 33079
She's Not There (Autumn 1990 re-recording); Tell Her No (Autumn 1990 re-recording); Time Of The Season (Autumn 1990 re-recording); plus other Colin Blunstone tracks

UK68 - "The DECCA Stereo Anthology" Big Beat 11/04/02
(2CD; new stereo remixes) CDWIK2 225
It's Alright With Me; She's Not There; You Make Me Feel Good; Summertime; Woman; Leave Me Be; Kind Of Girl; Sometimes; I'm Goin' Home; Road Runner; Sticks And Stones; Walking In The Sun; I Don't Want To Know; Tell Her No; What More Can I Do; I Remember When I Loved Her; I Want You Back Again (alternate); Can't Nobody Love You; The Way I Feel Inside; I Got My Mojo Working; You've Really Got A Hold On Me/ Bring It On Home To Me; I Can't Make Up My Mind; Work 'N' Play; I Want You Back Again (single version);/ She's Coming Home; I Must Move; Just Out Of Reach; Remember You (soundtrack version); Nothing's Changed; I'll Keep Trying; Don't Go Away; Whenever You're Ready; How We Were Before; I Love You; If It Don't Work Out; I Know She Will; Don't Cry For Me; Remember You (single version); Is This The Dream; Indication; I'll Call You Mine; Gotta Get A Hold On Myself; She Does Everything For Me; Goin' Out Of My Head; Leave Me Be (backing track take 1); Work 'N' Play (take 2 false start/ take 3); Just Out Of Reach (backing track/take 4); Whenever You're Ready (backing track/take 1)

UK69 - "Old And Wise" by COLIN BLUNSTONE (2CD)   Superior SU 29503   01/14/03
She's Not There (Autumn 1990 re-recording); Tell Her No (Autumn 1990 re-recording); Time Of The Season (Autumn 1990 re-recording); plus other Colin Blunstone tracks

UK70 - "New World" (CD; different packaging)   Big Beat   08/25/03
CDWIKM 234
New World (My America); When Love Breaks Down; I Can't Be Wrong; Lula Lula; Heaven's Gate; Time Of The Season (Autumn 1990 re-recording); Moonday Morning Dance; Blue; Nights On Fire; Losing You; Alone In Paradise; Knowing You; Love Conquers All; Hold My Hand aka Lula Lula (1978 demo); When My Boat Comes In (1978 demo)

UK71 - "Greatest Hits & The Light Inside"   French Recall   02/21/06
by COLIN BLUNSTONE (2CD)   9558
She's Not There (Autumn 1990 re-recording); Tell Her No (Autumn 1990 re-recording); Time Of The Season (Autumn 1990 re-recording); plus other Colin Blunstone tracks

UK72 - "Greatest Hits Plus"   Mystic MYS CD 194   11/13/06
by COLIN BLUNSTONE (CD)
She's Not There (Autumn 1990 re-recording); Tell Her No (Autumn 1990 re-recording); Time Of The Season (Autumn 1990 re-recording); plus other Colin Blunstone tracks

UK73 - "Odessey And Oracle" ("mini-LP" CD)   Big Beat CDHP 025   06/26/07
same tracks as **UK6**; "This Will Be Our Year" is mono instead of the inferior rechanneled version on the original LP

UK74 - "Into The Afterlife" (CD) by THE ZOMBIES/   Big Beat   07/02/07
COLIN BLUNSTONE as NEIL MacARTHUR/   CDWIKD 266
ROD ARGENT & CHRIS WHITE
Unhappy Girl*; She Loves The Way They Love Her*; Telescope (Mr. Galileo)*; Walking In The Sun (Orchestral Mix); It Never Fails To Please Me*; I Could Spend The Day*; I Know She Will (Orchestral Mix); To Julia (For When She Smiles)*; If It Don't Work Out (Orchestral Mix); Going To A Go-Go (live - French TV); plus 9 tracks by Neil MacArthur and one track by Chris White & Argent [* = Rod Argent & Chris demos recorded during the post-Zombies/ pre-Argent period]

UK75 - "Odessey And Oracle (Anniversary Edition)"   German Repertoire   03/03/08
(2CD)   REP 5089
Disc 1: same tracks as **UK5** plus I'll Call You Mine; Imagine The Swan; Conversation Off Floral Street; If It Don't Work Out; I Know She Will; Don't Cry For Me; Disc 2: same tracks as **UK6**

UK76 - "The Zombies And Beyond" (CD)   UMTV 1773931   05/26/08
Time Of The Season; She's Not There; Tell Her No; Summertime; Indication; I Love You; This Will Be Our Year; A Rose For Emily; Friends Of Mine; plus 5 tracks by Colin Blunstone (one with The Alan Parsons Project and one with Dave Stewart), 4 tracks by Argent, and 2 tracks by Colin Blunstone Rod Argent The Zombies (please see their separate sections for track details)

UK77 - "Odessey & Oracle {Revisited}" (2CD)   Red House   06/30/08
REDHCD 5
Care Of Cell 44; A Rose For Emily; Maybe After He's Gone; Beechwood Park; Brief Candles; Hung Up On A Dream; Changes; I Want Her She Wants Me; This Will Be Our Year; Butcher's Tale (Western Front 1914); Friends Of Mine; Time Of The Season; Tell Her No; She's Not There; Disc 2 tracks by Colin Blunstone Rod Argent The Zombies (please see their section for track details)

UK78 - "New World" (CD; different packaging)   German Repertoire   08/28/09
same tracks as **UK70**   REP 5159

UK79 - "Begin Here - The Complete Mono Decca   German Repertoire   02/21/11
Recordings 1964-1967" (2CD)   REP 5179
Disc 1: same tracks as **UK1** plus Road Runner; Summertime; I Can't Make Up My Mind; The Way I Feel Inside; Work 'N' Play; You've Really Got A Hold On Me; She's Not There; Sticks And Stones; Can't Nobody Love You; Woman; I Don't Want To Know; I Remember When I Loved Her; What More Can I Do; I Got My Mojo Working;/ Disc 2: You Make Me Feel Good; Leave Me Be; Kind Of Girl; Sometimes; It's Alright With Me; Tell Her No; She's Coming Home; I Must Move; I Want You Back Again (#1); Whenever You're Ready; I Love You; Is This The Dream; Don't Go Away; Nothing's Changed; Remember You (#1); Remember You (#2); Just Out Of Reach; Indication; How Were We Before; Gotta Get A Hold On Myself; Goin' Out Of My Head; She Does Everything For Me

UK80 - "Odessey & Oracle - The CBS Years   German Repertoire   02/21/11
1967-1969" (2CD)   REP 5182
Disc 1: same tracks as **UK5** plus I'll Call You Mine (mono mix); Disc 2: same tracks as **UK6** plus A Rose For Emily (Alternative Version 1); "R.I.P. - The Unreleased Album" - She Loves The Way They Love Her; Imagine The Swan; Smokey Day; Girl Help Me; I Could Spend The Day; Conversation Off Floral Street; If It Don't Work Out; I'll Call You Mine; I'll Keep Trying; I Know She Will; Don't Cry For Me; Walking In The Sun

UK81 -	"Bunny Lake Is Missing" (Original Soundtrack) (CD; stereo) same tracks as **US6**	Reel Time RTCD 1018	08/14/12
UK82 -	"Odessey And Oracle" (LP; mono) same tracks as **UK5**	German Repertoire V 102 M/REP 2206	12/10/13
UK83 -	"Odessey And Oracle" (LP; stereo) same tracks as **UK6**	German Repertoire V 102 S/REP 2207	12/10/13
UK84 -	"In Stereo" (4CD)	German Repertoire REP 5288	12/24/13

Disc 1: "True Stereo" Recordings - She's Not There; Woman; Tell Her No; Leave Me Be; Summertime; The Way I Feel Inside; Don't Go Away; I Must Move; How We Were Before; You Make Me Feel Good; You've Really Got A Hold On Me; I Got My Mojo Working; I'm Goin' Home; Is This The Dream; I Can't Make Up My Mind; Kind Of Girl (original US stereo mix); Nothing's Changed; Just Out Of Reach; She Does Everything For Me; I Remember When I Loved Her; I Love You; Indication; Whenever You're Ready; I Want You Back Again (#2); If It Don't Work Out; I'll Call You Mine; I'll Keep Trying; I Know She Will; Don't Cry For Me; Walking In The Sun; Kind Of Girl (original UK stereo mix); Remember You (#1);/ DISC 2: "Fake Stereo" Recordings - She's Not There; Summertime; It's Alright With Me; You've Really Got A Hold On Me; Sometimes; Woman; Tell Her No; I Don't Want To Know; Work 'N' Play; Can't Nobody Love You; What More Can I Do; I Got My Mojo Working; Sticks And Stones; Road Runner;/ DISC 3: 2002 Stereo Mixes (Part 1) - Road Runner; Summertime; I Can't Make Up My Mind; The Way I Feel Inside; Work 'N' Play; You've Really Got A Hold On Me; She's Not There; Sticks And Stones; Can't Nobody Love You; Woman; I Don't Want To Know; I Remember When I Loved Her; What More Can I Do; I Got My Mojo Working; I'm Goin' Home; Walking In The Sun; You Make Me Feel Good; Leave Me Be; Kind Of Girl; Sometimes; It's Alright With Me; Tell Her No;/ DISC 4: 2002 Stereo Mixes (Part 2) - She's Coming Home; I Must Move; I Want You Back Again (#1); I Want You Back Again (#2); Whenever You're Ready; I Love You; Is This The Dream; Don't Go Away; Nothing's Changed; Remember You (#1); Remember You (#2); Just Out Of Reach; Indication; How We Were Before; Gotta Get A Hold On Myself; Goin' Out Of My Head; She Does Everything For Me; I'll Keep Trying; If It Don't Work Out; I Know She Will; Don't Cry For Me; I'll Call You Mine

UK85 -	"Begin Here" (LP) same tracks as **UK1**	German Repertoire V 101 M/REP 2205	01/13/14
UK86 -	"Collected" by COLIN BLUNSTONE (3CD)	Dutch Universal 534 274-4	09/19/14

She's Not There; Tell Her No; Summertime; Time Of The Season; plus tracks spanning Colin Blunstone's solo and session career

UK87 -	"The Zombies" (LP; Record Store Day release on standard black vinyl) same tracks as **UK4** plus Kind Of Girl; I Want You Back Again (single version)	Not Bad BADLP013	04/16/16
UK88 -	"The Zombies" (LP; clear vinyl) same tracks as **UK4** plus Kind Of Girl; I Want You Back Again (single version)	Not Bad BADLP014	06/24/16
UK89 -	"Time Of The Season" (2LP; electric blue vinyl)	Not Bad BAD2LP206	02/17/17

She's Not There; Just Out Of Reach; Tell Her No; Is This The Dream; She's Coming Home; Whenever You're Ready; Friends Of Mine;/ Time Of The Season; I Love You; Gotta Get A Hold On Myself; Goin' Out Of My Head; Hung Up On A Dream; Kind Of Girl; Care Of Cell 44;// Sometimes; If It Don't Work Out; I Want You Back Again; Indication; You Make Me Feel Good; Leave Me Be; Beechwood Park;/ What More Can I Do; Woman; This Will Be Our Year; Imagine The Swan; Butcher's Tale (Western Front 1914); It's Alright With Me; I Remember When I Loved Her

UK90 -	"Collected" by COLIN BLUNSTONE (2LP; edited reissue on white vinyl)	Dutch Music On Vinyl MOVLP2169	06/28/18

She's Not There; Tell Her No; Summertime; Time Of The Season; plus tracks spanning Colin Blunstone's solo and session career

UK91 -	"Odessey And Oracle" (LP; Black Friday picture disc) same tracks as **UK6**	Not Now Music NOTLP263P	11/23/18
UK92 -	"In TheBeginning..." (5LP; various colored vinyl)	Demon DEMRECBOX32	02/22/19

RECORD 1 – Begin Here: same tracks as **UK1**
RECORD 2 – Early Days: same tracks as **US9**
RECORD 3 – Continue Here: Sometimes; It's Alright With Me; She's Coming Home; I Want You Back Again (single version); Nothing's Changed; Is This The Dream; Remember You (single version);/ Just Out Of Reach; Remember You (soundtrack version); How We Were Before; Gotta Get A Hold On Myself; Goin' Out Of My Head; I'll Call You Mine (original single version)
RECORD 4 – R.I.P.: She Loves The Way They Love Her; Imagine The Swan; Smokey Day; Girl Help Me; I Could Spend The Day; Conversation Off Floral Street;/ If It Don't Work Out; I'll Call You Mine; I'll Keep Trying; I Know She Will; Don't Cry For Me; Walking In The Sun
RECORD 5 – Odessey And Oracle: same tracks as **UK6**

US & CANADA:

US1 - "The Zombies" (mono) — Parrot PA 61001 — 02/08/65
She's Not There; Summertime; It's Alright With Me; You've Really Got A Hold On Me; Sometimes; Woman;/ Tell Her No; I Don't Want To Know; Work 'N' Play; Can't Nobody Love You; What More Can I Do; I Got My Mojo Working

US2 - "The Zombies" (rechanneled stereo) — Parrot PAS 61001 — 02/08/65
same tracks as **US1**

US3 - "England's Greatest Hitmakers" (mono) — London LL 3430 — 06/29/65
Nothing's Changed; plus tracks by other artists

US4 - "England's Greatest Hitmakers" (stereo) — London PS 430 — 06/29/65
Nothing's Changed; plus tracks by other artists

US5 - "Bunny Lake Is Missing" — RCA LOC-1115 — 10/04/65
(Original Soundtrack) (mono)
Nothing's Changed; Just Out Of Reach; Remember You; plus other tracks by Paul Glass

US6 - "Bunny Lake Is Missing" — RCA LSO-1115 — 10/04/65
(Original Soundtrack) (stereo)
same tracks as **US5**

US7 - "Odessey And Oracle" — Date TES 4013 — 07/15/68
Care Of Cell 44; A Rose For Emily; Maybe After He's Gone; Beechwood Park; Brief Candles; Hung Up On A Dream;/ Changes; I Want Her She Wants Me; This Will Be Our Year; Butcher's Tale (Western Front 1914); Friends Of Mine; Time Of The Season

US8 - "Odessey And Oracle" (alternate cover) — Date TES 4013 — 03/03/69
same tracks as **US7**

US9 - "Early Days" — London PS 557 — 06/02/69
Whenever You're Ready; Don't Go Away; She's Not There; I Love You; Leave Me Be; Indication;/ She Does Everything For Me; You Make Me Feel Good; Tell Her No; I Want You Back Again; Kind Of Girl; I Must Move

US10 - "The Zombies" (rechanneled stereo) — Parrot PAS 71001 — 08/06/73
same tracks as **US1**

US11 - "Time Of The Zombies" (2LP) — Epic KEG 32861 — 04/19/74
She's Not There; Tell Her No; Whenever You're Ready; Is This The Dream; Summertime; I Love You; You Make Me Feel Good; She's Coming Home;/ She Loves The Way They Love Her; Imagine The Swan; Smokey Day; If It Don't Work Out; I Know She Will; Don't Cry For Me; Walking In The Sun; I'll Call You Mine;// disc two same tracks as **US7**

US12 - "Time Of The Zombies" (2LP) — Epic PEG 32861 — 07/03/78
same tracks as **US11**

US13 - "Cruisin' 1965" — Canadian Ruby RR3-4088 — 11/02/81
She's Not There (1977 re-recording); plus tracks by other artists

US14 - "Cruisin' 1969" — Canadian Ruby RR3-4092 — 02/15/82
Time Of The Season (1977 re-recording); plus tracks by other artists

US15 - "Hit Reunion" — Era BU 5900 — 08/22/83
Time Of The Season (1977 re-recording); plus tracks by other artists

US16 - "The Best And The Rest Of The Zombies" — Backtrac P-17703 — 06/11/84
Time Of The Season; She's Not There; Tell Her No; If It Don't Work Out;/ Is This The Dream; Girl Help Me; I Could Spend The Day; I'll Keep Trying

US17 - "Zombies/Animals: Best Of 2 Super Groups" (cassette) — K-Tel BU 9304 — 03/18/85
She's Not There; Tell Her No; I Want You Back Again; I'm Goin' Home; Time Of The Season (1977 re-recording); plus five tracks by The Animals (Sky Pilot; San Francisco Nights; See See Rider; Don't Bring Me Down; Monterey)

US18 - "Live On The BBC" — Rhino RNLP 120 — 06/10/85
Intro/ Tell Her No (#1); Just Out Of Reach; Whenever You're Ready (#2); Can't Nobody Love You; What More Can I Do; This Old Heart Of Mine (Is Weak For You) (#2); For You My Love;/ It's Alright; American Rap/ Gotta Get A Hold On Myself (#3); Goin' Out Of My Head (#3); When The Lovelight Starts Shining Through Her Eyes; You Must Believe Me (#1); Soulville; I'm Goin' Home (#2) – all tracks recorded live for the BBC

US19 - "Odessey And Oracle" (LP)　　　　　　　　　　　　　　　　Rhino RNLP 70186　　　10/20/87
same tracks as **US7**

US20 - "Odessey And Oracle" (CD)　　　　　　　　　　　　　　　　Rhino RNCD 70186　　　10/20/87
same tracks as **US7** <u>plus</u>: I'll Call You Mine; Imagine The Swan
(After relocating their offices, Rhino reissued this CD on 01/28/92 as R2 70186 with the same packaging.)

US21 - "British Invasion Vol. 3" (CD)　　　　　　　　　　　　　　Rhino R2 70321　　　11/ 21/88
She's Coming Home; I Remember When I Loved Her; plus tracks by other artists

US22 - "Golden Years 1964" (CD)　　　　　　　　　　　　　　　　Dominion 655-2　　　06/05/90
She's Not There (1977 re-recording); plus tracks by other artists

US23 - "The Zombies Greatest Hits" (CD)　　　　　　　　　　　　DCC DZS-052　　　09/04/90
She's Not There; Don't Cry For Me; I Can't Make Up My Mind; You Make Me Feel Good; Tell Her No; Kind Of Girl; Leave Me Be; Sometimes; It's Alright With Me; I Don't Want To Know; I Love You; Indication; Nothing's Changed; Time Of The Season; Imagine The Swan (after a licensing renewal, this CD was re-promoted with the same packaging for a 02/25/97 re-release date.)

US24 - "Sensational 60's Vol. 4" (CD)　　　　　　　　　　　　　Dominion 3201-2　　　07/12/94
She's Not There (1977 re-recording); plus tracks by other artists

US25 - "Car Trax – City Limits" (CD)　　　　　　　　　　　　　Dominion 3448-2　　　02/17/95
She's Not There (1977 re-recording); plus tracks by other artists

US26 - "GREATest Hits * GREATest Recordings" (CD)　　　　　　TransLuxe 57803-2　　04/04/95
She's Not There; Gotta Get A Hold On Myself; I Remember When I Loved Her; Tell Her No; She's Coming Home; I Love You; Summertime; Whenever You're Ready; You've Really Got A Hold On Me; Leave Me Be; Time Of The Season; I Can't Make Up My Mind; Can't Nobody Love You; I Want You Back Again; Sometimes; plus an interview with Rod Argent

US27 - "The Ultimate History Of Rock 'N' Roll: Chapter Seven – The Great Bands" (CD)　　K-Tel 3807-2　　03/31/98
She's Not There (1977 re-recording); plus tracks by other artists

US28 - "The Ultimate History Of Rock 'N' Roll Collection" (10CD)　　K-Tel 8000-2　　03/31/98
She's Not There (1977 re-recording); plus tracks by other artists

US29 - "Absolutely The Best" (CD)　　　　　　　　　　　　　　Fuel 2000 FLD-1039　　07/13/99
She's Not There; Leave Me Be; Tell Her No; The Way I Feel Inside; She's Coming Home; Nothing's Changed; I Want You Back Again; Whenever You're Ready; If It Don't Work Out; I Love You; Is This The Dream; Remember You; Just Out Of Reach; Gotta Get A Hold On Myself; Time Of The Season; Imagine The Swan

US30 - "Millennium Pop Hits Volume 2" (CD)　　　　　　　　　Dominion 4367-2　　　06/20/00
Time Of The Season (1977 re-recording); plus tracks by other artists

US31 - "Greatest Hits" (dual layered hybrid CD/ SACD)　　　　Audio Fidelity AFZ 001　03/25/03
She's Not There; I Can't Make Up My Mind; Tell Her No; You Make Me Feel Good; Kind Of Girl; Leave Me Be; Sometimes; Don't Cry For Me; It's Alright With Me; I Don't Want To Know; I Love You; Nothing's Changed; I Remember When I Loved Her; Indication; Just Out Of Reach; What More Can I Do; She Does Everything For Me; Time Of The Season; She's Not There (single version); Time Of The Season (alternate mono mix)

US32 - "The Zombies Featuring She's Not There • Tell Her No" (CD)　　Varèse Sarabande　　03/25/03
　　　　　　　　　　　　　　　　　　　　　　　　　　　　　　　　302 066 436 2
same tracks as **US1** <u>plus</u> You Make Me Feel Good; Leave Me Be; She's Coming Home; I Must Move; I Want You Back Again; I Love You

US33 - "The Zombies" (pre-release title: "I Love You") (CD)　　Varèse Sarabande　　06/22/04
　　　　　　　　　　　　　　　　　　　　　　　　　　　　　　　　302 066 568 2
The Way I Feel Inside; How We Were Before; Is This The Dream; Whenever You're Ready; Woman; You Make Me Feel Good; Gotta Get A Hold Of Myself; Indication; Don't Go Away; I Love You; Leave Me Be; She's Not There; I Can't Make Up My Mind; I Remember When I Loved Her; Remember You; Just Out Of Reach; Goin' Out Of My Head; She Does Everything For Me

US34 - "Odessey And Oracle" (CD)　　　　　　　　　　　　　　Fuel 2000　302 061 413 2　06/29/04
same tracks as **US7** original album (except "This Will Be Our Year" is mono) <u>plus</u> I'll Call You Mine (Stereo Mix #1); Imagine The Swan (Stereo Mix #1); Conversation Off Floral Street; If It Don't Work Out; Don't Cry For Me; Smokey Day; She Loves The Way They Love Her; Time Of The Season (UK single mix); I'll Call You Mine (overdubbed); Imagine The Swan (Stereo Mix #2)

US35 - "The Zombies" (LP; Record Store Day release of 1,000 copies)　　Varèse Sarabande　　04/20/13
same tracks as **US1**　　　　　　　　　　　　　　　　　　　　　302 066 436 1

US36 -	"1960s Psychedelic Radio Commercials" (CD) Come On Time (edit); plus tracks by other artists	RockBeat ROC-3199	11/19/13
US37 -	"Odessey And Oracle" (LP; Record Store Day release of 2,500 copies) same tracks as **US7**	Varèse Sarabande 302 067 254 1	04/19/14
US38 -	"The Zombies" (LP; Record Store Day release of 1,500 copies) same tracks as **UK4**	Varèse Sarabande 302 066 568 1	04/19/14
US39 -	"R.I.P." (CD)	Varèse Sarabande 302 067 266 8	05/19/14

She Loves The Way They Love Her; Imagine The Swan; Smokey Day; Girl Help Me; I Could Spend The Day; Conversation Off Floral Street; If It Don't Work Out; I'll Call You Mine; I'll Keep Trying; I Know She Will; Don't Cry For Me; Walking In The Sun; Imagine The Swan (Single Mix); Smokey Day (Mono Mix); If It Don't Work Out (Single Mix); Don't Cry For Me (Single Mix)

US40 -	"R.I.P." (LP; Record Store Day release of 5,600 copies)	Varèse Sarabande 302 067 266 1	04/18/15

She Loves The Way They Love Her; Imagine The Swan; Smokey Day; Girl Help Me; I Could Spend The Day; Conversation Off Floral Street;/ If It Don't Work Out; I'll Call You Mine; I'll Keep Trying; I Know She Will; Don't Cry For Me; Walking In The Sun
(NOTE: this album exactly matches up with the proposed and cancelled Date Records "R.I.P." album from 1969.)

US41 -	"Odessey And Oracle" (LP) same tracks as **US7**	Varèse Sarabande 302 067 254 3	08/28/15
US42 -	"Odessey And Oracle" (LP; Newbury Comics exclusive edition of 1,000 copies on red/blue/yellow haze vinyl) same tracks as **US7**	Varèse Sarabande 302 067 254 5	11/20/15
US43 -	"The BBC Radio Sessions" (2LP; Black Friday release)	Varèse Sarabande 302 067 361 1	11/27/15

Road Runner; You Make Me Feel Good; Wee Baby Blues; She's Not There; Interview: The Zombies Find America; What More Can I Do; Interview: Before They Were Zombies; Tell Her No (#1); I'm Goin' Home (#2); For You My Love; Interview: Different Instruments; Tell Her No (#2);/ Soulville; Rip It Up; Interview: The Zombies Go To University; Can't Nobody Love You; Tell Her No (#3); You Must Believe Me (#1); Interview: Globetrotting Zombies; Whenever You're Ready; Just Out Of Reach; Just A Little Bit (#1);// It's All Right; Interview: The Zombies Talk About America; Will You Love Me Tomorrow (#1); When The Lovelight Starts Shining Through Her Eyes; If It Don't Work Out; Just A Little Bit (#2); Interview: Pop Profile - Colin Blunstone;/ Gotta Get A Hold On Myself (#3); Interview: Colin Talks About The Continent; Goin' Out Of My Head (#3); This Old Heart Of Mine (Is Weak For You) (#1); Loving You Is Sweeter Than Ever; This Old Heart Of Mine (Is Weak For You) (#2); Friends Of Mine; The Look Of Love; Kenny Everett Interview & Jingle Medley: Time Of The Season - A Rose For Emily - Jingle - This Will Be Our Year

US44 -	"Bunny Lake Is Missing" (Original Soundtrack) (CD) same tracks as **US5**	Intrada ISC 344	01/19/16
US45 -	"Hard To Find Jukebox Classics 1960-1964: 30 Amazing Stereo Hits" (CD) She's Not There (single version in stereo); plus tracks by other artists	Canadian Hit Parade 12317	02/19/16
US46 -	"The BBC Radio Sessions" (2CD) same tracks as **US43** plus I Must Move; She's Coming Home; Will You Love Me Tomorrow (#2); You Must Believe Me (#3); Sitting In The Park	Varèse Sarabande 302 067 361 8	05/20/16
US47 -	"Odessey And Oracle" (CD; 50th anniversary edition)	Varèse Sarabande 302 067 254 8	03/17/17

same tracks as **US7** plus: I'll Call You Mine; Prison Song; Care Of Cell 44 (alternate mix); A Rose For Emily (alternate version 2); I Want Her She Wants Me (mono mix); This Will Be Our Year (stereo mix); Time Of The Season (alternate mix); I'll Call You Mine; Imagine The Swan

US48 -	"The Zombies Greatest Hits" (LP)	Varèse Sarabande 302 067 463 1	04/21/17

She's Not There; You Make Me Feel Good; Tell Her No; Leave Me Be; She's Coming Home; I Want You Back Again; Whenever You're Ready; I Love You;/ Just Out Of Reach; Is This The Dream; Indication; The Way I Feel Inside; This Will Be Our Year; Time Of The Season; Imagine The Swan; If It Don't Work Out

US49 -	"The Zombies Greatest Hits" (LP; green vinyl) same tracks as **US48**	Varèse Sarabande 302 067 463 1	04/21/17
US50 -	"The Zombies Greatest Hits" (CD) same tracks as **US48**	Varèse Sarabande 302 067 463 8	04/13/18

US51 -	"The Zombies Greatest Hits" (LP; Newbury Comics exclusive edition of 1,000 copies on clear with white/gold splatter vinyl) same tracks as **US48**	Varèse Sarabande 302 067 463 5	04/13/18
US52 -	"Odessey And Oracle" (LP; Newbury Comics exclusive edition of 1,000 copies on technicolor explosion vinyl) same tracks as **US7**	Varèse Sarabande 302 067 254 7	05/25/18
US53 -	"Odessey And Oracle" (LP; Record Store Day Black Friday issue of 2,000 copies) same tracks as **US7**	Varèse Sarabande 302 067 254 3	11/23/18
US54 -	"Odessey And Oracle" (LP; Record Store Day Black Friday picture disc) same tracks as **US7**	Varèse Sarabande 302 067 254 6	11/23/18
US55 -	"The Complete Studio Recordings" (5LP) RECORD 1 – She's Not There/ Tell Her No (aka The Zombies): same tracks as **US1** RECORD 2 – I Love You (aka 1966 Swedish LP): same tracks as **UK4** RECORD 3 – Odessey And Oracle: same tracks as **US7** RECORD 4 – R.I.P.: same tracks as **US40** RECORD 5 – Oddities & Extras: Kind Of Girl; She's Coming Home; I Must Move; I Want You Back Again; I Can't Make Up My Mind; I Remember When I Loved Her; I'm Goin' Home;/ Remember You; Just Out Of Reach; Nothing's Changed; Goin' Out Of My Head; She Does Everything For Me; A Love That Never Was	Varèse Vintage/ Craft Recordings VSD00020	02/22/19
US56 -	"Rock & Roll Hall Of Fame 34th Annual Induction Ceremony, Brooklyn, New York, March 29, 2019" (CD) She's Not There; Time Of The Season; plus tracks by other artists	Rock & Roll Hall Of Fame 19075939482	03/29/19
US57 -	"Odessey And Oracle" (LP) same tracks as **US7**	Varèse Vintage VSD00020-03	11/13/19
US58 -	"The Zombies" (LP) same tracks as **US1**	Varèse Vintage/ Craft Recordings VSD00020-01/ 302 066 436 1	07/31/20
US59 -	"I Love You" (LP) same tracks as **UK4**	Varèse Vintage/ Craft Recordings VSD00020-02/ 302 066 568 1	07/31/20
US60 -	"R.I.P." (LP) same tracks as **US40**	Varèse Vintage/ Craft Recordings VSD00020-04/ 302 067 266 1	07/31/20
US61 -	"Oddities & Extras" (LP; Record Store Day release) same tracks as Record 5 of **US55**	Varèse Vintage VSD00020-05	06/12/21
US62 -	"Odessey And Oracle" (LP) same tracks as **US7**	Varèse Vintage/ Craft Recordings 302 067 254 3	07/15/22

NOTE: Two Zombies LPs by the Sweet Dandelion label in England cannot be confirmed as officially authorized releases from Marquis Enterprises, so they are not part of the discography above. They were: "Begin Here" (Sweet Dandelion SWDDL 715; released 11/30/08) and "R.I.P. - The Lost Album" (Sweet Dandelion SWDDL 718; released 03/01/10). The first album was exactly like the original Decca LP, and the second had the same track listing as the aborted US "R.I.P." album above. Both were released in 500-copy editions and were only sold by retailers specializing in reissues of this kind. I just thought you'd like to know!

DECCA/PARROT – RECORDED TRACKS

RECORDING CODES: M = mono, S = stereo, R = rechanneled stereo, C = countoff, * = longest mix – mono is different length than stereo.
For example, UK22 (S2) means that the second mix of this track is presented in stereo on album UK22.

BUNNY LAKE IS MISSING PROMO SPOT (03/31/65 – Decca Studio No. 2, West Hampstead, London – edited version of "Come On Time" with Laurence Olivier film excerpt)
UK & FOREIGN: UK55 (M)
US & CANADA: none

CALL OF THE NIGHT (demo; 11/66 – Regent Sound, Denmark Street, London – see "Girl Help Me")
UK & FOREIGN: UKEP5 (M); UK55 (M)
US & CANADA: none

CAN'T NOBODY LOVE YOU (12/10/64 – Decca Studio No. 2, West Hampstead, London)
UK & FOREIGN: UK1 (M); UK12 (M); UK23 (M); UK27 (M); UK30 (M); UK33 (M); UK34 (M); UK40 (M); UK44 (M); UK55 (M); UK60 (M); UK68 (S); UK79 (M); UK84 (R & S); UK85 (M); UK92 (M)
US & CANADA: US1 (M); US2 (R); US10 (R); US26 (M); US32 (M); US35 (M); US55 (M); US58 (M)

COME ON TIME (03/31/65 – Decca Studio No. 2, West Hampstead, London [vocals only] added to "Just Out Of Reach" backing track recorded 03/02/65 at Decca Studio No. 2, West Hampstead, London – see "Bunny Lake Is Missing Promo Spot")
UK & FOREIGN: UKEP3 (MC); UK55 (MC)
US & CANADA: US36 (M-edit)

DON'T CRY FOR ME (07/08/65 – Decca Studio No. 2, West Hampstead, London; 12/68 – Morgan Studios, Willesden [vocal overdubs])
UK & FOREIGN: UK7" (M3); UK9 (S2); UK17 (S1); UK18 (S1); UK24 (S1); UK39 (S1); UK41 (S1); UK43 (S1); UK44 (S1); UK55 (DISC2-S2 & DISC3-M3); UK68 (S4); UK75 (S2); UK80 (S2); UK84 (S2 & S4); UK92 (S2)
US & CANADA: US7" (M1); US11 (S2); US12 (S2); US23 (M1); US31 (M1); US34 (S2); US39 (S2 & M1); US40 (S2); US55 (S2); US60 (S2)
MONO/STEREO DIFFERENCE: first mono mix has a louder piano track when compared to stereo; the second mono mix is undubbed

DON'T GO AWAY (06/24/65 – Decca Studio No. 2, West Hampstead, London – see "You'll Go From Me" [demo])
UK & FOREIGN: UK7" (M1); UK4 (M1); UK13 (S2); UK14 (S2); UK19 (S2); UK20 (S2); UK22 (S2); UK24 (S2); UK40 (S2); UK44 (S2); UK55 (M1); UK63 (M1); UK68 (S3); UK79 (M1); UK84 (S2 & S3); UK87 (M1); UK88 (M1); UK92 (S2)
US & CANADA: US7" (M1); US9 (S2); US33 (M1); US38 (M1); US55 (M1); US59 (M1)
MONO/STEREO DIFFERENCE: mono has more echo on vocal

GOIN' OUT OF MY HEAD (#1 – single-tracked vocal with louder backing vocals; 10/23/66 – De Lane Lea, Portland Place, London; 11/66 – Advision Studios, London [vocal overdub with orchestration])
UK & FOREIGN: UK7" (M); UK55 (M); UK63 (M)
US & CANADA: US33 (M); US55 (M); US61 (M)

GOIN' OUT OF MY HEAD (#2 – double-tracked vocal with lower backing vocals; 10/23/66 – De Lane Lea, Portland Place, London; 11/66 – Advision Studios, London [vocal overdub with orchestration])
UK & FOREIGN: UK10 (M); UK11 (M); UK13 (M); UK14 (M); UK19 (R); UK20 (R); UK21 (R); UK22 (M); UK24 (R); UK41 (M); UK44 (M); UK68 (S); UK79 (M); UK84 (S); UK89 (M); M92 (M)
US & CANADA: none

GOTTA GET A HOLD ON MYSELF (05/04/66 – Lansdowne Studio, London)
UK & FOREIGN: UK7" (M1); UK4 (M1); UK10 (M1); UK11 (M1); UK13 (M1); UK14 (M1); UK19 (M1); UK20 (M1); UK22 (M1); UK24 (M1); UK40 (M1); UK44 (M1); UK55 (M1); UK63 (M1); UK68 (S2); UK79 (M1); UK84 (S2); UK87 (M1); UK88 (M1); UK89 (M1); UK92 (M1)
US & CANADA: US26 (M1); US29 (M1); US33 (M1); US38 (M1); US55 (M1); US59 (M1)

HOW WE WERE BEFORE (07/08/65 – Decca Studio No. 2, West Hampstead, London)
UK & FOREIGN: UK7" (M1); UK4 (M1); UK10 (S1); UK11 (S1); UK13 (S1); UK14 (S1); UK19 (S1); UK20 (S1); UK22 (S1); UK24 (S1); UK40 (S1); UK44 (S1); UK55 (M1); UK63 (M1); UK68 (S2); UK79 (M1); UK84 (S1 & S2); UK87 (M1); UK88 (M1); UK92 (M1)
US & CANADA: US7" (M1); US33 (M1); US38 (M1); US55 (M1); US59 (M1)

I CAN'T MAKE UP MY MIND (12/10/64 – Decca Studio No. 2, West Hampstead, London)
UK & FOREIGN: UK1 (M1); UK10 (S2C*); UK12 (M1); UK19 (S2); UK20 (S2); UK23 (S2); UK27 (S2); UK30 (S2); UK34 (S2); UK40 (S2); UK44 (S2); UK51 (S2); UK55 (M1); UK56 (S2); UK60 (M1); UK68 (S3); UK79 (M1); UK84 (S2 & S3); UK85 (M1); UK92 (M1)
US & CANADA: US23 (S2); US26 (S2); US31 (S2); US33 (M); US55 (M1); US61 (M1)
MONO/STEREO DIFFERENCE: mono has echo on vocal, first stereo mix is two seconds longer

I DON'T WANT TO KNOW (11/25/64 – Decca Studio No. 2, West Hampstead, London)
UK & FOREIGN: UK1 (M1); UK12 (M1); UK23 (M1); UK27 (M1); UK30 (M1); UK33 (M1); UK34 (M1); UK40 (M1); UK44 (M1); UK51 (M1); UK55 (M1); UK56 (M1); UK60 (M1); UK68 (S2C); UK79 (M1); UK84 (R1 & S2C); UK85 (M1); UK92 (M1)
US & CANADA: US1 (M1); US2 (R1); US10 (R1); US23 (M1); US31 (M1); US32 (M1); US35 (M1); US55 (M1); US58 (M1)

I DON'T WANT TO WORRY (1966 – home demo at 68 High Street, Markyate)
UK & FOREIGN: UK55 (M)
US & CANADA: none

I GOT MY MOJO WORKING (12/10/64 – Decca Studio No. 2, West Hampstead, London)
UK & FOREIGN: UK1 (M1); UK7 (M1); UK8 (S1); UK12 (M1); UK19 (S1); UK20 (S1); UK21 (S1); UK23 (S1); UK27 (S1); UK30 (S1); UK33 (S1); UK34 (R1); UK40 (S1); UK44 (S1); UK55 (M1); UK60 (M1); UK68 (S2); UK79 (M1); UK84 (R1 & S2); UK85 (M1); UK92 (M1)
US & CANADA: US1 (M1); US2 (R1); US10 (R1); US32 (M1); US35 (M1); US55 (M1); US58 (M1)

I KNOW SHE WILL (demo; 04/65 or 06/65 – Jackson's, Rickmansworth)
UK & FOREIGN: UK60 (M)
US & CANADA: none

I KNOW SHE WILL (07/08/65 – Decca Studio No. 2, West Hampstead, London; 12/68 and 01/69 – Morgan Studios, Willesden [vocal and string overdubs])
UK & FOREIGN: UK9 (S1); UK17 (S2); UK18 (S2); UK24 (S2); UK39 (S2); UK41 (S2); UK43 (S2); UK44 (S2); UK55 (DISC2-S1 & DISC3-M3); UK68 (S4); UK74 (S5; shown as "I Know She Will [Orchestral Mix]"); UK75 (S1); UK80 (S1); UK84 (S1 & S4); UK92 (S1)
US & CANADA: US11 (S1); US12 (S1); US39 (S1); US40 (S1); US55 (S1); US60 (S1)
MONO/STEREO DIFFERENCE: mono mix is undubbed; all stereo presentations are mixed differently

I LOVE YOU (07/08/65 – Decca Studio No. 2, West Hampstead, London)
UK & FOREIGN: UK7" (M1); UK4 (M1); UK9 (M1); UK10 (S2); UK13 (S2); UK14 (S2); UK19 (S2); UK20 (S2); UK22 (S2); UK23 (S2); UK30 (S2); UK34 (S2); UK40 (S2); UK42 (S2); UK44 (S2); UK51 (S2); UK54 (M1); UK55 (M1); UK56 (S2); UK63 (M1); UK68 (S3); UK76 (M1); UK79 (M1); UK84 (S2 & S3); UK87 (M1); UK88 (M1); UK89 (M1); UK92 (S2)
US & CANADA: US7" (M1); US9 (S2); US11 (M1); US12 (M1); US23 (S1); US26 (S2); US29 (M1); US31 (S2); US32 (M1); US33 (S2); US38 (M1); US48 (M1); US49 (M1); US50 (M1); US51 (M1); US55 (M1); US59 (M1)
MONO/STEREO DIFFERENCE: mono has guitar intro not on stereo

I MUST MOVE (03/02/65 – Decca Studio No. 2, West Hampstead, London)
UK & FOREIGN: UK7" (M1); UK13 (S2); UK14 (S2); UK22 (S2); UK23 (S2); UK30 (S2); UK34 (S2); UK40 (S2); UK42 (S2); UK44 (S2); UK55 (M1); UK63 (M1); UK68 (S3C); UK79 (M1); UK84 (S2 & S3C); UK92 (S2)
US & CANADA: US7" (M1); US9 (S2); US32 (M): US55 (M); US61 (M)
MONO/STEREO DIFFERENCE: mono has echo on guitar

I REMEMBER WHEN I LOVED HER (11/25/64 – Decca Studio No. 2, West Hampstead, London)
UK & FOREIGN: UK1 (M1); UK10 (M1); UK11 (M1); UK12 (M1); UK13 (S2); UK14 (S2); UK22 (S2); UK23 (S2); UK27 (S2); UK30 (S2); UK34 (S2); UK40 (S2); UK44 (S2); UK55 (M1); UK60 (M1); UK68 (S3); UK79 (M1); UK84 (S2 & S3); UK85 (M1); UK89 (M1); UK92 (M1)
US & CANADA: US7" (M1); US21 (M1); US26 (S2); US31 (S2); US33 (M1); US55 (M1); US61 (M1)
MONO/STEREO DIFFERENCE: mono has echo on vocal and louder percussion, stereo has no echo on vocal, louder organ and softer percussion with echo

I WANT YOU BACK AGAIN (#1; 11/25/64 – Decca Studio No. 2, West Hampstead, London)
UK & FOREIGN: UK55 (M1); UK68 (S2); UK79 (M1); UK84 (S2); UK87 (M1); UK88 (M1); UK89 (M1); UK92 (M1)
US & CANADA: US7" (M1); US29 (M1); US32 (M1); US48 (M1); US49 (M1); US50 (M1); US51 (M1); US55 (M1); US61 (M1)

I WANT YOU BACK AGAIN (#2; 03/02/65 – Decca Studio No. 2, West Hampstead, London)
UK & FOREIGN: UK13 (S1); UK14 (S1); UK22 (S1); UK24 (S1C); UK41 (S1); UK42 (S1); UK44 (S1); UK55 (M1C); UK68 (S2); UK84 (S1 & S2); UK92 (S1)
US & CANADA: US9 (S1); US17 (S1); US26 (S1)

I'LL CALL YOU MINE (05/04/66 – Lansdowne Studio, London; 12/68 – Morgan Studios, Willesden [piano and vocal overdubs])
UK & FOREIGN: UK7" (CBS: M1); UK7" (EPIC: S3); UK41 (S2); UK42 (S2); UK44 (DISC 1-S2 & DISC 2-S3); UK55 (DISC2-M1 & S3); UK63 (M1); UK68 (S4C); UK75 (S2); UK80 (M1 & S2); UK84 (S2 & S4C); UK92 (M1 & S2)
US & CANADA: US7" (M1); US11 (M1); US12 (M1); US20 (S2); US34 (S1 & S2); US39 (S2); US40 (S2); US47 (M1); US55 (S2); US60 (S2)
MONO/STEREO DIFFERENCE: mono has no echo; first stereo mix has one piano track; second stereo mix has three piano tracks and added backing vocals

I'LL KEEP TRYING (demo; 04/65 or 06/65 – Jackson's, Rickmansworth)
UK & FOREIGN: UK60 (M)
US & CANADA: none

I'LL KEEP TRYING (06/24/65 – Decca Studio No. 2, West Hampstead, London; 12/68 – Morgan Studios, Willesden [vocal overdubs])
UK & FOREIGN: UKEP3 (M1); UK54 (M1); UK55 (DISC2-S2 & DISC3-M1); UK68 (S3); UK80 (S2); UK84 (S2 & S3); UK92 (S2)
US & CANADA: US16 (S2); US39 (S2); US40 (S2); US55 (S2); US60 (S2)
MONO/STEREO DIFFERENCE: the mono mix has no vocal overdubs

I'M GOIN' HOME (Takes 1 & 2; 11/24/64 – Decca Studio No. 2, West Hampstead, London)
UK & FOREIGN: UKEP2 (M; Take 2 only); UK55 (MC)
US & CANADA: none

I'M GOIN' HOME (11/24/64 – Decca Studio No. 2, West Hampstead, London)
UK & FOREIGN: UK13 (S1); UK22 (S1); UK23 (S1); UK33 (S1); UK40 (S1); UK42 (S1); UK44 (S1); UK55 (M2); UK68 (S3); UK84 (S1 & S3)
US & CANADA: US17 (S1); US55 (S1); US61 (S1)
MONO/STEREO DIFFERENCE: mono is a different mix

IF IT DON'T WORK OUT (07/08/65 – Decca Studio No. 2, West Hampstead, London; 12/68 and 01/69 – Morgan Studios, Willesden [vocal and string overdubs])
UK & FOREIGN: UKEP3 (M2); UK9 (S1); UK17 (M1*); UK18 (M1*); UK24 (M1*); UK39 (M1*); UK41 (M1*); UK43 (M1*); UK44 (M1*); UK54 (S1); UK55 (DISC2-S1 & DISC3-M2C*); UK68 (S3); UK74 (S4; shown as "If It Don't Work Out [Orchestral Mix]"); UK75 (S1); UK80 (S1); UK84 (S1 & S3); UK89 (S1); UK92 (S1)
US & CANADA: US7" (M1*); US11 (S1); US12 (S1); US16 (S1); US29 (S1); US34 (S1); US39 (S1 & M1*); US40 (S1); US48 (M1*); US49 (M1*); US50 (M1*); US51 (M1*); US55 (S1); US60 (S1)
MONO/STEREO DIFFERENCE: first mono mix has overdubs and is slightly longer than the stereo; the second mono mix is undubbed. Orchestral mix has beginning studio chat.

INDICATION (05/04/66 – Lansdowne Studio, London)
UK & FOREIGN: UK7" (M1-2:59); UK4 (M1-2:59); UK10 (M1-2:59); UK11 (M1-2:59); UK13 (S1-2:59); UK14 (S1-2:59); UK19 (M1-2:59); UK20 (M1-2:59); UK22 (S1-2:59); UK24 (M1-2:59); UK40 (S1-3:01); UK44 (S1-2:59); UK51 (S1-3:00); UK55 (M1-2:59); UK56 (S1-3:00); UK63 (M1-3:02); UK68 (S2-3:00); UK76 (M1-2:59); UK79 (M1-2:59); UK84 (S1-2:59 & S2-3:00); UK87 (M1-2:59); UK88 (M1-2:59); UK89 (M1-2:59); UK92 (S1-2:59)
US & CANADA: US7" (M1-2:07); US9 (S1-2:59); US23 (S1-3:00); US31 (S1-3:02); US33 (M1-2:59); US38 (M1-2:59); US48 (M1-2:58); US49 (M1-2:58); US50 (M1-2:58); US51 (M1-2:58); US55 (M1-3:00); US59 (M1-3:00)

IS THIS THE DREAM (11/10/65 – Decca Studio No. 2, West Hampstead, London)
UK & FOREIGN: UK7" (M1); UK4 (M1); UK9 (M1); UK10 (M1); UK13 (S2); UK14 (S2); UK22 (S2); UK24 (M1); UK33 (M1); UK40 (S2); UK42 (S2); UK44 (S2); UK55 (M1); UK63 (M1); UK79 (M1); UK84 (S2); UK87 (M1); UK88 (M1); UK89 (M1); UK92 (M1)
US & CANADA: US7" (M1); US11 (M1); US12 (M1); US16 (M1); US29 (M1); US33 (M1); US38 (M1); US48 (M1); US49 (M1); US50 (M1); US51 (M1); US55 (M1); US59 (M1)
MONO/STEREO DIFFERENCE: mono has backing vocals and tambourine not on stereo

IS THIS THE DREAM (11/10/65 – Decca Studio No. 2, West Hampstead, London; 08/14/02 – The Red House Studio [tambourine overdubs])
UK & FOREIGN: UK68 (S); UK84 (S)
US & CANADA: none

IT'S ALRIGHT WITH ME (demo; 04/19/64 – Jackson's, Rickmansworth)
UK & FOREIGN: UKEP2 (M)
US & CANADA: none

IT'S ALRIGHT WITH ME (06/12/64 – Decca Studio No. 2, West Hampstead, London)
UK & FOREIGN: UKEP1 (M1); UK23 (M1); UK33 (M1); UK40 (M1); UK42 (M1); UK44 (M1); UK51 (M1); UK55 (M1); UK56 (M1); UK60 (M1); UK68 (S2); UK79 (M1); UK84 (R1 & S2); UK89 (M1); UK92 (M1)
US & CANADA: US1 (M1); US2 (R1); US10 (R1); US23 (M1); US31 (M1); US32 (M1); US35 (M1); US55 (M1); US58 (M1)

IT'S ALRIGHT WITH ME (ALTERNATE TAKE) (06/12/64 – Decca Studio No. 2, West Hampstead, London)
UK & FOREIGN: UK60 (M)
US & CANADA: none

JUST OUT OF REACH (TAKE 4 BACKING TRACK) (03/02/65 – Decca Studio No. 2, West Hampstead, London)
UK & FOREIGN: UK68 (SC)
US & CANADA: none

JUST OUT OF REACH (03/02/65 – Decca Studio No. 2, West Hampstead, London)
UK & FOREIGN: UK7" (M1); UK3 (M1); UK7 (M1); UK8 (S1); UK13 (S1); UK14 (S1); UK19 (S1); UK20 (S1); UK22 (S1); UK24 (S1); UK40 (S1); UK42 (S1); UK44 (S1); UK55 (M1); UK63 (M1); UK68 (S2); UK79 (M1); UK81 (S1); UK84 (S1 & S2); UK89 (M1); UK92 (M1)
US & CANADA: US7" (M1); US5 (M1); US6 (S1); US29 (M1); US31 (M1); US33 (M1); US44 (S1); US48 (M1); US49 (M1); US50 (M1); US51 (M1); US55 (M1); US61 (M1)

KIND OF GIRL (demo; 08/13/64 – Ryemuse Studios, South Molton Street, London)
UK & FOREIGN: UK55 (M)
US & CANADA: none

KIND OF GIRL (08/31/64 – Decca Studio No. 2, West Hampstead, London [backing track]; 09/05/64 – Decca Studio No. 2, West Hampstead, London [vocals])
UK & FOREIGN: UKEP1 (M1); UK7 (M1); UK8 (S3); UK19 (S3); UK20 (S3); UK23 (S3); UK30 (S3); UK40 (S3); UK42 (S3); UK44 (S3); UK51 (S3); UK55 (M1); UK56 (S3); UK60 (M1); UK68 (S4); UK79 (M1); UK84 (S2 & S3 & S4); UK87 (M1); UK88 (M1); UK89 (S3); UK92 (S2)
US & CANADA: US9 (S2); US23 (S2); US31 (S3); US55 (M1); US61 (M1)
MONO/STEREO DIFFERENCE: mono cymbal track not on stereo; first stereo mix with Blunstone humming before vocal; second stereo mix without humming

LEAVE ME BE (demo; 08/13/64 – Ryemuse Studios, South Molton Street, London)
UK & FOREIGN: UK55 (M)
US & CANADA: none

LEAVE ME BE (TAKE 1 BACKING TRACK) (08/31/64 – Decca Studio No. 2, West Hampstead, London)
UK & FOREIGN: UK68 (SC)
US & CANADA: none

LEAVE ME BE (08/31/64 – Decca Studio No. 2, West Hampstead, London [backing track]; 09/05/64 – Decca Studio No. 2, West Hampstead, London [vocals])
UK & FOREIGN: UK7" (M1); UK4 (M1); UK10 (S3); UK11 (S3); UK13 (S3); UK14 (S3); UK19 (S3); UK20 (S3); UK22 (S3); UK23 (S3); UK30 (S3); UK40 (S3); UK42 (S3); UK44 (S3); UK51 (S3); UK55 (M1); UK56 (S3); UK63 (M1); UK68 (S4); UK79 (M1); UK84 (S3 & S4); UK87 (M1); UK88 (M1); UK89 (S3); UK92 (S3)
US & CANADA: US7" (M2); US9 (S3); US23 (S3); US26 (S3); US29 (M1); US31 (S3); US32 (M2); US33 (M1); US38 (M1); US48 (M1); US49 (M1); US50 (M1); US51 (M1); US55 (M1); US59 (M1)
MONO/STEREO DIFFERENCE: first mono mix has no echo on vocals and louder vocals; second mono mix has different overall equalization

LOVE THAT NEVER WAS, A (demo; 10/66 – Regent Sound, Denmark Street, London)
UK & FOREIGN: UKEP5 (M); UK55 (M)
US & CANADA: US55 (M); US61 (M)

NOTHING'S CHANGED (backing track; 03/31/65 – Decca Studio No. 2, West Hampstead, London)
UK & FOREIGN: UK55 (MC)
US & CANADA: none

NOTHING'S CHANGED (03/31/65 – Decca Studio No. 2, West Hampstead, London)
UK & FOREIGN: UK2 (M1); UK3 (M1); UK7 (M1); UK8 (S1); UK19 (S1); UK20 (S1); UK24 (S1); UK41 (S1); UK42 (S1); UK44 (S1); UK51 (S1); UK54 (M1); UK55 (M1); UK56 (S1); UK68 (S2); UK79 (M1); UK81 (S1); UK84 (S1 & S2); UK92 (M1)
US & CANADA: US3 (M1); US4 (S1); US5 (M1); US6 (S1); US23 (S1); US29 (M1); US31 (S1); US44 (S1); US55 (M1); US61 (M1)

ONE DAY I'LL SAY GOODBYE (1966 – home demo at 68 High Street, Markyate – see "Maybe After He's Gone")
UK & FOREIGN: UKEP5 (M); UK54 (M); UK55 (M)
US & CANADA: none

OUT OF THE DAY (demo; 11/66 – Regent Sound, Denmark Street, London)
UK & FOREIGN: UK55 (M)
US & CANADA: none

REMEMBER YOU (#1; 03/31/65 – Decca Studio No. 2, West Hampstead, London)
UK & FOREIGN: UK3 (M1); UK55 (M1C); UK68 (S2); UK79 (M1); UK81 (S1); UK84 (S1 & S2); UK92 (M1)
US & CANADA: US5 (M1); US6 (S1); US44 (S1)

REMEMBER YOU (#2; 08/27/65 – Decca Studio No. 2, West Hampstead, London)
UK & FOREIGN: UK7" (M1); UK10 (M1); UK11 (M1); UK13 (M1); UK14 (M1); UK19 (M1); UK20 (M1); UK22 (M1); UK24 (M1); UK40 (M1); UK42 (M1); UK44 (M1); UK55 (M1); UK63 (M1; with special Record Mirror contest winner message); UK68 (S2); UK79 (M1); UK84 (S2); UK92 (M1)
US & CANADA: US7" (M1); US29 (M1); US33 (M1); US55 (M1); US61 (M1)

ROAD RUNNER (11/24/64 – Decca Studio No. 2, West Hampstead, London)
UK & FOREIGN: UK1 (M1); UK7 (M1); UK8 (R1); UK12 (M1); UK19 (R1); UK20 (R1); UK21 (R1); UK23 (R1); UK27 (R1); UK30 (R1); UK34 (R1); UK40 (R1); UK44 (M1); UK55 (M1); UK60 (M1); UK68 (S2); UK79 (M1); UK84 (R1 & S2); UK85 (M1); UK92 (M1)
US & CANADA: Can. 7" (M1)

SHE DOES EVERYTHING FOR ME (05/04/66 – Lansdowne Studio, London)
UK & FOREIGN: UK7" (M1); UK7 (M1); UK8 (S1); UK13 (S1); UK14 (S1); UK19 (S1); UK20 (S1); UK22 (S1); UK24 (S2); UK41 (S1); UK44 (S1); UK54 (M1); UK55 (M1); UK63 (M1); UK68 (S3); UK79 (M1); UK84 (S1 & S3); UK92 (M1)
US & CANADA: US9 (S1); US31 (S2); US33 (M1); US55 (M1); US61 (M1)
MONO/STEREO DIFFERENCE: the second stereo mix has much louder Rod Argent backing vocals and reversed channels

SHE'S COMING HOME (03/02/65 – Decca Studio No. 2, West Hampstead, London)
UK & FOREIGN: UK7" (M1); UK9 (M1); UK14 (R1); UK22 (R1); UK30 (R1); UK40 (R1); UK42 (M1); UK44 (M1); UK55 (M1); UK63 (M1); UK68 (S2); UK79 (M1); UK84 (S2); UK89 (M1); UK92 (M1)
US & CANADA: US7" (M1); US11 (M1); US12 (M1); US21 (M1); US26 (M1); US29 (M1); US32 (M1); US48 (M1); US49 (M1); US50 (M1); US51 (M1); US55 (M1); US61 (M1)

SHE'S NOT THERE (06/12/64 – Decca Studio No. 2, West Hampstead, London)
UK & FOREIGN: UK7" (M1); UK1 (M1); UK4 (M1); UK7 (M2); UK8 (S2); UK9 (M1); UK10 (S2C); UK11 (S2C); UK12 (M1); UK13 (S2); UK14 (S2); UK17 (M1); UK18 (M1); UK19 (S2C); UK20 (S2C); UK21 (S2C); UK22 (S2); UK23 (S2C); UK27 (S2C); UK30 (S2C); UK33 (S2C); UK34 (S2C); UK39 (S2C); UK40 (M1); UK42 (M1 & S2C); UK43 (M1); UK44 (S2C); UK51 (S2C); UK54 (M1); UK55 (M1; includes hidden Take 1 prior to the track); UK56 (S2C); UK60 (M1); UK63 (M1); UK76 (M1); UK79 (M1); UK84 (S2 & R); UK85 (M1); UK86 (M1); UK87 (M1); UK88 (M1); UK89 (S2); UK90 (M1); UK92 (M1 & S2C)
US & CANADA: US7" (PARROT, LONDON [first pressing], RHINO, RESTORATION HARDWARE SOUND: M1); US7" (LONDON [second pressing]: S2); US7" (COLLECTABLES: S2C); US1 (M1); US2 (R); US9 (S2); US10 (R); US11 (M1); US12 (M1); US16 (M1); US17 (S2); US23 (M1); US26 (S2); US29 (M1); US31 (M1 & S2); US32 (M1); US33 (S2); US35 (M1); US38 (M1); US45 (S1); US48 (M1); US49 (M1); US50 (M1); US51 (M1); US55 (M1 & M1); US56 (M1); US58 (M1); US59 (M1)
MONO/STEREO DIFFERENCE: mono has extra drum tracks

SHE'S NOT THERE (06/12/64 – Decca Studio No. 2, West Hampstead, London; 08/14/02 – The Red House Studio [drum overdubs])
UK & FOREIGN: UK68 (S); UK84 (S)
US & CANADA: none

SOMETIMES (demo; 08/13/64 – Ryemuse Studios, South Molton Street, London)
UK & FOREIGN: UKEP4 (M)
US & CANADA: none

SOMETIMES (Intro takes 1,2,4,5,6; 09/05/64 – Decca No.2, West Hampstead)
UK & FOREIGN: UK55 (MC)₁
US & CANADA: none

SOMETIMES (08/31/64 – Decca Studio No. 2, West Hampstead, London [backing track]; 09/05/64 – Decca Studio No. 2, West Hampstead, London, London [vocals])
UK & FOREIGN: UKEP1 (M1); UK23 (M1); UK30 (M1); UK33 (M1); UK40 (M1); UK42 (M1); UK44 (M1); UK51 (M1); UK55 (M1); UK56 (M1); UK60 (M1); UK68 (S2); UK79 (M1); UK84 (R1 & S2); UK89 (M1); UK92 (M1)
US & CANADA: US1 (M1); US2 (R1); US10 (R1); US23 (M1); US26 (M1); US31 (M1); US32 (M1); US35 (M1); US55 (M1); US58 (M1)

STICKS AND STONES (11/24/64 – Decca Studio No. 2, West Hampstead, London)
UK & FOREIGN: UK1 (M1); UK7 (M1); UK8 (R1); UK12 (M1); UK19 (R1); UK20 (R1); UK21 (R1); UK23 (R1); UK27 (R1); UK30 (R1); UK33 (R1); UK34 (R1); UK40 (R1); UK44 (M1); UK55 (M1); UK60 (M1); UK68 (S2); UK79 (M1); UK84 (R1 & S2); UK85 (M1); UK92 (M1)
US & CANADA: none

STICKS AND STONES (ALTERNATE TAKE) (11/24/64 – Decca Studio No. 2, West Hampstead, London)
UK & FOREIGN: UKEP2 (M); UK60 (M)
US & CANADA: none

SUMMERTIME (demo; 04/19/64 – Jackson's, Rickmansworth)
UK & FOREIGN: UK54 (M); UK55 (M)
US & CANADA: none

SUMMERTIME (06/12/64 – Decca Studio No. 2, West Hampstead, London)
UK & FOREIGN: UKEP1 (M1); UK1 (M1); UK7 (M1); UK8 (S2); UK9 (M1); UK10 (S2); UK12 (M1); UK19 (S2); UK20 (S2); UK23 (S2); UK27 (S2); UK30 (S2); UK33 (S2); UK34 (S2); UK40 (S2); UK42 (S2); UK44 (S2); UK55 (M1); UK60 (M1); UK68 (S3); UK76 (M1); UK79 (M1); UK84 (S2 & R & S3); UK85 (M1); UK86 (M1); UK90 (M1); UK92 (M1)
US & CANADA: US1 (M1); US2 (R); US10 (R); US11 (M1); US12 (M1); US26 (S2); US32 (M1); US35 (M1); US55 (M1); US58 (M1)
MONO/STEREO DIFFERENCE: mono has extra drum overdubs and drum roll at end

TELL HER NO (11/25/64 – Decca Studio No. 2, West Hampstead, London)
UK & FOREIGN: UK7" (M1); UK7 (M1); UK8 (S1); UK9 (M1); UK10 (S1); UK11 (S1); UK13 (S1); UK14 (S1); UK17 (S1); UK18 (S1); UK19 (S1); UK20 (S1); UK21 (S1); UK22 (S1); UK23 (S1); UK30 (S1); UK33 (S1); UK34 (S1); UK39 (S1); UK40 (S1); UK42 (S1); UK43 (S1); UK44 (S1); UK51 (S1); UK54 (M1); UK55 (M1); UK56 (S1); UK60 (M1); UK63 (M1); UK68 (S2); UK76 (M1); UK79 (M1); UK84 (S1 & R & S2); UK86 (M1); UK89 (S1); UK90 (M1); UK92 (S1)
US & CANADA: US7" (PARROT, LONDON [first pressing], RHINO: M1); US7" (LONDON [second pressing] & COLLECTABLES: S1); US1 (M1); US2 (R1); US9 (R1); US10 (R1); US11 (M1); US12 (M1); US16 (M1); US17 (S1); US23 (S1); US26 (S1); US29 (M1); US31 (S1); US32 (M1); US35 (M1); US48 (M1); US49 (M1); US50 (M1); US51 (M1); US55 (M1); US58 (M1)

THIS WILL BE OUR YEAR (demo; 11/66 – Regent Sound, Denmark Street, London)
UK & FOREIGN: UKEP5 (M); UK55 (M)
US & CANADA: none

WALKING IN THE SUN (11/25/64 – Decca Studio No. 2, West Hampstead, London; 12/68 and 01/69 – Morgan Studios, Willesden [vocal and string overdubs])
UK & FOREIGN: UKEP4 (M3); UK9 (S1*); UK17 (M2); UK18 (M2); UK24 (M2); UK39 (M2); UK41 (M2); UK43 (M2); UK44 (M2); UK55 (DISC2-S1* & DISC3-M3); UK68 (S4); UK74 (S5; as "Walking In The Sun [Orchestral Mix]"); UK80 (S1*); UK84 (S1* & S4); UK92 (S1*)
US & CANADA: US11 (S1*); US12 (S1*); US39 (S1*); US40 (S1*); US55 (S1*); US60 (S1*)
MONO/STEREO DIFFERENCE: first mono mix has overdubs and much less lead vocal echo than the undubbed second mono mix. The first stereo mix has the overdubs, but is differently mixed than either mono version. Orchestral mix only contains the 1969 overdubs and has a humorous longer ending.

WAY I FEEL INSIDE, THE (Studio chat, false start & rehearsal; 11/25/64 – Decca Studio No. 2, West Hampstead, London)
UK & FOREIGN: UKEP4 (M; rehearsal only); UK55 (MC)
US & CANADA: none

WAY I FEEL INSIDE, THE (12/10/64 – Decca Studio No. 2, West Hampstead, London)
UK & FOREIGN: UK7" (M1*); UK1 (M1*); UK4 (M1*); UK11 (M1*); UK12 (M1*); UK13 (S2); UK14 (S2); UK22 (S2); UK23 (S2); UK27 (S2); UK30 (M1*); UK34 (S2); UK40 (S2); UK44 (S2); UK55 (M1*); UK60 (M1*); UK63 (M1*); UK68 (S3*); UK79 (M1*); UK84 (S2 & S3*); UK85 (M1*); UK87 (M1*); UK88 (M1*); UK92 (M1*)
US & CANADA: US29 (M1*); US33 (M1*); US38 (M1*); US48 (M1*); US49 (M1*); US50 (M1*); US51 (M1*); US55 (M1*); US59 (M1*)
MONO/STEREO DIFFERENCE: mono has Blunstone "walking in" on intro and coin dropping at end with "walking out"

WHAT MORE CAN I DO (11/25/64 – Decca Studio No. 2, West Hampstead, London)
UK & FOREIGN: UK7" (M1); UK1 (M1); UK11 (M1); UK12 (M1); UK13 (M1); UK14 (M1); UK21 (M1); UK22 (M1); UK23 (M1); UK30 (M1); UK34 (M1); UK40 (M1); UK42 (M1); UK44 (M1); UK55 (M1); UK60 (M1); UK63 (M1); UK68 (S2); UK79 (M1); UK84 (R & S2); UK85 (M1); UK89 (M1); UK92 (M1)
US & CANADA: US1 (M1); US2 (R1); US10 (R1); US31 (M1); US32 (M1); US35 (M1); US55 (M1); US58 (M1)

WHENEVER YOU'RE READY (demo; 04/65 or 06/65 – Jackson's, Rickmansworth)
UK & FOREIGN: UK55 (M)
US & CANADA: none

WHENEVER YOU'RE READY (TAKE 1 BACKING TRACK) (06/24/65 – Decca Studio No. 2, West Hampstead, London)
UK & FOREIGN: UK68 (SC)
US & CANADA: none

WHENEVER YOU'RE READY (06/24/65 – Decca Studio No. 2, West Hampstead, London)
UK & FOREIGN: UK7" (M1); UK4 (M1); UK9 (M1); UK10 (S2); UK11 (S2); UK13 (S2); UK14 (S2); UK19 (S2C); UK20 (S2C); UK22 (S2); UK23 (S2C); UK30 (S2C); UK34 (S2C); UK40 (S2); UK42 (S2); UK44 (S2); UK51 (S2C); UK55 (M1); UK56 (S2C); UK63 (M1); UK68 (S3); UK79 (M1); UK84 (S2 & S3); UK87 (M1); UK88 (M1); UK89 (M1); UK92 (S2)
US & CANADA: US7" (M1); US9 (S2); US11 (M1); US12 (M1); US26 (S2); US29 (M1); US33 (M1); US38 (M1); US48 (M1); US49 (M1); US50 (M1); US51 (M1); US55 (M1); US59 (M1)
MONO/STEREO DIFFERENCE: mono has different echo on vocals

WOMAN (demo; 08/13/64 – Ryemuse Studios, South Molton Street, London)
UK & FOREIGN: UKEP2 (M); UK55 (M)
US & CANADA: none

WOMAN (08/31/64 – Decca Studio No. 2, West Hampstead, London [backing track]; 09/05/64 – Decca Studio No. 2, West Hampstead, London [vocals])
UK & FOREIGN: UK7" (M1); UK1 (M1); UK4 (M1); UK7 (M1); UK8 (S2); UK10 (S2); UK11 (S2); UK12 (M1); UK13 (S2); UK14 (S2); UK19 (S2); UK20 (S2); UK22 (S2); UK23 (S2); UK27 (S2); UK30 (S2); UK40 (S2); UK42 (S2); UK44 (S2); UK55 (M1); UK60 (M1); UK63 (M1); UK68 (S3); UK79 (M1); UK84 (S2 & R & S3); UK85 (M1); UK87 (M1); UK88 (M1); UK89 (S2); UK92 (M1)
US & CANADA: US1 (M1); US2 (R); US10 (R); US32 (M1); US33 (S2); US35 (M1); US38 (M1); US55 (M & M1); US58 (M1); US59 (M1)
MONO/STEREO DIFFERENCE: mono has extra drum tracks at end

WORK 'N' PLAY (12/10/64 – Decca Studio No. 2, West Hampstead, London)
UK & FOREIGN: UK1 (M1); UK12 (M1); UK23 (M1); UK27 (M1); UK30 (M1); UK33 (M1); UK40 (M1); UK44 (M1); UK55 (M1); UK60 (M1); UK68 (S2); UK79 (M1); UK84 (R1 & S2); UK85 (M1); UK92 (M1)
US & CANADA: US1 (M1); US2 (R1); US10 (R1); US32 (M1); US35 (M1); US55 (M1); US58 (M1)

WORK 'N' PLAY (TAKE 2 FALSE START/ TAKE 3) (12/10/64 – Decca Studio No. 2, West Hampstead, London)
UK & FOREIGN: UKEP4 (M; Take 3 only); UK68 (SC)
US & CANADA: none

YOU MAKE ME FEEL GOOD (06/12/64 – Decca Studio No. 2, West Hampstead, London)
UK & FOREIGN: UK7" (M1); UK4 (M1); UK9 (M1); UK10 (S2C); UK11 (S2C); UK13 (S2); UK14 (S2); UK19 (S2C); UK20 (S2C); UK21 (S2C); UK22 (S2); UK23 (S2C); UK30 (S2C); UK33 (S2C); UK34 (S2C); UK40 (S2C); UK42 (S2); UK44 (S2); UK51 (S2C); UK55 (M1); UK56 (S2C); UK63 (M1); UK68 (S3C); UK79 (M1); UK84 (S2 & S3C); UK87 (M1); UK88 (M1); UK89 (S2C); UK92 (S2)
US & CANADA: US7" (PARROT: M1); US7" (RESTORATION HARDWARE SOUND: S2); US9 (S2); US11 (M1); US12 (M1); US23 (S2); US31 (S2C); US32 (M1); US33 (S2); US38 (M1); US48 (M1); US49 (M1); US50 (M1); US51 (M1); U55 (M1); US59 (M1)

MONO/STEREO DIFFERENCE: mono has extra drum track and echo on vocals

YOU'LL GO FROM ME (demo; 04/65 or 06/65 – Jackson's, Rickmansworth – see "Don't Go Away")
UK & FOREIGN: UK55 (M)
US & CANADA: none

YOU'VE REALLY GOT A HOLD ON ME (includes BRING IT ON HOME TO ME) (12/10/64 – Decca Studio No. 2, West Hampstead, London)
UK & FOREIGN: UK1 (M1); UK7 (M1); UK8 (S1); UK12 (M1); UK19 (S1); UK20 (S1); UK21 (S1); UK23 (S1); UK27 (S1); UK30 (S1); UK33 (S1); UK34 (S1); UK40 (S1); UK44 (S1); UK55 (M1); UK60 (M1); UK68 (S2); UK79 (M1); UK84 (S1 & R1 & S2); UK85 (M1); UK92 (M1)
US & CANADA: US1 (M1); US2 (R1); US10 (R1); US26 (S1); US32 (M1); US35 (M1); US55 (M1); US58 (M1)

NOTE: The following tracks have not been released and/or master tapes are currently missing:

a) 10/16/64 demo session at Regent Sound, Denmark Street, London – tracks not known
b) MY GIRL (demo; early 1966)

CBS/DATE – RECORDED TRACKS
*= longest mix

BEECHWOOD PARK (07/67 or 08/67 – Olympic Studios, Barnes)
UK & FOREIGN: UK7" (M1); UK5 (M1); UK6 (S2); UK9 (S2); UK15 (S2); UK16 (S2); UK39 (S2); UK41 (S2); UK43 (S2); UK44 (S2); UK55 (S2); UK57 (S2); UK58 (M1 & S2); UK63 (M1); UK73 (S2); UK75 (M1 & S2); UK80 (M1 & S2); UK82 (M1); UK83 (S2); UK89 (S2); UK91 (S2); UK92 (S2)
US & CANADA: US7 (S2); US8 (S2); US11 (S2); US12 (S2); US19 (S2); US20 (S2); US34 (S2); US37 (S2); US41 (S2); US42 (S2); US47 (S2); US52 (S2); US53 (S2); US54 (S2); US55 (S2); US62 (S2)
MONO/STEREO DIFFERENCE: mono is a different mix

BRIEF CANDLES (08/16/67 – EMI Abbey Road No. 3, London [basic track]; 08/17/67 – EMI Abbey Road No. 3, London [reduction master])
UK & FOREIGN: UK5 (M1); UK6 (S2*); UK9 (S2*); UK15 (S2*); UK16 (S2*); UK39 (S2*); UK41 (S2*); UK42 (S2*); UK43 (S2*); UK44 (S2*); UK55 (S2*); UK57 (S2*); UK58 (M1 & S2*); UK73 (S2*); UK75 (M1 & S2*); UK80 (M1 & S2*); UK82 (M1); UK83 (S2*); UK91 (S2*); UK92 (S2*)
US & CANADA: US7 (S2*); US8 (S2*); US11 (S2*); US12 (S2*); US19 (S2*); US20 (S2*); US34 (S2*); US37 (S2*); US41 (S2*); US42 (S2*); US47 (S2*); US52 (S2*); US53 (S2*); US54 (S2*); US55 (S2*); US57 (S2*); US62 (S2*)
MONO/STEREO DIFFERENCE: mono has no echo on piano at end and is shorter than stereo

BUTCHER'S TALE (WESTERN FRONT 1914) (07/20/67 – EMI Abbey Road No. 3, London)
UK & FOREIGN: UK5 (M1); UK6 (S2); UK9 (S2); UK15 (S2); UK16 (S2); UK39 (S2); UK41 (S2); UK43 (S2); UK44 (S2); UK55 (S2); UK57 (S2); UK58 (M1 & S2); UK73 (S2); UK75 (M1 & S2); UK80 (M1 & S2); UK82 (M1); UK83 (S2); UK89 (S2); UK91 (S2); UK92 (S2)
US & CANADA: US7" (M2); US7 (S2); US8 (S2); US11 (S2); US12 (S2); US19 (S2); US20 (S2); US34 (S2); US37 (S2); US41 (S2); US42 (S2); US47 (S2); US52 (S2); US53 (S2); US54 (S2); US55 (S2); US57 (S2); US62 (S2)
MONO/STEREO DIFFERENCE: mono is a different mix with no echo

CARE OF CELL 44 (08/16/67 – EMI Abbey Road No. 3, London [backing track – see "Prison Song"]; 08/17/67 – EMI Abbey Road No. 3, London [reduction master])
UK & FOREIGN: UKEP6 (S2); UK7" (M-3:09); UK5 (M-3:09); UK6 (S1-3:58*); UK9 (S1-3:58*); UK15 (S1-3:58*); UK16 (S1-3:58*); UK39 (S1-3:53); UK41 (S1-3:58*); UK43 (S1-3:53); UK44 (S1-3:58*); UK54 (S1-3:54); UK55 (S1-3:54); UK57 (S1-3:54); UK58 (M-3:54 & S1-3:58*); UK63 (M-3:13); UK73 (S1-3:58*); UK75 (M-3:09 & S1-3:58*); UK80 (M-3:09 & S1-3:58*); UK82 (M-3:09); UK83 (S1-3:58*); UK89 (S1-3:56); UK91 (S1-3:57); UK92 (S1-3:57)
US & CANADA: US7" (M-3:09); US7 (S1-3:58*); US8 (S1-3:58*); US11 (S1-3:58*); US12 (S1-3:58*); US19 (S1-3:58*); US20 (S1-3:58*); US34 (S1-3:53); US37 (S1-3:53); US41 (S1-3:53); US42 (S1-3:53); US47 (S1-3:54 & S2-3:56); US52 (S1-3:58*); US53 (S1-3:58*); US54 (S1-3:58*); US55 (S1-3:58*); US57 (S1-3:58*); US62 (S1-3:58*)
MONO/STEREO DIFFERENCE: second, recently created stereo mix is on **UKEP6** and US 50th anniversary CD (**US47**)

CHANGES (11/07/67 – EMI Abbey Road No. 3, London [master])
UK & FOREIGN: UK5 (M1); UK6 (S2); UK9 (S2); UK15 (S2); UK16 (S2); UK39 (S2); UK41 (S2); UK43 (S2); UK44 (S2); UK55 (S2); UK57 (S2); UK58 (M1 & S2); UK73 (S2); UK75 (M1 & S2); UK80 (M1 & S2); UK82 (M1); UK83 (S2); UK91 (S2); UK92 (S2)
US & CANADA: US7 (S2); US8 (S2); US11 (S2); US12 (S2); US19 (S2); US20 (S2); US34 (S2); US37 (S2); US41 (S2); US42 (S2); US47 (S2); US52 (S2); US53 (S2); US54 (S2); US55 (S2); US57 (S2); US62 (S2)
MONO/STEREO DIFFERENCE: mono has different echo and is mixed much differently

CONVERSATION OFF FLORAL STREET (1968 – Central Sound, Denmark Street, London [basic track]; 12/68 – Morgan Studios, Willesden [percussion overdubs])
UK & FOREIGN: UK7" (M1*); UK9 (S2); UK17 (S2); UK18 (S2); UK24 (S2); UK39 (S2); UK41 (S2); UK43 (S2); UK44 (S2); UK55 (S2); UK63 (M1*); UK75 (S2); UK80 (S2); UK92 (S2)
US & CANADA: US7" (M1*); US34 (S1*); US39 (S2); US40 (S2); US55 (S2); US60 (S2)
MONO/STEREO DIFFERENCE: the original mono mix was extended, while the stereo was not. I created a longer stereo mix that is similar to the mono for the Fuel 2000 "Odessey And Oracle" CD.

FRIENDS OF MINE (06/01/67 – EMI Abbey Road No. 3, London [master])
UK & FOREIGN: UK7" (M1); UK5 (M1); UK6 (S2); UK9 (S2); UK15 (S2); UK16 (S2); UK39 (S2); UK41 (S2); UK43 (S2); UK44 (S2); UK54 (S2); UK55 (S2); UK57 (S2); UK58 (M1 & S2); UK63 (M1); UK73 (S2); UK75 (M1 & S2); UK76 (S2); UK80 (M1 & S2); UK82 (M1); UK83 (S2); UK89 (S2); UK91 (S2); UK92 (S2)
US & CANADA: US7" (M2); US7 (S2); US8 (S2); US11 (S2); US12 (S2); US19 (S2); US20 (S2); US34 (S2); US37 (S2); US41 (S2); US42 (S2); US47 (S2); US52 (S2); US53 (S2); US54 (S2); US55 (S2); US57 (S2); US62 (S2)
MONO/STEREO DIFFERENCE: mono is a different mix

GIRL HELP ME (1968 – Morgan Studios, Willesden – see "Call Of The Night [demo]")
UK & FOREIGN: UK17 (M1); UK18 (M1); UK24 (M1); UK39 (M1); UK41 (M1); UK43 (M1); UK44 (M1); UK55 (S2); UK80 (S2); UK92 (S2)
US & CANADA: US16 (S1); US39 (S2); US40 (S2); US55 (S2); US60 (S2)
MONO/STEREO DIFFERENCE: guitar on first stereo mix pans right to left and vice versa throughout the song and is a different mix than the second stereo mix, on which the guitar remains on the right channel and backing vocals are mixed differently

HUNG UP ON A DREAM (07/10/67 – EMI Abbey Road No. 3, London [master]; 07/11/67 – EMI Abbey Road No. 3, London [reduction master])
UK & FOREIGN: UKEP6 (S3); UK5 (M1); UK6 (S2); UK9 (S2); UK15 (S2); UK16 (S2); UK17 (S2); UK18 (S2); UK24 (S2); UK39 (S2 & S2); UK41 (S2); UK43 (S2 & S2); UK44 (S2); UK51 (S2); UK55 (S2); UK56 (S2); UK57 (S2); UK58 (M1 & S2); UK73 (S2); UK75 (M1 & S2); UK80 (M1 & S2); UK82 (M1); UK83 (S2); UK89 (S2); UK91 (S2); UK92 (S2)
US & CANADA: US7 (S2); US8 (S2); US11 (S2); US12 (S2); US19 (S2); US20 (S2); US34 (S2); US37 (S2); US41 (S2); US42 (S2); US47 (S2); US52 (S2); US53 (S2); US54 (S2); US55 (S2); US57 (S2); US62 (S2)
MONO/STEREO DIFFERENCE: mono has no echo, and newly created stereo mix (S3) is only on the EP

I COULD SPEND THE DAY (12/18/68 – Morgan Studios, Willesden)
UK & FOREIGN: UK17 (S); UK18 (S); UK24 (S); UK39 (S); UK41 (S); UK43 (S); UK44 (S); UK55 (S); UK80 (S); UK92 (S)
US & CANADA: US16 (S); US39 (S); US40 (S); US55 (S); US60 (S)

I WANT HER SHE WANTS ME (07/67 or 08/67 – Olympic Studios, Barnes)
UK & FOREIGN: UK5 (M1*); UK6 (S2); UK9 (S2); UK15 (S2); UK16 (S2); UK39 (S2); UK41 (S2); UK43 (S2); UK44 (S2); UK55 (S2); UK57 (S2); UK58 (M1* & S2); UK73 (S2); UK75 (M1* & S2); UK80 (M1* & S2); UK82 (M1*); UK83 (S2); UK91 (S2); UK92 (S2)
US & CANADA: US7 (S2); US8 (S2); US11 (S2); US12 (S2); US19 (S2); US20 (S2); US34 (S2); US37 (S2); US41 (S2); US42 (S2); US47 (M1* & S2); US52 (S2); US53 (S2); US54 (S2); US55 (S2); US57 (S2); US62 (S2)
MONO/STEREO DIFFERENCE: mono is a different mix, with echo and additional backing vocals ("heys")

IMAGINE THE SWAN (12/18/68 – Morgan Studios, Willesden)
UK & FOREIGN: UK7" (M1-3:10); UK9 (S1-3:10); UK17 (S2-3:11); UK18 (S2-3:11); UK24 (S2-3:11); UK39 (S2-3:10); UK41 (S2-3:11); UK43 (S2-3:10); UK44 (S2-3:11); UK55 (S1-3:10); UK63 (M1-3:13); UK75 (S1-3:10); UK80 (S1-3:09); UK89 (S2-3:11); UK92 (S1-3:10)
US & CANADA: US7" (DATE & RHINO: M1-3:10); US7" (EPIC: S1-3:10); US11 (S1-3:10); US12 (S1-3:10); US20 (S1*-3:13); US23 (S3-3:09); US29 (S1-3:09); US34 (S1*-3:13 & S3-3:09); US39 (S1*-3:13 & M1-3:10); US40 (S1*-3:13); US48 (M1-3:12); US49 (M1-3:12); US50 (M1-3:12); US51 (M1-3:12); US55 (S1-3:11); US60 (S1-3:09)
MONO/STEREO DIFFERENCE: the third stereo mix has organ on the intro which the other two versions lack

MAYBE AFTER HE'S GONE (07/67 or 08/67 – Olympic Studios, Barnes – see "One Day I'll Say Goodbye")
UK & FOREIGN: UK7" (M1); UK5 (M1); UK6 (S2); UK9 (S2); UK15 (S2); UK16 (S2); UK39 (S2); UK41 (S2); UK43 (S2); UK44 (S2); UK55 (S2); UK57 (S2); UK58 (M1 & S2); UK63 (M1); UK73 (S2); UK75 (M1 & S2); UK80 (M1 & S2); UK82 (M1); UK83 (S2); UK91 (S2); UK92 (S2)
US & CANADA: US7" (M1); US7 (S2); US8 (S2); US11 (S2); US12 (S2); US19 (S2); US20 (S2); US34 (S2); US37 (S2); US41 (S2); US42 (S2); US47 (S2); US52 (S2); US53 (S2); US54 (S2); US55 (S2); US57 (S2); US62 (S2)
MONO/STEREO DIFFERENCE: mono has echo and is mixed much differently

PRISON SONG (backing track for "Care Of Cell 44"; 08/16/67 – EMI Abbey Road No. 3, London [master], 08/17/67 – EMI Abbey Road No. 3, London [reduction master])
UK & FOREIGN: UK58 (SC)
US & CANADA: US47 (SC)

ROSE FOR EMILY, A (06/01/67 – EMI Abbey Road No. 3, London [basic track]; 07/10/67 – EMI Abbey Road No. 3, London [reduction master])
UK & FOREIGN: UK5 (M1); UK6 (S2); UK9 (S2); UK15 (S2); UK16 (S2); UK17 (S2); UK18 (S2); UK24 (S2); UK39 (S2 & S2); UK41 (S2); UK43 (S2 & S2); UK44 (S2); UK51 (S2); UK55 (S2); UK56 (S2); UK57 (S2); UK58 (M1 & S2); UK73 (S2); UK75 (M1 & S2); UK76 (S2); UK80 (M1 & S2); UK82 (M1); UK83 (S2); UK91 (S2); UK92 (S2)
US & CANADA: US7 (S2); US8 (S2); US11 (S2); US12 (S2); US19 (S2); US20 (S2); US34 (S2); US37 (S2); US41 (S2); US42 (S2); US47 (S2); US52 (S2); US53 (S2); US54 (S2); US55 (S2); US57 (S2); US62 (S2)
MONO/STEREO DIFFERENCE: mono has echo

ROSE FOR EMILY, A (alternative version 1; 06/01/67 & 07/10/67 – EMI Abbey Road No. 3, London)
UK & FOREIGN: UK55 (S); UK80 (S)
US & CANADA: none

ROSE FOR EMILY, A (alternative version 2; 06/01/67 & 07/10/67 – EMI Abbey Road No. 3, London)
UK & FOREIGN: UK58 (S)
US & CANADA: US7" (S), US47 (S)

ROSE FOR EMILY, A (original mono mix with cello; 06/01/67 & 07/10/67 – EMI Abbey Road No. 3, London)
UK & FOREIGN: UKEP6 (M)
US & CANADA: none

SHE LOVES THE WAY THEY LOVE HER (12/16/68 – Trident Studios, Wardour Street, London)
UK & FOREIGN: UK9 (S1-3:02); UK17 (M2-2:59); UK18 (M2-2:59); UK24 (M2-2:59); UK39 (M2-2:57); UK41 (M2-2:59); UK42 (M2-2:56); UK43 (M2-2:56); UK44 (M2-2:59); UK55 (S1-3:00); UK80 (S1-3:00); UK92 (S2-3:03)
US & CANADA: US11 (S1-3:02); US12 (S1-3:02); US34 (S1-2:59); US39 (S1-2:59); US40 (S1-2:59); US55 (S1-2:58); US60 (S1-2:58)
MONO/STEREO DIFFERENCE: mono has no crowd on intro, crowd comes in later than stereo, mono longer at end

SMOKEY DAY (12/18/68 – Morgan Studios, Willesden)
UK & FOREIGN: UK9 (S); UK41 (S); UK44 (S); UK55 (S); UK80 (S); UK92 (S)
US & CANADA: US11 (S); US12 (S); US34 (S); US39 (S & MC); US40 (S); US55 (S); US60 (S)

THIS WILL BE OUR YEAR (06/02/67 EMI Abbey Road No. 3, London [master]; 08/15/67 EMI Abbey Road No. 3, London [mono-to-mono reduction plus brass overdub])
UK & FOREIGN: UK5 (M1); UK6 (R1); UK9 (R1); UK15 (R1); UK16 (R1); UK17 (M1); UK18 (M1); UK24 (M1); UK39 (R1 & R1); UK41 (R1); UK43 (R1 & R1); UK44 (R1); UK55 (S2); UK57 (M1); UK58 (M1 & S2); UK73 (M1); UK75 (M1 & R1); UK76 (M1); UK80 (M1 & R1); UK82 (M1); UK83 (M1); UK89 (S2); UK91 (M1); UK92 (M1)
US & CANADA: US7" (M1); US7 (R1); US8 (R1); US11 (R1); US12 (R1); US19 (R1); US20 (R1); US34 (M); US37 (M1); US41 (M1); US42 (M1); US47 (M1 & S2); US48 (M1); US49 (M1); US50 (M1); US51 (M1); US52 (M1); US53 (M1); US54 (M1); US55 (M1); US57 (M1); US62 (M1)
MONO/STEREO DIFFERENCE: mono has brass overdub not on stereo version

TIME OF THE SEASON (08/67 – EMI Abbey Road No. 3, London [master])
UK & FOREIGN: UK7" (M1-3:32); UKEP6 (M1-3:30); UK5 (M1-3:32); UK6 (S2-3:32); UK9 (S2-3:32); UK15 (S2-3:28); UK16 (S2-3:28); UK17 (S2-3:28); UK18 (S2-3:28); UK19 (S2-3:28); UK20 (S2-3:28); UK21 (S2-3:28); UK24 (S2-3:10); UK34 (S2-3:30); UK39 (S2-3:32); UK41 (S2-3:28); UK42 (S2-3:31); UK43 (S2-3:26); UK44 (S2-3:28); UK51 (S2-3:09); UK54 (S2-3:32); UK55 (S2-3:32); UK56 (S2-3:09); UK57 (M1-3:30); UK58 (M1-3:32 & S2-3:32 & M3-3:31); UK63 (M1-2:55); UK73 (S2-3:32); UK75 (M1-3:32 & S2-3:32); UK76 (S2-3:31); UK80 (M1-3:32 & S2-3:32); UK82 (M1-3:32); UK83 (S2-3:32); UK86 (S2-3:32); UK89 (S2-3:28); UK90 (S2-3:32); UK91 (S2-3:32); UK92 (S2-3:34)
US & CANADA: US7" (DATE: M2-3:32); US7" (EPIC, ERIC & COLLECTABLES: S2-3:30); US7" (RHINO: M1-3:32); US7 (S2-3:32); US8 (S2-3:32); US11 (S2-3:32); US12 (S2-3:32); US16 (S2-3:28); US19 (S2-3:32); US20 (S2-3:32); US23 (S2-3:30); US26 (S2-3:31); US29 (S2-3:32); US31 (S2-3:32 & M3-3:32); US34 (S2-3:32 & M1-3:32); US37 (S2-3:32); US41 (S2-3:32); US42 (S2-3:32); US47 (S2-3:32 & M3-3:32); US48 (S2-3:31); US49 (S2-3:31); US50 (S2-3:31); US51 (S2-3:31); US52 (S2-3:32); US53 (S2-3:32); US54 (S2-3:32); US55 (S2-3:32); US56 (S2-3:32); US57 (S2-3:32); US62 (3:32)
MONO/STEREO DIFFERENCE: mono has more upfront organ throughout compared to first stereo mix. The third mix has drums running throughout the song.

TIME OF THE SEASON – US RADIO SPOT
UK & FOREIGN: UK55 (M)
US & CANADA: none

NOTE: The following tracks have not been released:

a) **GIRL HELP ME** (acetate version with Mac MacLeod on guitar) (1968 – Morgan Studios, Willesden)
b) **TO JULIA** (December 1968 – Morgan Studios, Willesden; with unused overdubs)

VARIOUS LABELS – RECORDED TRACKS
* = longest mix

ALONE IN PARADISE (recorded 1989)
UK & FOREIGN: UKCD5 (S-4:09); UK37 (S-4:07); UK38 (S-4:07); UK49 (S-4:07); UK70 (S-4:07); UK78 (S-4:07)
US & CANADA: none

BEECHWOOD PARK (LIVE) (recorded 03/08/08 at Shepherd's Bush Empire, London)
UK & FOREIGN: UK77 (S)
US & CANADA: none

BLUE (recorded 1989)
UK & FOREIGN: UK31 (S); UK32 (S); UK37 (S); UK38 (S); UK49 (S); UK70 (S); UK78 (S)
US & CANADA: none

BRIEF CANDLES (LIVE) (recorded 03/08/08 at Shepherd's Bush Empire, London)
UK & FOREIGN: UK77 (S)
US & CANADA: none

BUTCHER'S TALE (WESTERN FRONT 1914) (LIVE) (recorded 03/08/08 at Shepherd's Bush Empire, London)
UK & FOREIGN: UK77 (S)
US & CANADA: none

(INTERVIEW: THE ZOMBIES GO TO UNIVERSITY; recorded 02/26/65)/ CAN'T NOBODY LOVE YOU (recorded 02/26/65 at Studio 2, Aeolian Hall, London for "Top Gear" broadcast on 03/06/65 – also on BBC Transcription Service disc #20)
UK & FOREIGN: UK25 (M); UK26 (M); UK39 (M); UK43 (M); UK55 (M)
US & CANADA: US18 (M); US43 (M); US46 (M)

CARE OF CELL 44 (LIVE) (recorded 03/08/08 at Shepherd's Bush Empire, London)
UK & FOREIGN: UK77 (S)
US & CANADA: none

CHANGES (LIVE) (recorded 03/08/08 at Shepherd's Bush Empire, London)
UK & FOREIGN: UK77 (S)
US & CANADA: none

EARLY ONE MORNING – see WEE BABY BLUES (the song was titled incorrectly when released on "Zombie Heaven" in 1997)

FOR YOU MY LOVE (recorded 02/02/65 at Playhouse Theatre, London for "Saturday Club" broadcast on 02/06/65 – also on BBC Transcription Service disc #17)
UK & FOREIGN: UK25 (M); UK26 (M); UK39 (M); UK43 (M); UK55 (M)
US & CANADA: US18 (M); US43 (M); US46 (M)

FRIENDS OF MINE (recorded 10/10/67 at Studio 4, Maida Vale, London for Radio 1's "The David Symonds Show" broadcast during the week of 10/16/67 – 10/20/67 – also on BBC Transcription Service disc #155)
UK & FOREIGN: UK55 (M)
US & CANADA: US43 (M); US46 (M)

FRIENDS OF MINE (LIVE) (recorded 03/08/08 at Shepherd's Bush Empire, London)
UK & FOREIGN: UK77 (S)
US & CANADA: none

**(INTERVIEW: COLIN TALKS ABOUT THE CONTINENT; recorded 11/01/66)/ GOIN' OUT OF MY HEAD (VERSION 3; recorded 11/01/66 at Playhouse Theatre,
London for "Saturday Club" broadcast on 11/05/66 – also on BBC Transcription Service disc #106)**
UK & FOREIGN: UK25 (M); UK26 (M); UK39 (M); UK43 (M); UK55 (M)
US & CANADA: US18 (M); US43 (M); US46 (M)

GOING TO A GO-GO (LIVE) (recorded 10/30/66 at ORTF TV studio, Paris, France for "Dents De Lait, Dents De Loup" broadcast on 01/11/67)
UK & FOREIGN: UKEP3 (M); UK74 (M)
US & CANADA: none

(AMERICAN RAP aka INTERVIEW: THE ZOMBIES TALK ABOUT AMERICA) (recorded September 1965)/ GOTTA GET A HOLD ON MYSELF (VERSION 3; recorded 11/01/66 at Playhouse Theatre, London for "Saturday Club" broadcast on 11/05/66 – also on BBC Transcription Service disc #106)
UK & FOREIGN: UK25 (M); UK26 (M); UK39 (M); UK43 (M); UK55 (M)
US & CANADA: US18 (M); US43 (M); US46 (M)

HEAVEN'S GATE (recorded 1989)
UK & FOREIGN: UK31 (S-4:19); UK32 (S-4:19); UK37 (S-4:18); UK38 (S-4:18); UK49 (S-4:18); UK70 (S-4:18); UK78 (S-4:18)
US & CANADA: none

HOLD MY HAND (demo; recorded 1978 – see "Lula Lula")
UK & FOREIGN: UK70 (S); UK78 (S)
US & CANADA: none

HUNG UP ON A DREAM (LIVE) (recorded 03/08/08 at Shepherd's Bush Empire, London)
UK & FOREIGN: UK77 (S)
US & CANADA: none

I CAN'T BE WRONG (recorded 1989)
UK & FOREIGN: UKCD5 (S1-3:33); UK31 (S1-3:33); UK32 (S1-3:33); UK37 (S2-3:55); UK38 (S2-3:55); UK49 (S2-3:55); UK70 (S2-3:55); UK78 (S2-3:55)
US & CANADA: none

I MUST MOVE (recorded 04/20/65 at Studio 5, Maida Vale, London for "Saturday Club" broadcast on 05/01/65 – only four members appeared at this session)
UK & FOREIGN: UK55 (M)
US & CANADA: US46 (M)

I WANT HER SHE WANTS ME (LIVE) (recorded 03/08/08 at Shepherd's Bush Empire, London)
UK & FOREIGN: UK77 (S)
US & CANADA: none

I'M GOIN' HOME (VERSION 2; recorded 01/26/65 at Playhouse Theatre, London for "Saturday Club" but used only on BBC Transcription Service disc #13)
UK & FOREIGN: UK25 (M); UK26 (M); UK39 (M); UK43 (M); UK55 (M)
US & CANADA: US18 (M); US43 (M); US46 (M)

IF IT DON'T WORK OUT (recorded 09/20/65 at Studio 2, Aeolian Hall, London for "Saturday Club" broadcast on 10/02/65)
UK & FOREIGN: UK55 (M)
US & CANADA: US43 (M); US46 (M)

IT'S ALL RIGHT (recorded 09/20/65 at Studio 2, Aeolian Hall, London for "Saturday Club" broadcast on 10/02/65 – also on BBC Transcription Service disc #52)
UK & FOREIGN: UK25 (M); UK26 (M); UK39 (M); UK42 (M); UK43 (M); UK55 (M)
US & CANADA: US18 (M); US43 (M); US46 (M)

JUST A LITTLE BIT (VERSION 1; recorded 04/26/65 at Studio 5, Maida Vale, London for "Saturday Club"; broadcast 05/01/65 – only four members present for this session)
UK & FOREIGN: UKEP7 (M)
US & CANADA: US43 (M); US46 (M)

JUST A LITTLE BIT (VERSION 2; recorded 11/08/65 at Playhouse Theatre, London for "The Beat Show" broadcast on 11/11/65)
UK & FOREIGN: UK55 (M)
US & CANADA: US43 (M); US46 (M)

JUST OUT OF REACH (recorded 04/20/65 at Studio 5, Maida Vale, London for "Saturday Club" broadcast on 05/01/65 – only four members appeared at this session – also on BBC Transcription Service disc #47)
UK & FOREIGN: UK25 (M); UK26 (M); UK39 (M); UK43 (M); UK55 (M)
US & CANADA: US18 (M); US43 (M); US46 (M)

KENNY EVERETT INTERVIEW & JINGLE MEDLEY (Time Of The Season – A Rose For Emily – Jingle – This Will Be Our Year; recorded 04/19/68 at Broadcasting House, London for Radio 1's "The Kenny Everett Show" broadcast on 04/20/68)
UK & FOREIGN: UK55 (M)
US & CANADA: US43 (M); US46 (M)

KNOWING YOU (recorded 1989)
UK & FOREIGN: UK31 (S-2:34); UK32 (S-2:34); UK37 (S-2:33); UK38 (S-2:33); UK49 (S-2:33); UK70 (S-2:33); UK78 (S-2:33)
US & CANADA: none

LOOK OF LOVE, THE (recorded 10/10/67 at Studio 4, Maida Vale, London for Radio 1's "The David Symonds Show" broadcast during the week of 10/16/67 – 10/20/67 – also on BBC Transcription Service disc #155)
UK & FOREIGN: UKEP7 (M); UK55 (M)
US & CANADA: US43 (M); US46 (M)

LOSING YOU (recorded 1989)
UK & FOREIGN: UK31 (S-2:59); UK32 (S-2:59); UK37 (S-2:58); UK38 (S-2:58); UK49 (S-2:58); UK70 (S-2:57); UK78 (S-2:57)
US & CANADA: none

LOVE CONQUERS ALL (recorded 1990 – Livingstone Studios, London)
UK & FOREIGN: UK37 (S); UK38 (S); UK49 (S); UK70 (S); UK78 (S)
US & CANADA: none

LOVING YOU IS SWEETER THAN EVER (VERSION 1; recorded 11/01/66 at Playhouse Theatre, London for "Saturday Club"; broadcast 11/05/66)
UK & FOREIGN: UKEP7 (M)
US & CANADA: US43 (M); US46 (M)

LULA LULA (recorded 1989; see "Hold My Hand")
UK & FOREIGN: UKCD5 (S-4:05); UK31 (S-4:05); UK32 (S-4:05); UK37 (S-4:04); UK38 (S-4:04); UK49 (S-4:04); UK70 (S-4:02); UK78 (S-4:02)
US & CANADA: none

MAYBE AFTER HE'S GONE (LIVE) (recorded 03/08/08 at Shepherd's Bush Empire, London)
UK & FOREIGN: UK77 (S)
US & CANADA: none

MOONDAY MORNING DANCE (recorded 1989)
UK & FOREIGN: UKCD5 (S); UK31 (S); UK32 (S); UK37 (S); UK38 (S); UK49 (S); UK70 (S); UK78 (S)
US & CANADA: none

NEW WORLD aka NEW WORLD (MY AMERICA) (recorded 1989)
UK & FOREIGN: UKCD5 (S1-4:45); UK31 (S1-4:45); UK32 (S1-4:45); UK37 (S2-4:21); UK38 (S2-4:21); UK49 (S2-4:21); UK70 (S2-4:21); UK78 (S2-4:21)
US & CANADA: none

NIGHTS ON FIRE (recorded 1989)
UK & FOREIGN: UKCD5 (S-3:34); UK31 (S-3:34); UK32 (S-3:34); UK37 (S-3:32); UK38 (S-3:32); UK49 (S-3:32); UK70 (S-3:32); UK78 (S-3:32)
US & CANADA: none

POP PROFILE (COLIN BLUNSTONE INTERVIEW) (recorded 01/10/66 at Bush House, London – only used for BBC Transcription Disc CN 445: "Pop Profile" with George Harrison)
UK & FOREIGN: none
US & CANADA: US43 (M); US46 (M)

RIP IT UP (recorded 02/26/65 at Studio 2, Aeolian Hall, London for "Top Gear" broadcast on 03/06/65 – also on BBC Transcription Service disc #20)
UK & FOREIGN: UK55 (M)
US & CANADA: US43 (M); US46 (M)

ROAD RUNNER (recorded 09/29/64 at Playhouse Theatre, London for "Saturday Club" broadcast on 10/03/64)
UK & FOREIGN: UK55 (M)
US & CANADA: US43 (M); US46 (M)

ROSE FOR EMILY, A (LIVE) (recorded 03/08/08 at Shepherd's Bush Empire, London)
UK & FOREIGN: UK77 (S)
US & CANADA: none

SHE'S COMING HOME (recorded 04/20/65 at Studio 5, Maida Vale, London for "Saturday Club" broadcast on 05/01/65 – only four members appeared at this session)
UK & FOREIGN: UK55 (M)
US & CANADA: US46 (M)

SHE'S NOT THERE (recorded 09/29/64 at Playhouse Theatre, London for "Saturday Club" broadcast on 10/03/64)
UK & FOREIGN: UK55 (M)
US & CANADA: US43 (M); US46 (M)

SHE'S NOT THERE (1977 re-recording)
UK & FOREIGN: UK46 (S); UK47 (S); UK48 (S); UK50 (S); UK52 (S); UK53 (S); UK59 (S); UK61 (S); UK64 (S); UK65 (S)
US & CANADA: US13 (S); US22 (S); US24 (S); US25 (S); US27 (S); US28 (S)

SHE'S NOT THERE (Autumn 1990 re-recording – The Point Studios, London)
UK & FOREIGN: UK35 (S); UK36 (S); UK45 (S); UK62 (S); UK66 (S); UK67 (S); UK69 (S); UK71 (S); UK72 (S)
US & CANADA: none

SHE'S NOT THERE (LIVE) (recorded 03/08/08 at Shepherd's Bush Empire, London)
<u>UK & FOREIGN:</u> UK77 (S)
<u>US & CANADA:</u> none

SITTING IN THE PARK (VERSION 1; recorded 01/08/66 at Paris Theatre, London for "Easy Beat" broadcast on 01/09/66)
<u>UK & FOREIGN:</u> UK55 (M)
<u>US & CANADA:</u> US46 (M)

SOULVILLE (recorded 02/02/65 at Playhouse Theatre, London for "Saturday Club" broadcast on 02/06/65 – also on BBC Transcription Service disc #17)
<u>UK & FOREIGN:</u> UK25 (M); UK26 (M); UK39 (M); UK43 (M); UK55 (M)
<u>US & CANADA:</u> US18 (M); US43 (M); US46 (M)

(INTRO aka INTERVIEW: BEFORE THEY WERE ZOMBIES; recorded 01/26/65)/ **TELL HER NO (VERSION 1;** recorded 01/26/65 at Playhouse Theatre, London for "Saturday Club" broadcast on 02/06/65 – also on BBC Transcription Service discs #13 and #20)
<u>UK & FOREIGN:</u> UK25 (M); UK26 (M); UK39 (M); UK43 (M); UK55 (M)
<u>US & CANADA:</u> US18 (M); US43 (M); US46 (M)

(INTERVIEW: DIFFERENT INSTRUMENTS; recorded 02/02/65)/ **TELL HER NO (VERSION 2** – acoustic piano version; recorded 02/02/65 at Playhouse Theatre, London for "Saturday Club" but used only on BBC Transcription Service disc #17)
<u>UK & FOREIGN:</u> UK55 (M)
<u>US & CANADA:</u> US43 (M); US46 (M)

TELL HER NO (VERSION 3; recorded 02/26/65 at Studio 2, Aeolian Hall, London for "Top Gear;" broadcast 03/06/65)
<u>UK & FOREIGN:</u> none
<u>US & CANADA:</u> US43 (M); US46 (M)

TELL HER NO (Autumn 1990 re-recording – The Point Studios, London)
<u>UK & FOREIGN:</u> UK35 (S); UK36 (S); UK45 (S); UK62 (S); UK66 (S); UK67 (S); UK69 (S); UK71 (S); UK72 (S)
<u>US & CANADA:</u> none

TELL HER NO (LIVE) (recorded 03/08/08 at Shepherd's Bush Empire, London)
<u>UK & FOREIGN:</u> UK77 (S)
<u>US & CANADA:</u> none

THIS OLD HEART OF MINE (IS WEAK FOR YOU) (VERSION 1; recorded 11/01/66 at Playhouse Theatre, London for "Saturday Club" broadcast on 11/05/66 – also on BBC Transcription Service discs #106 and #155)
<u>UK & FOREIGN:</u> UK25 (M); UK26 (M); UK39 (M); UK43 (M); UK55 (M)
<u>US & CANADA:</u> US18 (M); US43 (M); US46 (M)

THIS OLD HEART OF MINE (IS WEAK FOR YOU) (VERSION 2; recorded 10/10/67 at Studio 4, Maida Vale, London for Radio 1's "The David Symonds Show" broadcast during the week of 10/16/67 – 10/20/67)
<u>UK & FOREIGN:</u> UKEP7 (M)
<u>US & CANADA:</u> US43 (M); US46 (M)

THIS WILL BE OUR YEAR (LIVE) (recorded 03/08/08 at Shepherd's Bush Empire, London)
<u>UK & FOREIGN:</u> UK77 (S)
<u>US & CANADA:</u> none

TIME OF THE SEASON (1977 re-recording)
<u>UK & FOREIGN:</u> none
<u>US & CANADA:</u> CAN7" (S); US14 (S); US15 (S); US17 (S); US30 (S)

TIME OF THE SEASON (1989 re-recording)
<u>UK & FOREIGN:</u> UK31 (S); UK32 (S)
<u>US & CANADA:</u> none

TIME OF THE SEASON (Autumn 1990 re-recording – The Point Studios, London)
<u>UK & FOREIGN:</u> UK35 (S); UK36 (S); UK37 (S); UK38 (S); UK45 (S); UK49 (S); UK62 (S); UK66 (S); UK67 (S); UK69 (S); UK70 (S); UK71 (S); UK72 (S); UK78 (S)
<u>US & CANADA:</u> none

TIME OF THE SEASON (LIVE) (recorded 03/08/08 at Shepherd's Bush Empire, London)
<u>UK & FOREIGN:</u> UK77 (S)
<u>US & CANADA:</u> none

WEE BABY BLUES (incorrectly listed as "Early One Morning" on "Zombie Heaven" in 1997; recorded 09/29/64 at Playhouse Theatre, London for "Saturday Club" broadcast on 10/03/64)
UK & FOREIGN: UK55 (M)
US & CANADA: US43 (M); US46 (M)

(INTERVIEW: THE ZOMBIES FIND AMERICA; recorded 01/26/65)/ WHAT MORE CAN I DO (recorded 01/26/65 at Playhouse Theatre, London for
"Saturday Club" broadcast on 02/06/65 – also on BBC Transcription Service disc #13)
UK & FOREIGN: UK25 (M; track only); UK26 (M; track only); UK39 (M; track only); UK43 (M; track only); UK55 (M; track only)
US & CANADA: US18 (M; track only); US43 (M; interview and track); US46 (M; interview and track)

WHEN LOVE BREAKS DOWN (1990 – Livingstone Studios, London)
UK & FOREIGN: UK37 (S); UK38 (S); UK49 (S); UK70 (S); UK78 (S)
US & CANADA: none

WHEN MY BOAT COMES IN (1978 demo)
UK & FOREIGN: UK70 (S); UK78 (S)
US & CANADA: none

WHEN THE LOVELIGHT STARTS SHINING THROUGH HER EYES (recorded 09/20/65 at Studio 2, Aeolian Hall, London for "Saturday Club" broadcast on 10/02/65 – also on BBC Transcription Service disc #52)
UK & FOREIGN: UK25 (M); UK26 (M); UK39 (M); UK43 (M); UK55 (M)
US & CANADA: US18 (M); US43 (M); US46 (M)

(INTERVIEW: GLOBETROTTING ZOMBIES; recorded 09/20/65)/ WHENEVER YOU'RE READY (VERSION 2; recorded 09/20/65 at Studio 2, Aeolian Hall, London for "Saturday Club" broadcast on 10/02/65 – also on BBC Transcription Service disc #47)
UK & FOREIGN: UK25 (M); UK26 (M); UK39 (M); UK43 (M); UK55 (M)
US & CANADA: US18 (M); US43 (M); US46 (M)

(INTERVIEW; recorded 09/20/65)/ WILL YOU LOVE ME TOMORROW (VERSION 1; recorded 09/20/65 at Studio 2, Aeolian Hall, London for "Saturday Club" broadcast on 10/02/65 – also on BBC Transcription Service disc #52)
UK & FOREIGN: UK55 (M)
US & CANADA: US43 (M); US46 (M)

WILL YOU LOVE ME TOMORROW (VERSION 2; recorded 11/08/65 at Playhouse Theatre, London for "The Beat Show;" broadcast on 11/11/65 only in northern regions)
UK & FOREIGN: none
US & CANADA: US46 (M)

YOU MAKE ME FEEL GOOD (recorded 09/29/64 at Playhouse Theatre, London for "Saturday Club" broadcast on 10/03/64)
UK & FOREIGN: UK55 (M)
US & CANADA: US43 (M); US46 (M)

YOU MUST BELIEVE ME (VERSION 1; recorded 04/20/65 at Studio 5, Maida Vale, London for "Saturday Club" broadcast on 05/01/65 – only four members appeared at this session – also on BBC Transcription Service disc #47)
UK & FOREIGN: UK25 (M); UK26 (M); UK39 (M); UK43 (M); UK55 (M)
US & CANADA: US18 (M); US43 (M); US46 (M)

YOU MUST BELIEVE ME (VERSION 3; recorded 11/08/65 at Playhouse Theatre, London for "The Beat Show;" broadcast 11/11/65 only in northern regions)
UK & FOREIGN: none
US & CANADA: US46 (M)

ZOMBIES RADIO APPEARANCES
(* = track has been lost)

"Saturday Club" (10/03/64; BBC Light Programme): Road Runner; You Make Me Feel Good; Wee Baby Blues aka Early One Morning; She's Not There (#1); I'm Goin' Home (#1)* – recorded 09/29/64 at BBC Playhouse Theatre, London

"Easy Beat" (12/13/64; BBC Light Programme): Sticks And Stones; Summertime; She's Not There (#2) – this session recorded 12/09/64 at BBC Playhouse Theatre, London was lost

"Saturday Club" (02/06/65; BBC Light Programme): What More Can I Do; Tell Her No (#1); For You My Love – recorded 02/02/65 at BBC Playhouse Theatre, London

BBC TRANSCRIPTION DISC:
"Top Of The Pops" Show #13 (02/08/65) (LP; BBC Transcription Services): What More Can I Do; interview with Don Moss ("The Zombies Find America"); Tell Her No (#1); I'm Goin' Home (#2) – the first two music tracks were recorded 02/02/65 at BBC Playhouse Theatre, London for broadcast on the 02/06/65 edition of "Saturday Club," the interview was recorded 01/65 at BBC Transcription Services, London, and the last track was recorded 01/26/65 at BBC Transcription Services, London specifically for this disc

"Easy Beat" (02/21/65; BBC Light Programme): the tracks recorded 02/17/65 at Playhouse Theatre, London for this session are lost

BBC TRANSCRIPTION DISC:
"Top Of The Pops" Show #17 (02/24/65) (LP; BBC Transcription Services): For You My Love; interview with Brian Matthew ("Different Instruments"); Tell Her No (#2); Soulville – music tracks recorded 02/02/65 at BBC Paris Studio, London for broadcast on the 02/06/65 edition of "Saturday Club" ("For You My Love" only) and the 02/28/65 edition of "Easy Beat" (the other two tracks), and the interview was recorded 02/65 at BBC Transcription Services, London

"Easy Beat" (02/28/65; BBC Light Programme): Tell Her No (#2); Soulville – recorded 02/02/65 at BBC Paris Studio, London

"Top Gear" (03/06/65; BBC Light Programme): Rip It Up; Can't Nobody Love You; Tell Her No (#3) – recorded 02/26/65 at Studio 2, Aeolian Hall, London

BBC TRANSCRIPTION DISC:
"Top Of The Pops" Show #20 (03/17/65) (LP; BBC Transcription Services): Rip It Up; interview with Brian Matthew ("The Zombies Return To University"); Can't Nobody Love You; Tell Her No (#3) – music tracks recorded 02/26/65 at Studio 2, Aeolian Hall, London for broadcast on the 03/06/65 edition of "Top Gear," and the interview was recorded 02/65 at BBC Transcription Services, London

"Saturday Club" (05/01/65; BBC Light Programme): Just Out Of Reach; Just A Little Bit (#1); I Must Move; She's Coming Home – recorded 04/20/65 at Studio 5, Maida Vale, London

"Easy Beat" (09/12/65; BBC Light Programme): You Must Believe Me (#1); Whenever You're Ready (#1) – recorded 09/11/65 at BBC Paris Studio, London

BBC TRANSCRIPTION DISC:
"Top Of The Pops" Show #47 (09/22/65) (LP; BBC Transcription Services): You Must Believe Me (#1); interview with Brian Matthew; Whenever You're Ready (#1); Just Out Of Reach – the first two music tracks were recorded 09/11/65 at BBC Paris Studio, London for broadcast on the 09/12/65 edition of "Easy Beat," the interview was recorded 09/65 at BBC Transcription Services, London, and the last track was recorded 04/20/65 at Studio 5, Maida Vale, London for the 05/01/65 edition of "Saturday Club"

"Saturday Club" (10/02/65; BBC Light Programme): It's All Right; Will You Love Me Tomorrow (#1); When The Lovelight Starts Shining Through Her Eyes; If It Don't Work Out – recorded 09/20/65 at BBC Paris Studio, London

BBC TRANSCRIPTION DISC:
"Top Of The Pops" Show #52 (10/27/65) (LP; BBC Transcription Services): It's All Right; interview with Brian Matthew ("The Zombies Talk About America"); Will You Love Me Tomorrow (#1); When The Lovelight Starts Shining Through Her Eyes – all music tracks recorded 09/20/65 at BBC Paris Studio, London for the 10/02/65 edition of "Saturday Club," and the interview was recorded 09/65 at BBC Transcription Service, London

"The Beat Show" (11/11/65; BBC Light Programme): Just A Little Bit (#2); Will You Love Me Tomorrow (#2); You Must Believe Me (#2); Whenever You're Ready (#2)* – recorded 11/08/65 at BBC Playhouse Theatre, London for broadcast in northern regions only

"Easy Beat" (01/09/66; BBC Light Programme): Sitting In The Park (#1); Ain't That Loving You Baby*; Is This The Dream* – recorded 01/08/66 at BBC Paris Studio, London

"Dateline London" (02/14/66) (BBC Transcription Service): a Colin Blunstone interview recorded on this date which has been lost

BBC TRANSCRIPTION DISC:
"Pop Profile" (04/29/66) (7' 33 1/3 RPM; BBC Transcription Services CN 445): Colin Blunstone interview with Brian Matthew (on one side of disc) – recorded 01/66 at BBC Transcription Services, London; the other side of the record has an interview with George Harrison recorded on 11/30/65

"The Joe Loss Show" (10/14/66; BBC Light Programme): Goin' Out Of My Head (#1)*; Gotta Get A Hold On Myself (#1)* – transmitted live

"Easy Beat" (10/30/66; BBC Light Programme): Goin' Out Of My Head (#2); Gotta Get A Hold On Myself (#2) – recorded 10/29/66 at BBC Paris Studio, London

"Saturday Club" (11/05/66; BBC Light Programme): Gotta Get A Hold On Myself (#2); This Old Heart Of Mine (#1); Sitting In The Park (#2)* – recorded 11/01/66 at BBC Playhouse, London

BBC TRANSCRIPTION DISCS:
"Top Of The Pops" Show #106 (11/09/66) (LP; BBC Transcription Services): Gotta Get A Hold On Myself (#2); Colin Blunstone interview with Brian Matthew; Goin' Out Of My Head (#2); This Old Heart Of Mine (#1) – the first and last tracks were recorded 11/01/66 at BBC Playhouse Theatre, London for broadcast on the 11/05/66 edition of "Saturday Club," the interview was recorded 10/66 at BBC Transcription Services in London, and the third track was recorded 10/29/66 at BBC Paris Studio, London for broadcast on the 10/30/66 edition of "Easy Beat"

"Top Of The Pops" Show #155 (10/18/67) (LP; BBC Transcription Services): This Old Heart Of Mine (#2); Friends Of Mine; The Look Of Love – recorded 10/10/67 at Studio 4, Maida Vale, London for broadcast on the 10/20/67 edition of "The David Symonds Show"

"The David Symonds Show" (10/20/67; BBC Radio One): Friends Of Mine; The Look Of Love; This Old Heart Of Mine (#2) – recorded 10/10/67 at Studio 4, Maida Vale, London

"The Pete Brady Show (Swingalong)" (10/21/67 – 10/27/67; BBC Radio One): Loving You Is Sweeter Than Ever (#1); Care Of Cell 44 (#1); This Old Heart Of Mine (#3)* – recorded 10/11/67 at Studio 2, Aeolian Hall, London

"Pop North" (11/27/67; BBC Radio One): Care Of Cell 44 (#2)*; Goin' Out Of My Head (#4)*; This Old Heart Of Mine (#4)* – recorded 11/20/67 at BBC Playhouse Theatre, London

"Monday, Monday" (11/27/67; BBC Radio One): Loving You Is Sweeter Than Ever (#2)*; Care Of Cell 44 (#3)*; The Monkey Time*; Since I Lost My Baby*; Say You Don't Mind* –recorded 11/16/67 at Studio 2, Aeolian Hall, London

"Jimmy Young" (12/11/67 – 12/15/67): Care Of Cell 44 (#4)* – recorded 11/12/67 at Studio 4, Maida Vale, London

"Pete Brady" (12/16/67 and 12/18/67 – 12/22/67): Care Of Cell 44 (#4)* – recorded 11/12/67 at Studio 4, Maida Vale, London

"The Kenny Everett Show" (04/21/68; BBC Radio One): Kenny Everett Interview with Rod Argent and Chris White; Jingle Medley – recorded 04/68 at BBC Broadcasting House, London

"Mastertapes – Series 1: The Zombies (The A-side)" (12/11/12; BBC Radio 4 FM): Colin, Rod and Chris White spoke to John Wilson about "Odessey And Oracle" and plaed some of the songs live – recorded 12/06/12 at BBC Maida Vale

"Mastertapes – Series 1: The Zombies (The B-side)" (12/17/12; BBC Radio 4 FM): Colin, Rod and Chris White spoke to John Wilson about "Odessey And Oracle," played some of the songs live, and answered audience questions

"Mastertapes" (05/27/13; BBC Radio 6 Music): repeat of 12/11/12 show

ZOMBIES TELEVISION, FILM, AND VIDEO APPEARANCES
(television broadcasts list the first broadcast dates and networks; films/videos list just the first release dates)

"Ready, Steady, Go!" (07/31/64; UK Associated-Rediffusion): She's Not There – filmed at Kingsway ATV House, London

"Top Of The Pops" (08/05/64; BBC One): filmed at BBC Studios, Dickenson Road, Manchester

"The Cool Spot" (08/11/64; BBC One): filmed 08/09/64 at Nottingham Ice Rink, Nottingham, UK

"3-Go-Round" (08/12/64; UK Southern TV): filmed in Southampton

"Ad Lib Club" (08/24/64): photos for the Queen

"Top Of The Pops" (08/26/64; BBC One): filmed live at BBC Studios, Dickenson Road, Manchester

"Top Of The Pops" (09/02/64; BBC One): a repeat of the 08/26/64 performance

"Ready, Steady, Go!" (09/11/64; UK Associated-Rediffusion): filmed at Kingsway ATV House, London

"Dig This" (09/17/64; Scottish TV)

"Five O'Clock Club" (10/17/64; UK Associated-Rediffusion): filmed 10/02/64 at Associated-Rediffusion TV Studios, Wembley

"Thank Your Lucky Stars" (10/31/64; UK ITV): filmed 10/25/64 at Alpha TV Studios, Aston, UK

"Sweden/Norway Tour" (11/28/64 – 12/07/64; various undocumented programs): 6 days in Sweden (TV and radio), and 3 days in Norway (TV and radio)

"Open House" (12/19/64; BBC Two): Leave Me Be – filmed 12/13/64 at BBC TV Centre, Wood Lane, London

"Shindig!" (01/06/65; US NBC): She's Not There – filmed 12/23/64

"Hullabaloo" (01/12/65; US NBC): Tell Her No – filmed 01/06/65 in color at NBC Studios, Rockefeller Center, New York, New York (rehearsals took place the previous two days before filming)

"Shindig!" (01/27/65; US ABC): Tell Her No

"Scene At 6.30" (02/04/65; UK Granada TV): filmed at Granada TV Centre, Manchester

"Ready, Steady, Go!" (02/05/65; UK Associated-Rediffusion): filmed at Kingsway ATV House, London

"Thank Your Lucky Stars" (02/27/65; UK ITV): filmed 02/21/65 at Alpha TV Studios, Aston, UK

"The Red Skelton Show" (03/65 [unaired]; US CBS): filmed 11/24/64 in the UK, but not used on the program

"Top Of The Pops" (04/22/65; BBC One): transmitted live from BBC TV Studios, Dickenson Road, Manchester

"Thank Your Lucky Stars" (04/24/65; UK ITV): filmed 04/18/65 at Alpha TV Studios, Aston, UK

"Shindig!" (05/19/65; US ABC): It's Alright With Me; Summertime – recorded 05/65

"Where The Action Is" (06/29/65; US ABC): She's Coming Home; She's Not There; Tell Her No – taped on a beach

"Ready, Steady, Go!" (09/03/65; UK Associated-Rediffusion): Whenever You're Ready – filmed 07/09/65 and 07/10/65 at Kingsway ATV House, London

"Gadzooks!" (09/06/65; BBC Two): Whenever You're Ready; I'm On My Way, Great God (the latter with Lulu and The Small Faces) – transmitted live from Shepherd's Bush Theatre, London

"Shindig!" (09/08/65; US ABC): She's Not There; Whenever You're Ready – filmed in black and white in Los Angeles, California on 08/16/65 and 08/19/65 (rehearsal on 08/15/65)

"Thank Your Lucky Stars Summerspin" (09/25/65; UK ITV): filmed 09/19/65 at Alpha TV Studios, Aston, UK

"Bunny Lake Is Missing" (10/03/65): Just Out Of Reach; Nothing's Changed; Remember You; Come On Time (promo film only) – filmed 04/09/65

– 04/10/65 at Associated-Rediffusion TV Studios, Wembley, UK

"Five O'Clock Club" (12/28/65; UK Associated-Rediffusion)

"Juke Box Jury" (01/15/66; BBC One): Colin and concert promoter Tito Burns were guest judges

"Where The Action Is" (05/05/66; US ABC): Is This The Dream; Don't Go Away – filmed lip-synchs in England during early spring 1966

"Hippodrome" (07/12/66; US CBS/ UK ITV): Gotta Get A Hold On Myself – filmed in color 01/66 at the circus in Battersea Park, UK

"Nuorten tanssihetki" (11/09/66; Finnish Tesvisio)

"Dents De Lait, Dents De Loup" (01/11/67; French ORTF): This Old Heart Of Mine; Going To A Go-Go (hosted by Emperor Rosko) – filmed 10/30/66 at ORTF, Paris, France

"Deja View" (12/21/85; US syndicated): She's Not There (newly created video)

"Deja View (The Ultimate '60s Party Video)" (05/16/87): She's Not There – a UK VHS release: Video Collection VC 4017; also with newly created videos of songs by Procol Harum, Lesley Gore, The Hollies, Sly & The Family Stone, Don McLean, The Beach Boys, The Box Tops, The Temptations, and other artists

"Rock 'N' Roll: The Greatest Years – '64 Volume 1" (07/15/88): She's Not There – a UK VHS release: VideoArts VC 4055

"English Invasion: The 60's" (11/21/88): She's Not There – a US VHS release: Goodtimes Home Video VHS 8064

"Rock 'N' Roll: The Greatest Years – '64 Volume 1" (08/23/89): She's Not There – a Japanese laserdisc release: VideoArts VAL-3107

"The Return Of The Zombies" (02/90; German TV): various TV appearances for "The Return Of The Zombies" album

"Deja View (The Ultimate '60s Party Video)" (10/22/90): She's Not There – a US VHS release: Warner Home Video 012569 0025 3

"Shindig! Presents British Invasion Vol. 2" (10/14/92): Tell Her No – a US VHS release: Rhino Home Video RNVD 1460

"Bunny Lake Is Missing" (06/24/95; UK Channel 4)

"Hullabaloo Vol. 6" (03/26/96): She's Not There – a US VHS release: MPI Home Video MP6390

"Single Luck: The Zombies – She's Not There" (02/17/98; Dutch NOS): the story of early Zombies days and the song is presented with interview segments by Gus Dudgeon, Colin Blunstone, Hugh Grundy, Rod Argent, and Chris White – a similar program was done for "Tell Her No," but there is no evidence that it was broadcast

"Hullabaloo Vols. 5 & 6" (03/31/98): She's Not There – a US laserdisc release: MPI Home Video 030306 6389 6

"Hullabaloo: A 1960s Music Flashback – Volumes 5-8" (05/22/01): She's Not There – a US DVD release: MPI Home Video DVD6389

"60's All Stars Volume 1" (06/02/03): She's Not There – a German DVD release: TDK Mediactive TDKDVR60AS1

"Sixties Rock" (06/13/04): She's Not There – a US DVD release: Passport Video DVD-1575

"The Beat Era" (09/13/04): She's Not There – a German DVD release: Delta Music 94111

"Barend en Van Dorp" (11/08/04; Dutch RTL4): archival footage

"Bunny Lake Is Missing" (01/25/05): film plus trailer – a US DVD release: Sony Pictures 09466

"British Invasion 1960s And 1970s Rarities" (11/08/05): She's Not There – a US DVD release: Passport Video DVD-1631

"My Music: My Generation - The 60s" (03/01/08; US PBS): archival footage

"Odessey & Oracle {Revisited}" (04/28/09): a UK DVD release: Red House REDHDVD 1 – same contents as the CD release

"My Music: A '60s Pop Flashback – Hullabaloo" (03/02/13; US PBS): archival footage

"The Sixties: The British Invasion" (07/10/14; CNN+): She's Not There

"Bunny Lake Is Missing" (11/11/14): a US Blu-ray release: Columbia Pictures 811956020222 (multi-format disc limited edition of 3,000 units)

"Psychedelic Britannia" (10/23/15; BBC Four): archival footage

"Bunny Lake Is Missing" (02/27/17): a UK Blu-ray release: Power House Films PHIDFE008

"Time Of The Season" (04/19/17; YouTube): the official lyric video

"The 2019 Rock & Roll Hall Of Fame Induction Ceremony Red Carpet Live" (03/29/19; US HBO) – broadcast from Barclays Center, Brooklyn, New York

"The 2019 Rock And Roll Hall Of Fame Induction Ceremony" (04/27/19; US HBO)

"The Top Ten Revealed: Epic Songs Of '69" (05/17/20; US AXS TV): Time Of The Season

"Rock Legends: The British Invasion" (01/30/22; US AXS TV) – archival footage

"A Year In Music: 1965" (06/28/22; US AXS TV): She's Not There (archival footage)

ZOMBIES RECORDING PLACEMENTS IN TELEVISION, FILM, AND VIDEO

"They Call Us Misfits" (03/25/68): Leave Me Be – Swedish film documentary

"More American Graffiti" (08/03/79): She's Not There

"The Big Chill" (09/09/83): Time Of The Season

"1969" (11/18/88): Time Of The Season

"The Krays" (04/27/90): She's Not There

"The Crossing" (10/18/90): She's Not There

"Awakenings" (12/12/90): Time Of The Season

"Quantum Leap: The Play's The Thing – September 9, 1969" (01/08/92; US NBC): Time Of The Season (uncredited)

"Heartbeat: Outsiders" (05/29/92; UK ITV): She's Not There (uncredited)

"Beverly Hills, 90210: The Game Is Chicken" (01/06/93; US Fox): She's Not There

"Friends – The One Where Monica Gets A Roommate" (09/22/94; US NBC): Time Of The Season (uncredited)

"Beverly Hills, 90210: Coming Out, Getting Out, Going Out" (03/13/96; US Fox): Time Of The Season

"Friends: The One With The Flashback" (10/31/96; US NBC): Time Of The Season (uncredited)

"South Park: The Mexican Staring Frog Of Southern Sri Lanka" (06/10/98): Time Of The Season

"1968: The Year That Shaped A Generation" (07/27/98; US PBS): Time Of The Season

"The Simpsons: D'oh-in' In The Wind" (11/15/98; US Fox): Time Of The Season (uncredited)

"A Walk On The Moon" (01/29/99): Time Of The Season

"The '60s" (02/07/99 – 02/08/99; US NBC): Time Of The Season

"Backdoor" (10/06/00): She's Not There

"The Shaft" (05/11/01): She's Not There

"Will & Grace: Marry Me A Little More" (11/21/02; US NBC): Time Of The Season

"Shanghai Knights" (01/30/03): Time Of The Season

"Crossing Jordan: Strangled" (02/03/03; US NBC): She's Not There (uncredited)

"American Dreams: The Carpetbaggers" (04/06/03; US NBC): She's Not There (a group of actors is actually pretending the play the original 1964 track!)

"Skeppsholmen" (10/16/03; Swedish SVT): Time Of The Season

"Kill Bill: Vol. 2" (04/08/04): About Her (this Malcolm McLaren track has a slowed-down sample of "She's Not There")

"Angel Dust" (09/10/94): Time Of The Season

"Riding The Bullet" (10/15/04): Time Of The Season

"Barend en Van Dorp" (11/08/04; Dutch RTL4): She's Not There (uncredited)

"The Life Aquatic With Steve Zissou" (11/20/04): The Way I Feel Inside

"Dear Wendy" (01/22/05): She's Not There; A Rose For Emily; Time Of The Season; Woman; The Way I Feel Inside; Indication

"Cold Case: Revolution" (02/20/05; US CBS): Time Of The Season

"The Eight - HaShminiya BiF'ula" (10/06/05; Israeli Children Channel): About Her (see above)

"Toots" (04/27/06): Time Of The Season

"The Life Before Her Eyes" (09/08/07): She's Not There

Melanie Fiona: "Give It To Me Right" (02/28/09; promotional video): heavily samples "Time Of The Season"

"Being Erica: Under My Thumb" (11/10/09; BBC Worldwide): Give It To Me Right (see above)

"So You Think You Can Dance: The Top 10 Perform" (12/01/09; syndicated): Give It To Me Right (see above)

"The Romantics" (01/24/10): This Will Be Our Year

"United States Of Tara: Yes" (03/22/10; US Showtime): Care Of Cell 44 (uncredited)

"South Park: 201" (04/21/10; US Comedy Central): Time Of The Season

"The Debt" (09/04/10): She's Not There

"Game Boys" (09/09/10): Tell Her No

"Confessions Of A Brazilian Call Girl" (02/25/11): Time Of The Season

"Paranoia" (06/07/11): She's Not There

"True Blood: She's Not There" (06/26/11; HBO): She's Not There

"Any Questions For Ben?" (02/09/12): Time Of The Season

"The Conjuring" (06/08/13): Time Of The Season

"Mad Men: A Day's Work" (04/20/14; US AMC): This Will Be Our Year (uncredited)

"NCIS: So It Goes" (10/07/14; US CBS): Time Of The Season (uncredited)

"Stone Quackers" (10/27/14 – 07/03/15; US FXX): Care Of Cell 44 (the theme for the show on FXX only – the Fox broadcast did not use this track as the program's theme)

"The Stairs" (11/10/14): Time Of The Season

"Bronze" (01/22/15): Give It To Me Right (Melanie Fiona's recording)

"Girls: Close Up" (02/22/15; HBO): Can't Nobody Love You

"The Red Road: Graves" (04/09/15; US Sundance TV): Hung Up On A Dream (uncredited)

"Beauty And The Beast: Destined" (09/10/15; US The CW): This Will Be Our Year (uncredited)

"Good Girls Revolt: Pilot" (11/04/15; Amazon): Time Of The Season (uncredited)

"Master Of None: Mornings" (11/06/15; Netflix): You Make Me Feel Good

"Atop The Fourth Wall – Batman: Shadow Of The Bat #58" (04/25/16; syndicated): Time Of The Season

"Wolves At The Door" (10/21/16): She's Not There

"Hot Summer Nights" (03/13/17): This Will Be Our Year (uncredited)

"The Vietnam War: The History Of The World (April 1969 – May 1970)" (09/26/17; US PBS): Time Of The Season

"All The Money In The World" (12/18/17): Time Of The Season

"DC's Legends Of Tomorrow: Daddy Darhkest" (02/12/18; The CW): Time Of The Season (uncredited)

"Boundaries" (03/12/18): This Will Be Our Year

"Beat Shazam" (06/12/18; US Fox): Time Of The Season

"Endeavour: Muse" (06/24/18; UK ITV): Time Of The Season

"The Innocents: The Start Of Us" (08/24/18; Netflix): She's Not There

"The Marvelous Mrs. Maisel: All Alone" (12/05/18; Amazon Prime Video): This Will Be Our Year

"Little Dog: Round Thirteen" (02/21/19; CBC): Time Of The Season (uncredited)

"The Sara Cox Show" (05/11/19; UK ITV1): This Will Be Our Year (uncredited)

"Where'd You Go, Bernadette" (08/16/99): She's Not There

"Giri/Haji" (01/10/20; BBC One): Time Of The Season (uncredited)

"Can You Hear Me: Enfin" (01/13/20; Netflix): Time Of The Season

"Fortunate Son: Chimes Of Freedom" (01/15/20; CBC): Time Of The Season

"Locke & Key: Welcome To Matheson" (02/07/20; Netflix): Time Of The Season (uncredited)

"Schitt's Creek: Happy Ending" (04/07/20; US Fox): This Will Be Our Year

"9-1-1: The Taking Of Dispatch 9-1-1" (04/13/20; US Fox): She's Not There

"Hitmen: Birthday" (08/06/20; UK Peacock): Time Of The Season (uncredited)

"Chilling Adventures Of Sabrina: Chapter Twenty-Nine: The Eldritch Dark" (12/31/20; Netflix): Time Of The Season")

"Cruella" (05/18/21): Time Of The Season

"Titane" (07/13/21): She's Not There

"This Is Going To Hurt" (06/23/22; BBC One): The Way I Feel Inside

SONGS WITHOUT MUSIC

by

Rod Argent, Colin Blunstone
Duncan Browne & David Jones

Bongi Books

ZOMBIES RECORDINGS IN COMMERCIALS

Grolsch beer (1995): a Dutch promo 5" CD single of "Time Of The Season" and "She's Not There" (Patio Music P.M. 95141) was given away with beer purchases during their "Four Seasons" campaign
Tampax (1999): Time Of The Season
Nissan Tilda (2004): Time Of The Season
Fidelity Investments (2005): Time Of The Season
Sprite (2006): Time Of The Season
Crest toothpaste (2006): Time Of The Season
Fidelity Investments (2006): Time Of The Season (a different commercial than the above)
Nike (2006): This Will Be Our Year
Magners Irish Cider (2007): Time Of The Season; This Will Be Our Year
Greece (2007): Time Of The Season
Russia (2008): Time Of The Season
Magners Irish Cider (2010): Time Of The Season
Nissan (2011): Time Of The Season
Toyota RAV4 (2013; Russia): Time Of The Season
Coco Mademoiselle (2014): She's Not There – a commercial for this Chanel Paris perfume
Grolsch beer (2021): Time Of The Season
Chelsea FC (2021): Time Of The Season

SAMPLES/REMIXES OF ZOMBIES TRACKS

"Seasons Of Time" by THE LADBROKE GROOVERS (1997): Time Of The Season
"Look Me Up" by SPEK (2001): She's Not There
"The Other White Meat" by SOUL PURPOSE FEAT. IMMORTAL TECHNIQUE (2003): Beechwood Park
"Monsieur Orange" by STARFLAM (2003): She's Not There
"About Her" by MALCOLM McLAREN (2004): She's Not There (used slowed-down extracts of the track)
"Who's Ya Daddy" by NECRO (2005): Time Of The Season
"The Way I Feel Inside" by VILE EVILS (2008): The Way I Feel Inside – in addition to the YouTube video edit, six download-only remixes of the track were offered by the dPulse label on 06/24/08: the standard remix; Radio Edit; Trippy Arrangement Mix; Arena Version; 3kStatic Remix; Video Edit
"Give It To Me Right" by MELANIE FIONA (2009): Time Of The Season
"Rolling Stone" by SCHOOLBOY Q (2011): Time Of The Season
"Wstyd" (sic) by GRUBY MIELZKY (2012): Smokey Day
"Rhyme Or Reason" by EMINEM (2013): Time Of The Season
"Time Of The Season (Chelsea FC & Harvey Gunn)" Remix (06/03/21) (download-only): officially licensed remix

There are lots of remixes of "Time Of The Season," but very few of them have been officially licensed. Please visit YouTube.com if you're interested!

ZOMBIES & RELATED PUBLICATIONS

UK sheet music published 1969 by Verulam Music – She's Not There; Leave Me Be; Tell Her No; She's Coming; Is This The Dream; Indication; Time Of The Season
US sheet music published 1969 by Al Gallico Music – She's Not There; Tell Her No; She's Coming Home; Is This The Dream; Time Of The Season
US song book "The Zombies Dollar Book Of Songs" published 1965 by Hansen Publications Inc.
US song book published 1969 by Hal Leonard Music: Time Of The Season; This Will Be Our Year; She's Not There; Walking In The Sun (not issued until 1974!); I Love You; What More Can I Do; It's Alright With Me; Tell Her No; If It Don't Work Out; I Want Her She Wants Me; Beechwood Park; Brief Candles; Butcher's Tale (Western Front 1914); Friends Of Mine; Hung Up On A Dream; Care Of Cell 44
"Songs Without Music" – published 1976 by Bongi Books – poems by Colin Blunstone, Rod Argent, Duncan Browne, and David Jones (see previous page)
"Action Plus" – published May 1984 and edited by Paul Hippensteel, Robinson, Illinois 62454. Front cover and featured article on The Zombies.
"Then Play On" by Mike Ober – published 1992 by Promised Land Productions, and includes an interview with Chris White
"Time Of The Season: The Zombies Collector's Guide" by Greg Russo – originally published May 1999 by Crossfire Publications, Floral Park, New York. You're now reading the 5th edition published in August 2022! Previous edition info is on page 2.
US song book "The Zombies Greatest Hits" – published March 2000 by Warner Bros.
"The Zombies: Hung Up On A Dream" by Claes Johansen – published June 2001 by SPF Publications Ltd., London
"The Odessey: The Zombies In Words And Images" by Rod Argent, Colin Blunstone, Hugh Grundy and Chris White with Scott B. Bomar and Cindy DaSilva – published 03/30/17 by Reel Art Press/ BMG Books, London, England, and Tom Petty wrote the foreward
"My British Invasion" by Harold Bronson – published 05/09/17 by Rare Bird Books, Los Angeles, California, and includes a chapter on The Zombies

NOTE: A free, limited-edition scrapbook of Zombies-related photos and articles coordinated by Alec Palao was made available to "Zombie Heaven" purchasers that requested it.

THE ZOMBIES CONCERT LISTING
(all UK unless otherwise noted)

1962
The Zombies R&B
with Paul Arnold:
(April) St. Albans County Grammar School for Boys, St. Albans
        Pioneer Youth Club, St. Albans

The Zombies R&B
with Chris White:
(April to   Old Verulamians Club, St. Albans (numerous gigs)
December)   St. Akbans Girls Grammar School, St. Albans

The Zombies
12/15   County Grammar School, St. Albans
12/22   Garden City Liberal Club, Welwyn Garden City
12/28   Hilltop, Hatfield

1963
01/18   St. Mary's Youth Club, St. Albans
02/09   Waverley Club, St. Albans
02/23   Free Church Youth Club, Welwyn Garden City
03/02   Waverley Club, St. Albans
04/05   St. Mary's Youth Club, St. Albans
04/06   Mercer's, St. Albans
04/13   Waverley Club, St. Albans
05/19   New Greens Hall, St. Albans
05/26   Cavalier Hall, St. Albans
05/27   Town Hall, St. Albans
06/15   Co-Op Hall, St. Albans
07/05   Parish Youth Club, Hatfield
07/20   Ballito's Sports Ground, St. Albans (supporting The Laurie Jay Combo)
07/22   High School, Welwyn Garden City
09/18   Memorial Hall, Hatfield
09/20   Kings Langley (Ovaltine Talent Contest)
09/21   Park Street Village Hall, St. Albans
09/24   St. Andrew's Youth Club, Luton
10/01   New Greens Hall, St. Albans
10/05   St. Michaels Youth Club, Hatfield
10/12   Mercer's, St. Albans
10/20   Cavalier Hall, St. Albans
10/27   Colney Willows, London
11/02   College Of Further Education, St. Albans
11/03   New Hermitage Ballroom, Hitchin
11/07   Co-Op Hall, St. Albans
11/09   Drill Hall, Ware
11/16   Marconi's, St. Albans
11/20   St. Luke's Youth Club, Luton
11/23   Ballito's, St. Albans
12/07   County Grammar School, St. Albans
12/08   Colney Willows, London
12/14   Southwest Herts College Of Further Education, Watford
12/16   Girls Grammar School, St. Albans
12/19   Art School, St. Albans
12/20   College Of Further Education, St. Albans
12/23   Market Hall, St. Albans
12/31   C.O. Social, Flamstead

1964
01/03   Faulkner Hall, St. Albans
01/10   St. Johns Hall, Hemel Hempstead
01/17   Halfway Youth Club, Luton
01/18   Old Verulamians, St. Albans
01/24   Market Hall, St. Albans
01/25   Ballito's, St. Albans (with The Niteshades and The Planets)
02/01   Ballito's, St. Albans (with Cadillac & The Playboys and The Whispers)
02/14   College Of Further Education, Welwyn Garden City
02/15   Sphere Social Club, St. Albans (With The Nitehawks Dance Orchestra)
02/21   Faulkner Hall, St. Albans
02/22   Old Verulamians, St. Albans
02/28   Ovaltine Factory, Kings Langley
02/29   Coronation Hall, Kingston-upon-Thames (with The Cheynes)
03/07   Village Hall, Flamstead
03/08   Francis Bacon School, St. Albans
03/14   College Of Further Education, St. Albans
03/15   California Ballroom, Dunstable (audition)
03/20   Girls Grammar School, St. Albans
03/26   Market Hall, St. Albans
04/04   Old Verulamians, St. Albans
04/05   Town Hall, Watford (Herts Beat Contest heat)
04/11   Village Hall, Redbourn
04/15   College Of Technology, Hatfield
04/17   Faulkner Hall, St. Albans
04/18   St. Lukes Youth Club, Luton
04/19   Jackson's Studio, Rickmansworth (recorded demos of "Summertime" and "It's Alright With Me")
04/21   New Greens Youth Club, St. Albans (with The Didds)
05/02   Old Albanians, St. Albans
05/09   Co-Op Hall, St. Albans
05/10   Town Hall, Watford (Herts Beat Contest final)
05/16   Old Verulamians, St. Albans
05/17   Ballito's, St. Albans
05/22   Breaks Youth Club, Hatfield
05/23   College Of Technology, Hatfield
05/24   Town Hall, Watford (with Billy J. Kramer & The Dakotas, Diane & The Londoners, The Shifters, The League Of Gentlemen, and The Ancient Britons)
05/29   Market Hall, St. Albans (with The Stormbreakers)
05/30   Ballito's, St. Albans (with Shane & The Shane Gang)
06/05   Colney Willows, London (with The Beachcombers)
06/06   Rickmansworth (afternoon show) **and** Old Verulamians, St. Albans (evening show)
06/13   College Of Further Education, St. Albans
06/18   Old Albanians, St. Albans (end of school)
06/20   Old Albanians, St. Albans
06/26   Market Hall, St. Albans
06/27   Old Verulamians, St. Albans
07/03   Market Hall, St. Albans
07/25   New Greens, St. Albans
07/31   Kingsway ATV House, London ("Ready, Steady, Go!")
08/01   Old Verulamians, St. Albans
08/02   Willows, London Colney
08/03   Botwell Youth Club, Hayes (first official professional gig)
08/05   BBC Studios, Manchester ("Top Of The Pops")
08/09   Ice Rink, Nottingham ("The Cool Spot"; broadcast on 08/11/64)
08/12   Southampton ("3-Go-Round")
08/21   Harbour Arena, Morecambe
08/22   Astoria, Rawtenstall
08/23   Futurist, Scarborough
08/24   Ad-Lib Club, London (photos for the Queen)
08/26   BBC TV Studios, Manchester (transmitted live on "Top Of The Pops")
08/28   Top Rank, Preston
08/29   Pavilion Gardens, Boston
08/30   Futurist, Scarborough

09/01	Lotus Ballroom, Forest Gate
09/02	Hermitage Ballroom, Hitchin (with The Hangmen)
09/03	Olympia, Reading
09/04	Hillside Ballroom, Hereford
09/05	Whitehall, East Grinstead (with The Orbits) **and** Club Noreik, Tottenham
09/07	Atlanta, Woking
09/09	Farnborough Town Hall, Farnborough
09/10	McIlroys, Swindon
09/11	ATV House Kingsway, London ("Ready Steady Go") **and** Carlton Club, Erdington (missed gig – after filming, the band got to Erdington [near Birmingham] too late and were pelted by bottles thrown by angry audience members)
09/12	Tyldesley Palace, Bury
09/13	Community Centre, Southall
09/14	Silver Blades, Liverpool
09/15	Lacarno, Montrose, Scotland
09/16	Kinema, Dunfermline, Scotland
09/17	Glasgow, Scotland ("Dig This")
09/18	Praith, Kirkaldy, Scotland
09/19	Corn Exchange, Haddington, Scotland
09/21	Tamworth
09/22	Nuneaton
09/23	Rialto, Liverpool
09/24	Southport
09/25	Oldhill, Birmingham
09/26	Atherstone
09/27	Twisted Wheel, Manchester
09/28	Altrincham and Warrington
09/29	BBC Playhouse Theatre, London (recording "Saturday Club"; broadcast 10/03/64) **and** Public Hall, Wallington
09/30	Corn Exchange, Stourbridge
10/01	Corn Exchange, Kidderminster
10/02	Associated-Rediffusion TV Studios, Wembley ("Five O'Clock Club") **and** California Ballroom, Dunstable (with The Escorts and James King & The Farinas)
10/03	Public Hall, Heacham
10/04	Hampstead Country Club, London
10/05	Bath Pavilion, Bath
10/06	High Wycombe Town Hall, High Wycombe
10/07	Corn Exchange, Bristol
10/08	Erdington
10/09	Ellesmere Port
10/10	Gainsborough
10/16	Regent Sound, London (demo session)

Package tour (10/17/64 – 11/23/64): The Zombies with The Searchers, Dionne Warwick, The Isley Brothers, Tony Sheverton, Alan Elsdon And The Voodoos, and Syd & Eddie

10/17	City Hall, Sheffield (2 shows: 6:10PM and 8:40PM)
10/18	Empire, Liverpool (2 shows: 5:40PM and 8:00PM)
10/19	ABC, Huddersfield (2 shows: 6:15PM and 8:30PM)
10/21	Odeon, Colchester (2 shows: 6:00PM and 8:25PM)
10/22	Odeon, Luton (2 shows: 6:30PM and 8:45PM)
10/23	Adelphi, Slough (2 shows: 6:30PM and 8:45PM)
10/24	Essoldo, Stoke (2 shows: 6:20PM and 8:30PM)
10/25	Alpha TV Studios, Aston ("Thank Your Lucky Stars"; broadcast 10/31) **and** Granada Woolwich, London (2 shows: 6:00PM and 8:30PM)
10/26	Gaumont, Taunton (2 shows: 6:25PM and 8:40PM)
10/27	Odeon, Exeter (2 shows: 6:15PM and 8:30PM)
10/28	ABC, Gloucester (2 shows: 6:15PM and 8:30PM)
10/29	Gaumont, Worcester (2 shows: 6:00PM and 8:30PM)
10/30	Granada, Maidstone (2 shows: 6:20PM and 8:30PM)
10/31	Winter Gardens, Bournemouth (2 shows)
11/01	Guildhall, Portsmouth (2 shows)
11/03	Regal, Cambridge (2 shows: 6:15PM and 8:30PM)
11/04	Regal, Leeds (2 shows: 6:20PM and 8:40PM)
11/05	ABC, Kingston (2 shows: 6:45PM and 9:00PM)
11/06	ABC, Chester (2 shows: 6:15PM and 8:30PM)
11/07	Gaumont, Doncaster (2 shows: 6:15PM and 8:30PM)
11/08	Odeon, Stockton (2 shows: 6:15PM and 8:30PM)
11/09	Odeon, Glasgow, Scotland (2 shows: 6:45PM and 9:00PM)
11/10	ABC, Chesterfield (2 shows: 6:10PM and 8:25PM)
11/11	ABC, Cleethorpes (2 shows: 6:15PM and 8:30PM)
11/12	Odeon, Birmingham (2 shows: 6:45PM and 9:00PM)
11/13	East Ham Granada, London (2 shows: 7:00PM and 9:10PM)
11/14	Theatre Royal, Norwich (2 shows: 6:20PM and 8:30PM)
11/15	Coventry Theatre, Coventry (2 shows: 6:00PM and 8:30PM)
11/16	Odeon, Nottingham (2 shows: 6:15PM and 8:30PM)
11/17	Colston Hall, Bristol (2 shows)
11/18	ABC, Croydon (2 shows: 6:45PM and 9:00PM)
11/19	Essoldo, Tunbridge Wells (2 shows: 6:20PM and 8:30PM)
11/20	Essoldo, Cannock (2 shows: 6:20PM and 8:30PM)
11/21	Newcastle City Hall, Newcastle (2 shows: 6:30PM and 8:45PM)
11/23	Odeon, Manchester (2 shows: 6:15PM and 8:45PM)
11/24	London (filming "The Red Skelton Show")
11/27	ATV House Kingsway, London ("Ready, Steady, Go!")
11/28	Trondheim, Norway (Scandinavian tour begins)
11/29	Norway
11/30-12/01	Sweden
12/02	Stockholm, Sweden
12/03-05	Sweden
12/06	Finland
12/07	Oslo, Norway
12/08	Denmark
12/13	BBC Television Centre, London ("Open House")
12/14	"Easy Beat" broadcast
12/18	Maple Ballroom, Northampton (with The Berkeley Squares)
12/19	Imperial Ballroom, Nelson

"Murray The K's Big Holiday Show" (12/25/64 – 01/03/65): The Zombies with Chuck Jackson, Ben E. King And The Drifters, The Shirelles, The Shangri-Las, Patti Labelle And The Bluebelles, The Nashville Teens, The Hullabaloos, and The Vibrations. The Brooklyn Fox shows were rehearsed on 12/24/64. Every day except for Sundays, 5 performances were given, and on 12/27/64 and 01/03/65, 6 performances took place.

12/25-31	Fox Theatre, Brooklyn, New York, USA

1965

01/01-03	Fox Theatre, Brooklyn, New York, USA
01/04-06	"Hullabaloo" (rehearsals on 01/04/65 and 01/05/65, with taping on 01/06/65; broadcast 01/12/65)
01/17	Agincourt Ballroom, Camberley
01/23	Dreamland Ballroom, Margate (with The Dolphins)
01/26	BBC Playhouse Theatre, London ("Saturday Club")
02/02	BBC Playhouse Theatre, London ("Saturday Club")
02/04	Granada TV Centre, Manchester ("Scene At 6.30")
02/05	ATV House Kingsway, London ("Ready, Steady, Go!")
02/06	Boston Gliderdrome Starlight Ballroom, Boston (with Johnny B. Great & The Quotations and Mal Ryder & The Spirits)
02/07	Droitwich
02/09	Glen Ballroom, Llanelli, Wales
02/12	Town Hall, Leamington Spa
02/13	Dudley

02/14	Agincourt Ballroom, Camberley
02/16	Assembly Rooms, Tunbridge Wells
02/17	BBC Playhouse Theatre, London ("Easy Beat"; broadcast 02/21/65 and 02/28/65)
02/18	Kidderminster
02/19	Trentham Gardens, Stoke
02/20	College Of Further Education, St. Albans
02/21	Alpha TV Studios, Aston ("Thank Your Lucky Stars"; broadcast 02/27/65)
02/24	Corn Exchange, Bristol
02/25	Pier Pavilion, Worthing
02/26	BBC Aeolian 2 Studios, London ("Top Gear"; broadcast 03/06/65) **and** Gravesend
02/27	Town Hall, Peterborough
02/28	Sussex Downs, Hassocks (with The Shades)
03/01	Pavilion, Bath
03/03	St. Michael's Centre, Sydenham
03/05	Loughborough and Leicester
03/06	Town Hall, Redhill
03/07	Working Mens Club, Kettering
03/09	Tower Of London, London (filming for Dick Clark: "Where The Action Is")
03/11	Garrison Club, London
03/12	Cromwellian Club, London (Otto Preminger audition)
03/13	March Hall, Cambridge
03/14	King David Suite, London
03/16	Aldershot
03/19	Paul Atkinson's house, At. Albans (his 19th birthday party)
03/20	Rawtenstall
03/21	Empire Pool, Wembley (10th Record Star Show, in aid of The Stars Organisation For Spastics; with Billy J. Kramer & The Dakotas, Elkie Brooks & The Master Sounds, The Fourmost, Kenny Ball & His Jazzmen, Long John Baldry & The Hoochie Coochie Men, Lonnie Donegan, Lulu & The Luvvers, The Merseybeats, P.J. Proby, The Pretty Things, Sandie Shaw, The Paramounts, The Searchers, The Seekers, Them, Tom Jones & The Squires, and Tommy Quickly)

Package tour (03/25/65 – 04/10/65): The Zombies with Dusty Springfield, The Searchers, Bobby Vee, Tony Jackson And The Vibrations, Heinz And The Wild Boys, Echoes, and compere George Meaton. The concert on 04/06/65 was not part of the tour.

03/25	Odeon, Stockton (2 shows: 6:15PM and 8:30PM)
03/26	City Hall, Newcastle (2 shows: 6:15PM and 8:40PM)
03/27	Gaumont, Doncaster (2 shows: 6:15PM and 8:30PM)
03/28	Empire, Liverpool (2 shows: 5:40PM and 8:00PM)
03/30	Wallington
04/01	Gaumont, Worcester (2 shows: 6:15PM and 8:45PM)
04/02	Town Hall, Birmingham (2 shows: 6:30PM and 8:45PM)
04/03	Gaumont, Bradford (2 shows: 6:15PM and 8:40PM)
04/04	Colston Hall, Bristol (2 shows: 5:40PM and 8:00PM)
04/06	St. Joseph's Hall, Basingstoke (with Men Friday)
04/07	Odeon, Colchester (2 shows: 6:00PM and 8:25PM)
04/08	City Hall, Salisbury (2 shows: 6:15PM and 8:40PM)
04/09-10	Associated-Rediffusion TV Studios, Wembley ("Bunny Lake Is Missing" rehearsal and filming)
04/09	Odeon, Taunton (2 shows: 6:25PM and 8:40PM – The Zombies missed these shows)
04/10	Sophia Gardens, Cardiff, Wales (2 shows: 6:15PM and 8:45PM)
04/15	Adelphi, West Bromwich and Carlton, Erdington (with The Couriers)
04/18	Alpha TV Studios, Aston ("Thank Your Lucky Stars"; broadcast 04/24/65)
04/19	Top Spot, Ross-On-Wye (with The Solents)
04/20	BBC Maida Vale Studio 5, London ("Saturday Club'; broadcast 05/01/65)
04/22	BBC TV Studios, Manchester (live "Top Of The Pops" broadcast)

Package tour: "Dick Clark's Caravan Of Stars 1965" (04/24/65 – 06/02/65): The Zombies with Dee Dee Sharp, Jewel Akins, and The Shangri-Las

04/24	Evansville, Indiana, USA
04/25	Municipal Auditorium, Nashville, Tennessee, USA
04/26	Murray State College, Murray, Kentucky, USA
04/27	Memphis Coliseum, Memphis, Tennessee, USA
04/28	Eau Claire, Wisconsin, USA
04/29	Pershing Auditorium, Lincoln, Nebraska, USA
04/30	Sioux City, Iowa, USA
05/01	City Auditorium, St. Joseph, Missouri, USA
05/02	Civic Auditorium Arena, Omaha, Nebraska, USA
05/03	Memorial Hall, Salina, Kansas, USA
05/04	Lawrence Stadium, Lawrence, Kansas, USA
05/05	The Pit, Bronco Bowl, Dallas, Texas, USA
05/06	Austin, Texas, USA
05/07	Heart Of Texas Coliseum, Waco, Texas, USA
05/08	Municipal Auditorium, San Antonio, Texas, USA
05/09	Music Hall, Houston, Texas, USA
05/10	San Angelo, Texas, USA
05/11	Fort Worth, Texas, USA
05/12	Odessa, Texas, USA (after one hour rehearsal time, Jerry Allison of The Crickets replaced Hugh Grundy, who had food poisoning while eating in Odessa)
05/13	Municipal Auditorium, Amarillo, Texas, USA
05/14	Denver, Colorado, USA
05/15	The Lagoon, Farmington, Utah, USA
05/16	Convention Center, Las Vegas, Nevada, USA
05/17	Melodyland, Anaheim, California, USA (2 shows: 5:00PM and 9:00PM)
05/18	Santa Barbara, California, USA
05/19	Centennial Coliseum, Reno, Nevada, USA
05/20	Merced, California, USA
05/21	Memorial Auditorium, Sacramento, California, USA
05/22	Armory, Salem, Oregon, USA
05/23	Spokane, Washington, USA
05/26	Vancouver, British Columbia, Canada
05/27	Calgary, Alberta, Canada
05/28	Edmonton, Alberta, Canada
05/29	Regina, Saskatchewan, Canada
05/30	Minot, South Dakota, USA
05/31	Grafton, North Dakota, USA
06/01	Winnipeg, Manitoba, Canada
06/02	Minneapolis, Minnesota, USA
06/27-28	La Locomotif, Paris, France

US tour with The Searchers (07/15/65 – 08/15/65):

07/15-17	McCormack Place, Chicago, Illinois, USA (also with The Kingsmen, and Chad & Jeremy, but Chad ended up performing with his wife Jill instead of Jeremy)
07/19	Municipal Auditorium, Nashville, Tennessee, USA (opening for The Beach Boys, with Ray Lynn also supporting)
07/21	Auditorium, Terre Haute, Indiana, USA
07/23	Coliseum, Montgomery, Alabama, USA (also with The Beach Boys, Del Shannon, and other bands)

07/24	Jacksonville Coliseum, Jacksonville, Florida, USA (two shows: 5PM and 9PM; The Beach Boys headlined with openers Lesley Gore, Del Shannon, The Shangri-Las, Del Reeves, Sam The Sham & The Pharaohs, and The Premieres)		transcription service interview with Brian Matthew)
07/25	Nora Mayo Hall, Winterhaven, Florida, USA	01/15	BBC TV Centre Studio 2, London (Colin and promoter Tito Burns appeared as guest judges on "Juke Box Jury")
07/26	Jai Alai Fronton, Orlando, Florida, USA	01/16	Whitehall, East Grinstead
07/27	Miami, Florida, USA	01/21	Westend Club, Coalville, Leicester (with The Ray King Soul Pact)
07/28	Municipal Auditorium, Pensacola, Florida, USA	02/10	Odeon, Leicester Square (UK premiere of "Bunny Lake Is Missing")
07/29	Municipal Auditorium, Panama City, Florida, USA	02/11	Cricketer's Inn, Southend (with The Orioles)
07/30	Fort Home Hesterley Armory, Tampa, Florida, USA	02/14	BBC Bush House, London (Colin recorded a "Dateline London" subscription service interview)
07/31	Municipal Auditorium, Columbus, Georgia, USA	02/19	Dreamland, Margate (with The Tribe)
08/01	Augusta, Georgia, USA	02/25	Miners Hall, Cinderford (with The Factotums)
08/04	Knoxville, Tennessee, USA	02/26	Brimingham School Of Advanced Technology, Birmingham
08/06	Norfolk, Virginia, USA (also with Tom Jones and Peter And Gordon)	04/08	Corn Exchange, Melton Mowbray
08/08	Charlotte, North Carolina, USA	04/09	Loughborough Town Hall, Loughborough
08/09	Arena, New Haven, Connecticut, USA	04/16	St. George's Ballroom, Hinckley
08/10	Armory, Burlington, Vermont, USA	05/30	Corn Exchange, Colchester (with Tommy Bishop And The Richochets and The Gatemouth)
08/11	Palace Auditorium, Biddeford, Maine, USA	06/10	Leeds University, Leeds
08/12	Boys Club, Piltsfield, Massachusetts, USA	06/11	St. Mary's College, Twickenham
08/13-15	Springlake Park, Oklahoma City, Oklahoma, USA	06/16	Birmingham University, Birmingham
08/16	ABC Television Center, Los Angeles, California, USA (filming "Shindig!"; broadcast 09/08/65 and 09/09/65)	06/17	Sussex University, Brighton
		06/18	California Ballroom, Dunstable
08/16-19	Whisky A Go-Go, West Hollywood, California, USA (with Johnny Rivers)	07/02	Birmingham University, Birmingham
		07/06	Brighton Box Club, Brighton (with The Who)
08/19	ABC Television Center, Los Angeles, California, USA (filming "Shindig!"; broadcast 09/08/65 and 09/09/65)	07/07	Locarno, Bristol (early show) and Byron, Greenford (late show; with 10 Boots)
08/30	St. Albans (Old Albanian Fete)	07/08	Southampton University, Southampton
09/01	Corn Exchange, Bristol	07/09	Fort Gardens, Gravesend
09/03	ATV House Kingsway, London ("Ready, Steady, Go!")	07/12	"Hippodrome" US TV broadcast
09/06	BBC TV Shepherds Bush Theatre, London (live filming of "Gadzooks!"; they performed "Whenever You're Ready" and joined Lulu and The Small Faces on the finale "I'm On My Way, Great God")	07/14	Byron, Greenford, West London (with Someone Else)
		07/20	Blue Lagoon, Newquay
		07/21	Princess Pavilion, Falmouth (with The Misfits)
		07/22	Winter Gardens, Penzance
09/11	BBC Playhouse Theatre, London (recorded "Easy Beat"; broadcast 09/12/65)	07/23	Beat Centre, Budleigh (with The New Law and Focus)
		07/24	Bridge Hotel, Looe
09/19	Alpha TV Studios, Aston (filmed "Thank Your Lucky Stars Summerspin"; broadcast 09/20/65)	08/06	Leas Cliff Hotel, Folkestone
		08/13	Chaul End Playing Field, Luton Boys Club, Luton
09/20	BBC Aeolian Studios, London (recorded "Saturday Club"; broadcast 10/02/65)	08/17	Pavilion, Hemel Hempstead (with Endevers Ltd.)
		08/19	The 7 Club, Wyle Cop, Shrewsbury
09/25	Bridlington	08/20	Victoria Cross Gallery, Wantage (with John Brown's Bodies)
09/26	Sunshine Floor, Tavern Club, Dereham (with Ricky Wilson and The Three Quarters)	10/14	BBC Playhouse Theatre, London (live recording of "The Joe Loss Show")
10/01	King's Lynn	10/15	Faculty Of Technology, Manchester (with Bread)
10/20	Stourbridge	10/28	Belgium
10/23	Redhill	10/29	Paris, France
10/28	Pier Pavilion, Worthing	10/30	"Dents De Lait Dents De Loup" TV filming in Paris, France (hosted by Emperor Rosko)
11/08	BBC Playhouse Theatre, Manchester (recorded "The Beat Show")	11/01	BBC Playhouse Theatre, London ("Saturday Club" recording; broadcast 11/05/66)
mid-Nov.	Swedish tour (6 days)		
11/20	Rhodes Centre, Bishop's Stortford (with Micky Jupp and The Orioles)	11/03	RAF Kenley, Kenley
		11/05	(start of Scandinavian tour)
11/22	Pavillion, Bath	11/20	(end of Scandinavian tour)
12/19	Warrington Sunday Club, Warrington (with The Klubs)	11/29	Mayfair Ballroom, Newcastle
12/23	Town Hall, Kidderminster (with The Apper Clause and The Jurymen)	12/02	Oxford University, Oxford
		12/03	Technical College, Bangor, Wales
12/28	Associated-Rediffusion TV Studios, Wembley (filmed "Five O'Clock Club")	12/07	Stonehouse Church Hall, Stonehouse
		12/09	Top Spot, Ross-on-Wye, Herefordshire (with The Insect)
1966		12/14	RCAT Student Union, Manchester (with Unit 4 Plus 2 and The Crestas)
01/03	Drill Hall, Dumfries, Scotland	12/16	Civic Hall, Consett
01/08	BBC Paris Studios, London (recorded tracks for "Easy Beat"; broadcast 01/09/66)	12/17	New Century Hall, Manchester (with The Signs and The Times)
01/10	BBC Bush House, London (Colin recorded a "Pop Profile"	12/19	Belfry, Sutton Coldfield

12/31	Town Hall, Birmingham (with The Searchers, Locomotive, and Longstack Humphries)		12/09	Teachers' Training College, Bingley

12/31   Town Hall, Birmingham (with The Searchers, Locomotive, and Longstack Humphries)

1967

01/07   Leicester College, Leicester
01/08   Wheatsheaf, Brandon (with The Bohemians)
01/27   Civic and Wulfrun Hall, Wolverhampton (with John Mayall's Bluesbreakers, Zoot Money & The Big Roll Band, The 'N' Betweens, The Savoy Jazz Band, and Ken Ingram's Jazz Band)
02/03   Southlands College, Wimbledon Common, Wimbledon, Southwest London
02/09   Pembroke Club, Chatham
02/17   Queen's Rink, West Hartlepool
02/18   Sheffield University, Sheffield
03/03-09   Araneta Coliseum, Cubao, Quezon City, Philippines (NOTE: The Zombies could not honor a 03/10/67 gig with The Move at Queen's College, Oxford)
03/12-14   Hong Kong
03/17   Plaza Restaurant, Makati, Philippines
03/18   The Nile Club, Manila, Philippines
03/19   El Dorado Club, Manila, Philippines (with The Crystals and The Dyna Souls)
03/25   Elm Hotel, Southend (with Sounds Around)
04/19   Students Union, Aberdeen, Scotland
04/21   Victoria Hall, Edinburgh, Scotland
04/22   Carioca Club, Auchinleck, Scotland
04/23   Kinema, Dunfermline, Scotland
05/12   Northampton Hall, Northampton
05/26   Avon Club, Whitehaven
05/27   Lincoln College, Oxford
06/10   Blue Lagoon, Newquay (with Jaguars)
06/18   Saville Theatre, London (did not take place)
06/30   Highbury Technical College, Cosham
07/12   De Valance Ballroom, Tenby, Wales
07/15   Hinckley Football Ground, Hinckley (with The Kinks and Whispering Jack Smith)
07/22   Leas Cliff Hall, Folkestone
09/30   West Midland Training College, Walsall
10/07   City Of Leeds Training College, Leeds
10/09   Top Rank, Cardiff, Wales (with The Searchers, Lucas with The Mike Cotton Sound, and Herbie Goins And The Night-Timers)
10/10   BBC Maida Vale Studio 4, London ("David Symonds Show" recording of "Friends Of Mine" and "The Look Of Love")
10/11   BBC Aeolian 2 Studios, London (recording of "Pete Brady Show")
10/13   High Hall, Edgbaston
10/14   Leicester University, Leicester
10/16   "David Symonds Show"
10/20   Harper Adams Agricultural College, Newport, Wales
10/21   recording "The Pete Brady Show" (broadcast on 10/27/67); **and** Aston University, Birmingham
10/28   Leeds University Union, Leeds
10/12   BBC Maida Vale Studio 4, London (radio programs: "Jimmy Young Show" and "Pete Brady Show")
11/16   BBC Aeolian 2 Studios, London (recording of "Monday, Monday"; broadcast 11/27/67)
11/20   BBC Playhouse Theatre, London (recording of "Pop North"; broadcast 11/23/67)
12/01   Carnatic Hall, Liverpool
12/02   Faculty of Tech, Manchester
12/03   Embassy Rooms, Sale, Greater Manchester
12/08   Braintree Institute, Braintree (with The Lloyde and Ministry Of Sound)
12/09   Teachers' Training College, Bingley
12/11   Didsbury College Of Education, Manchester
12/12   Keele University, Keele
12/14   Assembly Hall, Worthing (cancelled)
12/15   College Of Further Education, Ashton-Under-Lyne (cancelled)
12/20   Denbeigh Tech College, Wrexham, Wales
12/23   Hastings Pier, Hastings (cancelled; Pinkerton's Colours replaced The Zombies)

1997

11/25   Jazz Café, London (all five Zombies performed "She's Not There" and "Time Of The Season")

2004

01/27   "Time Of The Season Concert," House Of Blues, Los Angeles, California (benefit for Paul Atkinson at which all five Zombies performed "She's Not There" and "Time Of The Season"; Colin and Rod played "I Want To Fly," and Brian Wilson and his band performed "Don't Worry Baby")

The following dates are for the four surviving Zombies playing "Odessey And Oracle" in its entirety as part of concerts with the Zombies touring group assembled by Rod Argent and Colin Blunstone:

2008

"Odessey And Oracle" 40th Anniversary tour (03/02/08 – 03/09/08):

03/02-03   The Stables, Wavendon (warm-up gigs for the Shepherd's Bush concerts)
03/07-09   Shepherd's Bush Empire, London (03/08/08 concert filmed and recorded for release; with guitarist Keith Airey, keyboardist Darian Sahanaja, The Shotgun Horns [on "This Will Be Our Year"], Jim Rodford on backing vocals and percussion, Steve Rodford on percussion, and backing vocalist Vivienne Boucherat)

2009

"Odessey And Oracle And Beyond" tour (04/21/09 – 04/25/09):

04/21   O2 ABC, Glasgow, Scotland
04/23   Bristol Beacon, Bristol
04/24   The Bridgewater Hall, Manchester
04/25   HMV Hammersmith Apollo, London

2011

05/27   O2 Shepherd's Bush Empire, London (Hugh Grundy and Chris White guested with the Zombies touring band)

2015

US "Odessey And Oracle Tour 2015" (09/30/15 – 10/30/15):

09/30   Majestic Theatre, Dallas, Texas, USA
10/01   Paramount Theatre, Austin, Texas, USA
10/03   Provincetown Town Hall, Provincetown, Massachusetts, USA
10/06   The Wilbur Theatre, Boston, Massachusetts, USA
10/08   Lincoln Theatre, Washington, District of Columbia, USA
10/09   The Society for Ethical Culture, New York, New York, USA
10/10   Park Theatre at RI Center for the Performing Arts, Cranston, Rhode Island, USA
10/11   Keswick Theatre, Glenside, Pennsylvania, USA
10/13   The Ridgefield Playhouse, Ridgefield, Connecticut, USA
10/14   Carnegie Music Hall of Homestead, Munhall, Pennsylvania, USA
10/15   Kent Stage, Kent, Ohio, USA

10/16	Star Plaza Theatre, Merrillville, Indiana, USA		06/05	BBC Wogan House Studios, London (recording for "Lauren Laverne" program)
10/17	South Milwaukee Performing Arts Center, South Milwaukee, Wisconsin, USA		06/29	Music In The Gardens, Sheffield Botanical Gardens, South Yorkshire
10/19	Paramount Theatre, Denver, Colorado, USA		07/06	Festival d'été de Québec 2017, Parc de la Francophonie, Quebec City, Quebec, Canada
10/21	Benaroya Hall, Seattle, Washington, USA		07/08	Casino Nova Scotia, Halifax, Nova Scotia, Canada
10/22	Revolution Hall, Portland, Oregon, USA		07/11	RBC Royal Bank Bluesfest 2017, LeBreton Flats Park, Ottawa, Ontario, Canada (with many others)
10/24	Saban Theater, Beverly Hills, California, USA		07/14	Bergen Performing Arts Center, Englewood, New Jersey, USA (with Don DiLego)
10/25	Crest Theatre, Sacramento, California, USA		07/15	Infinity Music Hall & Bistro, Hartford, Connecticut, USA (with Don DiLego)
10/26	Cascade Theatre, Redding, California, USA		07/16	Great South Bay Music Festival 2017, Shorefront Park, Patchogue, New York, USA (with many others)
10/27	The Fillmore, San Francisco, California, USA		07/17	The Birchmere, Alexandria, Virginia, USA (with Don DiLego)
			07/18	Quebec Summer Music Festival 2017, Quebec City, Quebec, Canada
			09/29	London Palladium, London

2017

"Odessey And Oracle 50th Anniversary Tour" (03/10/17 – 09/29/17):

03/10	Scottish Rite Auditorium, Collingswood, New Jersey, USA
03/13	Rockefeller Center, New York, New York, USA
03/17	Keswick Theatre, Glenside, Pennsylvania, USA
03/18	Penn's Peak, Jim Thorpe, Pennsylvania, USA
03/20	Carolina Theatre, Durham, North Carolina, USA
03/21	Sandler Center for the Performing Arts, Virginia Beach, Virginia, USA
03/23	9:30 Club, Washington, District of Columbia, USA
03/24	H. Ric Luhrs Performing Arts Center, Shippensburg, Pennsylvania, USA
03/25	The Town Hall, New York, New York, USA
03/28	The Wilbur Theatre, Boston, Massachusetts, USA
03/30	Ridgefield Playhouse, Ridgefield, Connecticut, USA
03/31	Calvin Theatre, Northampton, Massachusetts, USA
04/01	Le National, Montreal, Quebec, Canada
04/02	Danforth Music Hall, Toronto, Ontario, Canada
04/04	Royal Oak Music Theatre, Royal Oak, Michigan, USA
04/05	Lorain Palace Theatre, Lorain, Ohio, USA
04/07	Golden Nugget Biloxi Hotel & Casino, Biloxi, Mississippi, USA
04/08	Variety Playhouse, Atlanta, Georgia, USA
04/09	James K. Polk Theater at Tennessee Performing Arts Center, Nashville, Tennessee, USA
04/11	Sangamon Auditorium, Springfield, Illinois, USA
04/13-14	Thalia Hall, Chicago, Illinois, USA
04/15	Barrymore Theatre, Madison, Wisconsin, USA
04/17	First Avenue, Minneapolis, Minnesota, USA
04/18	Club Regent Casino, Winnipeg, Manitoba, Canada
04/21	Commodore Ballroom, Vancouver, British Columbia, Canada
04/22	Showbox, Seattle, Washington, USA
04/23	Aladdin Theater, Portland, Oregon, USA
04/25	The UC Theatre Taube Family Music Hall, Berkeley, California, USA
04/27	Clive Davis Theater at the Grammy Museum, Los Angeles, California, USA
04/28	Stagecoach 2017, Empire Polo Club, Indio, California, USA
04/29	The Theatre at Ace Hotel, Los Angeles, California, USA
05/01	Warner Bros. Studios, Burbank, California, USA
05/04	The Heights Theater, Houston, Texas, USA
05/06	aTrolla Music Festival, Reunion Tower, Dallas, Texas, USA (with many others)
05/08	The Ridgefield Playhouse, Ridgefield, Connecticut, USA
05/09	The Wilbur Theatre, Boston, Massachusetts, USA
05/10	Calvin Theatre, Northampton, Massachusetts, USA
05/27	GetMAD! Festival 2017, But (sic), Madrid, Spain (with many others)
05/29	Forum de Barcelona, Barcelona, Spain (cancelled)
05/30	Zentral, Pamplona, Spain
06/01	Primavera Sound 2017, Auditori Forum, Barcelona, Spain (with many others)
06/04	Stables Theatre, Wavendon

2018

"Odessey And Oracle 50th Anniversary Finale Tour" (01/02/18 – 03/25/18):

01/02-07	Moody Blues Cruise 2018, Celebrity Eclipse, Miami, Florida, USA (with many others)
01/08	Key West Theater, Key West, Florida, USA
01/09	The Parker Playhouse, Fort Lauderdale, Florida, USA
01/10	The Plaza Theatre, Orlando, Florida, USA
01/11	Capitol Theatre, Clearwater, Florida, USA
01/12	Ponte Vedra Concert Hall, Ponte Vedra Beach, Florida, USA
01/14	30A Songwriter's Festival 2018, Grand Boulevard Main Stage, Miramar Beach, Florida, USA (with many others)

2019

03/29	34th Annual Rock And Roll Hall Of Fame Induction Ceremony, Barclays Center, Brooklyn, New York, USA

US tour: Something Great From '68 (including all of "Odessey And Oracle") (with Brian Wilson, Al Jardine, and Blondie Chaplin) (08/31/18 – 09/29/19):

08/31	The Joint at Hard Rock Hotel, Las Vegas, Nevada, USA
09/01	Fantasy Springs Resort Casino, Indio, California, USA
09/06	Comerica Theatre, Phoenix, Arizona, USA
09/07	Starlight Theater, Pala, California, USA
09/08	Arlington Theatre, Santa Barbara, California, USA
09/12	Greek Theatre, Los Angeles, California, USA
09/13	Fox Theater, Oakland, California, USA
09/14	Ironstone Amphitheatre, Murphys, California, USA
09/16	Paramount Theatre, Seattle, Washington, USA
09/17	Arlene Schnitzer Concert Hall, Portland, Oregon, USA
09/19	Sandy Amphitheater, Sandy City, Utah, USA
09/20	Paramount Theatre, Denver, Colorado, USA
09/22	Riverside Theater, Milwaukee, Wisconsin, USA
09/23	Taft Theatre, Cincinnati, Ohio, USA
09/24	Royal Oak Music Theatre, Royal Oak, Michigan, USA
09/26	Beacon Theatre, New York, New York, USA
09/27	Palace Theater, Waterbury, Connecticut, USA
09/28	Tower Theatre, Upper Darby, Pennsylvania, USA
09/29	Robert E. Parilla Performing Arts Center, Rockville, Maryland, USA

THE SOLO RECORDINGS OF THE ZOMBIES

ROD ARGENT

(All recordings by Argent, except: * = as by Rod Argent; ** = as by San José featuring Rodriguez Argentina; *** = as by Barbara Thompson and Rod Argent; **** = as by Shadowshow; ***** = as by Rod Argent and John Dankworth; ****** = as by Silsoe; ******* = as by Robert Howes & Rod Argent; ******** = as by Rod Argent & Peter Van Hooke featuring Clem Clempson; ********* = as by Rod Argent and Peter Van Hooke); + = Ringo Starr & His All-Star Band

All Argent group LPs produced by Chris White and Rod Argent, except "Counterpoints," which was produced by White and Argent with Tony Visconti

SINGLES

TITLES	UK & FOREIGN LABEL/NO.	RELEASE DATE	US & CANADA LABEL/NO.	RELEASE DATE
Liar/ Schoolgirl			Date 2-1659	11/17/69
Schoolgirl/ Like Honey	German Epic 5-9979	02/18/70		
Celebration/ Where Are We Going Wrong	CBS S 5423	01/22/71		
Sweet Mary (edit)/ Rejoice			Epic 5-10718	03/15/71
Celebration/ Kingdom	Ger. Epic EPC 7120	04/02/71	Epic 5-10746	06/21/71
Hold Your Head Up/ Closer To Heaven - Keep On Rollin' (#1)	Epic S EPC 9315	10/02/71		
Hold Your Head Up (2:52 edit)/ Keep On Rollin' (#1)	Epic S EPC 7786	02/11/72	Epic 5-10852	04/10/72
Tragedy (edit)/ Rejoice	Epic S EPC 8115	05/26/72		
Hold Your Head Up (3:15 edit)/ Closer To Heaven			Epic 5-10852	06/05/72
Tragedy (edit)/ He's A Dynamo (edit)			Epic 5-10919	10/16/72
God Gave Rock And Roll To You (edit)/ Christmas For The Free	Epic S EPC 1243	02/23/73	Epic 5-10972	03/26/73
It's Only Money Pt. 2 (edit)/ Losing Hold			Epic 5-11019	06/18/73
It's Only Money Pt. 2 (edit)/ Candles On The River	Epic S EPC 1628	06/22/73		
Christmas For The Free (stereo)/ (mono) (promo only)			Epic 5-10972	11/26/73
Thunder And Lightning (edit)/ Keeper Of The Flame	Epic S EPC 2147	02/22/74		
Hold Your Head Up (edit)/ God Gave Rock And Roll To You (edit)			Epic 15-2332	04/22/74
Man For All Reasons (edit)/ Music From The Spheres	Epic S EPC 2448	06/14/74	Epic 5-11137	06/03/74
Thunder And Lightning (edit)/ The Coming Of Kohoutek			Epic 8-50025	09/02/74
Keep On Rollin' (#2)/ I Am The Dance Of Ages (live)	Epic S EPC 2849	11/22/74		
Highwire (edit)/ Circus (withdrawn)	Epic S EPC 3407	06/20/75		
Rock & Roll Show/ It's Fallin' Off	RCA 2624	10/31/75		
God Gave Rock And Roll To You (edit)/ Hold Your Head Up (edit)	Epic S EPC 3954	02/13/76		
Hold Your Head Up (edit)/ It's Only Money Pt. 1	Epic S EPC 4321	06/11/76		
Gymnopédies No. 1*/ Light Fantastic*	MCA MCA 294	05/28/77		
Argentine Melody (Canción de Argentina)**/ Strung	MCA MCA 369	05/19/78		

(NOTE: Rod Argent is not on the B-side of the above single.)

TITLES	UK & FOREIGN LABEL/NO.	RELEASE DATE	US & CANADA LABEL/NO.	RELEASE DATE
Home*/ No. 1*	MCA MCA 393	09/29/78		
Silence*/ Recollection*	MCA MCA 403	01/12/79		
Hold Your Head Up (edit)/ Tragedy (edit)	Epic EPC 7062	02/06/79		
With You***/ Ghosts***	MCA MCA 761	01/29/82		
Ghosts (Full Version)***/ With You*** - Poltergeist*** (12")	MCA MCAT 761	02/19/82		
Hold Your Head Up (Parts 1 & 2)/ Dance In The Smoke	Old Gold OG 9187	07/16/82		
Secure In You****/ Noonday Riser****	German TM 7TM 2	11/04/83		
Echoes****/ Echoes Dub**** (7")	TM 7TM 4	03/03/84		
God Gave Rock And Roll To You (edit)/ Hold Your Head Up (edit)	CBS A 4580	07/27/84		
Aztec Gold******/ On Wings Of The Wind******	CBS A 7231	06/13/86		
The Two Of Us******/ Genesis - AON******	Sierra FED 30	12/12/86		
Hold Your Head Up (2:52 edit)/ Keep On Rollin' (#1)	Epic S EPC 7786	07/17/87		
Baby Don't You Cry No More*/ Teenage Years*	MMC MMCS 1	09/02/88		
God Gave Rock And Roll To You (edit)/ Tragedy (edit)	Epic S EPC 1243	11/18/88		
Tragedy (edit)/ Rejoice	Epic S EPC 8115	11/18/88		
Into The Sun*******/ Pale Horizon*******	Honey Bee HONEY 12	12/04/89		
Not With A Bang********/ The Piglet Files********	Weekend WEEK 100	03/05/90		
Tutti Al Mondo*********/ Hot Foot*********	Weekend WEEK 101	06/04/90		
The Zombies And Beyond: Album Sampler (promo CD-R; with "Hold Your Head Up" and tracks by The Zombies, Colin Blunstone, and Dave Stewart Featuring Colin Blunstone)	Universal no #	05/26/08		
More Than A Feeling (by Boston)/ God Gave Rock And Roll To You (7"; part of Record Store Day ten 7" box "'70s Rock Classic 45s")	Demon CLASSIC45007	04/22/17		

PROMOTIONAL SINGLES

"Heads Up" (7" EP) (1970; US Epic AS 4)
Tracks: Be Free; plus tracks by Catfish, Shuggie Otis, Jam Factory, Susan Carter, and Redbone

"Playback" (7' EP) (1972; US Columbia AS 32)
Tracks: Smokey Day (by Colin Blunstone; Argent backing band); plus tracks by John Paul Hammond, Wayne Cochran & The C.C. Riders, and Looking Glass)

"Play:Back" (sic) (7" EP) (1974; US Columbia AS 69)
Tracks: Keeper Of The Flame; plus tracks by Allee Willis, Janis Ian, and Michael Murphey

ALBUMS

TITLES	UK & FOREIGN LABEL/NO.	RELEASE DATE	US & CANADA LABEL/NO.	RELEASE DATE
Argent	CBS CBS 63781	01/16/70	Epic BN 26525	11/24/69
Ring Of Hands	Epic S EPC 64190	02/05/71	Epic E 30128	03/15/71
All Together Now	Epic S EPC 64962	04/21/72	Epic KE 31556	06/26/72
In Deep	Epic S EPC 65475	03/23/73	Epic KE 32195	03/26/73
In Deep (quad)	Epic Q 65475	03/23/73	Epic EQ 32195	03/26/73
Nexus (UK and US editions have different covers)	Epic S EPC 65924	02/22/74	Epic KE 32573	04/22/74
Encore (2LP)	Epic S EPC 88063	11/22/74	Epic PEG 33079	12/09/74
Circus	Epic S EPC 80691	04/04/75	Epic PE 33422	03/10/75
Counterpoints	RCA RS 1020	10/31/75	U.A. UA-LA-560-G	02/02/76
The Argent Anthology - A Collection Of Greatest Hits			Epic PE 33955	02/09/76
An Anthology - The Best Of Argent (cancelled)	Epic S EPC 81202	04/16/76		
An Anthology - The Best Of Argent	Epic S EPC 81321	05/17/76		
"Best Of British Rock" (exclusive Rod Argent tracks: "The Prince" and "Five Finger Blues")			Vee Jay Int'l VJS-1209	06/13/77
Hold Your Head Up	Embassy EMB 31640	04/14/78		
Moving Home*	MCA MCF 2854	01/05/79		
Ghosts***	MCA MCF 3125	02/12/82		
Moving Home* (reissue)	MCA MCL 1695	07/16/82		
Shadowshow****	TM 3	11/04/83		
Metro*****	Sepia RSR 2013	11/04/83		
Second Sight ****** (library music release only)	KPM 1332	<</<</84		
An Anthology - The Best Of Argent (reissue)	Epic EPC 32517	09/14/84		
A New Age ****** (CD; library music release only)	TIM 1049	<</<</86		
The Argent Anthology - A Collection Of Greatest Hits (CD)			Epic EK 33955	06/30/87
Barbara Thompson's Special Edition**** by BARBARA THOMPSON (CD; with three Shadowshow tracks)	German veraBra vBr 2017 2	<</<</87		
Network Heroes ****** (CD; library music release only)	KPM 1392	<</<</88		
Red House (CD; US release has different packaging)	MMC CDMMC 1012	08/19/88	Relativ. 88561-1039-2	04/23/91
Network Heroes ****** (CD; reissue)	KPM 27	<</<</88		
The Advance Of Man ****** (CD; library music release only)	KPM 45	<</<</88		
"20 Great TV Themes" ********* (LP/CD; with "Aztec Gold," "Eye Witness," "Goal Crazy," and "The Two Of Us")	Weekend WEEK LP2/	<</<</89		
An Anthology - The Best Of Argent (CD; reissue)	Epic 465444 2	11/20/89		
The Theme Music From "Rescue"******* (LP/CD)	Honey Bee HONEY L/D 14	01/15/90		
An Anthology - The Best Of Argent (CD; reissue)	Epic 902293 2	04/16/90		
Road Back Home (cassette; retitled version of "Counterpoints")			Capitol Special Markets 4XLL-57290	<</<</90
New Horizons ****** (CD; library music release only)	Chappell Recorded Mus. CHAP AV055	<</<</91		
Music From The Spheres (CD)	Elite ELITE 004CD	05/13/91		
Argent (CD)	BGO BGO CD 110	07/29/91		
The Best Of King Biscuit Live - Volume 3 (CD; with "Hold Your Head Up" live in London 05/01/74)			Sandstone D233007-2	09/24/91
An Anthology - The Best Of Argent (CD; reissue)	Epic 471141 2	03/23/92		
"Favourite TV Themes" ********* (CD; with "Goal Crazy," "Tutti Al Mondo," and "Hot Foot")	Music Club MCCD069	06/15/92		
The Premiere Collection Encore by ANDREW LLOYD WEBBER (LP/CD; with "Argentine Melody")	Really Useful/Polydor 314 517 366-1/2	11/16/92 11/16/92	Polydor 314 517 336-2	03/09/93
Music From The Spheres (CD; reissue)	Elite ELITE 004CD	08/30/93		
Encore (CD; withdrawn)	BGO BGO CD 206	11/08/93		
An Anthology - The Best Of Argent (CD; reissue)	Epic 902293 2	03/14/94		

Title	Label/Cat#	Date	Alt Label/Cat#	Alt Date
All Together Now (CD)	Epic 477377 2	09/05/94		
1964-67 by THE ZOMBIES (CD; with 4 live Argent tracks)	More Music MOCD 3009	01/30/95		
In Concert (CD)	Windsong WINCD 067	03/06/95		
GREATest Hits * GREATest Recordings by THE ZOMBIES (CD; with Argent interview)			TransLuxe 57803-2	04/04/95
In Deep (CD)	Epic 480529 2	06/05/95		
All Together Now (CD; plus bonus tracks)			Koch KOC-CD-7941	05/20/97
The Complete BBC Sessions (CD)	Strange Fruit SFRSCD 039	09/29/97		
Nexus (CD)	Epic 489442 2	01/26/98		
"Cool Britannia" by THE YARDBIRDS/ THE SMALL FACES/ THE ZOMBIES (3CD; includes the above "1964-67" CD)	Summit Deluxe SDCDBX 3659	04/23/98		
Classically Speaking* (CD)	Red House 001	06/01/98		
Ring Of Hands (CD; reissue - bonus track: "He's A Dynamo")			Collectables 6087	11/09/99
In Deep (CD: reissue - bonus track: "Hold Your Head Up")			Collectables 6088	11/09/99
Encore (CD; reissue)			Collectables 6089	11/09/99
Hold Your Head Up (CD)			Sony Custom Mktg. A 31052	06/17/00
Argent/ Ring Of Hands (2CD; reissue)	BGO BGOCD 480	07/14/00		
"Crazy Drums/ Crazy Drummer" by BOBBY GRAHAM (CD; with 3 live tracks featuring Rod Argent & Jazz Experience)	German Rollercoaster 3040	12/12/00		
Hold Your Head Up - The Best Of Argent (CD; different cover/tracks)	Jap. Epic EICP 7037	03/20/02		
Encore (CD; reissue)	BGO BGOCD 588	09/08/03		
Hold Your Head Up (CD; reissue of Sony compilation)			Collectables 9482	04/13/04
Metro ***** (CD; reissue)	Qnote QNT 10105	06/21/04		
Argent/ Circus (2CD; reissue)			Wounded Bird 6525	06/21/05
In Deep/ Nexus (2CD; reissue)	Edsel MEDCD 759	08/29/05		
"The Ultimate Football Songs" ****** (CD; with "Aztec Gold")	Sony 82876 76144 2	02/20/06		
Collectables Classics (4CD box set)			Collectables 0397	06/13/06
All Together Now (CD; reissue - 5 bonus tracks: "Closer To Heaven," "Christmas For the Free," "Celebration," "Kingdom" and "Hold Your Head Up")	Acadia ACAM 8134	01/29/07		
Into The Afterlife (CD; includes "Telescope [Mr. Galileo]" by Chris White & Argent, as well as 6 other Argent/White demos from the post-Zombies/pre-Argent period)	Big Beat CDWIKCD 266	07/02/07		
Ghosts*** (CD; reissue)	Jap. Geffen UICY-93372	12/05/07		
Greatest – The Singles Collection (with many radio single edits)			Varèse Sara. 066880	03/18/08
The Zombies And Beyond (CD; with the Argent tracks "God Gave Rock And Roll To You," "Hold Your Head Up," "Keep On Rollin'" and "Pleasure")	UMTV 1773931	05/26/08		
Argent (CD; reissue)	Jap. Sony SICP 1908	06/25/08		
Ring Of Hands (CD; reissue)	Jap. Epic EICP 1014	06/25/08		
All Together Now (CD; reissue)	Jap. Epic EICP 1015	06/25/08		
In Deep (CD; reissue)	Jap. Epic EICP 1016	06/25/08		
Nexus (CD; reissue)	Jap. Epic EICP 1017	06/25/08		
Encore (CD; reissue)	Jap. Epic EICP 1018	06/25/08		
Circus (CD; reissue)	Jap. Epic EICP 1019	06/25/08		
Ringo Starr & His All Starr Band: Live 2006 (CD; Rod plays keyboards throughout and performs "She's Not There" and "Hold Your Head Up" – the CD has edited highlights of the set)+			Koch KOC-CD-4542	07/08/08
Original Album Classics (5CD; reissues of "Argent," "Ring Of Hands," "All Together Now," "In Deep" and "Nexus")	Epic 88697445472	03/30/09		
God Gave Rock And Roll To You - The Greatest Hits (CD)	Sony/Camden 88697695742	08/30/10		
High Voltage Festival (2CD; reunion concert recorded on 07/25/10)	Concert Live CLCD 284	10/18/10		
"The Old Grey Whistle Test Live" (3CD; with live version of "God Gave Rock And Roll To You" that is also on "In Concert")	BBC/Rhino WMTV193	04/29/12		
All Together Now (CD; reissue)	Esoteric ECLEC 2321	05/08/12		
The Argent Anthology - A Collection Of Greatest Hits (CD; reissue)	Dutch Music On CD MOCCD 13060	08/29/13		
In Deep (CD; reissue)	Talking Elephant TECD 241	02/28/14		
Circus (CD; reissue)	Talking Elephant TECD 279	04/17/15		

Red House (CD; reissue)	Grey Scale GSGZ029CD	06/30/17
Argent (CD; reissue)	Dutch Music On CD MOCCD 13819	10/11/19
In Deep/ Nexus/ Ring Of Hands (2 SACD hybrid discs with both stereo and quad mixes of the albums)	Vocalion 2CDSML 8568	12/18/19
Counterpoints (CD; not from an album master)	Jap. Vivid Sound/ VSCD-5958/ Big Pink BIG PINK 708	05/26/21
Hold Your Head Up - The Best Of Argent (2LP/CD)	Demon DEMREC 1006/ Edsel EDSL0104	06/03/22

VIDEOS

TITLES	UK & FOREIGN LABEL/NO.	RELEASE DATE	US & CANADA LABEL/NO.	RELEASE DATE
A Keyboard Approach (66-minute instructional video)	Starnite Ltd. SNT010	08/11/92		
"70's Rock – Rock Legends" (DVD; with "God Gave Rock And Roll To You")	Regeneration CRP1655	01/28/03		
"The Old Grey Whistle Test Volume 2" (DVD; with "God Gave Rock And Roll To You")	Video/Film Express 500606	09/16/03		
"Classic Rock –The Ultimate Anthology" (DVD: with "Hold Your Head Up")	Ragnarock DVDL010D	03/15/04		
Inside Free 1968 - 1972 (CD/DVD; with Rod Argent interview)	Classic Rock Legends 1609	02/01/05	Classic Rock Legends 1609	02/01/05
Inside Argent (CD/DVD; with live performances)	Classic Rock Legends 1814	04/05/05	Classic Rock Legends	04/05/05
"The Old Grey Whistle Test (The Definitive Collection)" (4DVD; with "God Gave Rock And Roll To You")	BBC BBCDVD1867	11/21/05		
"The Old Grey Whistle Test - The Complete Collection" (3DVD; with "God Gave Rock And Roll To You")	BBC E2351	08/29/06		
Argent - Total Rock Review (DVD; with live performances)	Storm Bird STB 2182	09/18/06		
"Burt Sugarman's The Midnight Special: 1973" (DVD; with "Hold Your Head Up")			Guthy-Renker Entertain. MU.0009	10/27/06
"Burt Sugarman's The Midnight Special: Legendary Performances 1973-1981" (9DVD; "Hold Your Head Up")			Guthy-Renker Entertain. MUBOX001	06/05/07
Ringo Starr & His All Starr Band: Live 2006 (DVD; Rod plays keyboards throughout and performs "She's Not There" and "Hold Your Head Up")+			Koch KOC-DV-4543	07/08/08
"The Midnight Special" (1DVD/6DVD/11 DVD; with "Hold Your Head Up")			StarVista Entertainment/ Time-Life 30730-X/ 30732-X/30902-X	09/09/14

SINGLES SESSIONS AND COMPOSITIONS

(* = produced by Rod Argent & Chris White; ** = co-produced with Peter Van Hooke; *** = co-produced with Neil Innes and Peter Van Hooke; **** = co-produced with Will Birch and Peter Van Hooke; ***** = co-produced with Mike Hurst and Peter Van Hooke)

TITLES	UK & FOREIGN LABEL/NO.	RELEASE DATE	US & CANADA LABEL/NO.	RELEASE DATE
SECOND CITY SOUND - Tchaikovsky One/ Shadows (promo only; B-side written by Argent – same as below)	Jackson DW 5123	12/03/65		
SECOND CITY SOUND - Tchaikovsky One/ Shadows	Decca F 12310	12/31/65	London 45 LON 9813	01/31/66
THE MINDBENDERS - I Want Her She Wants Me/ The Morning After (A-side written by Argent)	Fontana TF 780	12/30/66	Fontana F-1571	01/23/67
DAVE COLMAN UND DAS ORCHESTER MARK WIRTZ - Mister Galilei/ Alaska Quinn (the A-side with the original title "Mister Galileo" was written by Rod Argent, Chris White, and translated into German by Fleming, and the B-side was a German version of Bob Dylan's "Mighty Quinn")	German Columbia C 23 755	04/26/68		
FREE FERRY - Mary, What Have You Become*/ Friend*	CBS 4456	03/15/69	Date 2-1658	11/17/69
SYKES & MEDINA - Everything's Fine, Fine, Fine*/ I Can Feel The Thickness*	CBS 4529	09/26/69		
FREE FERRY - Haverjack Drive*/ Flying*	CBS 4647	01/02/70	Epic 5-10579	02/20/70
DUFFY POWER - Hell Hound*/ Hummingbird*	CBS S 5176	09/18/70	Epic 5-10650	08/31/70
DUFFY POWER - Hummingbird*/ Hell Hound*	Epic S EPC 7139	04/09/71		
METAL - Mike (Like Honey)/ Dix Ans Ont Passé (Liar)	French Disques Meys	08/<</72		

(A-side written by Chris White and Rod Argent, with French lyrics by Michèle Senlis, and the B-side written by Russ Ballard with French lyrics by Senlis, translates to "Ten Years Have Passed") 10.039

Artist - Title	Label/Cat#	Date	Label/Cat#	Date
THE HOLLIES - Star/ Love Is The Thing	Polydor 2058 719	04/15/76		
ROGER DALTREY - Written On The Wind/ Dear John	Polydor 2121 319	04/08/77		
NEWPORT MALE VOICE CHOIR - Love Me Tender/ Still, Still, Still	Polydor 2058 964	12/02/77		
ANDREW LLOYD WEBBER - Theme And Variations 1-4/ Variation 16	MCA MCA 345	01/13/78	MCA 40866	04/24/78
THE WHO - Who Are You (edit)/ Had Enough	Polydor WHO 1	06/30/78	MCA 40948	08/14/78
ANDREW LLOYD WEBBER - Variation 23/ Variation 5	MCA MCA 376	07/07/78		
MARTI WEBB - Take That Look Off Your Face/ Sheldon Bloom (keyboards on both sides)	Polydor POSP 100	01/18/80	Polydor PD 2062	02/11/80
BRIAN CONNOLLY - Hypnotised/ Fade Away	Carrere CAR 231	04/16/82		
BARBARA COURTNEY-KING, ROD ARGENT, RAY COOPER, JULIAN LLOYD WEBBER AND THE GABRIELLI STRING QUARTET - Pastourelle/ Mirabel Bridge	RCA 308	01/21/83		
JONAS - Bang The Drum All Day*****/ Rockin' Little Rebel	Lamborghini LMG 19	01/25/85		
NEIL INNES - Dear Father Christmas***/ City Of The Angels	Making Waves SURF 104	12/13/85		
ELECTRIC BLUEBIRDS - Tell It Like It Is****/ Wake Me, Shake Me**** (in addition to co-production, Argent played keyboards on the A-side)	Making Waves SURF 117	07/25/86		
BARBARA DICKSON - Time After Time (Theme From The TV Series "Animal Squad")/ She Moves Thro' The Fair (Rod Argent wrote the A-side with Robert Howes)	K-tel BABS 1	09/05/86		
MORT SHUMAN - Sorrow**/ Just An Hour**	Sierra FED 26	10/17/86		
DROWSY MAGGIE - Sing An Irish Song/ Cockles And Mussels (Molly Malone) (by Drowsy Maggie with Martha Hoffnung) (Argent and Howes produced both sides)	Solitaire/Starblend STAR 11	<</ <</87		
TANITA TIKARAM - Good Tradition**/ Valentine Heart** (three different 7" single packages)	WEA YZ 196/ 196G/ 196L	06/27/88		
TANITA TIKARAM - Twist In My Sobriety**/ Friends** - For All These Years** (12")	WEA YZ 321 T	10/14/88		
TANITA TIKARAM - Twist In My Sobriety** - The Kill In Your Heart** (10")	WEA YZ 321 TT	10/14/88		
TANITA TIKARAM - Twist In My Sobriety** - Friends** - The Kill In Your Heart** (CD5)	WEA YZ 321 CD	10/14/88		
TANITA TIKARAM - Cathedral Song**/ Sighing Innocents** (7")	WEA YZ 331	01/06/89		
TANITA TIKARAM - Cathedral Song** - Sighing Innocents**/ Let's Make Everybody Smile Today** (7" EP)	WEA YZ 331B	01/06/89		
TANITA TIKARAM - World Outside Your Window (remix)**/ For All These Years** (7")	WEA YZ 363	03/10/89		
TANITA TIKARAM - World Outside Your Window (remix)**/ For All These Years** - Good Tradition (live) (12")	WEA YZ 363 T	03/10/89		
TANITA TIKARAM - World Outside Your Window (remix)** - For All These Years** - Good Tradition (live) - He Likes The Sun (live) (boxed CD5)	WEA YZ 363 CDB	03/10/89		
TANITA TIKARAM - World Outside Your Window (remix)** - For All These Years** - World Outside Your Window (extended) (CD5)	WEA YZ 363 CD	03/10/89		
TANITA TIKARAM - We Almost Got It Together**/ Love Story** - Over You All** (12"/CD5)	WEA YZ 443 T/CD	01/05/90		
TANITA TIKARAM - Little Sister Leaving Town** - I Love The Heaven's Solo** - Hot Pork Sandwiches** - Twist In My Sobriety** (CD5)	WEA YZ 459 CD	02/19/90		
TANITA TIKARAM - Sunset's Arrived (edit)**/ Once And Not Speak** (7")	French EastWest 9031-71831-7	06/13/90		
TANITA TIKARAM - Thursday's Child (New Version)**/ Once And Not Speak** (7")	EastWest YZ 481	06/13/90		
TANITA TIKARAM - Thursday's Child (New Version)**/ Once And Not Speak** - Cathedral Song (live in Norway) (12"/CD5)	EastWest YZ 481T/ 481CD	06/13/90		
FRANCES RUFFELLE - Stranger To The Rain (Extended)/ Stranger To The Rain (7") - In Another World** (12"/CD5)	London LONX/ LONCD 278	09/24/90		
TANITA TIKARAM - Only The Ones We Love** - Me In Mind** - Cathedral Song (instrumental)** (CD5)	E. West YZ 558 CD	01/28/91		
TANITA TIKARAM - I Love The Heaven's Solo** - Only In Name** - To Wish This** - I'm Going Home** (CD5)	E. West YZ 569 CD	03/18/91		
LABI SIFFRE - Most People Sleep Alone**/ Schooldays** (7")	China WOK 2003	07/15/91		
LABI SIFFRE - Most People Sleep Alone** - City Of Dreams -	China WOKCD 2003	07/15/91		

A Matter Of Love... - Schooldays** (CD5)				
MORT SHUMAN - Promised Land**/ The World Is Waiting For Love (7")	E. West 74150-7	08/19/91		
MORT SHUMAN - Promised Land** - The World Is Waiting For Love - Just An Hour** (CD5)	E. West 74151-2	08/19/91		
NANCI GRIFFITH - Late Night Grande Hotel**/ It's Just Another Morning Here** (7"/cassette single)	MCA MCS/MCSC 1566	09/30/91		
NANCI GRIFFITH - Late Night Grande Hotel**/ It's Just Another Morning Here** - Wooden Heart** (12")	MCA MCST 1566	09/30/91		
NANCI GRIFFITH - Late Night Grande Hotel** - It's Just Another Morning Here** - Wooden Heart - From A Distance (live) (CD5)	MCA MCSTD 1566	09/30/91		
MORT SHUMAN - Amalie**/ Sorrow** (7")	German EastWest 9031-75519-7	10/25/91		
NANCI GRIFFITH - Heaven**/ Down 'n' Outer** (7")	MCA MCS 1596	11/25/91		
NANCI GRIFFITH - Heaven**/ Down 'n' Outer** - Tumble And Fall** (12")	MCA MCST 1596	11/25/91		
NANCI GRIFFITH - Heaven** - Down 'n' Outer** - Tumble And Fall** - Love At The Five And Dime (CD5)	MCA MCSTD 1596	11/25/91		
TANITA TIKARAM - You Make The Whole World Cry - Rock Me 'Til I Stop - This Stranger (Alternative Version)** (CD5)	EastWest YZ644CD	02/10/92		
TANITA TIKARAM - You Make The Whole World Cry - Me, You & Lucifer - This Stranger (Alternative Version)** (CD5)	EastWest YZ644CDX	02/10/92		
MICHAEL BALL - One Step Out Of Time/ No More Steps To Climb** (7"; wrote B-side with Don Black)	Polydor PO 206	04/17/92		
MICHAEL BALL - One Step Out Of Time/ No More Steps To Climb** - We Break Our Own Hearts (CD5)	Polydor PZCD 206	04/17/92		
SHAKY FEATURING ROGER TAYLOR - Radio**/ Oh Baby Don't (Outtake) (7")	Epic 658436 7	09/28/92		
JOSHUA KADISON - Jessie**/ When A Woman Cries** (cassette single)	SBK TC-SBK 43	05/11/93	SBK 4KM-50429	05/11/93
TOBIAH JAMES - I See You Naked - Trust - I See You Naked (Remix) (CD-R test pressing – available as a download)**	private release	<</<</93		
JOSHUA KADISON - Jessie**/ When A Woman Cries** (7")	SBK 43	02/18/94		
JOSHUA KADISON - Jessie (Edit)** - Jessie (Album Version)** - When A Woman Cries** - All I Ever Ask (CD5)	SBK CDSBK 43	02/18/94		
JOSHUA KADISON - Jessie (Edit)** - Jessie (Album Version)** (CD5)	Dutch SBK 7243 8 81565 2 3	02/18/94		
JOSHUA KADISON - Picture Postcards From L.A.** - Mama's Arms** (first CD5 of two)	Dutch SBK 7243 8 81616 2 6	09/09/04		
JOSHUA KADISON - Picture Postcards From L.A.** - Picture Postcards From L.A. (live) - Mama's Arms** (second CD5 of two)	Dutch SBK 7243 8 81617 2 5	09/09/04		
JOSHUA KADISON - Picture Postcards From L.A.** - Invisible Man (live) - Picture Postcards From L.A. (live) (CD5)	Australian SBK 8817942	10/10/94	SBK 4KM-58238	10/10/94
JOSHUA KADISON - Picture Postcards From L.A.**/ Jessie** (7" translucent yellow vinyl jukebox edition)			SBK/ CEMA Special Markets S7-18130	10/22/94
JOSHUA KADISON - Beau's All Night Radio Love Line** - Picture Postcards From L.A.** (CD5)	Australian SBK 8821172	10/31/94		
JOSHUA KADISON - Beautiful In My Eyes (Edit)**/ Invisible Man** (7")	SBK 50	10/31/94		
JOSHUA KADISON - Beautiful In My Eyes (Edit)**/ All I Ever Ask - Jessie (Original Demo)** (cassette single/CD5)			SBK 4KM/K2-58099	02/28/95
GILBERT O'SULLIVAN – I Wish I Could Cry (4th Version)** - Matrimony (CD5)	Dutch Gold 9909257	04/<</95		
JOSHUA KADISON - Jessie** - Picture Postcards From L.A.** Mama's Arms** (first CD5 of two)	SBK CDSBK 53	04/10/95		
JOSHUA KADISON - Jessie (Edit)** - Picture Postcards From L.A. (live) - Invisible Man (live) (second CD5 of two)	SBK CDSBK 53	04/10/95		
JOSHUA KADISON - Jessie** - Picture Postcards From L.A.** (cassette single; both tracks on both sides of the tape)	SBK TC-SBK 53	04/10/95		
JOSHUA KADISON - Beautiful In My Eyes (Edit)** - Beautiful In My Eyes (Album Version)** - Jessie (Album Version)** (first CD5 of two)	SBK CDSBKS 55	08/04/95		
JOSHUA KADISON - Beautiful In My Eyes (Edit)** - Painted Desert Serenade** – All I Ever Ask (second CD5 of two)	SBK CDSBK 55	08/04/95		
JOSHUA KADISON - Beautiful In My Eyes (Edit)** - Jessie (Album Version)** (cassette single; both songs on both sides of the tape)	SBK 724388225144	08/04/95		
SORAYA - Suddenly - De Repente (CD5)	Spanish Mercury 575 438-2	04/29/96		

TANITA TIKARAM - Twist In My Sobriety (The Remixes): (Phil Kelsey Vocal)** - (Tikaramp Radio)**/ (Tikaramp Vocal)** - (Extended Bumps Fluidity Mix)** (12"/CD5)	EastWest EWO64T/ EWO064CD	09/20/96		
TANITA TIKARAM - Twist In My Sobriety (The Remixes): (Tikaram Vocal)** - (Tikaram Dub)**/ (Phil Kelsey Vocal)** - (Tikaram Radio)**// (Extended Bumps Fluidity Mix)** - (SFX Sobriety Mix)**/ (Phil Kelsey Instrumental)** - (Bumps Fluidity Radio Mix) (two 12" discs)	German EastWest SAM 1865	09/20/96		
EZIO - Call You Tomorrow (Radio Edit)** - Moonstruck** - Clowns (live) - If You Want** (first CD5 of two)	Univ. MCSTD 40143	06/06/97		
EZIO - Call You Tomorrow (Radio Edit)** - Circus (live) - Moon (live) - Call You Tomorrow (live) (second CD5 of two)	Univ. MCSXD 40143	06/06/97		
SORAYA - Avalanche** - Stay Awhile (live) - Calm Before The Storm (live) (CD5)			Island 572 117-2	06/09/97
SORAYA - Stay Awhile** - Quédate** - Reason To Believe** (CD5)	Ger. Island 571 217-2	06/23/97		
SORAYA - Suddenly (LP)** - Suddenly (De Repente)** - Avalanche (live) (CD5)	London 571 697-2/ LONCD 400	08/25/97		
EZIO - Deeper** - Moonstruck (cassette single)	Univ. MCSC 40123	12/10/97		
EZIO - Deeper** - Moonstruck - Clowns (live) - If You Want** (CD5)	Univ. MCSTD 40123	12/10/97		
SORAYA - J'aimerais Tant** - Wall Of Smiles (Acoustic)** (CD5)	Fr. Island 568 816-2	03/20/98		
LUKA BLOOM - Water Ballerina** - Blackberry Time** (CD5)	Columbia 666699.1	05/11/98		
SORAYA - So Far Away (Radio Edit)** - Wall Of Smiles (Acoustic)** - Lejos De Aquí** (CD5)	German Mercury 568 833-2	05/25/98		
SORAYA - Paris, Cali, Milan (promo 12"/CD5 containing different mixes of the above song): Spanish Radio Mix** - Spanish Club Mix** - Spanish Extended Remix** - Spanish Original Version** - English Radio Mix** - English Club Mix** - English Extended Remix** - English Original Version**			Island PRO LAT 18/ CDP-LAT 175	07/21/98
THE HIGH DIALS - The Holy Ground EP: The Holy Ground - Sing For Loveless Seasons - Picture Of A Fading Man - The Sound Of Daisy Leaving (CD5; Hammond B-3 solo on "Picture Of A Fading Man")			Rainbow Quartz Int'l	07/10/07
SPÖÖN FAZER - "Bam-Boo" (7" EP): Rising Sun - Kyoto/ Festival - Back To The Beginning (drum programming)	Anna Logue ANNA 018.2008	09/08/08		
DEF LEPPARD - Rock & Roll Hall Of Fame 29 March 2019: Hysteria - Rock Of Ages - Photograph/ Pour Some Sugar On Me - All The Young Dudes* (Record Store Day 12" of 4,000 copies - keyboards on the last track; recorded live at the induction ceremony at Barclays Center, Brooklyn, New York on 03/29/19)	Bludgeon Riffola 0602508192067	08/29/20	Bludgeon Riffola 0602508192067	08/29/20

ALBUM SESSIONS AND COMPOSITIONS

(see COLIN BLUNSTONE section for Rod Argent's contributions to Colin Blunstone singles and the albums "One Year," "Ennismore," "Journey," "Never Even Thought," "Late Nights In Soho," "Colin Blunstone Sings His Greatest Hits," "Live At The BBC," and "The Light Inside")
(*= co-produced with Peter Van Hooke, + = co-produced with Robert Howes):

TITLES	UK & FOREIGN LABEL/NO.	RELEASE DATE	US & CANADA LABEL/NO.	RELEASE DATE
EDWIN ASTLEY AND HIS ORCHESTRA - Secret Agent Meets The Saint (Original Music From The TV Shows) (with "Mio Amore Sta Lontano" - an Italian version of "I Remember When I Loved Her" with Italian lyrics by Zombies publisher Joseph Angelo Roncoroni, and sung by Angelique)			RCA LPM/LSP-3467	10/04/65
DUSTY SPRINGFIELD - Ev'rything's Coming Up Dusty (with Argent's "If It Don't Work Out")	Philips RBL/SRBL 1002	10/15/65		
DUSTY SPRINGFIELD - You Don't Have To Say You Love Me (with Argent's "If It Don't Work Out")			Philips PHM 200-210/ PHS 600-210	06/20/66
EDWIN ASTLEY AND HIS ORCHESTRA - Music From Secret Agent (with "Mio Amore Sta Lontano" by Angelique)			RCA LPM/LPS-3630	06/20/66
THE MINDBENDERS - With Woman In Mind (first issued version of Argent's "I Want Her She Wants Me")	Fontana TL/ STL 5403	04/07/67		
MIKE HURST - In My Time (on "All I Can Do Is Sing" and "Scarlet Revisited")	Capitol ST-21819	06/18/71		
KEITH CHRISTMAS - Pigmy (keyboards on "Song For A Survivor" and "Forest And The Shore")	B & C CAS 1041	09/10/71		
DUSTY SPRINGFIELD - Sheer Magic (retitled reissue of "Ev'rything's Coming Up Dusty")	Audio Club GB 6856 020	04/21/72		
TRAPEZE - You Are The Music...We're Just The Band	Threshold THS 8	12/01/72	Threshold THS 8	12/01/72

(Argent plays electric piano on "Coast To Coast" and piano on "Feelin' So Much Better Now")

Release	UK Cat.	UK Date	US Cat.	US Date
JOHN LEES - A Major Fancy (cancelled - see below)	Harvest SHVL 811	06/01/73		
MICHAEL FENNELLY - Lane Changer (backing vocals on "Touch My Soul" and "Won't You Please Do That" and mellotron on "Dark Night")	Epic EPC 80230	07/26/74	Epic KE 32703	02/25/74
JOHN HOWARD - Kid In A Big World (synthesizer on "Guess Who's Coming To Dinner")	CBS 80473	02/28/75		
THE HOLLIES - Write On (Argent piano and Moog on "Star")	Polydor 2442 141	01/09/76		
DIRTY TRICKS - Night Man (US edition is a compilation)	Polydor 2383 398	06/25/76	Polydor PD-1-6082	11/01/76
EASY STREET - Easy Street (organ on "Feels Like Heaven")	Polydor 2383 415	10/08/76	Capricorn CP 0174	10/18/76
LIMEY - Silver Eagle (backing vocals)	RCA PL 25032	02/04/77		
ROGER DALTREY - One Of The Boys (US LP has "Say It Ain't So, Joe" instead of "Written On The Wind")	Polydor 2442 146	05/13/77	MCA 2271	06/27/77
MAE McKENNA - Walk On Water	Transatlantic TRA 345	05/27/77		
JOHN LEES - A Major Fancy (Rod Argent organ on "Untitled No. 1 - Heritage")	Harvest SHSM 2018	07/22/77		
GARY BOYLE - The Dancer	Gull GULP 1020	09/16/77		
SPLINTER - Two Man Band (LP; uncredited synth on "Round & Round")	Dark Horse K56403	10/14/77	Dark Horse DH 3073	10/17/77
INTERGALACTIC TOURING BAND - Intergalactic Touring Band (lead vocal on "Silver Lady")	Charisma CDS 4009	11/19/77	Passport PB 9823	10/19/77
NEWPORT MALE VOICE CHOIR - Love Me Tender (synthesizer on "The Long And Winding Road," "Yesterday," "Bridge Over Troubled Water," and "Still, Still, Still," and piano on the first three and the last titles, plus piano on "Scarborough Fair" – the LP was produced by John Entwistle)	Polydor 2383 483	01/13/78		
ANDREW LLOYD WEBBER - Variations	MCA MCF 2824	01/27/78	MCA 3042	04/24/78
CHRIS REA - Whatever Happened To Benny Santini? (Argent on the title track and "Because Of You")	Magnet MAG 5021	04/21/78	U.A. UA-LA-879-H	07/17/78
THE WHO - Who Are You (Argent is on the title track, "Had Enough," "Love Is Coming Down" and "Guitar And Pen." Rod is not credited on "Love Is Coming Down," but he has confirmed his participation on the track.)	Polydor WHOD 5004	08/18/78	MCA 3050	08/25/78
JACK LANCASTER - Skinningrove Bay	Acrobat ACRO 1	10/20/78		
ANDREW LLOYD WEBBER - Variations (LP; reissue)			MCA 31089	07/02/79
MARTI WEBB - Tell Me On A Sunday	Polydor POLD 5031	02/08/80	Polydor PD-1-6260	02/18/80
PHOENIX - In Full View	Charisma CAS 1150	02/15/80		
MATTHEW FISHER - Matthew Fisher (Argent on backing vocals)	Vertigo 9198 652	02/15/80	A&M SP 4801	02/25/80
ROGER DALTREY - One Of The Boys (LP; reissue)			MCA 37031	08/04/80
LEA NICHOLSON - The Concertina Record (Rod synth on the three "Brandenburg 4th Concerto" tracks)	Kicking Mule SNKF 165	10/17/80		
MARTI WEBB - Won't Change Places (Argent wrote and produced produced "Angry And Sore" and "Masquerade")	Polydor 2442 186	11/21/80		
ORIGINAL LONDON CAST - "Cats" (2LP)	Polydor CATX 001	07/24/81	Geffen 2GHS 2017	06/15/82
JACK LANCASTER - Skinningrove Bay (reissue)	Kamera KAM 003	02/12/82		
VARIOUS ARTISTS featuring BARBARA COURTNEY-KING, Soprano - "Pastourelle" (Rod plays on "Pastourelle," "The Young Shepherdess," "Bailero," "I Am So Sad," "Unhappy The Man" and "Lullaby")	German RCA Red Seal RL 25413	04/16/82	MMG MMG 1145	08/<</83
FRIDA - Something's Going On (Argent wrote "Baby Don't You Cry No More")	Epic EPC 85966	09/10/82	Atlantic 80018-1	09/27/82
CHRIS REA - Whatever Happened To Benny Santini? (LP/CD; reissue)	Magnet MAG/ CDMAG 5021	06/17/83		
VERITY - Interrupted Journey (In addition to Rod, the LP features former Argent members Jim Rodford, Rob Henrit, Russ Ballard and John Verity.)	PRT LBP 100	11/18/83	Compleat CPLI 1-1007	03/12/84
CLEO LAINE & JOHN WILLIAMS - Let The Music Take You (produced by John Dankworth and Rod Argent; Argent is also on piano, Fender Rhodes and synthesizer - the album features Argent's "Baby Don't You Cry No More.")	CBS 25751	12/09/83	CBS FM 39211	03/19/84
ORIGINAL LONDON CAST - "Cats" (2CD; reissue)	Polydor 817 810-2	06/18/84	Geffen 2017-2	09/25/90
ELIZABETH PAGE AND THE HOLBORNE CONSORT OF RECORDERS - Playing The Recorder (keyboards)	Music For Pleasure MFP 4156611	07/27/84		
ORIGINAL LONDON CAST - "Starlight Express" (2LP/2CD)	Starlight/Polydor LNER 1/821 597-2	07/30/84		
VERITY - Truth Of The Matter (in addition to Rod Argent, the LP also features former Argent members Jim Rodford, Rob Henrit and John	PRT LBP 7971	10/18/85		

Release	UK Catalog	UK Date	US Catalog	US Date
Verity) VERITY - Honesty & Emotion (similar to the above album, but with the bonus track "Stay With Me Baby")	Portuguese PRT PT/LP 2014	10/18/85		
ELIZABETH PAGE AND THE HOLBORNE CONSORT OF RECORDERS - Playing The Recorder (reissue)	Classics For Pleasure CFP 4513	<</<</86		
VARIOUS ARTISTS - "Themes (Eighteen TV/Film Themes)" (LP; "Aztec Gold" and "The Two Of Us")	Sierra FEDM 1	<</<</86		
ELECTRIC BLUEBIRDS - Electric Bluebirds (remixed by Argent and Van Hooke; keyboards on one track)	Making Waves SPRAY 105	07/25/86		
BARBARA DICKSON - The Right Moment (LP/CD; with the Argent/Howes composition "Time After Time")	K-Tel ONE/ONCD	11/24/86		
ORIGINAL LONDON CAST - "The Phantom Of The Opera" (2LP/2CD)	Polydor PODV 9/ 831 273-2	02/13/87	Polydor 831 273-1 Y-2/ 831 273-2	04/27/87
ANDREW LLOYD WEBBER - Variations (CD; reissue)	MCA DMCL 1816	03/20/87	MCA MCAD 31089	08/24/87
JACK LANCASTER - Wild Connections (LP/CD; retitled version of "Skinningrove Bay")	Bold Reprieve BR/ BRMCD 001	06/20/87		
MARTI WEBB - Tell Me On A Sunday (CD; reissue)	German Polydor 833 447-2	<</<</87		
ORIGINAL LONDON CAST - Highlights From "The Phantom Of The Opera" (LP/CD)	Polydor 831 563-1/ 831 563-2	11/14/87	Polydor 831 563-1/ 831 563-2	10/10/88
CHRIS REA - Whatever Happened To Benny Santini? (CD; reissue)	Magnet 242 368 2	02/15/88		
MO FOSTER - Bel Assis (CD)	MMC CDMMC 1013	05/17/88	Relativity 88561-1041-2	04/23/91
VARIOUS ARTISTS - The Country Supersession (LP; reissue of Mike Hurst's "In My Time")	MMG/ Sundown SDLP 059	06/14/88		
ORIGINAL LONDON CAST - Highlights From "Cats" (CD)	Polydor 839 415-2	08/19/88		
TANITA TIKARAM - Ancient Heart (LP/CD; Argent string arrangements)*	WEA WX 210/210CD	09/16/88	Reprise 25839 1/2	12/06/88
ORIGINAL SOUNDTRACK - "Homeboy" (LP/CD; Argent sang and played on his composition "Living In The Real World" with the group The Brakes)*	Virgin V/CDV 2574	11/25/88		
FRIDA - Something's Going On (CD; reissue)	CBS CDCBS 85966	12/09/88		
VARIOUS ARTISTS - The World Of BBC TV Themes (LP/CD; with Barbara Dickson's recording of "Time After Time")	BBC REB/CD 705	<</<</89		
VERITY - Rock Solid (LP/CD; backing vocals)	Sierra LBR/CDLBR 100	<</<</89		
TANITA TIKARAM - The Sweet Keeper (LP/CD; Argent played keyboards, plus string arrangements and conducting)*	WEA WX/CD 330	02/02/90	Reprise 26091 1/2	01/30/90
VARIOUS ARTISTS - "The Last Temptation Of Elvis" (2LP/2CD; with Tanita Tikaram's "Loving You" - Argent on piano)*	NME LP/CD 038-039	03/23/90		
DUSTY SPRINGFIELD - Ev'rything's Coming Up Dusty (LP/CD; reissue)	BGO BGOLP/ BGOCD 74	05/21/90		
VARIOUS ARTISTS - "Love Stories" (CD; one track with Robert Howes: "Dragonflies At Dusk")	KPM KPM 123 CD	<</<</90		
VARIOUS ARTISTS - "Twenty Top TV Themes" (CD; with "Tutti Al Mondo [ITV World Cup 90]," "Hot Foot," "Goal Crazy," and "The Piglet Files" – all Argent/ Van Hooke works)	Weekend WEEK CD 3	<</<</90		
VARIOUS ARTISTS - Public Television's Greatest Hits, Vol. 1 (CD; Rod wrote "Soldiers," which was performed by The United Kingdom Symphony Orchestra)			RCA Victor 60470-2	09/25/90
JULIAN LLOYD WEBBER - Lloyd Webber Plays Lloyd Webber (LP/CD; Argent on "Variations 1-4," "Starlight Express," and "Close Every Door")	Philips 432 291-1/2	10/25/90	Philips 426 484-2	10/25/90
TANITA TIKARAM - Everybody's Angel (LP/CD; co-produced with Tikaram - Argent on keyboards, plus string arrangements and conducting)*	East West WX 401/ 903173498 2	02/08/91	Reprise 26468 1/2	03/12/91
THE CHILDREN'S COMPANY - The Adventures Of Roger And The Rottentrolls (CD; narrated by Colin Baker)+	MFP/EMI MFP 5952	<</<</91		
WAYNE FONTANA AND THE MINDBENDERS - Hit Single Anthology (CD; with "I Want Her She Wants Me")	Fontana 848 161-2	04/29/91		
LABI SIFFRE - Man Of Reason* (LP/CD)	China WOL/WOLCD 1015	07/29/91		
MORT SHUMAN - Distant Drum (LP/CD; all but 3 tracks produced by Argent and Peter Van Hooke; Rod provided keyboards and/or backing vocals on 8 tracks. CD bonus track produced by Argent/Van Hooke: "Just An Hour")*	E. West 82290-1/2	08/19/91	Atlantic 82290-2	08/20/91
NANCI GRIFFITH - Late Night Grande Hotel (CD; Rod played keyboards and provided string arrangements)*	MCA MCAD-10306	09/16/91	MCA MCAD-10306	09/17/91
ORIGINAL LONDON CAST - "Starlight Express" (2CD; reissue)	Japanese Polydor POCP-1169/70	02/26/92		

Release	Catalog	Date	Catalog (alt)	Date (alt)
JACK LANCASTER - Skinningrove Bay (CD; reissue)	C5 C5CD 580	03/16/92		
MICHAEL BALL - Michael Ball (LP/CD; wrote "No More Steps To Climb" with Don Black)*	Polydor 511 330-1/2	05/22/92		
CHRIS REA - Whatever Happened To Benny Santini? (CD; reissue)	Pickwick 242 368 2	06/18/92		
FRIDA - Something's Going On (CD; reissue)	Polydor 800 102-2	01/18/93		
JOSHUA KADISON - Painted Desert Serenade (CD; Argent produced 7 of the album's 9 tracks, played keyboards and did string arrangements)*			SBK 7 80920 2	05/18/93
BARBARA DICKSON - The Right Moment (CD; reissue)	Castle C.. CLACD 310	10/19/93		
MARTI WEBB - Tell Me On A Sunday (CD; reissue)	Polydor 833 447-2	<</<</93		
WAYNE FONTANA AND THE MINDBENDERS - The Best Of Wayne Fontana And The Mindbenders			Fontana 314 522 666-2	10/04/94
JOSHUA KADISON - Painted Desert Serenade (CD; late US issue)	SBK SBKCD 22	11/14/94		
TRAPEZE - You Are The Music...We're Just The Band (CD; reissue)	Deram 820 956-2	03/18/94	Deram 820 956-2	03/22/94
JULES SHEAR - Healing Bones (CD; Argent on keyboards)*			Island 314 523 120-2	08/23/94
JACK LANCASTER - Wild Connections (CD; retitled version of "Skinningrove Bay" - credited as Phil Collins, Gary Moore and Rod Argent)	Tring JHD 063	09/23/94		
MO FOSTER - Bel Assis (CD; reissue –bonus track: "Nomad")	German In-Akustik INAK 11003 CD	03/06/95		
GILBERT O'SULLIVAN - The Very Best Of Gilbert O'Sullivan (CD; with "I Wish I Could Cry")*	Dutch Arcade 01.9080.6	05/<</95		
DUFFY POWER - Just Stay Blue (CD; contains unreleased tracks recorded with the Argent lineup and produced by Rod Argent and Chris White)	Retro 802	06/05/95		
SORAYA - On Nights Like This (CD; Argent on keyboards and did string orchestration)*			Island 314 529 000-2	02/06/96
SORAYA - En Esta Noche (CD; Spanish-language edition of "On Nights Like This" - Argent on keyboards and string orchestration)*			Polydor 314 527 831-2	02/06/96
PAUL CARRACK - Blue Views (CD; Argent on keyboards)	EMI EIRSCD 1075	03/11/96	Ark 21/IRS 1007-2	05/20/97
MATTHEW FISHER - Matthew Fisher/ Strange Days (CD; reissue – Rod Argent is on the first album, while Chris White co-produced the second and co-wrote many songs with Fisher for "Strange Days")	BGO BGOCD 308	03/20/96		
NAIMEE COLEMAN - Silver Wrists (CD; keyboards)	Lime CDCHR 6119	06/23/96		
THE WHO - Who Are You (CD with an Argent-related bonus track: the Olympic '78 Mix of "Guitar And Pen")	MCA MCAD-11492	11/18/96	MCA MCAD-11492	11/19/96
HOUSE OF SATIRE - "The Doomsday Clock" (CD; Argent played Hammond organ on "Ghost Train To Hell," "Danger," "Race Against Time (2)," "Not In My Backyard" and "Knife Edge")	Satire CD 1	04/14/97		
EZIO - Diesel Vanilla (CD; also string arrangements)*	MCA MCD 60038	06/06/97		
SORAYA - On Nights Like This (CD; belated UK issue)	Lon. 314 529 000-2	06/16/97		
ORIGINAL SOUNDTRACK - Secret Agent: Music From The TV Series (CD; reissue)			Razor & Tie 2151-2	08/19/97
THE MINDBENDERS - The Mindbenders/ With Woman In Mind (CD; reissue)	BGO BGOCD 389	09/15/97		
SORAYA - Torre De Marfil (CD; co-produced with Soraya – Argent on keyboards and string arrangements)*			PolyGram Latino 314 539 067-2	10/21/97
JACK LANCASTER - Skinningrove Bay (CD; reissue)	Zok ZCDJL013	11/26/97		
ROGER DALTREY - One Of The Boys (CD; reissue)	German Repertoire REP-4643-WY	01/15/98		
DUSTY SPRINGFIELD - Ev'rything's Coming Up Dusty (CD; reissue)	Philips 536 852-2	04/12/98		
SORAYA - Wall Of Smiles (CD; co-produced with Soraya –Argent on keyboards and string arrangements)*	PolyGram 558 451-2	05/25/98	Canadian Polydor 558 451-2	08/18/98
LUKA BLOOM - Salty Heaven (CD; Argent played keyboards on the entire album and arranged strings)	Sony LUKABCD01	06/15/98		
MORT SHUMAN - Distant Drum (CD; reissue)*	Thunderbird CSAM111	06/15/98		
SORAYA - Wall Of Smiles (CD; with two extra tracks – "Suddenly" and a French-language version of "So Far Away" entitled "J' aimerais tant")*	Japanese PolyGram PHCR-1873	08/01/98		
ORIGINAL LONDON CAST - "Cats" (2CD; reissue)	Really Useful/ Polydor 817 810-2	10/05/98		
ANDREW LLOYD WEBBER - Variations (CD; remastered reissue)	MCA MCLD 19396	02/15/99		
FRIDA - Something's Going On (CD; remastered reissue)			Polydor 314 580 010-2	03/16/99
DUSTY SPRINGFIELD - You Don't Have To Say You Love Me (CD; reissue)			Polydor 314 538 911-2	03/23/99
CLEM CLEMPSON - Acoustic Connection (CD; library music	KPM Music KPM 418	<</<</99		

release – Rod played piano and organ)
ORIGINAL LONDON CAST - "Starlight Express" (2CD; reissue)   Polydor 821 597-2   08/31/99
LUKA BLOOM - Salty Heaven (CD; belated US issue)   Shanachie 5739   09/21/99
LUKA BLOOM - Salty Heaven (CD; bonus track)   German Pinorrekk PRCD 3405031   09/21/99

Release	Label/Cat#	Date	Label/Cat#	Date
JOHN LEES - A Major Fancy (CD; repackage)	Eagle EAGCD107	10/18/99		
THE HOLLIES - Write On (CD; reissue)	Fr. Magic 5244142	12/05/99		
LEA NICHOLSON - The Concertina Record (CD; reissue)	Jamring JRINGCD001	02/14/00		
MICHAEL BALL - Secrets Of Love (CD; Rod wrote "No More Steps To Climb" with Donald Black)	Spectrum 5441002	03/14/00		
EZIO - Higher (CD; string arrangements and mellotron)	Salami 4	04/17/00		
ORIGINAL LONDON CAST - "The Phantom Of The Opera" (2CD; reissue)	R. Useful 543 928-2	02/06/01	Really Useful 543 928-2	02/06/01
JULIAN LLOYD WEBBER - Julian Lloyd Webber Plays Andrew Lloyd Webber (CD; reissue)	Philips 468 362-2	05/08/01	Philips 289 468 362-2	05/08/01
ORIGINAL SOUNDTRACK - The Saint/ Secret Agent - Original Music From The TV Series (CD; reissue)			Collectables 2830	03/19/02
MIKE HURST - Home/ In My Time (CD; reissue)	Angel Air 98	04/08/02		
TARKUS - A Gaze Between The Past And The Future (CD; 500 made)	Braz.. Medusa MR 003	12/ 10/02		
TARKUS - A Gaze Between The Past And The Future (CD)	French Rock Symphony RSLN 080	12/ 10/02		
INTERGALACTIC TOURING BAND - Intergalactic Touring Band (CD; reissue)	Voiceprint VP251 CD	01/27/03		
MAC MAC LEOD - The Incredible Musical Odyssey Of The Original Hurdy Gurdy Man (CD; with a demo of Rod Argent and Chris White's "Telescope" performed with the early version of Argent that he was briefly in. Also included is "Tick Tock Man," written by Argent and White.)	RPM RPM 258	05/11/03		
SHAKIN' STEVENS - Hits & More! (3CD; with "Radio")*	Sony 509962 2	06/16/03		
MO FOSTER - Bel Assis (CD; reissue)	Angel Air SJPCD 151	08/11/03		
TRAPEZE - You Are The Music…We're Just The Band (CD; reissue)	Lemon CDLEM 4	09/01/03		
GILBERT O'SULLIVAN - Caricature: The Box (3CD; with "I Wish I Could Cry" – repromoted in 2007)*	Bygum BGR 120	10/15/03	Rhino Handmade 77849	10/15/03
PAUL CARRACK - It Ain't Over (Special Edition) (CD; piano on "Georgia")	Carrack PCARCD6	10/27/03		
JOHN HOWARD - Kid In A Big World (CD; reissue)	RPM RPM 271	11/ 03/03		
EDWARD ROGERS - Sunday Fables (CD; with backing vocals by Colin Blunstone and Rod Argent on "Make It Go Away")			Not Lame 88	03/02/04
ORIGINAL SOUNDTRACK - Kill Bill, Vol. 2 (CD; with slowed down version of The Zombies' "She's Not There" for Malcolm McLaren's "About Her")	Maverick 48676-2	04/19/04	Maverick 48676-2	04/13/04
ANIMALS & FRIENDS - Instinct (CD; keyboards)	Organic Mt. MPS001	05/03/04		
DIRTY TRICKS - Night Man (CD; reissue)	Majestic Rock 30	06/08/04		
MOON DOGS - The Blues'll Get Ya' (CD; organ: "Travelling Show")	Market Square MSMCD 131	12/ 13/04		
FRIDA - Something's Going On (CD; reissue - 2 bonus tracks)	Polydor 9868767	05/02/05		
SHAKIN' STEVENS - The Collection (CD)	Sony Int'l 519822	05/10/05		
PAUL CARRACK - Blue Views (CD: reissue - 2 bonus tracks)	Carrack-UK PCARD 11	05/17/05		
SHAKIN' STEVENS - Collectable Shakin' Stevens (CD/DVD)	Sony 5176613000	06/06/05		
TARKUS - A Gaze Between The Past And The Future (CD; bonus cut)	French Musea FGBG 4537	08/29/05		
ROGER DALTREY - One Of The Boys (CD; reissue – 2 bonuses)	Castle CMRCD 1139	10/03/05		
ORIGINAL LONDON CAST - "Cats" (2CD; reissue)	R. Useful 987 443-3	12/20/05	R. Useful B0006633-02	12/20/05
ORIGINAL LONDON CAST - "Starlight Express" (2CD; reissue)	R. Useful 987 444-8	12/20/05		
GARY BOYLE - The Dancer (CD; reissue)	Jap. Airmail Archive AIRAC-1159	02/28/06		
VARIOUS ARTISTS - Wild Connection (CD; reissue)	Brisa 039	05/15/06		
TARKUS - A Gaze Between The Past And The Future (CD)			Medusa MEA 4537	07/28/06
ROGER DALTREY - One Of The Boys (CD; 4 bonus tracks)			Hip-O 000665102	08/29/06
DUFFY POWER - Vampers & Champers (2CD; includes tracks recorded with the band Argent, produced by Argent/White)	RPM RPM 320	09/25/06		
TRAPEZE - You Are The Music…We're Just The Band (CD; reissue)	Japanese Threshold UICY-93187	12/13/06		
PAUL CARRACK - Old, New, Borrowed And Blue (CD/special souvenir edition CD; on "The Reason Was You" and the remix of "No Easy Way Out")	Carrack-UK PCARD 15/15X	10/29/07		
ANDREW LLOYD WEBBER - Variations (CD; reissue)	Japanese Geffen UICY-93371	11/ 28/07		

Artist - Title	Label/Cat#	Date	Label/Cat# 2	Date 2
TANITA TIKARAM - Ancient Heart*/ Everybody's Angel* (CD; reissue)	German Rhino 2564-69459-5	08/04/08		
THE MINDBENDERS - With Woman In Mind (CD; with bonuses)	Japanese Fontana UICY-94018	03/25/09		
THE WHO - Who Are You (standard LP/4LP at 45 RPM)	Polydor WHOD 5004	03/27/09	Classic CRLP90147/ 2490 147-45	03/27/09
VERITY - Interrupted Journey (CD; reissue)	Jap. Air Mail Archive AIRAC-1541	06/10/09		
PHOENIX - Phoenix/ In Full View (CD; reissues)			Renaissance RMED262	08/25/09
THE MINDBENDERS - A Groovy Kind Of Love – The Complete LP's & Singles 1966-1968 (2CD)	RPM Retro D865	02/22/10		
INTERGALACTIC TOURING BAND - Intergalactic Touring Band (CD; reissue)	Jap. Air Mail Archive AIRAC-1571	03/17/10		
JOHN LEES - A Major Fancy (2CD; alternate mix of Rod's track)	Esoteric ECLEC 22233	11/29/10		
JACQUI DANKWORTH - It Happens Quietly (CD; Argent liner notes)	Specific Jazz SPEC014	08/15/11		
ORIGINAL LONDON CAST - "The Phantom Of The Opera" (2CD; 25th anniversary edition)	R. Useful 543 928-2	11/15/11		
VERITY - Interrupted Journey (CD-R; reissue)	VaVoom (no #)	01/02/12		
THE WHO - Who Are You (LP; reissue)	Polydor 3715630	01/19/12		
GARY BOYLE - The Dancer (CD; reissue)	Esoteric ECLEC2307	01/30/12		
KEITH CHRISTMAS - Pigmy (CD; reissue)	Talking Elephant TECD196	04/30/12		
JOHN LEES - A Major Fancy (2CD; reissue)	Jap. Air Mail Archive AIRAC-1673	08/09/12		
VARIOUS ARTISTS - Songs Of The Century: An All-Star Tribute To Supertramp (CD; on the track "School")			Purple Pyramid CLP 8808-2	08/14/12
PHILIP SCHOFIELD - Safety First At Home (download only; with Rod Argent, Robert Howes and Tim Renwick)	The Children's Co. download	11/04/12		
TONY ROBINSON - Fairy Tales I (download only; with Rod Argent and Robert Howes)	The Children's Co. download	11/04/12		
BILL ODDIE - What's The Time Mr. Wolf? (download only; with Rod Argent, Robert Howes and Tim Renwick)	The Children's Co. download	11/04/12		
COLIN BAKER - Roger And The Rottentrolls (download only; with Rod Argent and Robert Howes - reissue of the 1991 MFP CD)	The Children's Co. download	11/04/12		
ANDY CRANE - Fairy Tales II (download only; with Rod Argent and Robert Howes)	The Children's Co. download	11/04/12		
NEKTAR - A Spoonful Of Time (LP/CD; on the track "Riders On The Storm" - the first date shown is the CD release)			Purple Pyramid 9223-1/8932-2	11/27/12/ 01/15/13
VARIOUS ARTISTS - Little Boys Bedtime Songs & Stories (download only; with Rod Argent and Robert Howes)	Vanilla OMP download	06/02/13		
VARIOUS ARTISTS - "Fly Like An Eagle: An All-Star Tribute To Steve Miller Band (CD; "Rock'n Me" with Steve Hillage)			Purple Pyramid CLP 0640-2	07/30/13
PAUL CARRACK - Blue Views (CD; reissue)	Carrack-UK PCARCD11R	05/05/14		
LUKA BLOOM - Salty Heavem (CD; reissue)	Dutch Music On CD MOCCD 13013	06/26/14		
PAUL CARRACK - It Ain't Over (CD; reissue)	Carrack-UK PCARCD5	10/07/14		
PAUL CARRACK - Old, New, Borrowed And Blue (CD; reissue)	Carrack PCARCD15	10/07/14		
CHRIS REA - Whatever Happened To Benny Santini? (CD; reissue)			Culture Factory CFU2-LA879	11/18/14
CHRIS REA - Whatever Happened To Benny Santini? (CD; reissue)	Japanese Magnet WPCR-16196	02/11/15		
THE WHO - Who Are You (LP; reissue)	Polydor 3715630	03/23/15	Polydor B0022560-01	03/23/15
MICHAEL FENNELLY - Lane Changer (CD; reissue)			Wounded Bird WOU 2703	05/12/15
FRIDA - Something's Going On (CD/DVD/7")	Polar 00602547418456	10/23/15		
FRIDA - Something's Going On (CD + DVD)	Polar 00602547583734	10/23/15		
DUSTY SPRINGFIELD - 5 Classic Albums (5CD; including the album "Ev'ything's Coming Up Dusty")	Spectrum 00600753635469	02/19/16		
JOHN VERITY - Truth Of The Matter (CD-R; reissue without bonuses)	VaVoom (no #)	03/19/16		
VERITY - Rock Solid (CD-R; reissue)	VaVoom (no #)	03/19/16		
SPLINTER - Two Man Band (CD; reissue)	Jap. Vivid Sound VSCD-5688/ Big Pink BIG PINK 439	09/28/16		
ROBBY KRIEGER - In Session (CD; bonus track – Rod is on "School")			Purple Pyramid CLO 0514	02/17/17
MATTHEW SWEET - Tomorrow Forever (2LP/CD; Argent played			Honeycomb Hideout	06/16/17

piano on "Haunted" and "Hello")

Release	Label/Cat#	Date	Label/Cat# 2	Date 2
VARIOUS ARTISTS - "Fly Like An Eagle: An All-Star Tribute To Steve Miller Band" (CD; reissue)			Purple Pyramid CLO 0623	06/29/17
FRIDA - Something's Going On (LP; violet vinyl)	Polar 00602557569926/ 00602557444247	07/28/17		
FRIDA - Something's Going On (LP; reissue)	Polar 00602557444247	08/11/17	Polar 00602557444247	08/11/17
SPLINTER - Two Man Band (CD; reissue with 3 bonus tracks)	Grey Scale GSGZ044CD	08/12/17		
JOHN HOWARD - Kid In A Big World (LP; reissue)	Spanish You Are The Cosmos YATC41	04/20/18		
PAUL WELLER - True Meanings (2LP; organ on "The Soul Searchers" and mellotron and piano on "White Horses")	Parlophone 0190295635947	09/14/18		
PAUL WELLER - True Meanings (CD; 5 bonus tracks)	Parl. 0190295615161	09/14/18	Parl. 0190295615161	09/14/18
PAUL WELLER - True Meanings (CD; 2 bonus tracks)	Japanese Parlophone WPCR-18080	09/14/18		
JOHN HOWARD - Kid In A Big World (CD; reissue with 5 bonuses)	Japanese Wasabi WSBAC-0094	09/26/18		
TANITA TIKARAM - Ancient Heart* (CD; reissue with 2 bonuses)	Dutch Music On CD MOCCD13697	12/07/18		
TANITA TIKARAM - Ancient Heart* (LP; reissue – transparent vinyl without bonus tracks)	Dutch Music On Vinyl MOVLP2337	12/07/18		
DUSTY SPRINGFIELD - Ev'rything's Coming Up Dusty (CD; reissue – 2 bonus tracks)	Japanese Oldays ODRS98049	12/29/18		
TANITA TIKARAM - Ancient Heart* (LP; reissue)	Dutch Music On Vinyl MOVLP2337	01/25/19		
THE CHRIS WHITE EXPERIENCE - Volume One (CD/download; Rod Argent is on Chris White's "When My Boat Comes In")	Sunfish CWE001CD	03/29/19		
VARIOUS ARTISTS - "Songs Of The Century – A Tribute To Supertramp (CD; repackaged reissue)			Purple Pyramid CLO 1318	07/05/19
THE CHRIS WHITE EXPERIENCE - Volume Two (CD/download; Argent is on John Verity's "Heard Your Song," Chris White's "Hold My Hand [Lula Lula]," and JJ White's "Killing Rose")	Sunfish CWE002CD	08/31/19		
ROBBY KRIEGER - In Session (LP; reissue on blue vinyl – no extras)			Purple Pyramid CLO 0514	11/15/19
THE CHRIS WHITE EXPERIENCE - Volume Three (CD/download; Rod is on Colin Blunstone's "Unhappy Girl" and Kevin Finn's "Let's Have A Party")	Sunfish CWE003CD	12/18/19		
PAUL CARRACK - Live 2000-2020: The Independent Years (5CD; Rod is on the tracks from the Royal Albert Hall)	Carrack-UK PCARCD33	01/24/20		
ORIGINAL LONDON CAST - "Cats" (2LP; reissue)	Polydor 0852388	02/14/20	Polydor 0852388	02/14/20
TANITA TIKARAM - Ancient Heart* (LP; reissue on white vinyl)	Dutch Music On Vinyl MOVLP2337	03/13/20		
MATTHEW FISHER - Matthew Fisher/ Strange Days (CD; reissues)	Japanese Wasabi WSBAC-0130	03/25/20		
KEITH CHRISTMAS - Pigmy (CD; reissue)	Japanese Wasabi WSBAC-0132	04/24/20		
THE CHRIS WHITE EXPERIENCE - Volume Four (download-only; Rod Argent is on Chris White's "Mr. Galileo," Duffy Power's "Hummingbird," and Argent's "Alexis, You're A Circus")	Sunfish (no #)	07/03/20		
TRAPEZE - You Are The Music…We're Just The Band (2CD; reissue)	Purple PURPLE024T	09/18/20		
THE CHRIS WHITE EXPERIENCE - Volume Five (download-only; Rod Argent was involved with Duffy Power's "Love Song" and Free Ferry's "Magic Carpet Ride")	Sunfish (no #)	12/25/20		
VARIOUS ARTISTS - "Still Wish You Were Here: A Tribute To Pink Floyd" (CD/ blue vinyl LP/ clear vinyl LP/ red vinyl LP; Rod vocal and keyboards on "Shine On You Crazy Diamond [Parts 6-9]")			Cleopatra CLO 2309	05/28/21
GARY BOYLE - The Dancer (CD; reissue)	Japanese Belle Antique BELLE 223650	04/25/22		

HH001-LP/CD

ROD ARGENT RADIO APPEARANCES, INCLUDING SOLO AND GROUP RECORDINGS

"John Peel's Sunday Concert" (07/05/70; BBC Radio One): recorded 06/25/70 live at Paris Theatre, London

"Sounds Of The 70s" (07/08/70; BBC Radio One): repeat of above, hosted by John Peel

"Sounds Of The 70s" (09/09/70; BBC Radio One): Where Are We Going Wrong; Rejoice (#1) – recorded 08/27/70 at BBC Paris Studio, London (hosted by Bob Harris)

BBC TRANSCRIPTION DISCS:
"Top Of The Pops" Show #307 (09/23/70) (LP; BBC Transcription Services): Where Are We Going Wrong; Rejoice (#1) – both tracks recorded 08/27/70 for broadcast on the 09/09/70 edition of "Sounds Of The 70s"

"Pick Of The Pops For Your D.J." Show #307 (09/18/70) (LP; BBC Transcription Services): Where Are We Going Wrong; Rejoice (#1) – recorded 08/27/70 at BBC Paris Studio, London for broadcast on the 09/09/70 edition of "Sounds Of The 70s"

"Sounds Of The 70s" (12/21/70; BBC Radio One): Sweet Mary; Rejoice (#2); Stepping Stone

"Sounds Of The 70s" (01/25/71; BBC Radio One): Rejoice (#3); Chained (#1) – recorded 01/12/71 at Studio 5, Maida Vale, London (hosted by Bob Harris)

BBC TRANSCRIPTION DISC:
"Top Of The Pops" Show #326 (02/03/71) (LP; BBC Transcription Services): Rejoice (#3); Chained (#1) – recorded 01/12/71 at Studio 5, Maida Vale, London for broadcast on the 01/25/71 edition of "Sounds Of The 70s"

"In Concert" (02/14/71; BBC Radio One): Lothlorien; Chained (#2); Rejoice (#4); The Fakir (#1); Sweet Mary (#1); Time Of The Season (hosted by John Peel)

"In Concert" (02/17/71; BBC Radio One): repeat of above

"Sounds Of The 70s" (02/17/71; BBC Radio One)

"Sounds Of The 70s" (03/01/71; BBC Radio One): Stepping Stone; Rejoice (#5); Chained (#3) (Bob Harris hosted)

"Sounds Of The 70s" (06/08/71; BBC Radio One): Cast Your Spell Uranus – recorded 05/31/71 at Studio 5, Maida Vale, London (hosted by Mike Harding)

BBC TRANSCRIPTION DISCS:
"Pick Of The Pops For Your D.J." Show #345 (06/16/71) (LP; BBC Transcription Services): Cast Your Spell Uranus – recorded 05/31/71 at Studio 5, Maida Vale, London for broadcast on the 06/08/71 edition of "Sounds Of The 70s"

"Top Of The Pops" Show #345 (06/16/71) (LP; BBC Transcription Services): Cast Your Spell Uranus – recorded 05/31/71 at Studio 5, Maida Vale, London for broadcast on the 06/08/71 edition of "Sounds Of The 70s"

"Sounds Of The 70s" (06/29/71; BBC Radio One): hosted by Mike Harding

"Sounds Of The 70s" (09/27/71; BBC Radio One): hosted by Bob Harris

"Sounds Of The 70s" (10/18/71; BBC Radio One): hosted by Bob Harris

"Sounds Of The 70s" (11/30/71; BBC Radio One): Say You Don't Mind (Argent was the backing band for Colin Blunstone) – hosted by Bob Harris

"Sounds Of The 70s" (03/06/72; BBC Radio One): Hold Your Head Up (#1); Tragedy (#2); Keep On Rollin' (#1) – recorded 02/23/72 at Studio 2, Aeolian Hall, London (hosted by Bob Harris)

BBC TRANSCRIPTION DISC:
"Top Of The Pops" Show #384 (03/08/72) (LP; BBC Transcription Services): Hold Your Head Up (#1); Tragedy (#1) – recorded 02/23/72 at Studio 2, Aeolian Hall, London for broadcast on the 03/06/72 edition of "Sounds Of The 70s"

"Sounds Of The 70s" (04/10/72; BBC Radio One): Liar; Rejoice (#6); Keep On Rollin' (#2); Tragedy (#2) – recorded 04/04/72 in London (hosted by Bob Harris)

"John Peel" (04/25/72; BBC Radio One): hosted by John Peel

"In Concert" (07/01/72; BBC Radio 1): hosted by Bob Harris

"The United States Air Force Presents Wolfman Jack: Series #11" (07/72) (2LP; US Air Force Recruiting Service): Hold Your Head Up (edit)

BBC TRANSCRIPTION DISC:
"Top Of The Pops" Show #403 (07/26/72) (LP; BBC Transcription Services): Tragedy (#2); interview – first track recorded 02/23/72 at Studio 2, Aeolian Hall, London, and the interview was recorded 07/72 at BBC Transcription Services in London

"In Concert" (01/06/73; BBC Radio One): Be My Lover, Be My Friend; Sweet Mary (#2); Tragedy (#3); I Am The Dance Of Ages; The Fakir (#2); Hold Your Head Up (#2); He's A Dynamo – recorded 12/14/72 live at Paris Theatre, London (hosted by Bob Harris)

BBC TRANSCRIPTION DISC:
"Stereo Pop Special – 34" (02/73) (LP; BBC Transcription Services CN 1716/S): Be My Lover, Be My Friend; Sweet Mary (#2); Tragedy (#3); I Am The Dance Of Ages; The Fakir (#2); Hold Your Head Up (#2); He's A Dynamo – recorded 12/14/72 live at Paris Theatre, London

"Johnnie Walker" (03/01/73 – 03/02/73; BBC Radio One)

"Sounds Of The 70s" (03/12/73; BBC Radio One): It's Only Money (Part 1); It's Only Money (Part 2); God Gave Rock And Roll To You; Christmas For The Free – recorded 03/07/73 at BBC Studio, London (hosted by Bob Harris)

BBC TRANSCRIPTION DISC:
"Top Of The Pops" Show #436 (03/14/73) (LP; BBC Transcription Services): God Gave Rock And Roll To You; It's Only Money (Part 2); Christmas For The Free – recorded 03/07/73 at BBC Studio, London for broadcast on the 03/12/73 edition of "Sounds Of The 70s"

"Alan Freeman" (03/19/73 – 03/23/73; BBC Radio One): Argent was the guest for the week

"Dave Lee Travis" (04/09/73 – 04/13/73; BBC Radio One): Argent was the guest for the week

RADIO COMMERCIAL DISC:
"1973 Pepsi-Cola Radio" (Spring 1973) (Pepsi-Cola PA 1907): Argent and other artists recorded 30-second and 60-second Pepsi commercials for this disc

"Nightbird & Co.: Cosmic Connections" (week of 10/06/74) (2LP; United States Army Reserve Programs #177-180): Argent is Program #179 on one LP side and features Rod Argent and Russ Ballard

"Encore"/ "In Flight" (12/74) (LP; Armed Forces Radio and Television Service RL 29-5): one side each from Argent's "Encore" and Alvin Lee & Co.'s "In Flight" LPs

BBC TRANSCRIPTION DISCS:
"Top Of The Pops" Show #534 (01/29/75) (LP; BBC Transcription Services): Rod Argent interview with Michael Wale; Keep On Rollin' (#3) – recorded 02/23/75 at BBC Studio, London

"Top Of The Pops" Show #746 (03/01/79) (LP; BBC Transcription Services): Silence ("Moving Home" album track)

"The Spinners And Friends" (01/14/82; BBC Radio Two): Rod Argent on piano

"Classic Concert" (08/03/86; BBC Radio One): Andy Peebles presented the Argent "In Concert" program recorded on 12/14/72

"King Biscuit Flower Hour" (07/88) (CD; DIR Radio Network): live in London 05/01/74; the program also features Mott The Hoople

"Colin Blunstone Session" (01/30/91; BBC): She's Not There; Time Of The Season; Andorra; Caroline Goodbye (with Colin Blunstone, Jim Rodford, and John Verity)

"Desert Island Discs" (week of 04/19/93) (LP; MJI Broadcasting D.I.D. – 172): Rod played his favorite songs, and the end of Side 1 included a promo for the show

"Maestro" (05/03/96; BBC Radio Two): Rod Argent was a team captain for six episodes of the music quiz program

"Maestro" (05/10/96; BBC Radio Two)

"Maestro" (05/17/96; BBC Radio Two)

"Maestro" (05/24/96; BBC Radio Two)

"Maestro" (05/31/96; BBC Radio Two)

"Maestro" (06/07/96; BBC Radio Two)

"Jammin'" (10/05/06; BBC Radio Two): Rod joined comedian Steve Furst, Rowland Rovron, Steve Brown and Dave Catlin for a jam session and chat, and included was Rod's Louis Armstrong-influenced take of Green Day's "Boulevard Of Broken Dreams"!

"Saturday Live" (02/21/09; BBC Radio 4): Rod Argent chose his "Inheritance Tracks"

"Classic Rock Sequence" (07/25/09; BBC Radio 6 Music): archival Argent BBC session

"Classic Rock Sequence" (10/10/09; BBC Radio 6 Music): archival Argent BBC session

"Sounds Of The 70s With Johnnie Walker" (11/08/09; BBC Radio Two): Rod discussed his '70s career with the band Argent

"A Tribute To Sir John Dankworth" (02/26/10; BBC Radio Two): Rod was one of many artists that appeared at the 40th anniversary concert recorded at The Stables on the day that Dankworth passed away (02/06/10)

"Classic Rock Sequence" (03/20/10; BBC Radio 6 Music): archival Argent BBC session

"Gideon Coe" (04/28/11; BBC Radio 6 Music): archival 1972 Argent BBC session

"Liz Kershaw" (05/14/11; BBC Radio 6 Music): Rod Argent talked about his fantasy party!

"Bethan Elfyn" (08/06/11; BBC Radio Wales): Rod talked about the Rheola Festival

"The Old Grey Whistle Test 40" (08/31/11; BBC Radio Two): Rod Argent and Russ Ballard appeared on Bob Harris' program to talk about the 40th anniversary of "The Old Grey Whistle Test," and the interview was recorded on 06/27/11

"Late Show – Keith Middleton" (11/05/11; BBC Coventry & Warwickshire): Rod appeared

"Roger Day" (02/01/12; BBC Surrey): Rod was interviewed about being in two great bands

"Justin Dealey" (04/21/12; BBC Three Counties Radio): Rod and Jim Rodford made "Justin's Jukebox" selections

"6 Music Live Hour" (11/15/12; BBC Radio 6 Music): archival Argent BBC session from the Paris Theatre in London during 1972

"Steve Lamacq's Rock College" (08/08/13; BBC Radio Two): Rod was the Guest Lecturer for the program

"6 Music Live Hour" (12/08/14; BBC Radio 6 Music): Paris Theatre 1972

"Robert Elms" (04/25/15; BBC Radio London): Rod played live in studio

"6 Music Live Hour" (11/06/15; BBC Radio 6 Music): archival Argent BBC session

"The Janice Forsyth Show" (11/09/15; BBC Radio Orkney): Rod was interviewed

"Ken Bruce" (02/23/16; BBC Radio Two): Rod picked "The Tracks Of My Years"

"6 Music Live Hour" (07/28/16; BBC Radio 6 Music): Paris Theatre 1972

"Alan Thompson" (10/30/16; BBC Radio Wales): Rod was interviewed

"6 Music Live Hour" (04/02/18; BBC Radio 6 Music): Paris Theatre 1972

"Cerys Matthews" (06/16/19; BBC Radio 6 Music): archival Argent BBC session

"First Cast" (12/29/19; BBC Radio Two): Rod was interviewed about the musical "Cats"

"6 Music Live Hour" (01/16/20; BBC Radio 6 Music): Paris Theatre 1972

"First Cast" (01/30/21; BBC Radio Two): a repeat of Rod's interview about "Cats"

ROD ARGENT TELEVISION, FILM, AND VIDEO APPEARANCES
(television broadcasts list the first broadcast dates and networks; films/videos list just the first release dates)

"Disco 2" (02/25/71; BBC Two): Argent's contribution to this program was on film

"Set Of 6" (05/30/72; UK Granada TV): Stepping Stone; Liar; Rejoice; Hold Your Head Up; Sweet Mary; Keep On Rollin'

"Top Of The Pops" (06/22/72; BBC One): Tragedy

"Two G's And The Pop People" (06/24/72; UK ITV): Rod was a guest

"The Midnight Special: Pilot" (08/19/72; US NBC): Hold Your Head Up

"The Old Grey Whistle Test" (03/06/73; BBC Two): God Gave Rock And Roll To You; It's Only Money; Hold Your Head Up

"Popgala '73" (03/16/73; Dutch VARA): God Gave Rock And Roll To You; Keep On Rollin' – Argent session recorded 03/10/73 at Sporthal de Vliegermolen, Voorburg, Netherlands

"The Midnight Special" (06/02/73; US NBC): God Gave Rock And Roll To You; Hold Your Head Up; It's Only Money (Part 2) – filmed 05/13/73 at NBC Studios, Burbank, California

"Don Kirshner's Rock Concert" (12/29/73; syndicated): God Gave Rock And Roll To You; I Am The Dance Of Ages; I Don't Believe In Miracles; The Fakir; Drum Solo; It's Only Money (Parts 1 & 2); Hold Your Head Up – recorded 11/07/73 at The Palace Theatre in New York, New York

"The Old Grey Whistle Test" (02/24/74; BBC Two): Gonna Meet My Maker

"The Old Grey Whistle Test" (04/03/74; BBC Two): Music From The Spheres

"The Old Grey Whistle Test" (06/14/75; BBC Two): Hold Your Head Up

"Top Of The Pops" (06/22/78; BBC One): Argentine Melody (Canción de Argentina) (by San José featuring Rodriguez Argentina)

"Top Of The Pops" (07/06/78; BBC One): same as the 06/22/78 episode

"The Old Grey Whistle Test" (02/13/79; BBC Two): Rod Argent appeared

"The Old Grey Whistle Test" (02/18/79; BBC Two): repeat of above

"Tell Me On A Sunday" (02/12/80; BBC One): Rod played piano for Marti Webb

"Won't Change Places" (02/16/81; BBC Two): Marti Webb with Andrew Lloyd Webber, Paul Nicholas, Julian Lloyd Webber and Rod Argent at the Watermill Theatre near Newbury

"Won't Change Places" (04/08/81; BBC One): repeat of above

"Friday Night...Saturday Morning" (11/20/81; BBC Two)

"The Old Grey Whistle Test" (03/18/82; BBC Two): Barbara Thompson and Rod Argent from Riverside Studios, Hammersmith

"Six Fifty-Five" (08/03/83; BBC Two): Rod Argent piano with Stephanie Lawrence

"Six Fifty-Five" (08/15/83; BBC Two): Barbara Courtney-King performed the album "Pastourelle" with Rod Argent, Julian Lloyd Webber, and The Gabrieli String Quartet

"BBC Television's Carol Competition 1983" (12/23/83; BBC One): the eighth competition that offered young people from the UK the chance to compose their own Christmas Carols – Rod Argent, Kiki Dee and Peter Skellern were the judges

"Soldiers" (09/18/85 – 12/18/85; BBC One): Rod composed music for 10 episodes of this documentary, including the theme

"The Two Of Us" (10/31/86 – 03/18/90; UK ITV): Rod Argent composed the theme and incidental music with Peter Van Hooke

"Celebration In Watercolor" (07/10/87): Rod composed music for this short documentary

"Bust: Family Business" (10/09/87; UK ITV): title and incidental music by Argent and Van Hooke

"Reaching For The Skies" (09/12/88 – 11/28/88; BBC Two): title music with Van Hooke

"Not With A Bang: The World Disappears" (03/25/90; UK ITV): Argent and Van Hooke music

"The Piglet Files: Now You See It" (10/12/90; UK ITV): Argent and Van Hooke music

"It'll Be Alright On The Night 6" (12/02/90; UK ITV): Argent/ Van Hooke title music

"The Piglet Files: The Hunt For Red Decoder" (05/31/91; UK ITV): Argent and Van Hooke music

"Reaching For The Skies" (07/03/91 – 09/11/91; BBC Two): rebroadcast

"The Piglet Files: Guerrilas In The Mist" (03/29/92; UK ITV): Argent and Van Hooke music

"The Piglet Files: Sex, Spies And Videotape" (04/12/92; UK ITV): Argent and Van Hooke music

"A Keyboard Approach" (08/11/92): a UK VHS release: Starnite Ltd. SNT010 – 66-minute instructional video

"It'll Be Alright On The Night 7" (01/02/93; UK ITV): Argent/ Van Hooke title music

"The Utterly Worst Of Alright On The Night" (04/10/94; UK ITV): Argent/ Van Hooke title music

"The Kids From Alright On The Night" (11/26/94; UK ITV): Argent/ Van Hooke title music

"It'll Be Alright On The Night 8" (12/10/94; UK ITV): Argent/ Van Hooke title music

"Alright On The Night's Cockup Trip" (10/12/96; UK ITV): Argent/ Van Hooke title music

"It'll Be Alright On The Night 10" (11/29/97; UK ITV): Argent/ Van Hooke title music

"21 Years Of Alright On The Night" (01/24/98; UK ITV): Argent/ Van Hooke title music

"It'll Be Alright On The Night 11" (10/02/99; UK ITV): composed title music with Van Hooke

"It'll Be Alright On The Night 12" (01/27/01; UK ITV): composed title music with Van Hooke

"It'll Be Alright On Election Night" (06/07/01; UK ITV): Argent/ Van Hooke title music

"It'll Be Alright On The Night 13" (08/17/01; UK ITV): Argent/ Van Hooke title theme

"Alright On The Night's Silver Jubilee Special" (09/14/02; UK ITV): Argent/ Van Hooke title theme

"70's Rock – Rock Legends" (01/28/03): Hold Your Head Up – a UK DVD release: Regeneration CRP1655

"The Old Grey Whistle Test Volume 2" (09/16/03): God Gave Rock And Roll To You – a UK DVD release: Video/Film Express 500606

"Classic Rock – The Ultimate Anthology" (03/15/04): Hold Your Head Up – a UK DVD release: Ragnarock DVDL010D

"Inside Free 1968-1972" (02/01/05): Rod Argent interview – a UK/US CD/DVD release: Classic Rock Legends 1609

"Inside Argent" (04/05/05): Stepping Stone; Liar; Sweet Mary; Rejoice; Hold Your Head Up; Keep On Rollin'; God Gave Rock And Roll To You; I Don't Believe In Miracles; plus numerous interviews – a UK/US CD/DVD release: Classic Rock Legends 1814

"The Old Grey Whistle Test (The Definitive Collection)" (11/21/05): God Gave Rock And Roll To You – a UK 4DVD release: BBC BBCDVD1867

"It'll Be Alright On The Night 19" (12/31/05; UK ITV): Argent/ Van Hooke title theme

"The 60s: The Beatles Decade – Teenage Rebels 1960-1962" (07/10/06; UKTV History: Rod contributed to four out of the five episodes

"The 60s: The Beatles Decade – Sex, Spies And Rock And Roll" (07/11/06; UKTV History)

"The 60s: The Beatles Decade – Swinging Britain 1965-1966" (07/12/06; UKTV History)

"The 60s: The Beatles Decade – The Party's Over 1969-1970" (07/14/06; UKTV History)

"The Old Grey Whistle Test – The Complete Collection" (08/29/06): God Gave Rock And Roll To You – a UK 3DVD release: BBC E2351

"Argent – Total Rock Review" (09/18/06): Stepping Stone; Liar; Rejoice; Hold Your Head Up; Sweet Mary – an unauthorized UK DVD release: Storm Bird STB 2182

"Burt Sugarman's The Midnight Special: 1973" (10/27/06): Hold Your Head Up – a US DVD release: Guthy-Renker Entertainment MU.0009

"Burt Sugarman's The Midnight Special: Legendary Performances 1973-1981" (06/05/07): Hold Your Head Up – a US 9DVD release: Guthy-Renker Entertainment MUBOX001

"Mellodrama" (02/14/08 –02/20/08): Rod contributed to this documentary about the mellotron

"Ringo Starr & His All Starr Band Live 2006" (07/08/08): She's Not There; Hold Your Head Up – a US DVD release: Koch KOC-DV-4543; recorded 07/16/06 at Mohegan Sun, Uncasville, Connecticut, and Rod played keyboards throughout the tour

"Mellodrama: The Mellotron Movie" (01/19/10): a US DVD release: Bazillion Points (no #)

"The Old Grey Whistle Test: 70s Gold" (09/23/11; BBC Four): archival Argent appearance

"It'll Be Alright On The Night 2011: Part 1" (12/28/11; UK ITV): Argent/ Van Hooke title theme

"It'll Be Alright On The Night 2011: Part 2" (12/31/11; UK ITV): Argent/ Van Hooke title theme

"The Midnight Special" (09/09/14): Hold Your Head Up – respective US 1DVD/6DVD/11DVD releases: StarVista Entertainment/ TimeLife 30730-X/30732-X-30902-X

"It'll Be Alright On The Night 39" (12/30/15; UK ITV): Argent/ Van Hooke title theme

"It'll Be Alright On The Night 40" (06/04/16; UK ITV): Argent/ Van Hooke title theme

ADDITIONAL NOTES

A cassette exists of Rod Argent's demos for the 1981 stage work "Masquerade."

Rod Argent played keyboards on the UK Eurovision song entry "No Dream Impossible" written by Russ Ballard and sung by 16-year-old Lindsay Drakkas. The contest took place on 05/11/01.

The Children's Company and Vanilla OMP albums above were recorded in 1989 and 1990, and with one exception (the 1991 MFP CD listed with Rod's album sessions), were not commercially released at the time.

SAMPLES OF ROD ARGENT-RELATED TRACKS

"Run The Sphere" by MONSTA ISLAND CZARS (2001): Dance In The Smoke (by Rod Argent and Chris White)
"De 1st Installment" by J DILLA (2002): Cast Your Spell Uranus (by Rod Argent and Chris White)
"Raw Addict" by JAYLIB (2013): God Gave Rock And Roll To You (by Russ Ballard)
"Sunlight & Breakfast In 3D" by VIDEO EZY (2014); Network Heroes (by Rod Argent and Robert Howes)
"What's It All About" by GIRL TALK (2018): Hold Your Head Up (by Rod Argent and Chris White)
"Spread Your Wings" by KANYE WEST (2019): Like Honey (by Rod Argent and Chris White)

UNISSUED ROD ARGENT SONGS FILED WITH BMI

I'll Be Kind
I'll Be There
I Won't Be Your Alibi
Piglet Files (bumper music, incidental music, opening and closing themes, background cues – all with Peter Van Hooke)

ARGENT SONG PLACEMENTS IN FILM

"Towards The Morning" (11/06/81): Towards The Morning (Rod Argent wrote the title theme for this short film)

"Queens Logic" (02/01/91): Hold Your Head Up

"The Master" (05/07/92): Dragonflies At Dusk (Rod Argent wrote this song with Robert Howes for their CD "A New Age")

"Trees Lounge" (05/11/96): Hold Your Head Up

"Rocko's Modern Life: Heff In A Handbasket/ Wallaby On Wheels" (07/18/96; US Nickelodeon): Requiem For A Hero - Part II (a) (uncredited; used in the first cartoon listed, and the track is also on the KPM CD "Network Heroes")

"The Castle" (04/10/97): Hold Your Head Up

"Outside Providence" (08/16/99): Hold Your Head Up

"Joe Dirt" (04/11/01): Hold Your Head Up

"Slap Shot 2: Breaking The Ice" (03/26/02): Good Morning America (Rod Argent wrote this song with Robert Howes for the KPM CD "Network Heroes")

"House Of D" (05/07/04): Hold Your Head Up

"Gym Teacher" (09/12/08): Good Morning America (from the Argent/Howes KPM CD "Network Heroes")

"Men Of A Certain Age: A League Of Their Owen" (06/15/11; US TNT): Hold Your Head Up – uncredited

"That's My Boy" (06/04/12): Hold Your Head Up

"Anchorman 2: The Legend Continues" (11/24/13): Hold Your Head Up

"Trust: The House Of Getty" (03/25/18; BBC Two/ US FX): Hold Your Head Up

"I'm Dying Up Here: Now You See Me, Now You Don't" (06/24/18; US Showtime): Hold Your Head Up

"She's Gotta Have It: #NationTime" (05/24/19; Netflix): Hold Your Head Up

"Mrs. America: Bella" (05/13/20; BBC Two): Hold Your Head Up

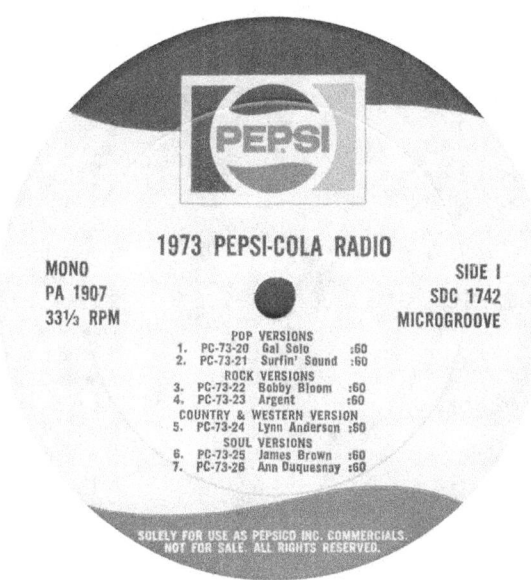

ROD ARGENT CONCERT LISTING
(all UK and by the band Argent unless otherwise noted;
* = Rod Argent solo or guest)

1969

September – October: warm-up gigs in Germany and Italy:
The PN Hit House, Munich, Germany
Italian club gigs

1970

03/08	University Of Dayton, Dayton, Ohio, USA
03/12-14	Boston Tea Party, Boston, Massachusetts, USA (with Mother Earth and Mocha Chip)
03/19-21	Fillmore East, New York, New York, USA (with The Moody Blues and Lee Michaels)
03/22-25	Ungano's, New York, New York, USA
03/26	Allen Theatre, Cleveland, Ohio, USA (with The Moody Blues and John Mayall)
03/27	Aragon Ballroom, Chicago, Illinois, USA
04/10-11	Ludlow Garage, Cincinnati, Ohio, USA
04/16-19	Fillmore West, San Francisco, California, USA
04/22-26	Whisky A Go Go, West Hollywood, California, USA
05/16	Cardiff University, Cardiff, Wales
05/23-24	Whitsun Festival, Plumpton Racecourse, Plumpton, Lewes
06/01	The Marquee, London
06/05	Lyceum Ballroom, London (with Procol Harum, Hard Meat, and Supertramp)
06/07	Roundhouse, London (with Fotheringay, Elton John, The Humblebums, and Amory Kane)
06/27	Van Dike Club, Plymouth
07/02	Haverstock Hill Country Club, London (with Hobgoblin)
07/04	Farnborough Tech College, Farnborough (with Stackridge)
07/06	Friars, Aylesbury
07/08	Resurrection Club, London
07/09	Grasshopper, Crawley
07/11	Kursaal, Southend-on-Sea (with Juicy Lucy and Stackridge)
07/19	Cloud Nine Club, Peterborough
07/22	The Castle, Tooting
07/24	Star, Croydon
07/25	Farx, Potters Bar (with Bram Stoker)
08/02	Mothers, Birmingham
08/18	Hampstead Country Club, Hampstead
08/20	Old Granary, Bristol
08/21	Turku International Pop & Rock Festivaalit, Ruissalo, Turku, Finland (with Blue Mink and Burnin' Red Ivanhoe)
08/23	Ruisrock Festival 1970, Ruissalo, Turku, Finland
08/26	Resurrection Club, Barnet
09/06	Farx, Southall
09/08	Fishmongers Arms, Wood Green
10/02	Thames Polytechnic, London (with Climax Chicago Blues Band)
10/11	Bletchley Youth Centre, Bletchley
10/13	Hampstead Country Club, Hampstead (with Jasper)
10/14	Mothers, Birmingham
10/17	University College London Union, London
10/20	South Parade Pier, Portsmouth (with Black Sabbath)
10/31	Free Trade Hall, Manchester (with Kevin Ayers And The Whole World)
11/05	Old Granary, Bristol
11/07	Brunel College, Uxbridge (with Genesis)
12/11	Tottenham Sisters Club, London (with Teargas)
12/12	Exeter University, Exeter (with Fairport Convention)
12/15	1832 Club, Windsor (with Skinny Cat)
12/17	Warrington Carlton, Warrington
12/18	Flamingo, Hereford
12/20	Farx, Southall
12/27	The Black Prince, Bexley

1971

01/02	Temple Club, London (with Sweet Slag)
01/03	Pavilion, Hemel Hempstead
01/15	Van Dike Club, Plymouth
01/19	Tricorn Club, Portsmouth
01/31	Lyceum Ballroom, London (with Slade and Barclay James Harvest)
02/01	Birmingham Odeon, Birmingham
02/02	Civic Hall, Wolverhampton
02/03	Pavilion, Weston-Super-Mare
02/07	Wake Arms, Epping
02/12	Odeon Walsall, Walsall and The Marquee, London and South Parade Pier, Portsmouth
02/13	Bristol Polytechnic, Bristol
02/14	Black Prince, Bexley
02/19	Imperial College, London
02/20	Leicester Tech College, Leicester
02/23	Civic Hall, Tunbridge Wells (with Skid Row and Alan Bown)
02/26	Hull University, Hull
03/06	Anglia University, Norwich (with Barclay James Harvest)
03/07	Black Swan, Sheffield
03/09	The Place, Hanley
03/16	Chiswick Polytechnic, Chiswick (with Barclay James Harvest)
03/19	Shades Discotheque, Northampton
03/23	Tricorn Club, Portsmouth
03/25	Denbighshire College, Denbighshire, Wales
03/28	The Greyhound, Croydon
04/01	The Marquee, London (with Satisfaction)
04/03	Kingham Hall, Watford
04/04	Roundhouse, London (with The Edgar Broughton Band, Gypsy, and Budgie)
04/18	Zoom, Frankfurt, Germany (Russ Ballard is electrocuted on stage)
05/11	Nightingale, Wood Green
05/24	The Marquee, London
05/29	Dagenham Roundhouse, London
06/01	Starlight Ballroom, Crawley
06/03	High Wycombe Town Hall, High Wycombe
06/05	Resurrection Club, Hitchin
06/06	Guildford Civic Hall, Guildford
06/18	Il Rondo, Leicester
06/19	Temple Club, London
07/04	The Lyceum, London (with Trapeze)
07/11	Wake Arms, Epping
07/12	Forum, Cannock
07/25	Old Granary, Bristol
08/12	Kensington Town Hall, Kensington
08/15	Greyhound, Croydon
08/28-29	Weeley 1971, Clacton-on-Sea (with many others)
09/10	Red Lion, Leytonstone (with Third World War)
09/11	High Wycombe Town Hall, High Wycombe (with Man)

UK tour (09/24/71 – 11/15/71) with Climax Chicago [Blues Band]:

09/24	Stoke Civic Hall, Stoke
09/28	St. George's Hall, Bradford
09/30	Bath Pavilion, Bath
10/02	Slough College, Slough
10/10	Caley Cinema, Edinburgh, Scotland
10/14	Southampton Guild Hall, Southampton
10/15	Preston Public Hall, Preston
10/16	Sheffield University, Sheffield
10/17	Cheltenham Town Hall, Cheltenham
10/18	St. Andrew's Hall, Norwich
10/19	Winter Gardens, Malvern
10/21	Oaken Gates Town Hall, Oaken Gates
10/22	Aberystwyth University, Aberystwyth, Wales
10/23	Cardiff University, Cardiff, Wales
10/25	Leeds Town Hall, Leeds
10/26	Newcastle City Hall, Newcastle
10/27	New Victoria, Halifax
10/28	Kinetic Circus, Birmingham
10/29	Bristol University, Bristol
10/30	Bangor University, Bangor

10/31	Wolverhampton Civic Hall, Wolverhampton	06/18	Kinetic Circus, Kenilworth
11/01	Liverpool Stadium, Liverpool	06/19	Wolverhampton City Hall, Wolverhampton
11/03	Winter Gardens, Bournemouth	06/20	Queen's College, Cambridge
11/04	Warwick University, Warwick	07/16	The Lyceum, London (with The Gary Moore Band)
11/09	Free Trade Hall, Manchester	07/20	Liverpool Stadium, Liverpool
11/12	Westfield College, London	07/28	Community Centre, Slough
11/13	Farnborough Tech College, Farnborough	08/02	Gaelic Park, The Bronx, New York, USA (with The Jeff Beck Group, Flash, and Blue Öyster Cult)
11/15	Rainbow Theatre, London (also with Duffy Power)	08/04	Curtis Hixon Convention Hall, Tampa, Florida, USA (with Poco)

1972

01/01	Belfry, Sutton Coldfield	08/13	Hollywood Palladium, Los Angeles, California, USA (with The Jeff Beck Group and Foghat)
01/07	JB's, Dudley	08/14	Berkeley Community Theatre, Berkeley, California, USA
01/09	Coatham Hotel, Redcar	08/17	Sam Houston Coliseum, Houston, Texas (supporting It's A Beautiful Day and Canned Heat)
01/14	North London Polytechnic, London (with Patto and Keith Christmas) **and** Red Lion, Leytonstone	08/22	The Agora, Cleveland, Ohio, USA
01/19	Flintshire Tech College, Flintshire	08/24	Reflections, Cincinnati, Ohio, USA
01/20	Winsford City Hall, Winsford (with Climax Chicago [Blues Band])	08/30	Knoxville Civic Coliseum, Knoxville, Tennessee, USA
01/22	Bradford University, Bradford	09/01	Syria Mosque, Pittsburgh, Pennsylvania, USA
01/28	Child's Hall, Reading	09/02	Municipal Auditorium, New Orleans, Louisiana, USA (with The Doors and The Phlorescent Leech And Eddie)
01/29	Rijnhal, Arnhem, Netherlands	09/07	Mississippi Coliseum, Jackson, Mississippi, USA
02/01	Nightingale, Wood Green	09/09	Indianapolis Raceway Festival, Bush Stadium, Indianapolis, Indiana, USA (with numerous acts)
02/03	Glen Ballroom, Llanelli, Wales		
02/04	Salford University, Salford	09/14	Academy Of Music, New York, New York, USA (with T-Rex and The Doobie Brothers)
02/05	Glasgow University Union, Glasgow, Scotland		
02/06	Black Swan, Sheffield	09/30	Melody Maker Poll Concert 1972, The Oval, London (with Wishbone Ash, Genesis, Focus, Fudd, and Emerson, Lake & Palmer)
02/17	Wallington Public Hall, Wallington		
02/18	Civic Centre, St. Albans		
02/19	Imperial College, London	10/06	Aston University, Birmingham
02/26	Paradiso, Amsterdam, Netherlands	10/07	Roundhouse, Dagenham
03/02	Toby Jug, Tolworth	10/13	Lancaster University, Lancaster (with Hackensack)
03/14	Chelsea Village, Bournemouth	10/14	University of Kent, Canterbury and Rutherford College, Rutherford
03/24	Ipswich Civic College, Ipswich (with Man and Skid Row)		
03/25	Kingston Polytechnic, Kingston	10/20	Community Centre, Slough
03/27	Civic Centre, Chelmsford (with Trapeze)	10/21	Nottingham University, Nottingham
03/31	Chez Club, Leytonstone	10/22	Greyhound, Croydon (with The Sensational Alex Harvey Band)
04/01	Woodford Centre, Stockport		
04/02	Greyhound, Croydon	10/27	Queens Hotel, Southend-on-Sea
04/05	Boobs, Bristol	10/28	Corn Exchange, Cambridge (with Snake Eye)
04/10	Gravesend Civic Centre, Gravesend	11/02	Sundown, Mile End (with Nazareth)
04/13	Glen Ballroom, Llanelli, Wales (with Van Der Graaf Generator, Chicken Shack, Black Widow, and Sassafras)	11/03	Mayfair Ballroom, Newcastle (with Babe Ruth)
		11/04	Leicester University, Leicester
04/14	Corn Exchange, Devizes	11/05	Electric Flag, Wheeling, West Virginia, USA
04/15	Watford Tech College, Watford (with Glencoe and Renia)	11/10	Hatfield Polytechnic, Hatfield
04/16	Barbarella's, Birmingham	11/12	Sundown, Edmonton, London
04/17	Free Trade Hall, Manchester (with Gallagher & Lyle)	11/15	Winter Gardens, Bournemouth
04/20	Kensington Court, Newport	11/16	Alhambra, Birmingham (with Capability Brown)
04/21	Mandarin, Liverpool	11/17	Bath University, Bath
04/22	Leeds University, Leeds	11/24	Imperial College, London (with John And Beverley Martin, Ellis, Biggles, and Rainmaker)
04/23	Caird Hall, Dundee, Scotland		
04/26	Cardiff University, Cardiff, Wales	11/25	Liverpool Stadium, Liverpool (with Greasy Bear)
05/11	Locarno, Coventry (with Vinegar Joe)	11/27	Free Trade Hall, Manchester
05/12	Christ's College, Cambridge	12/01	Sundown, Edmonton, London
05/13	St. Mary's College, Twickenham (with Sandy Denny, Paladin, and Hookfoot)	12/14	Paris Theatre, London (recording "In Concert" program)
		12/16	Northamptonshire County Cricket Ground, Northampton
05/15	Victoria Hall, Hanley		
05/16	Mayfair, Newcastle		
05/17	Pier Pavilion, Felixstowe	**1973**	
05/19	Camden Town Hall, London (with Capability Brown)	01/26	Academy Of Music, New York, New York, USA
05/20	Rock, Wellingborough	01/27	Free Trade Hall, Manchester
05/22	Pinkpop 1972, Burgemeester Damen Sportpark, Geleen, Netherlands	02/02	Leeds Polytechnic, Leeds
		02/08	Glen Ballroom, Llanelli, Wales
05/27	Dagenham Roundhouse, London	02/10	South Parade Pier, Southsea
06/01	Paris Theatre, London	02/16	Goldsmiths College, London
06/02	Festival della musica d'avanguardia e nuove tendenze 1972, Stadio della Pallacorda, Rome, Italy	02/24	Loughborough University, Loughborough
		03/02	Salford University, Salford
06/10	Starlight Rooms, Boston	03/06	Overton Park Shell, Memphis, Tennessee, USA
06/12	Cambridge Tech College, Cambridge	03/10	Pop Gala '73, Sporthal de Vliegermolen, Voorburg, Netherlands
06/15	Victoria Hall, Hanley		
06/16	Mayfair Ballroom, Newcastle	03/31	Alumni Hall, St. John's University, Queens, New York, USA (with The Kinks)
06/17	Pier Pavilion, Felixstowe		

04/05	Harrisburg State Farm Arena, Harrisburg, Pennsylvania, USA (with The Beach Boys)
04/06	The Spectrum, Philadelphia, Pennsylvania, USA (with The Beach Boys and Spooky Tooth)
04/13	McCarter Theatre, Princeton University, Princeton, New Jersey, USA
04/21	Lake Spivey Park, Jonesboro, Georgia, USA (with Fanny, Bloodrock, and Blue Öyster Cult)
05/01	Auditorium Theatre, Chicago, Illinois, USA
05/04	Sam Houseton Coliseum, Houston, Texas, USA (with Boz Scaggs)
05/05	University of Texas at Arlington, Arlington, Texas, USA (with Boz Scaggs)
05/06	Municipal Auditorium, San Antonio, Texas, USA (with Boz Scaggs)
05/11	Tucson Convention Center, Tucson, Arizona, USA
05/12	Anaheim Convention Center, Anaheim, California, USA
05/13	NBC Studios, Burbank, California, USA (filming for "The Midnight Special")
05/18	Carnegie Hall, New York, New York, USA (with The Doobie Brothers)
05/19	Capitol Theatre, Passaic, New Jersey, USA (with The Doobie Brothers)
05/20	Ohio University, Athens, Ohio, USA
05/22	Allen Theatre, Cleveland, Ohio, USA (with The Doobie Brothers)
05/23	Armory Fieldhouse, Cincinnati, Ohio, USA (with The Doobie Brothers and Sons Of Champlin)
05/25	St. Paul Auditorium, St. Paul, Minnesota, USA
05/26	Arie Crown Theater, Chicago, Illinois, USA
06/02	Convention Center, Louisville, Kentucky, USA (supporting The Guess Who)
06/03	Overton Park Shell, Memphis, Tennessee, USA
07/27	London Music Festival 1973, Alexandra Palace, London (with Family, Glencoe, Ellis, and Fumble)
08/08	Alexandra Palace, London (with Thin Lizzy and Wizzard)
08/18	Jazz-Bilzen 1973, Dell, Bilzen, Belgium
09/08	Rock-Festival Scheeßel, Eichenring, Scheeßel, Germany (with many other acts)
09/16	Fairfield Concert Hall, London (with Glencoe)
09/17	Colston Hall, Bristol (with Glencoe)
09/19	Dome, Brighton (with Glencoe)
09/20	Guildhall, Southampton (with Glencoe)
09/21	Rainbow Theatre, London (with Glencoe)
09/22	Guildhall, Portsmouth (with Glencoe)
09/23	Birmingham Town Hall, Birmingham (with Glencoe)
09/24	De Montfort Hall, Leicester (with Glencoe)
09/25	Sheffield City Hall, Sheffield (with Glencoe)
09/26	Newcastle City Hall, Newcastle (with Glencoe)
09/27	Leeds Town Hall, Leeds (with Glencoe)
09/28	Free Trade Hall, Manchester (with Glencoe)
09/29	Empire, Edinburgh, Scotland (with Glencoe)
09/30	Apollo Theatre, Glasgow, Scotland (with Glencoe)
10/06	Liverpool Stadium, Liverpool (with Glencoe)
10/20	NE London Polytechnic, Dagenham (with Duncan Browne and Hummingbird)
10/26	Top Rank, Doncaster
11/02	Masonic Temple Theatre, Detroit, Michigan, USA (with Frank Zappa)
11/05	Auditorium Theatre, Chicago, Illinois, USA (with Joe Walsh And Barnstorm)
11/07	D.A.R. Constitution Hall, Washington, District of Columbia, USA
11/09	Onondaga War Memorial Auditorium, Syracuse, New York, USA (with Frank Zappa)
11/10	The Spectrum, Philadelphia, Pennsylvania, USA (with John Mayall and Brian Auger's Oblivion Express)
11/11	Palace Concert Center, Providence, Rhode Island, USA (with John Mayall)
11/16	Allan Kirby Field House, Lafayette College, Easton, Pennsylvania, USA (with Renaissance)
11/17	Academy Of Music, New York, New York (with Wishbone Ash)
11/18	Glassboro State College, Glassboro, New Jersey, USA (Russ Ballard cut his nose badly)
11/21	Municipal Auditorium, Atlanta, Georgia, USA
11/22	Bayfront Center, St. Petersburg, Florida, USA
11/23	Seminole Turf Club, Casselberry, Florida, USA
11/24	Auditorium, Chicago, Illinois, USA (with The Doobie Brothers)
12/16	Roundhouse, London (with Beggars Opera, Trapeze, Fable, and The John Verity Band)
12/29	The Palace Theater, New York, New York, USA

1974

01/25	Birmingham Town Hall, Birmingham
01/26	Malvern Winter Gardens, Great Malvern (with Walrus Gumboot and Sidewinder)
01/27	Guild Hall, Plymouth
01/31	Empire Theatre, Liverpool University, Liverpool
02/01	University Of Edinburgh, Edinburgh, Scotland
02/02	Loughborough University, Loughborough
02/04	Apollo, Glasgow, Scotland
02/07	Portsmouth Guild Hall, Portsmouth
02/08	University Of Exeter, Exeter
02/09	Colston Hall, Bristol
02/14	Apollo Theatre, Glasgow, Scotland
02/15	Free Trade Hall, Manchester
02/16	University Of Hull, Kingston upon Hull
02/21	Victoria Hall, Hanley
02/23	The Pier Ballroom, Hastings (with The John Verity Band) and University Of East Anglia, Norwich
02/24	Theatre Royal Drury Lane, London
03/09	St. Albans City Hall, St. Albans
03/11	Top Rank Suite, Swansea, Wales
03/14	Top Of The World, Stafford
03/16	Hastings Pier, Hastings
03/22	Tower Theatre, Upper Darby, Pennsylvania, USA (with The Soft Machine)
03/23	Academy Of Music, New York, New York, USA (with Redbone)
04/02	BBC Television Theatre, London (filming for "The Old Grey Whistle Test")
04/07	The Greyhound, Croydon
05/07	The Tower Theater, Philadelphia, Pennsylvania (with Manfred Mann's Earth Band)
05/08	The Joint In The Woods, Parsippany, New Jersey, USA
05/10	Sunshine In, Asbury Park, New Jersey, USA (with Graham Central Station and Brian Auger's Oblivion Express)
05/14	Agora, Toledo, Ohio, USA
05/15	The Brewery, Lansing, Michigan, USA
05/18	Michigan Palace, Detroit, Michigan, USA (with The Chambers Brothers)
05/24	Sunshine In, Asbury Park, New Jersey, USA
05/26	Saratoga Performing Arts Center, Saratoga Springs, New York, USA (Russ Ballard's last concert)
11/22	Winter Gardens, Bournemouth (first show with revised lineup)
11/23	New Theatre, Oxford
11/24	Civic Hall, Wolverhampton
11/25	Barry Memorial Hall, Barry, Wales
11/28	Caird Hall, Dundee, Scotland
11/29	Apollo Theatre, Glasgow, Scotland
12/01	Caley Cinema, Edinburgh, Scotland
12/02	Newcastle City Hall, Newcastle
12/03	Hard Rock, Manchester
12/05	Town Hall, Cheltenham (with Clancy)
12/06	Rainbow Theatre, London
12/08	Colston Hall, Bristol
12/09	Preston Guild Hall, Preston
12/10	Sheffield City Hall, Sheffield
12/11	Liverpool Stadium, Liverpool (with Clancy)
12/12	Brangwyn Hall, Swansea, Wales
12/13	Plymouth Guild Hall, Plymouth

12/20	Birmingham Town Hall, Birmingham
12/21	St. Albans City Hall, St. Albans

1975

01/17	University of Salford, Salford
01/23	St. George's Hall, Bradford
01/25	Guildford Civic Hall, Guildford
01/29	Crewe And Alsager College Of Higher Education, Crewe
01/31	Brunel University Students' Hall, Uxbridge (with Back Door)
02/01	Leicester Polytechnic Arena, Leicester
02/08	Imperial College London, London
02/21	Capitol Theatre, Passaic, New Jersey, USA (with Queen and Kansas)
02/28	Capitol Theatre, Port Chester, New York, USA
03/14	Aragon Ballroom, Chicago, Illinois, USA
03/16	Anderson Arena, Bowling Green, Ohio, USA
03/16	Bowen Field House, Ypsilanti, Michigan, USA
03/19-22	Alex Cooley's Electric Ballroom, Atlanta, Georgia, USA (with Les Variations)
03/28	Capitol Theatre, Port Chester, New York, USA
04/13	Roundhouse, London
06/17	Tiffanys, Stevenage
09/07	Guildford Civic Hall, Guildford
09/09	Johnson Hall, Yeovil (with Dirty Tricks)
09/10	Torquay Town Hall, Torquay
09/11	Regal Theatre, Redruth
09/12	Plymouth Town Hall, Plymouth
09/26	Apollo Victoria Theatre, London
10/02	Victoria Hall, Stoke-on-Trent (with Dirty Tricks)
10/07	Mecca Locarno, Portsmouth
10/10	Mayfair Ballroom, Newcastle
10/11	University of Leicester, Leicester
10/14	Preston Guild Hall, Preston
10/17	London College Of Printing, London
10/19	Civic Hall, Wolverhampton
10/22	Apollo Theatre, Glasgow, Scotland
10/23	Caird Hall, Dundee, Scotland
10/24	Citadel, Edinburgh, Scotland
10/25	Manchester University, Manchester
10/26	Empire Theatre, Liverpool
10/27	Cardiff University, Cardiff, Wales
10/29	University Of Reading, Reading
10/30	Cambridge Corn Exchange, Cambridge
11/01	Leas Cliff Hall, Folkestone
11/10	Forum de Montreal, Montreal, Quebec, Canada (with Rainbow)
11/12	Beacon Theatre, New York, New York, USA (with Rainbow)
11/15	Tower Theatre, Upper Darby, Pennsylvania, USA (with Rainbow)
11/21	Paramount Northwest, Seattle, Washington (opening for Steppenwolf)
11/22	Paramount Theatre, Portland, Oregon, USA
11/24	Medford Armory, Medford, Oregon (opening for Steppenwolf)
11/28-30	The Starwood, West Hollywood, California, USA
12/04	Armadillo World Headquarters, Austin, Texas, USA

1976

01/02	Heavy Metal Festival, Kensington Olympia, London (with Bad Company and Black Sabbath)
04/26-27	Alex Cooley's Electric Ballroom, Atlanta, Georgia, USA
05/19	Camden Town Hall, London

1979

02/08	The Venue, London* (Rod Argent & Friends = Chester Thompson, Morris Pert, John Goodsall, Alphonso Johnson, Peter Robinson, Robin Lumley, plus guest Colin Blunstone)
mid-year	gigs in St. Albans and London to promote "Moving Home"
09/15	The Venue, London* (Rod Argent & Friends)

1981

05/11-06/14	"Cats," New London Theatre, London (Rod was first piano for the first 5 weeks of the musical)

1984

03/27-04/30	"Starlight Express," Apollo Victoria Theatre, London (Rod was first piano for the first 5 week of the musical

1997

Dec.	(The band Argent reunited to play private charity gigs, including a Christmas show at The Stables in Wavendon at which Rod Argent asked Colin Blunstone to sing "She's Not There")

1998

Dec.	Bedfordshire* (Rod appeared at a church benefit concert with Jennie Linden)

1999

10/17	The Stables, Wavendon* (Rod put on a 3-part concert)

2001

05/04	Royal Albert Hall, London* (Rod was a guest of Paul Carrack)

2003

04/11-12	The Stables, Wavendon* (with a string quartet; also with the band Argent)

2006

North American tour: Ringo Starr & His All Starr Band (06/14/06 – 07/20/06)*:

06/14-15	Casino Rama, Orillia, Ontario, Canada
06/16	DTE Energy Music Theatre, Clarkson, Michigan, USA
06/17	Rosemont Theatre, Rosemont, Illinois, USA
06/20	Fiddler's Green, Denver, Colorado, USA
06/21	Sandia Casino, Albuquerque, New Mexico, USA
06/21	Luther Burbank PAC, Santa Rosa, California, USA
06/22	The Mountain Winery, Saratoga, California, USA
06/23	Cache Creek Casino, Brooks, California, USA
06/24	Gibson Amphitheatre, Universal City, California, USA
06/25	Fantasy Springs Casino, Indio, California, USA
06/27	Humphrey's By The Bay, San Diego, California, USA
06/27	Wente Brothers Winery, Livermore, California, USA
06/28	Pala Grand Cabaret, Pala, California, USA
06/29	Humphrey's By The Bay, San Diego, California, USA
06/30-07/01	The Beach At Mandalay Bay, Las Vegas, Nevada, USA
07/02	Sandia Casino Amphitheater, Albuquerque, New Mexico, USA
07/03	Nokia Live, Grand Prairie, Texas, USA
07/07	Ruth Eckerd Hall, Clearwater, Florida, USA
07/08	Mizner Amphitheatre, Boca Raton, Florida, USA
07/09	King Center, Melbourne, Florida, USA
07/11	Lyric Opera House, Baltimore, Maryland, USA
07/11-12	State Theatre, Easton, Pennsylvania, USA
07/12	North Fork Theatre, Westbury, New York, USA
07/14	North Fork Theatre, Westbury, New York, USA
07/15	Trump Taj Mahal, Atlantic City, New Jersey, USA
07/16	Mohegan Sun Arena, Uncasville, Connecticut, USA
07/18	PNC Bank Arts Center, Holmdel, New Jersey, USA
07/19	Bank Of America Pavillion, Boston, Massachusetts, USA
07/20	Radio City Music Hall, New York, New York, USA

2010

02/06	The Stables, Wavendon*
07/25	High Voltage Festival 2010, Victoria Park, London (with many other acts)
12/04	Cheese And Grain, Frome
12/05	The Brook, Southampton
12/07	The Robin 2, Bilston

12/08	The Assembly, Royal Leamington Spa
12/13	HMV Forum, London

2012

01/27	Manchester Academy 3, University of Manchester Students' Union, Manchester
01/28	The Great British Rock & Blues Festival 2012, Butlins Resort Skegness, Skegness
01/29	O2 ABC2, Glasgow, Scotland
02/01	The Glee Club, Cardiff, Wales (cancelled)
02/02	The Robin 2, Bilston
02/04	O2 Shepherd's Bush Empire, London (with Martin Turner's Wishbone Ash)

2013

06/02	Aylesbury Waterside Theatre, Aylesbury

COLIN BLUNSTONE

SINGLES

(* = as by Neil MacArthur; ** = as by Alan Parsons Project; *** = as by Dave Stewart, guest vocals: Colin Blunstone; **** = as by Mitchell-Coe Mysteries; ***** = as by Keats)

TITLES	UK & FOREIGN LABEL/NO.	RELEASE DATE	US & CANADA LABEL/NO.	RELEASE DATE
She's Not There*/ World Of Glass*	Deram DM 225	01/10/69	Deram 45-7524	01/20/69
Ma Non É Giusto (Italian version of A-side)*/ World Of Glass*	Ital. Deram DM 230	01/24/69		
Don't Try To Explain*/ Without Her*	Deram DM 262	06/20/69	Deram 45-85050	09/01/69
It's Not Easy*/ 12.29*	Deram DM 275	10/17/69	Deram 45-85054	10/27/69
Mary Won't You Warm My Bed/ I Hope I Didn't Say Too Much Last Night	Epic S EPC 7095	03/19/71		
Caroline Goodbye/ Though You Are Far Away	Epic S EPC 7520	10/08/71		
Say You Don't Mind/ Let Me Come Closer	Epic S EPC 7765	01/28/72		
Caroline Goodbye/ Misty Roses			Epic 5-10826	02/21/72
Say You Don't Mind/ Though You Are Far Away			Epic 5-10868	05/08/72
I Don't Believe In Miracles/ I've Always Had You	Epic S EPC 8434	10/20/72	Epic 5-10948	01/22/73
Andorra/ How Could We Dare To Be Wrong	Dutch Epic EPC 1183	01/12/73		
How Could We Dare To Be Wrong/ Time's Running Out	Epic S EPC 1197	01/19/73		
I Want Some More (edit)/ Pay Me Later	Dut. Epic EPC 1513	04/20/73	Epic 5-10981	04/23/73
Andorra (edit)/ Caroline Goodbye			Epic 5-11004	06/04/73
Wonderful (edit)/ Beginning	Epic S EPC 1775	09/21/73		
Weak For You (edit)/ Keep The Curtains Closed Today	Dutch Epic EPC 2132	02/23/74		
It's Magical/ Summersong	Epic S EPC 2413	05/24/74		
When You Close Your Eyes/ Good Guys Don't Always Win	Epic S EPC 4576	09/11/76		
Planes/ Dancing In The Dark	Epic S EPC 4752	11/05/76		
Beautiful You/ It's Hard To Say Goodbye	Epic S EPC 5009	02/18/77		
Lovin' And Free/ Dancing In The Dark	Epic S EPC 5199	04/22/77		
I Can Almost See The Light/ Good Guys Don't Always Win	Australian Rocket ROKN-11546	09/19/77		
I'll Never Forget You/ You Are The Way For Me	Epic S EPC 6320	05/05/78	Rocket JH-11356	08/14/78
Ain't It Funny/ Who's That Knocking?	Epic S EPC 6535	07/21/78		
Ain't It Funny/ Touch And Go	Dut. Rocket 6079 665	07/21/78		
Photograph (edit)/ Touch And Go	Epic S EPC 6793	11/10/78	Rocket JH-11412	10/23/78
Photograph (edit)/ Lovelight	Australian Rocket Xpress 6079 656	03/28/79		
Boogaboo/ Can We Still Be Friends	Dut. Rocket 6079 694	11/16/79		
What Becomes Of The Broken Hearted***/ There Is No Reward	Broken BROKEN 1	12/03/80		
What Becomes Of The Broken Hearted***/ There Is No Reward	Stiff BROKEN 1	02/20/81		

(NOTE: Colin Blunstone is not on the B-side of the above single. The records have different picture sleeves.)

Miles Away****/ Excerpt From "Exiled"*****	Panache PAN 1	09/25/81		

(NOTE: Colin Blunstone is not on the B-side of the above single.)

Say You Don't Mind/ Let Me Come Closer	Epic S EPC 7765	04/16/82		
Tracks Of My Tears/ The Last Goodbye (7")	PRT 7P 236	05/14/82		
Tracks Of My Tears/ The Last Goodbye (12")	PRT 12P 236	05/14/82		
Touch/ Touch (instrumental mix) (7")	PRT 7P 264	02/18/83		
Touch/ Touch (instrumental mix) (12")	PRT 12P 264	02/18/83		
Turn Your Heart Around (edit)*****/Ask No Questions*****	EMI EMI 5484	07/20/84		
Where Do We Go From Here/ Helen Loves Paris (7")	Sierra FED 22	05/16/86		
Where Do We Go From Here/ Helen Loves Paris - Where Do We Go From Here (instrumental) (12")	Sierra FEDT 22	05/16/86		
She's Not There/ Who Fires The Gun (7"; both sides produced by Rod Argent and Peter Van Hooke)	Sierra FED 27	10/17/86		
She's Not There/ Who Fires The Gun (12"; same as above)	Sierra FEDT 27	10/17/86		
Cry An Ocean/ Make It Easy (7")	IRS IRM 151	05/05/88		
Cry An Ocean (Extended Version)/ Make It Easy - What Becomes Of The Broken Hearted ***(12")	IRS IRMT 151	05/05/88		
Say You Don't Mind/ Still Burning Bright (7")	JSE ESS 2001	01/14/91		
Say You Don't Mind/ Still Burning Bright - Caroline Goodbye (12")	JSE ESST 2001	01/14/91		
Old And Wise (1990 version)/ She's Not There (1990 Version) (CD5)	Belgian Indisc DICD 8246	01/14/91		
Caroline Goodbye (1990 version)/ Andorra (1990 Version) (7")	Belgian Indisc DIS 8278	03/22/91		
Every Living Moment/ Perfect Vision (by Louise Tucker) (7"/cassette single)	Gen'l. Portfolio LRFP LEUK 1 / LEUK C 1	05/25/92		
Every Living Moment - Every Living Moment (Children's Mix) -	Gen'l. Portfolio LRFP	05/25/92		

Perfect Vision (by Louise Tucker) (CD5)	LEUK CD 1	
("Every Living Moment" is a charity single for a leukemia research foundation.)		
The Radio Was Playing Johnny Come Lately - Tearing The Good Things Down (CD5)	Permanent CDS PERM 25	09/11/95
What Becomes Of The Broken Hearted***- The Locomotion (by Dave Stewart with Barbara Gaskin) (CD5)	Old Gold 12623 63222	09/18/95
If I Said - The Best Is Yet To Come (CD5; cancelled)	Permanent CDS PERM 27	01/15/96
Walking In The Rain (remix) - You Make Love So Good - She's Not There (CD5; the last track with Argent and White backing vocals)	Mystic MYS CD 505	11/30/98
The Zombies And Beyond: Album Sampler (promo CD-R; with "Say You Don't Mind," "What Becomes Of The Broken Hearted"*** and tracks by The Zombies and Argent)	Universal no #	05/26/08
Turn Your Heart Around***** (promo CD3; with "Keats" CD)	Jap. Air Mail Archive AIRPROMO-024	05/25/11
So Much More (download only)	iTunes download	01/04/13

PROMOTIONAL SINGLES

"Playback" (7" EP) (1972; US Columbia AS 32)
<u>Tracks:</u> Smokey Day; plus tracks by John Paul Hammond, Wayne Cochran & The C.C. Riders, and Looking Glass)

"Play:Back" (sic) (7" EP) (1974; US Columbia AS 70)
<u>Tracks:</u> Smooth Operation; plus tracks by Rupert Holmes, Blue Öyster Cult, and Tanya Tucker

"The Ghost Of You And Me" (CD-R) (2009; Ennismore CDENNIS1P): one-track promo

"The Best Is Yet To Come" (CD-R) (2012; Ennismore CDENNIS2P): one-track promo

"So Much More" (CD-R) (2012; Ennismore CDENNIS3P): one-track promo

ALBUMS
(* = as by Keats)

TITLES	UK & FOREIGN LABEL/NO.	RELEASE DATE	US & CANADA LABEL/NO.	RELEASE DATE
One Year (Rod Argent & Chris White produced; covers of two Zombies songs ["She Loves The Way They Love Her" and "Smokey Day"], Rod Argent wrote "Her Song" and Argent personnel played on "She Loves The Way They Love Her," "Caroline Goodbye" and "Mary Won't You Warm My Bed.")	Epic S EPC 64557	11/05/71	Epic E 30974	01/24/72
Ennismore (UK and US editions have different covers; Rod Argent provides piano and backing vocals, especially on "I Don't Believe In Miracles" and besides producing, Argent and White wrote "Andorra")	Epic S EPC 65278	10/20/72	Epic KE 31994	02/26/73
Journey (UK, US and European editions have different covers; US version has the tracks "You Who Are Lonely" and "It's Magical" instead of "Beware." Chris White produced except for "You Who Are Lonely," "It's Magical" and "Beware," the latter an Argent/White production. White and Argent wrote "Wonderful" and "Beware" - Rod played keyboards on both.)	Epic S EPC 65805	02/23/74	Epic KE 32962	08/26/74
Planes (US issue cancelled)	Epic S EPC 81592	02/18/77	Rocket PIG-2244	04/11/77
Never Even Thought (Rod Argent backing vocals on all tracks except the title track and "Do Magnolia Do")	Epic S EPC 82835	06/09/78	Rocket BXL1-2903	07/31/78
It's His "Time Of The Season" (promo 12" with tracks from the album "Never Even Thought" on one side and tracks by Lorna Wright on the other. Colin's tracks are "Photograph," "I'll Never Forget You," "Who's That Knocking?," "Never Even Thought" and "You Are The Way For Me.")			Rocket DJL1-2959	08/21/78
I Don't Believe In Miracles	Embassy S CBS 31760	10/19/79		
Late Nights In Soho (with Rod Argent guesting and producing)	Dutch/Australian Rocket 9103 510	12/07/79		
"Stiffs On 45 On 33" (LP; with "What Becomes Of The Broken Hearted")	Stiff STIFF 1	<</<</82		
I Don't Believe In Miracles (reissue)	Epic S EPC 32192	10/15/82		
Various Artists - "20 One Hit Wonders Vol. 2" (with the Neil MacArthur version of "She's Not There")	See For Miles CM 124	12/09/83		

Title	UK Cat.	UK Date	US Cat.	US Date
Keats* (US LP has "Give It Up" instead of "Hollywood Heart")	EMI EJ 2 40174 1	07/13/84	EMI America ST-17136	09/10/84
Golden Highlights	Dutch Epic 54702	05/17/85		
"Deram Dayze" (with the Neil MacArthur version of "She Not There")	Decal LIK 9	03/06/87		
"I.R.S. - The Singles" (LP/CD; with "Cry An Ocean")	I.R.S. MIRL/DMIRL 1501	<</<</88		
Ennismore (CD)	Epic 465580 2	06/13/89		
Colin Blunstone Sings His Greatest Hits (LP/CD; with Argent lineup on "Caroline Goodbye," "Andorra" and "I Don't Believe In Miracles," Argent backing vocals on "What Becomes Of The Broken Hearted" and Zombies lineup on "She's Not There," "Tell Her No" and "Time Of The Season")	Essential ESSLP/ ESSCD 139	04/01/91		
"Split Second" (CD; film soundtrack with one Blunstone track: "Nights In White Satin")	Milan 873 117	07/13/92		
"The Stiff Records Box Set" (4CD box; with "What Becomes Of The Broken Hearted")	Stiff BOX 1	08/04/92	Rhino R2 71062	08/04/92
"Just Like A Woman" (CD; film soundtrack with one Blunstone track: "Politics Of Love." This was the only track released from sessions with writer/producer Charlie Skarbek.)	RCA 74321110702	04/23/93		
Colin Blunstone Sings His Greatest Hits (CD; reissue of above)	Castle Commun. CLACD 351	08/16/93		
Miracles (CD)	Pickwick PWKS 4170	09/20/93		
I Don't Believe In Miracles (CD)	Epic 474692 2	06/13/94		
"You Can't Hurry Love: The Motown Covers Album" (CD; with "What Becomes Of The Broken Hearted")	Stateside 31652	11/16/94		
One Year (CD)	Jap. Epic ESCA 7575	02/01/95		
Live At The BBC (CD; cancelled – no release date set)	Strange Fruit	<</ <</95		
Some Years: It's The Time Of Colin Blunstone (CD)			Legacy EK 66449	06/06/95
Echo Bridge (CD; US issue has uncredited bonus track: "She's Not There" [1986 version])	Permanent PERMCD 38	10/16/95	Renaissance RMED00125	06/10/97
Live At The BBC (CD; Argent group on "Say You Don't Mind")	Windsong WINCD 079	12/18/95		
Keats* (CD; with bonus track: edit of "Turn Your Heart Around")	See For Miles SEECD 447	08/26/96		
Keats* (CD; includes "Give It Up" and "Hollywood Heart" plus bonus interviews with Alan Parsons and Ian Bairnson)			Renaissance RMED00111	01/07/97
The Light Inside (CD; Rod Argent backing vocals)	Mystic MYS CD 125	06/01/98		
Echo Bridge (CD; reissue)	Indelible INDELCD4	07/20/98		
One Year (CD)	Epic 491694 2	08/17/98		
Greatest Hits (CD; "Walking In The Rain" and "She's Not There '98" replaced "Still Burning Bright" and "Don't Feel No Pain No More" from the 1991 CD. Chris White and Don Airey produced the new tracks.)	Mystic MYS CD 138	12/06/99		
The Very Best Of Colin Blunstone (CD; retitled version of "Some Years: It's The Time Of Colin Blunstone")	Sony 4894872	04/23/00		
One Year (CD)	Sony 4916942	05/16/00		
Say You Don't Mind (CD; reissue of "Greatest Hits" CD)	Armoury ARMCD029	11/13/00		
Ennismore (CD)	Jap. Epic ESCA 7877	07/18/01		
On Air (CD; reissue of "Live At The BBC")	Strange Fruit SFRSCD 20	12/20/01		
Anthology (CD; reissue of "Colin Blunstone Sings His Greatest Hits")	Brilliant Classics BT 33079	02/02/02		
Journey (CD)	Jap. Epic EICP 7035	03/20/02		
Best Of Colin Blunstone (CD)	Jap. Epic EICP 7036	03/20/02		
"Producers Archives Volume 1" by MIKE HURST (CD; with "Never My Love" [previously unreleased] and "Don't Try To Explain.")	Angel Air SJPCD 123	11/18/02		
One Year (CD; reissue)	Dutch Epic 510577 2	11/26/02		
Old And Wise (2CD)	Superior SU 29503	01/14/03		
Various Artists - "Zigzag: 20 Junkshop Soft Rock Singles (CD; with "It's Not Easy")	RPM RPM 262	08/25/03		
Ennismore (CD)	German Sony SMM 5128182	08/25/03		
Super Hits (CD)	Sony 5120222	09/01/03		
Echo Bridge (CD)	Big Beat CDWIKM 238	02/02/04		
Greatest Hits & The Light Inside (2CD)	French Recall 9558	02/21/06		
One Year (CD; bonus track: "I Hope I Didn't Say Too Much Last Night")	Jap. CBS MHCP-985	05/01/06		

Title	Label/Catalog	Date	Alt Label	Alt Date
Greatest Hits Plus (CD; same as 1991 CD plus new piano and vocal arrangements of "Miles Away" and "How We Were Before" with Rod Argent)	Mystic MYS CD 194	11/13/06		
Super Hits (CD)	Camden 7370539	01/14/07		
One Year (CD)	Italian Water 193	03/20/07		
Into The Afterlife (CD; includes all 7 of the Neil MacArthur singles tracks plus "Never My Love" and the previously unissued "Hung Upside Down")	Big Beat CDWIKCD 266	07/02/07		
The Light Inside (CD; reissue)	Jap. Mystic/ Isol Discus Organization POCE-19003	08/22/07		
Ennismore/ Journey (CD)	Acadia 8187	02/12/08		
The Zombies And Beyond (CD; with the tracks "I Don't Believe In Miracles," "Say You Don't Mind," "Caroline Goodbye," "Old And Wise" [with The Alan Parsons Project] and "What Becomes Of The Broken Hearted" [with Dave Stewart])	UMTV 1773931	05/26/08		
The Light Inside (CD; reissue)	Jap. Mystic/ Isol Discus Organization GQCP-59021	06/25/08		
The Ghost Of You And Me (CD)	Ennismore ENNISCD1	03/09/09		
Original Album Classics (3CD; contains the albums "One Year," "Ennismore" and "Journey" with 2 bonus tracks)	Epic 88697617132	07/26/10		
The Best Of Colin Blunstone (CD)	Camden 88697695772	08/30/10		
One Year (CD; reissue)	Jap. Epic EICP 1386	10/20/10		
Ennismore (CD; reissue)	Jap. Epic EICP 1387	10/20/10		
Journey (CD; reissue – 4 bonus tracks)	Jap. Epic EICP 1388	10/20/10		
Keats* (CD; reissue of Renaissance label edition from 1997)	Jap. Air Mail Archive AIRAC-1623	05/25/11		
I Don't Believe In Miracles (CD; reissue of Embassy LP)	Talking Elephant TECD205	08/21/12		
On The Air Tonight (CD)	Ennismore ENNISCD2	10/15/12		
Ennismore (CD; reissue)	Dutch Music On CD MOCCD 13062	07/ 13/13		
One Year (LP; reissue)	4 Men With Beards 4M 237	11 /10/13		
Ennismore (LP; reissue)	Dutch Music On Vinyl MOVLP882	01/13/14		
On The Air Tonight (CD; belated US issue)			Zip ZIPR 91	01/21/14
Ennismore/Journey (CD; reissues)	Voiceprint VP604CD	06/23/14		
One Year (CD; reissue)	Dutch Music On CD MOCCD 13116	07/22/14		
Collected (3CD; contains tracks from Colin's entire career, with many lead vocal sessions for others)	Dutch Universal 534 274-4	09/19/14		
Planes/ Never Even Thought (2CD; reissues)	Cherry Red CDMRED 665	08/28/15		
Keats* (CD; reissue –no bonus tracks)	Jap. Parlophone WPCR-16737	10/ 21/15		
Collected (2LP; edited reissue –white vinyl)	Dutch Music On Vinyl MOVLP2169	06/28/18		
"Volume One" by THE CHRIS WHITE EXPERIENCE (CD/download; lead vocals on "Why Can't You Lie To Me" and "Taking The Wings From Butterflies")	Sunfish CWE001CD	03/29/19		
"Volume Two" by The CHRIS WHITE EXPERIENCE (CD/download; lead vocals on "Don't Go Looking" and "Normal Heart")	Sunfish CWE002CD	08/31/19		
"Volume Three" by THE CHRIS WHITE EXPERIENCE (CD/download; lead vocal on "Unhappy Girl")	Sunfish CWE003CD	12/18/19		
"Volume Four" by THE CHRIS WHITE EXPERIENCE (download-only; lead vocal on "New World")	Sunfish (no #)	07/03/20		
"Volume Five" by THE CHRIS WHITE EXPERIENCE (download-only; lead vocal on "When I Was All Alone")	Sunfish (no #)	12/25/20		
Keats* (LP; reissue)			Renaissance RDEG-111	12/04/20
"In My Time – Recordings, Productions And Songs 1962-1985" by MIKE HURST *4CD; lead vocal on "World Without Love")	Strawberry CRJAMC005	08/17/21		
One Year (CD; with 14 additional pre-album demos)			Sundazed SC 5606	11/05/21
One Year (2LP; with 14 additional pre-album demos)			Sundazed LP 5608	03/11/22

SINGLES SESSIONS
(* = track featuring Colin Blunstone)

TITLES	UK & FOREIGN LABEL/NO.	RELEASE DATE	US & CANADA LABEL/NO.	RELEASE DATE
MIKE BATT & FRIENDS FEATURING COLIN BLUNSTONE - Losing Your Way In The Rain*/ The Dean Of Night	Epic S EPC 8155	02/01/80		
ALAN PARSONS PROJECT - Old And Wise*/ Children Of The Moon	Arista ARIST 494	12/17/82		
ALAN PARSONS PROJECT - Old And Wise*/ You're Gonna Get Your Fingers Burned			Arista AS 1048	02/07/83
FRANCIE CONWAY - Something I Heard/ One Night Love*	Irish WEA CON 1	<</ <</83		
THE CROWD - You'll Never Walk Alone*/ Messages* (7")	Spartan BRAD 1	05/24/85		
THE CROWD - You'll Never Walk Alone*/ Messages* (12")	Spartan BRAD 112	05/24/85		
DON AIREY - Julie (If You Leave Me)*/ Sea Of Dreams (Part I) (7")	German MCA 257 7867-0	01/15/88		
DON AIREY - Julie (If You Leave Me) (Extended Version)* - (7" Edited version)*/ Sea Of Dreams (Parts I & II)	German MCA 257 785-0	01/15/88		
NADIEH - Turn Me Loose - Wasted Water - Splendid Morning* (CD5; vocal duet on "Splendid Morning")	Dutch Mercury 874 181-2	03/04/89		
THE BOLLAND PROJECT - Emma My Dear (Love Theme)*- For A Moment In Time - Emma My Dear (Instrumental) (CD5)	Dutch Dino 9070 362	01/13/92		
TIMECODE 64 - She's Not There (Radio Mix)*/ Slide (cassette)	F.B.I. MCFBI 10	02/15/93		
TIMECODE 64 - She's Not There (Club Mix)* - (Alternate Mix)* - (Acapella Mix)*/ Slide - Slide Experience (12")	F.B.I. 12 FBI 10	02/15/93		
TIMECODE 64 - She's Not There (Radio Mix)* - (Club Mix)* - (Acoustic Mix)* - (Alt. Mix)*- Slide - Slide Experience (CD5)	F.B.I. CDFBI 10	02/15/93		
DEF LEPPARD - Rock & Roll Hall Of Fame 29 March 2019: Hysteria - Rock Of Ages - Photograph/ Pour Some Sugar On Me - All The Young Dudes* (Record Store Day 12" of 4,000 copies - backing vocals on the last track; recorded live at the induction ceremony at Barclays Center, Brooklyn, New York on 03/29/19)	Bludgeon Riffola 0602508192067	08/29/20	Bludgeon Riffola 0602508192067	08/29/20

PROMOTIONAL SESSION SINGLE

"Tiger In The Night And Other Selections From The Original Motion Picture Score 'Keep The Aspidistra Flying'" (CD5) (1998; UK EMI MIKE BATT 1)
<u>Tracks</u>: Tiger In The Night - Theme From "Keep The Aspidistra Flying" (by Mike Batt with The Royal Philharmonic Orchestra) - Booking At Modigliani's (by Mike Batt with The Royal Philharmonic Orchestra) - A Bower Made For Us (by Mike Batt with The Royal Philharmonic Orchestra)

ALBUM SESSIONS

TITLES	UK & FOREIGN LABEL/NO.	RELEASE DATE	US & CANADA LABEL/NO.	RELEASE DATE
VARIOUS ARTISTS - "Rondor D'Oeuvre" (publishing demo LP; Colin wrote "Come Homeward Darling" with Richard Kerr)	Rondor Music Ron100	<</ <</74		
RICHARD KERR - Reflections Of Richard Kerr (publishing demo LP; Blunstone co-wrote "Ain't It Funny," "I Really Wanted You" and "Let Me In")	Rondor Music Ron101	<</ <</74		
VARIOUS ARTISTS - "Cover Stories" (publishing demo LP; Colin and Phil Dennys wrote "Make This The Story Of A Lifetime")	Rondo Music (no #)	<</ <</74		
ROGER DALTREY - One Of The Boys (with Blunstone's song "Single Man's Dilemma"; US has "Say It Ain't So, Joe" instead of "Written On The Wind")	Polydor 2442 146	05/13/77	MCA 2271	06/27/77
MAE McKENNA - Walk On Water (backing vocals with Rod Argent on "I Want To Believe In You")	Transatlantic TRA 345	05/27/77		
ALAN PARSONS PROJECT - Pyramid (Blunstone lead vocal on "The Eagle Will Rise Again" and backing vocal on "Shadow Of A Lonely Man")	Arista SPART 1054	05/26/78	Arista AB-4180	06/19/78
MIKE BATT & FRIENDS - Tarot Suite (lead vocal on "Losing Your Way In The Rain")	Epic EPC 86099	09/07/79	Epic NJE 36312	02/18/80
ROGER DALTREY - One Of The Boys (reissue)			MCA 37031	08/04/80
MITCHELL-COE MYSTERIES - Exiled (lead vocal: "Miles Away")	RCA PL 25297	09/06/80		
ALAN PARSONS PROJECT - Eye In The Sky (lead vocal: "Old And Wise")	Arista 204 606	05/21/82	Arista AL 9599	06/07/82
IVA TWYDELL - Duel (backing vocals)	Redsky SKY 777-2	<</ <</82	Can. Tunesmith TS 6015	<</ <</82
ALAN PARSONS PROJECT - Eye In The Sky (LP/CD; reissue - CD only in UK)	Arista 610 004-2	11/04/83	Arista AL8/ARCD-8033	11/07/83
ALAN PARSONS PROJECT - Pyramid (reissue)			Arista AL8-8042	11/07/83

Album	Label/Cat#	Date	Label/Cat#	Date
ALAN PARSONS PROJECT - Ammonia Avenue (LP/CD; lead vocal on "Dancing On A High Wire")	Arista 206 100/ 610 105-2	02/24/84	Arista AL8/ARCD-8204	03/12/84
ALAN PARSONS PROJECT - Pyramid (LP/CD; reissue)			Arista AL8/ARCD-8225	03/12/84
ALAN PARSONS PROJECT - Vulture Culture (LP/CD; lead vocal on "Somebody's Out There")	Arista 206 577/ 610 228-2	05/15/85	Arista AL8/ARCD-8263	02/25/85
ALAN PARSONS PROJECT - Eye In The Sky (LP/CD; reissue)	Arista 208 718/ 258 718	01/09/87		
ALAN PARSONS PROJECT - Pyramid (CD; reissue)	Arista 610 141-2	02/13/87		
ALAN PARSONS PROJECT - Pyramid (LP/CD; reissue)	Arista 208 983/ 258 983	10/02/87		
DON AIREY - K2: Tales Of Triumph And Tragedy (vocal on "Julie [If You Leave Me] [Love Theme]")	German MCA Int'l. MCD 15457	01/29/88		
ALAN PARSONS PROJECT - Ammonia Avenue (LP/CD; reissue)	Arista 208 885/ 258 885	03/04/88		
ALAN PARSONS PROJECT - Vulture Culture (LP/CD; reissue)	Arista 208 884/ 258 884	03/04/88		
KAREL FIALKA - Human Animal (Blunstone backing vocals)	IRS MIRF 1036	11/18/88	IRS 42252	01/02/89
NADIEH - No Way Back (CD; duet on "Splendid Morning")	Dutch Mercury 838 326-2	05/05/89		
MIKE BATT & FRIENDS - Tarot Suite (CD; reissue)	Germ. Epic 450092 2	09/24/89		
THE LONDON SYMPHONY ORCHESTRA - Rock Symphonies Vol. II (LP/CD; lead vocal on "Groovy Kind Of Love")	German Portrait PRT 465961 1/2	10/05/89		
THE BOLLAND PROJECT - Darwin - The Evolution (Blunstone lead vocal on "Way Of The Evolution" and "Emma My Dear [Love Theme]")	Dutch Dino 9070 117	11/30/91		
VARIOUS ARTISTS - "Night Of The Proms '93" (lead vocals on "She's Not There")	Belgian EMI EVA 828 333-2	12/06/93		
DUNCAN BROWNE - Songs Of Love & War (CD; vocals on "Misunderstood," "Love Leads You" and "I Fall Again")	Zomart ZOMCD 007	09/05/94		
STEVE HACKETT - Genesis Revisited (CD; lead vocal on "For Absent Friends," with "Riding The Colossus" instead of "Los Endos")	Japanese Mercury PHCR-1454	08/25/96		
DUNCAN BROWNE - Songs Of Love & War (CD; 2 bonus tracks)	Jap. MSI MSI-15100	06/25/97		
STEVE HACKETT - Genesis Revisited (CD; US title: "Watcher Of The Skies: Genesis Revisited")	Reef SRECD 704	09/03/97	Guardian 8 21943 2	10/21/97
ROGER DALTREY - One Of The Boys (CD; reissue)	German Repertoire REP-4643-WY	01/15/98		
MIKE BATT/ ROYAL PHILHARMONIC ORCHESTRA - "Keep The Aspidistra Flying" soundtrack (CD; lead vocal: "Tiger In The Night")	EMI Classical CDC 556 613-2	03/30/98		
SIR JOHN BETJEMAN & MIKE READ - Words And Music (CD; Blunstone vocals on "Peggy" and "In Memory")	Eagle EAGCD 029	06/22/98		
MIKE BATT/ ROYAL PHILHARMONIC ORCHESTRA - "A Merry War" soundtrack (CD; UK film title: "Keep The Aspidistra Flying")			Angel CDQ 7243 4 94697 2 3	09/22/98
MARTIN DARVILL & FRIENDS - The Greatest Show On Earth (CD; backing vocals)	Music Of Life 004	10/05/98		
MIKE BATT/ ROYAL PHILHARMONIC ORCHESTRA - Mike Batt's Philharmania - Volume 1 (CD; vocal: "Owner Of A Lonely Heart")	German Stella Music 559 618-2	01/11/99		
DON AIREY - K2: Tales Of Triumph And Tragedy (CD/download; repackage with bonus track)	MCK (no #)	04/12/99		
ALAN PARSONS - The Time Machine (CD; with bonus track - Colin Blunstone lead vocal on "Ignorance Is Bliss")	Artful ARTFULCD 28	08/23/99	Miramar 23146-2	09/28/99
MARTIN DARVILL & FRIENDS - The Greatest Show On Earth (CD; reissue)	Mystic MYS CD 135	05/02/00		
ALAN PARSONS - The Time Machine (CD; reissue)			Roadrunner 2004320	05/28/01
SIR JOHN BETJEMAN & MIKE READ - Songs (CD; retitled reissue of "Words And Music")	NMC PILOT 148	11/18/02		
ERIC WOOLFSON - Poe: More Tales Of Mystery And Imagination (CD; vocal on "Somewhere In The Audience")	Limelight LREC 0374	09/29/03		
EDWARD ROGERS - Sunday Fables (CD; backing vocals with Rod Argent on "Make It Go Away")			Not Lame 88	03/02/04
MARTIN DARVILL & FRIENDS - The Greatest Show On Earth (CD; reissue)	Mystic MYS CD 135	02/23/05		
STEVE HACKETT - Genesis Revisited (CD; reissue)	Snapper Classics SDPCD 126	03/08/05		
ALAN PARSONS PROJECT - Eye In The Sky (double-sided DVD in two different HDAD formats)			Classic HDAD 2011	08/09/05
ROGER DALTREY - One Of The Boys (CD; reissue with 2 bonuses)	Castle CMRCD 1139	10/03/05		
SIR JOHN BETJEMAN & MIKE READ - Songs (2CD; reissue)	Right Rec. RIGHT 043	08/14/06		
ROGER DALTREY - One Of The Boys (CD; reissue with 4 bonuses)			Hip-O 000665102	08/29/06

ALAN PARSONS PROJECT - Eye In The Sky (LP; reissue)	German Speakers Corner AL 9599	01/08/07		
ALAN PARSONS PROJECT - Vulture Culture (CD; 5 bonus tracks)	Arista 82876838592	03/09/07	Arista 82876838592	03/09/07
ALAN PARSONS PROJECT - Eye In The Sky (CD; 6 bonus tracks)	Arista 82876815272	03/20/07	Arista 82876815272	03/20/07
ALAN PARSONS PROJECT - Pyramid (CD; 7 bonus tracks)	Arista 82876815252	03/07/08	Arista 82876815252	03/07/08
ALAN PARSONS PROJECT - Eye In The Sky (LP; reissue)	German Arista 88697269431	03/28/08		
ALAN PARSONS PROJECT - Ammonia Avenue (CD; 8 bonus tracks)	Arista 82876838622	09/18/08	Arista 82876838622	09/18/08
ALAN PARSONS PROJECT - Pyramid (LP; reissue)	Dutch Music On Vinyl MOVLP335	07/22/11		
ALAN PARSONS PROJECT - Eye In The Sky (LP; reissue)	Dutch Music On Vinyl MOVLP188	01/09/12		
ALAN PARSONS PROJECT - Ammonia Avenue (LP; reissue)	Dutch Music On Vinyl MOVLP560	08/13/12		
STEVE HACKETT - Genesis Revisited (CD; reissue)	German Inside Out/ Wolfwork IOMCD 373/ 0506418	02/25/13		
ALAN PARSONS PROJECT - Vulture Culture (LP; reissue)	Dutch Music On Vinyl MOVLP880	11/04/13		
ALAN PARSONS - The Time Machine (2LP; reissue with bonus track)	Dutch Music On Vinyl MOVLP1010	07/14/14		
STEVE HACKETT - Genesis Revisited (2 dark green vinyl LPs + CD)	German Inside Out/ Wolfwork IOMLP 373/ 0506411	09/01/14		
EMILE HAYNIE - We Fall (LP/CD/LP + 12"; lead vocal on "Nobody Believes You")			Interscope B002265501/ B002265502/ B002198811	02/24/15
DON AIREY - K2: Tales Of Triumph And Tragedy (CD; reissue)	Dutch Music On CD MOCCD13276	02/26/16		
ERIC WOOLFSON - Poe: More Tales Of Mystery And Imagination (LP; reissue)	Limelight LREC 0375LP	12/03/16		
DUNCAN BROWNE - Songs Of Love & War (CD; reissue)	Grey Scale GSGZ010CD	02/17/17		
DON AIREY - K2: Tales Of Triumph And Tragedy (CD+DVD; 7 bonus tracks – 100 copies only)	Gonzo Multimedia HST454CD-DVD	06/16/17		
ALAN PARSONS PROJECT - Eye In The Sky (2CD + Blu-ray Audio + two 45 RPM 12" + 7" flexidisc)	Arista 88985421862	12/01/17	Arista 88985421862	12/01/17
ALAN PARSONS PROJECT - Eye In The Sky (LP; reissue – white vinyl)	German Arista 88985375431	12/08/17		
ALAN PARSONS PROJECT - Eye In The Sky (Blu-ray Audio)	Real Gone RGM-0725	08/03/18	Real Gone RGM-0725	08/03/18
ALAN PARSONS PROJECT - Ammonia Avenue (Blu-ray Audio – original album plus 2 videos)	Esoteric BECLEC2706	03/27/20		
ALAN PARSONS PROJECT - Ammonia Avenue (3CD + 2 Blu-ray + two 12" vinyl)	Esoteric ECLEC2705	03/27/20		
ALAN PARSONS PROJECT - Eye In The Sky (SACD hybrid disc)			MFSL UDSACD 2221	04/07/21
ALAN PARSONS - The Time Machine (2LP; either black vinyl or blue translucent vinyl – bonus track)	Dutch Music On Vinyl MOVLP1010	07/09/21		
ALAN PARSONS - The Time Machine (CD; reissue – bonus track)	Dutch Music On CD MOCCD14078	07/09/21		
ALAN PARSONS PROJECT - Eye In The Sky (two 45 RPM 12" vinyl)			MFSL 2-500	06/07/22

COMMERCIAL JINGLES

South West Electricity Board (SWEB) (1984)
British Telecom (1990): She's Not There
Midlands Gas
Quick-Brew Tea
Noxzema: Time Of The Season
Toblerone (1996)

COLIN BLUNSTONE RADIO APPEARANCES, INCLUDING SOLO AND GROUP RECORDINGS

"Sounds Of The 70s" (09/20/71; BBC Radio One): hosted by Bob Harris

"Sounds Of The 70s" (11/30/71; BBC Radio One): Say You Don't Mind (Argent backing band) – hosted by Bob Harris

"Johnnie Walker" (12/27/71 – 12/31/71; BBC Radio One): Colin was the guest for the week

"Johnnie Walker" (01/17/72 – 01/21/72; BBC Radio One): Colin was the guest for the week

"Dave Lee Travis" (11/06/72 – 11/10/72; BBC Radio One): Colin was the guest for the week

"John Peel" (11/14/72; BBC Radio One): Andorra; I Don't Believe In Miracles; How Wrong Can One Man Ever Be – all recorded 10/23/72 at BBC Studio, London with these musicians: Derek Griffiths (lead guitar), Pete Wingfield (electric piano), Terry Poole (bass), Jim Toomey (drums). Of these tracks, only "I Don't Believe In Miracles" has been released.

"Johnnie Walker" (11/27/72 – 12/01/72; BBC Radio One): Colin was the guest for the week

"Johnnie Walker" (12/11/72 – 12/15/72; BBC Radio One): Colin was the guest for the week

"John Peel" (12/26/72; BBC Radio One): same as 11/14/72 plus "Say You Don't Mind" (also recorded the same day)

"Jimmy Young" (02/05/73 – 02/09/73; BBC Radio One): Colin was the guest for the week

"4th Dimension" (02/10/73; BBC Radio 4 FM): Colin talked about songwriting

"4th Dimension" (02/17/73; BBC Radio 4 FM): Colin was part of a segment dealing with recording

TRANSCRIPTION DISC:
"Top Of The Pops" Show #433 (02/21/73) (LP; BBC Transcription Services): How Could We Dare To Be Wrong; Pay Me Later – both tracks recorded 01/31/73 at BBC Studio, London

"4th Dimension" (02/24/73; BBC Radio 4 FM): Colin was part of a segment about record promotion

"Sounds On Sunday" (03/18/73; BBC Radio One): session introduced by John Peel

"John Peel" (03/27/73; BBC Radio One): Pay Me Later; I Want Some More; Looking For Someone To Love – recorded 03/06/73 at BBC Studio, London

"John Peel" (06/05/73; BBC Radio One): same as 03/27/73 show

"Sounds On Sunday" (10/14/73; BBC Radio One)

"John Peel" (11/06/73; BBC Radio One): Wonderful; Weak For You; Shadow Of A Doubt; Setting Yourself Up To Be Shot Down – recorded 10/22/73

"John Peel" (01/08/74; BBC Radio One): same as 11/06/73 show

"John Peel" (02/07/74; BBC Radio One): same as 11/06/73 show

"Bob Harris" (08/12/74; BBC Radio One)

"Sounds Of The 60s" (09/19/87; BBC Radio Two): Colin played some of his favorite '60s songs

"Greater London Radio" (01/91; Greater London Radio [GLR]): interview; Let Me Come Closer To You; Keep The Curtains Closed Today

"Bob Harris" (01/30/91; BBC Radio One) She's Not There; Time Of The Season; Andorra; Caroline Goodbye – recorded 01/30/91 with Rod Argent, Hugh Grundy, Jim Rodford, and John Verity

"Debbie Thrower" (10/20/95; BBC Radio Two): interview

"The Mix – 134" (10/96) (CD; BBC Radio International/ BBC World Service TCDM 9644): I Don't Believe In Miracles – recorded 10/23/72 at BBC Studio, London

"Fresh Air With Terry Gross" (01/28/98; US National Public Radio): 45-minute interview

"Paul Gambaccini's Inside Track" (05/14/98; BBC Radio Two): Colin called in to Paul's program to talk about "The Light Inside"

"Richard Allinson" (06/22/98; BBC Radio Two): Colin spoke about his new album

(NOTE: Colin also gave many informal interviews about "The Light Inside" to BBC stations in Newcastle, Derby, Leicester, and Liberty.)

"Brian Matthew" (09/30/07; BBC Radio Two): archival interview that Brian did with Colin

"Ken Bruce" (09/01/08 – 09/05/08; BBC Radio Two): Colin picked his ten favorite discs as his "Tracks Of My Years" – two per day

"Ken Bruce" (10/13/08 – 10/17/08; BBC Radio Two): repeated from the previous month

"Steve Lamacq" (02/05/09; BBC Radio 6 Music): Colin guested

"Steve Wright In The Afternoon" (02/10/09; BBC Radio Two): Colin appeared

"De Plantage" (03/14/09; Dutch Radio 2): live recording at Radio 2 Muziekcafé in Amsterdam, Netherlands

"Jonathan Ross" (03/21/09; BBC Radio Two): Colin played live

"Suzi Quatro" (05/21/09; BBC Radio Two): Colin discussed his American music influences

"Late Show – Keith Middleton" (01/01/11; BBC Coventry & Warwickshire): Colin appeared

"Men @ Work" (01/29/11; UK Premier Radio): Colin was interviewed by Nick Battle for this one-hour special

"Bernie Keith" (02/01/11; BBC Radio Northampton): Colin discussed his upcoming solo tour

"Roger Day" (02/07/11; BBC Surrey): Colin talked about his upcoming solo tour

"Old Grey Whistle Test 40" (08/31/11; BBC Radio Two): Bob Harris interview with Colin about the early days of the program

"Bernie Keith" (01/25/12; BBC Radio Northampton): Colin talked about his upcoming gig at The Stables

"Andy Potter" (02/15/12; BBC Radio Derby): Colin spoke about his upcoming gig at The Flowerpot in Derby

"Mike Wyer" (05/23/12; BBC Hereford & Worcester): Colin was interviewed about his solo career and recording for the Rocket label

"Sounds Of The 70s With Johnnie Walker" (01/27/13; BBC Radio Two): Colin picked his favorite '70s tracks

"Andy Potter" (02/11/13; BBC Radio Derby): Colin's gig at The Flowerpot in Derby was promoted

"Tribute To Eva Cassidy" (04/12/03; BBC Radio Leeds/ BBC Radio Humberside, and 04/18/03 on BBC regional stations): this tribute included an interview with Colin

"Tim Smith" (01/11/14; BBC Radio Oxford): Colin appeared

"James Watt" (03/24/16; BBC Radio Stoke): Colin appeared

"The Dominic King Show" (04/06/16; BBC Radio Kent): Colin appeared

"Andy Potter" (04/07/16; BBC Radio Derby): Colin appeared

"Justin Dealey" (04/09/16; BBC Three Counties Radio): Colin appeared

"Tim Smith" (04/30/16; BBC Radio Oxford): Colin appeared

"Chris Berrow" (10/28/16; BBC Radio Lincolnshire): Colin appeared

"James Watt" (01/30/17; BBC Radio Stoke): Colin appeared

"Sounds Of The 70s With Johnnie Walker" (10/15/17; BBC Radio Two): Colin spoke about the '70s

"Tammy Gooding" (11/24/17; BBC Hereford & Worcester): Colin talked about Northern Soul

"Tim Smith" (04/07/18; BBC Radio Oxford): Colin appeared

"Robert Elms" (04/22/19; BBC Radio London): Colin talked about his solo tour

"Gary Hickson" (08/16/20; BBC Radio Lancashire): an archival Colin interview

COLIN BLUNSTONE TELEVISION, FILM, AND VIDEO APPEARANCES
(television broadcasts list the first broadcast dates and networks; films/videos list just the first release dates)

"Juke Box Jury" (01/15/66; BBC One): Colin and concert promoter Tito Burns were guest judges

"Dim Dam Dom" (03/01/69; French TV): She's Not There (lip-synch of Deram version)

"The Old Grey Whistle Test" (09/20/71; BBC Two): Misty Roses; Smokey Day; Say You Don't Mind; Though You Are Far Away – all tracks recorded 08/31/71 with 7 musicians, including The Patrick Halling String Quartet; presented by Bob Harris

"The Old Grey Whistle Test" (12/14/71; BBC Two): Misty Roses; Say You Don't Mind (rebroadcast of two tracks recorded on 08/31/71)

(NOTE: with the exception of the two 12/14/71 re-aired tracks, the above recordings are not in the BBC's archives.)

"Top Of The Pops" (02/17/72; BBC One)

"Top Of The Pops" (03/02/72; BBC One)

"Engelbert With The Young Generation" (03/26/72; BBC One): Say You Don't Mind

"Lift Off With Ayshea" (04/12/72; UK Granada TV)

"Lift Off With Ayshea" (11/22/72; UK Granada TV)

"TopPop" (01/12/73; Dutch AVRO)

"Russell Harty Plus" (01/13/73; UK ITV)

"Top Of The Pops" (01/25/73; BBC One): How Could We Dare To Be Wrong

"The Old Grey Whistle Test" (02/19/73; BBC Two): She's Not There; A Sign From Me To You; How Wrong Can One Man Be; She Loves The Way They Love Her – recorded 02/03/73; presented by Bob Harris (all are unreleased)

"The Old Grey Whistle Test" (03/27/73; BBC Two): Pay Me Later; I Want Some More; Looking For Someone To Love – recorded 03/06/73; presented by John Peel (all are unreleased)

"Music My Way" (08/22/73; BBC One): guest appearance

"Glamour..." (08/24/73; UK Anglia Television)

"The Old Grey Whistle Test" (11/06/73; BBC Two): Wonderful; Weak For You; Shadow Of A Doubt; Setting Yourself Up To Be Shot Down – recorded 10/22/73; presented by John Peel (only the first track has been released)

"TopPop" (11/10/73; Dutch AVRO): Wonderful

"Lift Off With Ayshea" (11/14/73; UK Granada TV)

"The Old Grey Whistle Test" (03/10/74; BBC Two): Brother Lover; Something Happens When You Touch Me – recorded the same day

"See You Sunday" (05/05/74; BBC One): live appearance

"The Old Grey Whistle Test" (06/24/74; BBC Two): Keep The Curtains Closed Today; Beginning; Weak For You; Beware (with Duncan Browne) – recorded 04/24/74 and presented by Bob Harris (all are unreleased)

"Rock On With 45" (12/25/74; UK Granada TV): Colin was one of many guests

"The Bob Braun Show" (11/20/78; WLWT-TV, Cincinnati, Ohio)

"Losing Your Way In The Rain" by MIKE BATT (1980; BBC): live vocal with orchestra

"Friday Night, Saturday Morning" (03/14/80; BBC Two)

"What Becomes Of The Broken Hearted" by DAVE STEWART featuring COLIN BLUNSTONE (12/80; promotional video)

"Top Of The Pops" (12/25/80; BBC One): What Becomes Of The Broken Hearted (with Dave Stewart)

"Top Of The Pops" (03/19/81; BBC One): What Becomes Of The Broken Hearted (with Dave Stewart)

"Top Of The Pops" (04/02/81; BBC One): rebroadcast of above

"My Kind Of Music: Barbara Dickson" (09/05/81; BBC One): The Last Goodbye; I'll Be Back (Lennon/McCartney song duet with Dickson)

"Iltatähti" (12/01/81; Finnish YLE): What Becomes Of The Broken Hearted (with Dave Stewart)

"Top Of The Pops" (12/25/81; BBC One): What Becomes Of The Broken Hearted (with Dave Stewart)

"Pop Quiz" (05/15/82; BBC One): Colin on a game show hosted by Mike Read

"My Kind Of Music" (11/18/83; BBC One): repeat of 1981 program

"Turn Your Heart Around" by KEATS (07/84; promotional video): an A-side for EMI

"You'll Never Walk Alone" by THE CROWD (05/85): a charity single

"Cry An Ocean" (05/88; promotional video): an IRS A-side

"TopPop" (10/91; Dutch AVRO): Old And Wise (original version)

"Belfleur" (10/10/91; Dutch AVRO): Old And Wise (1991 version)

"Just Like A Woman" (09/25/92): Politics Of Love

"Night Of The Proms '93" (10/22/93; Belgian TV): She's Not There (Santana-type arrangement); All You Need Is Love (with Sting and Gary Brooker); Silence & I – recorded live the same day at Sportpalais, Antwerp, Belgium for a concert sponsored by Heineken

"Tellyphonin'" (12/10/95; UK HTV West): She's Not There

"A Merry War" (09/08/97): Tiger In The Night

"Night Fever" (01/17/98; UK Channel 5): She's Not There – hosted by Graham "Suggs" McPherson

"VH-1" (06/28/98; UK VH-1): She's Not There; Your Love Is Like The Sun (in early June 1998, Colin and his band recorded four or five songs at the VH-1 studios, but only these two were broadcast

"De Plaatgast" (02/00; Belgian TV): Old And Wise

"Top Ten: Heartbreakers" (02/10/01; UK Channel 4): Colin was interviewed about "What Becomes Of The Broken Hearted"

"This Is Your Life" (04/11/01; BBC One): Colin was a guest for the program honoring Paul Jones

"The Savages" (04/24/01 – 05/29/01; BBC Two): Days (Colin's version of the popular Kinks song)

"The British Invasion" (05/01; UK ITV): Colin was interviewed

"TOTP2" (03/20/02; BBC Two): What Becomes Of The Broken Hearted (archival performance with Dave Stewart)

"The 60s: The Beatles Decade – Swinging Britain 1965-1966" (07/12/06; UKTV History): Colin and Rod contributed

"The 60s: The Beatles Decade – The Party's Over 1969-1970" (07/14/06; UKTV History): Colin and Rod contributed (Colin is not on the other two episodes that Rod was on)

"Christopher's Music" (01/29/16): Colin appeared during a documentary about composer Christopher Gunning

"Life Stories With Des Tong" (09/28/16; Birmingham TV): interview

"Butt Boy" (09/21/19): It's Not Easy (uncredited)

"The Crown: Cri de Coeur" (11/17/19; Netflix): She's Not There (Colin's solo version from 1991)

"In Conversation" (07/22/20; YouTube): interview recorded 02/02/19 at World Café, Philadelphia, Pennsylvania with Mike D of Reelblack

"Vinyl: An Unlikely History" (currently in production; planned for 2023): Colin Blunstone interview

COLIN BLUNSTONE UNRELEASED COMPOSITIONS LISTED WITH BMI

Absence Makes The Heart Grow Fonder (with Stephen Levine, Julian Lindsay and Ian Richie)
Back On My Feet Again
Change My Heart (with Stephen Levine and Julian Lindsay)
Do You Really Know The One You Love (with Andy Nye)
Five Years Ago
Girls In Cars (with Stuart Elliott)
Give Me One Word (with Richard Kerr)
Giving My All For Love (with Stuart Elliott)
Hurricane (with Stuart Elliott)
If Love's Worth Dying For (with Christopher Eaton)
In My Heart (with Stuart Elliott)
Last Thing On My Mind (with Richard Kerr)
Lonely To Be Alone (with Stuart Elliott)
Love Like A Loaded Gun (with Andy Nye)
Naked Heart (with Andy Nye)
Never Been Kissed In The Same Place
No Future In The Past (with Stuart Elliott)
Now More Than Ever (with Christopher John Winter)
Point Of No Return (with Stuart Elliott)
Remember To Forget
Shadows In The Night
Sue, Ana And Jane
That's The Way To Love A Girl
This Time Around (with Stuart Elliott)
Towers Of Love (with Andy Nye)
We Don't Care (with Richard Frierson, Ian Richie and Christopher Rios)
When Love Has Gone (with Philip Dennys)
Win Or Lose It All (with Stuart Elliott)
Your Time Will Come (with Stuart Elliott)

COLIN BLUNSTONE CONCERT LISTING
(all UK unless otherwise noted)

1972
03/24	Paradiso, Upstairs, Amsterdam, Netherlands

UK tour (05/02/72 – 05/26/72) with Electric Light Orchestra and F.F.Z.:

05/02	Colston Hall, Bristol
05/03	Brighton Dome, Brighton
05/06	Albert Hall, Nottingham
05/07	Guildford Civic Hall, Guildford
05/08	De Montfort Hall, Leicester
05/09	Free Trade Hall, Manchester
05/10	Sheffield City Hall, Sheffield
05/11	Portsmouth Guildhall, Portsmouth
05/12	Plymouth Guildhall, Plymouth
05/14	Fairfield Halls, Croydon
05/17	Music Hall, Aberdeen, Scotland
05/18	Newcastle City Hall, Newcastle
05/19	Green's Playhouse, Glasgow, Scotland
05/20	Empire Theatre, Edinburgh, Scotland
05/22	Solihull Civic Hall, Solihull
05/23	Winter Gardens, Bournemouth
05/26	Public Hall, Preston
09/03	Chiltern Rooms, High Wycombe
09/07	Granary, Bristol
09/08	JB's, Dudley
09/09	Civic Hall, Guildford
10/14	Clarence's, Halifax
10/20	Goldsmiths College, London (with Flash and Home)
10/22	George Hotel, Burslem
10/26	Vine Club, Newport, Monmouth
10/27	Red Lion, Leytonstone
10/29	Black Prince, Bexley (with Climax Chicago [Blues Band])
10/30	The Marquee, London
11/15	Sundown, Mile End
11/16	Sundown, Edmonton, London
11/17	Sundown, Brixton
11/28	Zero Six, Southend-on-Sea
12/17	Torrington, London

1973
01/08	Hardrock Concert Theatre, Manchester
02/03	Queen Margaret Union, Glasgow, Scotland
02/04	Kinema, Dunfermline, Scotland
02/09	Colston Hall, Bristol (with Stealers Wheel)
02/10	Rainbow Theatre, London (with Stealers Wheel)
02/11	Palace Theare, Watford (with Stealers Wheel)
02/13	Free Trade Hall, Manchester (with Stealers Wheel)
02/16	Town Hall, Birmingham (with Stealers Wheel)
02/19	Royal Festival Hall, London (Colin opened for The Bee Gees)
02/24	Leeds University Union, Leeds
03/10	Pop Gala '73, Sporthal de Vliegermolen, Voorburg, Netherlands
03/26-31	Paul's Mall, Boston, Massachusetts, USA (opening for Doug Sahm)
04/20-21	Winterland, San Francisco, California, USA (with Sha Na Na, Commander Cody And The Lost Planet Airmen, and Gentle Giant)
04/24-29	The Troubadour, West Hollywood, California, USA (opened for Tim Buckley)
05/02-07	Max's Kansas City, New York, New York, USA
05/25	Queen Elizabeth Hall, London
06/11	Pinkpop 1973, Burgemeester Damen Sportpark, Geleen, Netherlands
07/13	Sarasani, Texel, Netherlands
07/25	Global Village, Charing Cross, London (with Moonstone)
07/28	Civic Hall, St. Albans
07/30	Top Hat, Spennymoor
08/19	Jazz-Bilzen 1973. Dell, Bilzen, Belgium
09/02	Roundhouse, London (with Badfinger, Blue, and Good Habit)
09/09	Rock-Festival Scheeßel, Eichenring, Scheeßel, Germany
09/13	Heavy Steam Machine, Hanley
09/15	Clarence's, Halifax
09/16	Palace Theare, Watford
09/23	Civic Hall, Wolverhampton
09/25	Colston Hall, Bristol
10/05	Leeds Polytechnic, Leeds
10/06	Dudley College, Dudley
10/10	Wolverhampton Polytechnic, Wolverhampton
10/20	Pavilion, Hemel Hempstead (with The Steve Gibbons Band)
10/27	Queen Margaret Union, Glasgow, Scotland
11/09	Sundown, Edmonton, London
12/07	Bedford College, London
12/17	Top Hat, Spennymoor

1974
01/09	Théâtre Marni, Elsene/Ixelles, Belgium
01/16	De Lantaren, Rotterdam, Netherlands
02/02	City Hall, St. Albans
02/17	Chancellor Hall, Chelmsford
03/31	Town Hall, Birmingham (with John Hetherington)
04/01	Queens Hall, Barnstaple (with John Hetherington)
04/08	Guildhall, Plymouth (with John Hetherington)
04/09	Barbarella's, Birmingham (with John Hetherington)
04/09	Lewisham Concert Hall, London (with John Hetherington)
04/10	Town Hall, Watford (with John Hetherington)
04/11	Victoria Hall, Stoke-on-Trent (with John Hetherington)
04/14	Oakengates Town Hall, Oakengates (with John Hetherington)
04/16	Royal Spa Centre, Royal Leamington Spa (with John Hetherington)
04/21	Davenport Theatre, Stockport (with John Hetherington)
04/26	Paisley College of Technology, Paisley (with John Hertherington)
04/27	Nottingham University, Nottingham (with John Hetherington)

1993
"Night Of The Proms" gigs: Colin sang "Silence And I" and "She's Not There":

10/22-24	Night Of The Proms 1993 Antwerp #1, Sportpaleis, Merksem, Belgium
10/27	Night Of The Proms 1993 Maastricht, MECC, Maastricht, Netherlands
10/28-29	Night Of The Proms 1993 Antwerp #2, Sportpaleis, Merksem, Belgium
10/30-31	Night Of The Proms 1993 Rotterdam, Ahoy, Rotterdam, Netherlands

1997
02/21	The Borderline, London
10/08	The Irish Centre, Leeds
10/09	The Cellar Club, South Shields
10/17	The Borderline, London
10/18	Robin Hood, Brierley Hill
10/24	Towngate Theatre, Basildon
10/25	The Brook, Southampton
10/26	Liscombe Park, Leighton Buzzard
11/04-09	Café Royal, London
11/11-16	Café Royal, London
11/25	Jazz Café, London (Colin dd his regular set before all five Zombies members played)

11/29	Hare & Hounds, Coventry **and** The Wharf Arts Centre, Tavistock		11/28	Leisure Centre, Hereford
			11/30	BIC, Bournemouth
			12/01	Cliffs Pavilion, Southend
			12/02	Regent Theatre, Ipswich

1998

05/21	Cellar, South Shields
05/22	Boardwalk, Sheffield
05/23	Robin Hood, Brierley Hill
05/27	Assembly Halls, Tunbridge Wells
05/28	Beck Theatre, Hayes
05/29	Wyvern Theatre, Swindon
05/30	The Brook, Southampton
05/31	The Stables, Wavendon
06/03	Dingwalls, London
06/04	Winding Wheel, Chesterfield
06/05	Pavilion Theatre, Worthing
06/07	Ashcroft Theatre, Croydon
08/28	Open Air, Zeist, Netherlands
11/01	Ronnie Scott's, Birmingham
11/07	The Robin 2, Bilston
11/08	Theatre Royal, Windsor
11/10-14	Café Royal, London
11/26	Riddle's Music Bar, Stoke
11/27	Artezium Club, Luton
11/28	Mean Fiddler, London

1999

02/12-14	The Fez, New York, New York, USA (the 02/13 show was by invitation only)
05/15	The Brook, Southampton

UK "Maximum Rhythm & Blues Tour" with The Manfreds (10/09/99 – 12/16/99):

10/09	De Montfort Hall, Leicester
10/10	Civic Theatre, Darlington (2 shows)
10/11	City Hall, Hull
10/12	Empire Theatre, Sunderland
10/14	Waterfront Hall, Belfast, Northern Ireland
10/15	Caird Hall, Dundee, Scotland
10/16	Royal Concert Hall, Glasgow, Scotland
10/17	Music Hall, Aberdeen, Scotland
10/18	Festival Theatre, Edinburgh, Scotland
10/19	Bridgewater Hall, Manchester
10/27	Guildhall, Preston
10/28	Philharmonic Hall, Liverpool
10/31	The Orchard, Dartford (2 shows)
11/01	Fairfield Halls, Croydon
11/02	Congress Theatre, Eastbourne
11/04	Assembly Hall, Worthing
11/05	Royal Concert Hall, Nottingham
11/06	Theatre Royal, Norwich (2 shows)
11/07	New Victoria, Woking (2 shows)
11/09	Hexagon, Reading
11/10	St. David's Hall, Cardiff, Wales
11/11	The Cresset, Peterborough
11/13	Corn Exchange, Kings Lynn
11/14	Swan Theatre, High Wycombe (2 shows)
11/16	The Guildhall, Portsmouth
11/17	Royal Albert Hall, London
11/18	Assembly Halls, Tunbridge Wells
11/19	Alban Arena, St. Albans (2 shows)
11/20	Derngate, Northampton (2 shows)
11/21	Apollo, Oxford
11/23	North Wales Theatre, Llandudno, Wales
11/24	The Royal, Hanley
11/25	Symphony Hall, Birmingham
11/26	The Anvil, Basingstoke
11/27	New Coliseum, St. Austell
12/13	Assembly Rooms, Derby
12/14	City Halls, Sheffield
12/16	Oasis Centre, Swindon

2000

Sept.	Netherlands tour

2002

03/08	Port Fairy Folk Festival 2002, Southcombe Park Sports Reserve, Port Fairy, Australia
04/12	The Brook, Southampton
04/25	De Boerderij, Zoetermeer, Netherlands
04/26	Struve Party House, Sappemeer, Netherlands
04/27	ECR Building, Zolder, Belgium

UK "The Manfreds Maximum R&B Tour '02" with The Manfreds, Chris Farlowe, and Long John Baldry (04/30/02 – 07/18/02):

04/30	City Hall, Salisbury
05/01	Victoria Hall, Stoke-on-Trent
05/03	Cliffs Pavilion, Southend
05/04	The Orchard, Dartford (2 shows)
05/05	Royal Concert Hall, Nottingham
05/07	The Hawth, Crawley
05/08	Central Theatre, Chatham
05/09	Civic, Guildford
05/10	The Cresset, Peterborough
05/11	Town Hall, Middlesborough
05/13	Grand Theatre, Swansea, Wales
05/14	Corn Exchange, Cambridge
05/17	Opera House, Newcastle
05/18	Derngate Theatre, Northampton (2 shows)
05/19	Hippodrome, Bristol
05/20	North Wales Theatre, Llandudno, Wales
05/21	Philharmonic Hall, Liverpool
05/23	City Hall, Sheffield
05/24	Assembly Hall, Tunbridge Wells
05/25	Pavilion Theatre, Bournemouth
05/27	Auditorium, Grimsby
05/28	Royal Concert Hall, Glasgow, Scotland
05/29	St. George's Hall, Bradford
05/30	Guildhall, Preston
05/31	The Embassy, Skegness
06/05	Hexagon Theatre, Reading
06/06	The Anvil, Basingstoke
06/07	Guildhall, Portsmouth
06/08	Congress, Eastbourne
06/09	Palladium, London
06/10	Fairfield Halls, Croydon
06/16	Opera House, Buxton
06/17	The Hall For Cornwall, Truro
06/18	Symphony Hall, Birmingham
06/20	Town Hall, Cheltenham
06/21	St. David's Hall, Cardiff, Wales
06/22	Alban Arena, St. Albans
06/24	Assembly Hal, Worthing
06/25	De Montfort Hall, Leicester
07/05	Claremont Landscape Garden, Esher, Surrey (Alan Price replaced Long John Baldry for this show only)
07/18	Claremont Landscape Garden, Esher

2003
UK "Maximum Rhythm 'n' Blues" tour with The Manfreds, Alan Price, and P.P. Arnold:

10/02	Central Theatre, Chatham
10/07	Hexagon Theatre, Reading
10/09	Swan Theatre, High Wycombe
10/10	Auditorium, Grimsby
10/11	Assembly Hall, Tunbridge Wells
10/12	Assembly Hall, Worthing
10/14	Colosseum, Watford
10/16	The Cresset, Peterborough
10/17	Apollo Theatre, Oxford
10/18	Queen's Theatre, Barnstable (2 shows)
10/19	De Montfort Hall, Leicester
10/23	Fairfield Halls, Croydon
10/24	Rivermead, Reading
10/26	Princess Theatre, Torquay
10/27	Corn Exchange, Cambridge
10/28	The Orchard, Dartford
10/30-31	Pavilion, Bournemouth
11/02	Guildhall, Preston
11/03	Symphony Hall, Birmingham
11/04	Grand Theatre, Swansea, Wales
11/05	City Hall, Salisbury
11/06	Victoria Theatre, Halifax
11/09	International Centre, Harrogate
11/12	North Wales Theatre, Llandudno, Wales
11/13	Opera House, Manchester
11/14	Embassy, Skegness
11/23	Usher Hall, Edinburgh, Scotland
11/24	Royal Concert Hall, Glasgow, Scotland
11/25	Caird Hall, Dundee, Scotland
11/26	Opera House, Buxton
11/27	Royal Concert Hall, Nottingham
11/29	The Anvil, Basingstoke
11/30	Palladium, London
12/01	Philharmonic Hall, Liverpool
12/02	Newcastle City Hall, Newcastle
12/03	Derngate, Northampton
12/04	City Hall, Sheffield
12/07	Theatre Royal, Bath (2 shows)
12/09	Pavilion, Plymouth
12/10	Town Hall, Cheltenham
12/11	Civic, Guildford

2007
10/12	100 Club, London

2009
02/11	The Brook, Southampton
02/14	The Ferry, Broomielaw, Glasgow, Scotland
02/18	The Globe, Cardiff, Wales
02/19	The Stables, Wavendon
02/20	100 Club, London
02/21	Boom Boom Club, London
02/23	Whelan's, Dublin, Ireland
03/14	Radio 2 Muziekcafé, Amsterdam, Netherlands (live radio recording for Dutch Radio 2)

2010
02/12	The Flowerpot, Derby
02/13	Cheese And Grain, Frome
02/14	The Brook, Southampton
02/18	The Globe, Cardiff, Wales
02/19	100 Club, London

2011
02/03	The Globe, Cardiff, Wales
02/08	The Stables, Wavendon
02/09	The Brook, Southampton
02/10	The Robin 2, Bilston
02/11	The Ferry, Glasgow, Scotland
02/12	Backstage @ The Green Hotel, Kinross, Scotland
02/13	Stanley Theatre, Liverpool
02/17	Beaverwood Club, Chiselhurst
02/18	Boom Boom Club, London
02/19	Astor Community Theatre, Deal
02/20	Jazz Café, London
02/23	Zalen Schaaf, Leeuwarden, Netherlands
02/24	P60, Amstelveen, Netherlands
02/25	De Boerderij, Zoetermeer, Netherlands
02/26	Gigant Popzaal, Apeldoorn, Netherlands
02/27	Lakei, Helmond, Netherlands

2012
02/07	The Stables, Wavendon
02/09	The Robin 2, Bilston
02/10	The Duchess, York
02/12	Backstage @ The Green Hotel, Kinross, Scotland
02/15	Jazz Café, London
02/18	The Flowerpot, Derby
02/21	The Glee Club, Cardiff, Wales
02/24	Boom Boom Club, London
02/25	Cox's Yard, Stratford-upon-Avon
02/26	The Brook, Southampton
02/28	Glee Club, Cardiff, Wales (cancelled)
09/27	Astor Community Theatre, Deal, UK
11/02	De Boerderij, Zoetermeer, Netherlands (cancelled)
11/03	Theater De Willem, Papendrecht, Netherlands (cancelled)
11/04	Schouwburg De Meerse Grote Zaal, Hoofddorp, Netherlands (cancelled)
11/06	Limburgzaal, Parkstad Limburg Theaters, Heerlen, Netherlands (cancelled)
11/09	Stadsgehoorzaal, Kampen, Netherlands (cancelled)
11/11	Luxor Live, Arnhem, Netherlands (cancelled)
11/14	Theater De Kom, Nieuwegein, Netherlands (cancelled)
11/18	De Kleine Komedie, Amsterdam, Netherlands (cancelled)
11/30	The Trades Club, Hebden Bridge (cancelled)

2013
01/19	Corneel, Lelystad, Netherlands
01/27	The Great British Rock & Blues Festival 2013, Butlins Resort Skegness, Skegness
01/28	The Trades Club, Hebden Bridge
01/30	Jazz Café, London
02/01	Swindon Arts Centre, Swindon
02/03	Uppermill Civic Hall, Oldham
02/05	The Stables, Wavendon
02/07	Garage Music Venue, Swansea, Wales
02/08	The Globe, Cardiff, Wales
02/10	Backstage @ The Green Hotel, Kinross, Scotland
02/14	The Robin 2, Bilston
02/16	The Flowerpot, Derby (with Limehouse Lizzy)
08/22	The Cellars at Eastney, Southsea
08/24	Pinkpop Classic Festival 2013, Megaland, Landgraaf, Netherlands
10/04	P60, Amstelveen, Netherlands
10/05	Cultuurpodium Boerderij Dommelsch Zaal, Zoetermeer, Netherlands
10/06	De Pul, Uden, Netherlands
10/11	Wycombe Arts Centre, High Wycombe

2014
03/16	Jazz Café, London (with Mike Hough)

Date	Venue
05/08	Tupelo Music Hall, Londonderry, New Hampshire, USA
05/09	Bridge Street Live, Collinsville, Connecticut, USA
05/10	Robert E. Parilla Performing Arts Center, Rockville, Maryland, USA
05/11	World Café Live, Philadelphia, Pennsylvania, USA
05/13	City Winery, New York, New York, USA
05/14	Boulton Center For The Performing Arts, Bay Shore, New York, USA
05/15	City Winery, Chicago, Illinois, USA
05/21	The Jam House, Edinburgh, Scotland
05/30	The Jam House, Edinburgh, Scotland
06/04	Jazz Café, London
06/06	The Flowerpot, Derby
06/08	The Robin 2, Bilston
08/31	The Day The Music Died 2014, Ahoy, Rotterdam, Netherlands
10/02	Poppodium Metropool, Hengelo, Netherlands
10/03	Luxor Live, Arnhem, Netherlands
10/04	De Boerderij, Zoetermeer, Netherlands
10/05	P3, Purmerend, Netherlands

2016

Date	Venue
01/22	Tivoli Theatre, Wimborne Minster
01/23	The Citadel, St. Helens
01/24	The Great British Rock & Blues Festival 2016, Butlins Resort Skegness, Skegness
02/04	P60, Amstelveen, Netherlands
02/05	Podium De Vorstin, Hilversum, Netherlands
02/06	Manifesto, Hoorn, Netherlands
02/07	Stadstheater, Zoetermeer, Netherlands
02/09	Cultuurplein Zwaneberg, Heist-op-den-Berg, Belgium
02/11	De blauwe kei, Veghel, Netherlands
02/12	Iduna, Drachten, Netherlands
04/15	The Flowerpot, Derby
04/16	Hessle Town Hall, Hessle
04/17	Stables Theatre, Wavendon
04/19	Waterside Arts Centre, Manchester
04/20	The Robin 2, Bilston
04/22	The Brook, Southampton
04/23	Trading Boundaries, Fletching
04/24	The Borderline, London
10/28	St. Edward's Church, Stow-on-the-Wold
10/29	Howden Shire Hall, Howden (with Carl Palmer)
10/30	Boom Boom Club, Sutton

2017

Date	Venue
01/20	The Brook, Southampton
01/22	100 Club, London
01/26	Backstage @ The Green Hotel, Kinross, Scotland
01/27	Selby Town Hall, Selby
02/02	Mezz, Breda, Netherlands
02/03	Luxor Live, Arnhem, Netherlands
02/04	De Boerderij, Zoetermeer, Netherlands
02/05	De Cacaofabriek, Helmond, Netherlands
02/06	Concertgebouw, Amsterdam, Netherlands
02/10	St. John's Church, Godalming
02/11	Tivoli Theatre, Wimborne Minster
02/12	Tithe Barn, Bishop's Cleeve
02/15	The Robin 2, Bilston
02/16	The Flowerpot, Derby
02/17	Trading Boundaries, Fletching
02/18	Alban Arena, St. Albans
10/22	100 Club, London
11/10	Lowdham Village Hall, Lowdham
11/11	Grayshott Village Hall, Hindhead
11/12	Floral Pavilion, New Brighton
11/15	Sage Gateshead, Gateshead
11/16	The Ferry, Glasgow, Scotland
11/17	Backstage @ The Green Hotel, Kinross, Scotland
11/23	The Beaverwood, Chislehurst
11/24	Boom Boom Club, Sutton
11/25	Long Street Blues Club, Devizes
11/27	The Robin 2, Bilston

2018

Date	Venue
04/06	Podium De Vorstin, Hilversum, Netherlands
04/07	Pop-en Cultuurhuis Px, Volendam, Netherlands
04/08	ECI Cultuurfabriek, Roermond, Netherlands
04/09	Spirit Of 66, Verviers, Belgium
04/12	P60, Amstelveen, Netherlands
04/13	Neushoorn Grote Zaal, Leeuwarden, Netherlands
04/14	De Boerderij, Zoetermeer, Netherlands
04/20	The Flowerpot, Derby
04/21	The Astor Community Theatre, Deal
04/22	Epic Studios, Norwich
04/24	Grayshott Village Hall, Hindhead
04/25	The Borderline, London
04/26	Stables Theatre, Wavendon
04/27	Tivoli Theatre, Wimborne Minster

2019

Date	Venue
01/31	Daryl's House Club, Pawling, New York, USA
02/01	My Father's Place at The Roslyn Hotel, Roslyn, New York, USA
02/02	World Café Live, Philadelphia, Pennsylvania, USA
02/04	One Longfellow Square, Portland, Maine, USA
02/05	City Winery, Boston, Massachusetts, USA
02/07	City Winery, Washington, District of Columbia, USA
02/08	City Winery, New York, New York, USA
02/14	On The Blue Cruise 2019, MS Mariner Of The Seas, Miami, Florida, USA
04/04	Backstage @ The Green Hotel, Kinross, Scotland (with Bruce Sudano)
04/05	Arts Centre, Pocklington (with Bruce Sudano)
04/06	Hull Minster, Kingston upon Hull (with Bruce Sudano)
04/07	Earl Haig Memorial Hall, Cardiff, Wales (with Bruce Sudano)
04/09	Grayshott Village Hall, Hindhead (with Bruce Sudano)
04/10	Stables Theatre, Wavendon (with Bruce Sudano)
04/11	The Robin 2, Bilston (with Bruce Sudano)
04/12-13	Trading Boundaries, Fletching (with Bruce Sudano)
04/24	The King's Hall, Herne Bay (with Bruce Sudano)
04/25	Tivoli Theatre, Wimborne Minster (with Bruce Sudano)
04/26	The Borderline, London (with Bruce Sudano)
11/14	P60, Amstelveen, Netherlands
11/15	De Boerderij, Zoetermeer, Netherlands
11/16	Manifesto, Hoorn, Netherlands
11/17	CC Het Bolwerk, Vilvoorde, Belgium
11/19	Podium De Vorstin, Hilversum, Netherlands
11/20	De Bosuil, Weert, Netherlands
11/21	Zalen Schaaf, Leeuwarden, Netherlands
11/22	Metropool Jupiler Stage, Hengelo, Netherlands

COLIN BLUNSTONE ROD ARGENT THE ZOMBIES DISCOGRAPHY
(* as Colin Blunstone & Rod Argent; ** as The Zombies featuring Colin Blunstone & Rod Argent; *** as The Zombies)

SINGLES

TITLES	UK & FOREIGN LABEL/NO.	RELEASE DATE	US & CANADA LABEL/NO.	RELEASE DATE
Sanctuary * - Sanctuary (White Magic Mix) * - Love Can Heal The Pain * (CD5)	Red House CDREDH 100	03/25/01		
Mystified * - Only The Rain * (CD5)	Red House CDREDH 101	11/05/01		
Home * - Living In The Real World * (CD5)	Red House CDREDH 102	05/06/02		
In My Mind A Miracle (Radio Edit)** - In My Mind A Miracle (Live Version - recorded at The Bloomsbury Theatre, London on June 6, 2003)**	Red House CDREDH 103	04/12/04		
Southside Of The Street (Single Edit)** - As Far As I Can See (Single Edit)**	Red House CDREDH 104	08/13/04		
Breathe Out, Breathe In ** (promo CD5)	Red House CDREH 1 P	05/09/11		
A Moment In Time (Single Version)** (promo CD5/download)	Red House CDREH 2 P	08/12/11		
Any Other Way** (promo CD5)	Go! Entertainment GO 70505	04/28/14		
Now I Know I'll Never Get Over You (Radio Mix) *** (promo CD-R; incorrectly titled "Never Get Over You" on the disc)	no label or #	01/08/16		
I Want You Back Again (2015)***/ I Want You Back Again (1965) (7"; Record Store Day release)			The End 538268571	04/22/17

ALBUMS

TITLES	UK & FOREIGN LABEL/NO.	RELEASE DATE	US & CANADA LABEL/NO.	RELEASE DATE
Out Of The Shadows * (CD)	Red House REDHCD 2	03/25/01	Koch KOCCD 8470	03/25/03

TRACKS: Home; A Girl Like That; Helpless; Sanctuary; Living In The Real World; Mystified; Only The Rain; Baby Don't You Cry No More; Danger Zone; Love Can Heal The Pain

Out Of The Shadows * (CD; 2 bonus tracks – see below)	Japanese JVC Victor VICP-61637	11/21/01		

TRACKS: different order of same original tracks; plus piano and vocal arrangements of "I Want To Fly" and "Wings Against The Sun"

As Far As I Can See...** (CD)	Red House REDHCD 3	03/04/04	Rhino 76573	09/14/04

TRACKS: In My Mind A Miracle; Memphis; Southside Of The Street; I Want To Fly; Time To Move; I Don't Believe In Miracles; As Far As I Can See; With You Not Here; Wings Against The Sun; Together; Look For A Better Way

Live At The Bloomsbury Theatre, London ** (2CD; recorded on 06/07/03)	Red House REDHCD 4	02/03/05	Rhino 74839	04/03/07

TRACKS: Andorra; This Will Be Our Year; I Love You; What Becomes Of The Broken Hearted; Mystified; A Rose For Emily; Beechwood Park; Time Of The Season; I Want To Fly; In My Mind A Miracle; Keep On Rollin'; Hold Your Head Up;/ Sanctuary; Pleasure; Say You Don't Mind; Misty Roses; I Don't Believe In Miracles; Old And Wise; Care Of Cell 44; Indication; Tell Her No; She's Not There; Just Out Of Reach; God Gave Rock And Roll To You; Summertime

Zombies And Beyond ** (CD)	UMTV 1773931	05/26/08		

TRACKS: I Want To Fly (Single Edit); Southside Of The Street; plus tracks by The Zombies, Colin Blunstone, Alan Parsons Project, Argent, and Dave Stewart with Colin Blunstone

Odessey & Oracle {Revisited} ** (2CD; the live tracks "I Love You," "Sticks And Stones," "Can't Nobody Love You," "What Becomes Of The Broken Hearted," "Misty Roses," "Her Song," "Say You Don't Mind," "Keep On Rollin'," and "Hold Your Head Up")	Red House REDHCD 5	06/30/08		
Breathe Out, Breathe In ** (CD)	Red House REDHCD 6	05/09/11		

TRACKS: Breathe Out, Breathe In; Any Other Way; Play It For Real; Shine On Sunshine; Show Me The Way; A Moment In Time; Christmas For The Free; Another Day; I Do Believe; Let It Go

Recorded Live In Concert At Metropolis Studios, London ** (CD/DVD; recorded 01/08/11)	Salvo/ Union Square SALVOSVX005	06/04/12		

TRACKS: I Love You; Can't Nobody Love You; Mystified; What Becomes Of The Broken Hearted; Any Other Way; A Rose For Emily; Care Of Cell 44; This Will Be Our Year; Beechwood Park; I Want Her She Wants Me; Time Of The Season; Whenever You're Ready; Tell Her No; I Do Believe; Say You Don't Mind; Hold Your Head Up; I Don't Believe In Miracles; She's Not There; Summertime (same tracks on DVD, but the DVD has bonus interviews with Colin and Rod)

Extended Versions *** (CD; recorded 2012 live in the UK)   Sony Commercial Music Group 88725473262   11/21/12
TRACKS: Time Of The Season; Can't Nobody Love You; Breathe In, Breathe Out; I Love You; A Rose For Emily; Care Of Cell 44; This Will Be Our Year; Tell Her No; Hold Your Head Up; She's Not There

Live In The UK *** (CD; repackage of previous CD)   Red House REDHCD 7   04/28/13
TRACKS: same as "Extended Versions" CD

Recorded Live In Concert At Metropolis Studios, London ** (2LP; reissue)   Go Entertainment GO2VIN7340   04/28/14
TRACKS: same as the CD/DVD release from 06/04/12

"Collected" ** by COLIN BLUNSTONE (3CD)   Dutch Universal 534 274-4   09/19/14
TRACKS: Home; Mystified; Sanctuary; In My Mind A Miracle; I Want To Fly; Memphis; Any Other Way; plus many other tracks from Colin Blunstone's career

Still Got That Hunger *** (CD)   Cherry Red CDBRED671   10/09/15   The End TE708-2   10/09/15
TRACKS: Moving On; Chasing The Past; Edge Of The Rainbow; New York; I Want You Back Again (2015); And We Were Young Again; Maybe Tomorrow; Now I Know I'll Never Get Over You; Little One; Beyond The Borderline

Still Got That Hunger *** (LP; reissue –baby blue vinyl)   The End TE708-1   01/08/16
TRACKS: same as CD edition above

Still Got That Hunger *** (LP; reissues of 500 copies each – first release was 180g vinyl; the second release was 140g vinyl)   Plane Groovy PLG043   02/12/16/ 03/12/16
TRACKS: same as CD edition above

"Collected" by COLIN BLUNSTONE (2LP; edited –white vinyl)   Dutch Music On Vinyl MOVLP2169   06/28/18
TRACKS: Home; Sanctuary; In My Mind A Miracle; Any Other Way; plus many other tracks from Colin Blunstone's career

Live From Studio Two *** (CD/DVD; sold at gigs and online)   Red House 195269161408   04/01/22
TRACKS: Moving On; I Want You Back Again; Edge Of The Rainbow; I Love You; Say You Don't Mind; Different Game; You Could Be My Love; I Want To Fly; Tell Her No; Care Of Cell 44; This Will Be Our Year; I Want Her She Wants Me; Time Of The Season; Merry Go Round; Runaway; Hold Your Head Up; She's Not There; The Way I Feel Inside

VIDEOS

TITLES	UK & FOREIGN LABEL/NO.	RELEASE DATE	US & CANADA LABEL/NO.	RELEASE DATE
As Far As I Can See... (DVD; recorded 06/07/03 at The Bloomsbury Theatre in London. The disc also includes their "2 Meter XL" TV appearance in the Netherlands on 02/12/02.)	Stax Entertainment Ltd. STX2099	08/15/05		
Live At The Bloomsbury Theatre, London (DVD of above concert, but without "Say You Don't Mind," "Misty Roses," "Old And Wise," "Just Out Of Reach," "Summertime," and "2 Meter XL" tracks)			Rhino 972712	04/03/07
"The British Beat Live! Best Of The 60s" (contains "She's Not There," "Tell Her No" and "Time Of The Season" from the Bloomsbury concert; broadcast on US PBS TV stations)			Shout Factory 826663-10353	09/04/07
Odessey & Oracle {Revisited} (DVD; with live performances of "I Love You," "Sticks And Stones," "Can't Nobody Love You," "What Becomes Of The Broken Hearted," "Misty Roses," "Her Song," "Say You Don't Mind," "Keep On Rollin'," and "Hold Your Head Up")	Red House REDHDVD 1	04/28/09	MVD Visual/ Red House MVDV4896	04/28/09
Filmed Live At Metropolis Studio (DVD; recorded 01/08/11)	Metropolis Group 37115345-43	05/23/11		
Recorded Live In Concert At Metropolis Studios, London ** (CD/DVD; recorded 01/08/11)	Salvo/ Union Square SALVOSVX005	06/04/12	Canadian Convexe CVX902141	06/04/12

COLIN BLUNSTONE   ROD ARGENT   THE ZOMBIES RADIO/PODCAST APPEARANCES

"Total Rock Radio" (03/17/01; www.totalrock.com/ satellite): interview

"Johnnie Walker" (04/16/01; BBC Radio Two): Baby Don't You Cry No More; She's Not There; interview – Colin and Rod (voice and piano only) promoted "Out Of The Shadows"

"The Nicky Campbell Show" (11/01/01; BBC Radio 5): interview

"The Richard Allinson Show" (11/06/01; BBC Radio Two): chat and live performance

"Denk Aan Henk Show" (02/13/02; Dutch Radio 3 FM): She's Not There; Sanctuary; I Don't Believe In Miracles; interview (all songs live); plus recorded for later use: Home; Old And Wise; She's Not There; Baby Don't You Cry No More

"Schiffers FM Live" (02/14/02; Dutch Radio 2): interview

"KLM Airlines" (02/02): a one-hour program for the airline which promoted "Out Of The Shadows" and spotlighted some Colin Blunstone solo tracks and Rod Argent's "Classically Speaking" CD; used for in-flight entertainment during June 2002

"Belgian Radio" (05/03/02; Belgian Radio 1): acoustic session and interview taped on 04/27/02

"The Jonathan Ross Show" (04/10/04; BBC Radio Two): interview and live performance

"Capitol Gold Radio" (04/14/04; UK Capitol Gold Radio [London]): interview

"Gary Crowley" (04/14/04; BBC Radio London): interview

"The Simon Mayo Program" (04/22/04; BBC Radio Two): interview

"The Richard Allinson Show" (04/26/04; BBC Radio Two): interview

"The Danny Baker Show" (04/27/04; BBC Radio London): interview

"Loose Ends" (05/01/04; BBC Radio 4): interview

"The Simon Mayo Chart Show" (05/03/04; BBC Radio Two): music and interview

"Dutch Radio" (05/05/04 – 05/08/04; Dutch radio): press and inteviews in the Netherlands

"Loose Ends" (08/14/04; BBC Radio 4): tied in with the "Southside Of The Street" single

"The Johnny Walker Show" (08/31/04; BBC Radio Two); two live songs, an interview, plus the studio version of "Southside Of The Street"

"Rhino Records Interview" (09/04; rhino.com): an interview to promote "As Far As I Can See..."

"Radio Promos" (11/04; Netherlands/Germany): promotional broadcasts and shows in the Netherlands and Germany

"Café De Paris Live" (07/24/05; Capital Gold Radio [London]): the live performance was broadcast on radio and was also available online

"Bob Harris Sunday" (02/16/08; BBC Radio Two): Colin Blunstone and Rod Argent appeared

"The Tom Robinson Show" (02/19/08; BBC Radio 6 Music): The Zombies played live

"Mark Lamarr And Jo Brand" (05/24/08; BBC Radio Two): The Zombies appeared on Jonathan Ross' program with these fill-in hosts

"Stephen Merchant" (06/29/08; BBC Radio 6 Music): Rod Argent and Colin Blunstone live studio session

"Stephen Merchant" (07/06/08; BBC Radio 6 Music): repeat of above program

"Johnnie Walker" (08/17/08; BBC Radio Two): She's Not There; Time Of The Season (both live in the studio)

"Face To Face" (12/08/08, 12/10/08, and 12/12/08; rockondigital.com): Colin and Rod were interviewed by host Rick Wakeman

"Face To Face" (10/08/09 and 10/26/09; rockondigital.com): Colin and Rod were interviewed again by host Rick Wakeman

"The Huey Show" (01/04/09; BBC Radio 6 Music): Rod and Colin talked about playing "Odessey And Oracle" live

"Gideon Coe" (01/19/09; BBC Radio 6 Music): BBC archival material

"Gideon Coe" (02/09/09; BBC Radio 6 Music): BBC archival material

"George Lamb" (10/08/09; BBC Radio 6 Music): Zombies live session in the Hub

"Danny Baker" (04/14/11; BBC Radio London): Zombies live in the studio

"Jools Holland" (04/18/11; BBC Radio Two): Sticks And Stones (Colin and Rod joined Jools in this live version)

"Lauren Laverne" (04/20/11; BBC Radio 6 Music): Zombies live in the studio

"Met Het Oog Op Morgen" (06/30/11; Dutch Radio 1): interview and live performance

"Stenders Late Vermaak" (07/01/11; Dutch 3FM): interview and live performance for the program hosted by Rob Stenders

"Tros Muziekcafe" (07/02/11; Dutch Radio 2): interview and live performance from De Vorstin-Hilversum

"Andy Potter" (08/18/11; BBC Radio Derby): Colin and Rod appeared

"Andy Potter" (08/20/11; BBC Radio Derby): repeat of the above

"Roger Day" (09/01/11; BBC Sussex/ BBC Radio Solent): Rod and Colin talked about the new Zombies album

"6 Music Live Hour" (09/28/11; BBC Radio 6 Music): archival BBC session

"Late Show – Keith Middleton" (11/05/11; BBC Coventry & Warwickshire): Rod talked about The Zombies

"Roger Day" (02/01/12; BBC Surrey/ BBC Radio Oxford): Rod talked about the latest Zombies tour

"Robert Elms" (05/21/12; BBC Radio London): Zombies live in the studio

"6 Music Live Hour" (07/29/12; BBC Radio 6 Music): archival BBC session

"6 Music Live Hour" (08/18/12; BBC Radio 6 Music): archival BBC session

"6 Music Live Hour" (09/25/12; BBC Radio 6 Music): archival BBC session

"Tiny Desk Concert" (10/09/12; US National Public Radio [NPR]): concert

"Daytrotter Studio" (05/06/13; Daytrotter Studio, Rock Island, Illinois): 5 live tracks

"Stephen Bumfrey" (05/10/13; BBC Radio Norfolk): Zombies live in the studio session

"Robert Elms" (05/22/13; BBC Radio London): Zombies live in the studio session

"Radcliffe And Maconie" (05/22/13; BBC Radio 6 Music): Colin and Rod appeared

"Simon Mayo Drivetime" (05/22/13; BBC Radio 2): Colin and Rod talked about their new album and tour

"Steve Lamacq's Rock College" (06/06/13; BBC Radio 2): Colin recalled recording a Zombies classic

"Nick Coffer" (01/09/14; BBC Three Counties Radio): Colin talked about his career and an upcoming Zombies performance in Stevenage

"6 Music Live Hour" (06/06/14; BBC Radio 6 Music): archival BBC session

"Gideon Coe" (10/14/14; BBC Radio 6 Music): archival BBC session

"6 Music Live Hour" (04/03/15; BBC Radio 6 Music): archival BBC session

"Radcliffe And Maconie" (07/29/15; BBC Radio 6 Music): The Zombies appeared and discussed "Still Got That Hunger"

"Mike Sweeney" (08/03/15; BBC Radio Manchester): Colin talked to fill-in Andy Crane about the new Zombies album and tour

"Alan Thompson" (09/13/15; BBC Radio Wales): Colin spoke with Alan about the new Zombies album

"6 Music Live Hour" (10/15/15; BBC Radio 6 Music): archival BBC session

"Loose Ends" (11/07/15; BBC Radio 4 FM): Zombies appearance

"Robert Elms" (11/09/15; BBC Radio London): Zombies live session in studio

"Moving On" (11/12/15; YouTube; promotional video)

"The Guestlist With Sean Cannon" (01/25/16; podcast): Colin and Rod on this early podcast episode

"Nick Piercey" (04/06/16; BBC Radio Oxford): Colin and Rod appeared

"Ralph McLean – Rock And Soul" (04/28/16; BBC Radio Ulster): Colin and Rod looked back on their careers

"The Strange Brew" (05/01/16; podcast): Rod only

"Robert Elms" (08/02/16; BBC Radio London): Colin and Rod played live

"Gideon Coe" (10/24/16; BBC Radio 6 Music): archival BBC session

"Songcraft: Spotlight On Songwriters" (03/06/17; podcast): Rod only

"Lauren Laverne" (06/05/17; BBC Radio 6 Music): This Will Be Our Year; Time Of The Season – a live Zombies studio session with Colin and Rod

"The Janice Forsyth Show" (11/13/17; BBC Radio Orkney): Colin appeared about The Zombies

"Wynne Evans" (04/17/18; BBC Radio Wales): Colin talked about the upcoming Zombies tour and the date in Cardiff that June

"My London" (06/09/18; BBC Radio London): Colin and Rod spoke to Gary Crowley about their experiences in London

"Lynn Bowles" (06/10/18; BBC Radio Wales): Colin and Rod were interviewed

"The Afternoon Show" (12/19/18; BBC Radio Orkney): Colin discussed The Zombies' induction into the Rock 'N' Roll Hall Of Fame and the upcoming colored vinyl 5LP set

"Tammy Gooding" (01/17/19; BBC Hereford & Worcester): a salute to The Zombies' induction

"Mike Naylor" (01/19/19; BBC Three Counties Radio): Colin discussed the induction

"Stephen McCauley" (02/25/19; BBC Radio Foyle): saluted The Zombies at their induction in New York

"This Must Be The Gig" (01/30/19; podcast): Colin only

"The Trap Set With Joe Wong" (03/27/19; podcast): Colin and Rod

"Mike Naylor" (03/30/19; BBC Three Counties Radio): saluted The Zombies

"Saturday Night With Justin Dealey" (03/30/19; BBC Radio Norfolk): Justin was in New York with The Zombies at their induction

"Rolling Stone Music Now" (05/01/19; podcast): Colin and Rod

"Artist Interviews & Performances" (08/22/19; podcast): Colin only

"Lynn Bowles" (04/26/20; BBC Radio Wales): Colin talked about 50 years in the music business, and especially his time in The Zombies

"Sending Signals" (10/06/20; podcast): all four surviving Zombies appeared to discuss the making of "Odessey And Oracle"

"The Bob Lefsetz Podcast" (08/05/21; podcast): Rod only

"Rock & Roll High School With Pete Ganbarg" (09/02/21; podcast): Colin and Rod

"Music Is My Life" (09/13/21; podcast): Colin only

"Breaking It Down With Frank MacKay" (09/13/21; podcast): Colin only

"The Strange Brew" (09/14/21; podcast): Colin only

"Dublab: In Conversation" (09/16/21; podcast): Colin and Rod

"Inside The Studio" (09/24/21; podcast): Colin only

"Raconteurs" (10/02/21; podcast): Colin only

"The Sixties Recording Podcast" (11/01/21; podcast): Colin only

"Little Steven's Underground Garage: Coolest Conversation" (11/15/21): Colin only

"Robert Elms" (11/26/21; BBC Radio London): Colin spoke about The Zombies' 2022 UK tour (which was later postponed to 2023)

"Life Of The Record" (01/11/22; podcast): Colin spoke about the making of "One Year" and his work with The Zombies

"Stereo Embers: The Podcast With Alex Green" (01/12/22; podcast): Colin only

"Greatest Music Of All Time" (02/28/22; podcast): Colin only

"Caropop" (03/17/22; podcast): Colin only

"Desperately Seeking Paul: Paul Weller Fan Podcast" (05/02/22; podcast): Rod only

"Cultural Manifesto" (05/26/22; podcast): Colin only

"Better Each Day" (07/14/22; podcast): Colin only

NOTE: Colin and Rod also appeared on Smooth FM, Talk Sport with James Whale, among others.

COLIN BLUNSTONE   ROD ARGENT   THE ZOMBIES TELEVISION, FILM, AND VIDEO APPEARANCES
(television broadcasts list the first broadcast dates and networks; films/videos list just the first release dates)

"Later...With Jools Holland" (04/27/01; BBC Two): Sanctuary; She's Not There – live and piano versions of both were offered, and the segment was filmed three days before by Colin and Rod

"2 Meter XL" (02/12/02 and 02/16/02; Dutch RTL5): She's Not There; Home; Sanctuary; Summertime; Time Of The Season – hosted by Jan Douwe Koreske, this program aired just the first two tracks and retained the others for later use (a subsequent airing for days later, and the whole program on the DVD "As Far As I Can See..."), and Rod also performed the song "Lover" with Dutch artist Birgit

"The Dan And Dusty Show" (08/20/04; UK ITV): Southside Of The Street; She's Not There (live versions by Colin and Rod) – the program was hosted by two puppets (!)

"The Dan And Dusty Show" (10/08/04; UK ITV): a repeat of the above

"As Far As I Can See..." (08/15/05): a UK DVD release: Stax Entertainment Ltd. STX2099 – filmed 06/07/03 at The Bloomsbury Theatre, London, plus tracks from the "2 Meter XL" sessions listed above

"Straight Talk With Cito Beltran" (02/09/06; Philippine ABS CBN): interview

"Eat Bulaga!" (02/10/06; Philippine GMA Network): interview

"My Music: The British Beat" (03/03/07; US PBS): She's Not There; Tell Her No; Time Of The Season – from the Bloomsbury Theatre concert

"Live At The Bloomsbury Theatre, London" (04/03/07) – a US DVD release: Rhino 972712 – an edited version of the DVD "As Far As I Can See..."

"The British Beat Live! Best Of The 60s" (09/04/07): She's Not There; Tell Her No; Time Of The Season – a US DVD release: Shout Factory 826663-10353; from the Bloomsbury Theatre concert

"Suggs In The City" (06/12/08; UK ITV): a Zombies performance

"Odessey & Oracle {Revisited}" (04/28/09): a UK DVD release: Red House REDHDVD 1, and a US DVD release: MVD Visual/ Red House MVDV4896

"The One Show" (04/07/10; BBC One): Colin and Rod were interviewed about "Odessey And Oracle" and "She's Not There"

"Filmed Live At Metropolis Studio" (05/23/11): a UK DVD release: Metropolis Group 37115345-43; reissued with the CD edition the next year

"Rijnmond Live uit Lloyds-Rotterdam" (07/01/11; Dutch RTV): Time Of The Season (Rod and Colin only)

"Late Night With Jimmy Fallon" (09/12/11; US NBC): Breathe Out, Breathe In; Time Of The Season; This Will Be Our Year

"Gershwin's Summertime: The Song That Conquered The World" (11/23/11; BBC Four): Colin and Rod were involved

"How The Brits Rocked America – Go West: How The West Was Won" (01/27/12; BBC Four): Colin and Rod contributed

"Recorded Live In Concert At Metropolis Studios, London" (06/04/12): a UK CD/DVD release: Salvo/ Union Square SALVOSVX005, and a Canadian CD/DVD release: Convexe CVX902141

"Good Day L.A." (09/09/13; KTTV-TV, Los Angeles, California): She's Not There; interview

"Style-City Music Presents" (10/01/13; syndicated): live performance

"The Stern Grove Festival Videos" (11/14/14; sterngrove.org): Moving On; Time Of The Season

"My Music Archives: The Best Of The '60s" (11/30/13; US PBS): live performance

"All ATX: The British Invasion" (02/19/15; US PBS)

"The Late Show With Stephen Colbert" (10/30/15; US CBS): Moving On

"Later...With Jools Holland" (11/03/15; BBC Two): Colin and Rod performed

"The Nation's Favourite Beatles Number One" (11/11/15; UK ITV 1): Colin and Rod contributed

"The Story Of The Zombies" (12/11/15): Colin and Rod interview for the Cherry Red label

"Conan" (05/01/17; US TBS): Time Of The Season

"Hits, Hype & Hustle: An Insider's Guide To The Music Business – Revivals And Reunions" (02/02/18; BBC Four): Colin and Rod talked about how word of mouth led to their revival

"CBS Saturday Morning" (03/17/18; US CBS): live performance

"The Zombies – Track By Track At Gibson" (11/30/18): short film in which Colin and Rod talk about the songs on their "Greatest Hits" album)

"The Tonight Show Starring Jimmy Fallon" (04/01/19; US NBC): Time Of The Season

"Stern Grove - Best Of The Fest" (08/16/20; sterngrove.org): Time Of The Season

**COLIN BLUNSTONE   ROD ARGENT   THE ZOMBIES
CONCERT LISTING**
(all UK unless otherwise noted)

1999
05/01	The Stables, Wavendon (relaunching of the venue)
05/07	Robin Hood, Brierley Hill
05/08	Hare & Hounds, Coventry
05/15	The Brook, Southampton
05/21	Worcester Park Club, Surrey

2000
05/05	Huntingdon Halls, Worcester
05/06	The Stables, Wavendon
05/09	Telford's Warehouse, Chester
05/10	City Memorial Hall, Sheffield
05/11	Picture House, Beverley
05/12	The Brook, Southampton
05/13	The Wharf, Tavistock
05/15	Jazz Café, London
05/18	Bourbon Street, Glasgow, Scotland
05/19	The Dome, Whitley Bay
05/20	Robin Hood, Brierley Hill
05/21	Delano, Bromley
05/26	Worcester Park, Surrey
06/01	Pavilion, Bournemouth
06/02	Palace Theatre, Newark
06/03	De Montfort Halls, Leicester
06/04	Wyvern Theatre, Swindon
06/06	Hippodrome, Bristol
06/08	Penningtons, Bradford
06/09	Corn Exchange, Kings Lynn
06/10	Opera House, York
06/11	Corn Exchange, Ipswich
06/15	Beck Theatre, Hayes
06/16	Alban Arena, St. Albans
06/18	Wyllyotts, Potters Bar
06/20	Ashcroft Theatre, Croydon
06/22	Derngate Theatre, Northampton
06/23	Ryde Theatre, Isle of Wight
06/24	Civic Hall, Guilford
06/25	Alexandra Theatre, Birmingham
09/21	De Boerderij, Zoetermeer, Netherlands
Sept.	Netherlands tour
Nov.-Dec.	UK tour

2001
03/25	The Charlotte, Leicester
03/28	The Stables, Wavendon
03/29	Phoenix Arts, Exeter
03/30	Martlett Hall, Burgess Hill
03/31	The Robin, Brierley Hill
04/01	Cheese & Grain, Frome
04/04	Jazz Café, London
04/05	The Flowerpot, Derby
04/06	Alban Arena, St. Albans
04/07	Huntingdon Hall, Worcester
04/10	Limelight Club, Crewe
04/11	The Witchwood, Ashton-under-Lyne
04/12	Picture House, Beverley
04/13	Astor Theatre, Deal
04/14	The Brook, Southampton
04/20	De Beurs, Middenmeer, Netherlands
04/21	Festival, Middelharnis, Netherlands
04/22	Plein 79, Hertogenbosch, Netherlands
04/25	Opera House, Newcastle
04/26	The Lemon Tree, Aberdeen, Scotland
04/27	Memorial Hall, Sheffield
04/28	The Standard, London
05/24-27	The Village Underground, New York, New York, USA
11/09	Plinston Hall, Letchworth
11/11	Princes Hall, Aldershot
11/13	Telfords Warehouse, Chester
11/14	Limelight Club, Crewe
11/15	Bar Cuba, Macclesfield
11/16	Mount Stuart, Cardiff, Wales
11/17	Patti Pavilion, Swansea, Wales
11/23	The Robin 2, Bilston
11/27	Alban Arena, St. Albans
11/30	The Y Theatre, Leicester (Mark Johns' last gig)

2002
01/31-02/01	Star Pine's Café, Tokyo, Japan (Keith Airey's first gig)
02/02	Club Quattro, Osaka, Japan
03/10	Jazz Café, London
04/10	Boardwalk, Sheffield
04/11	Picture Playhouse, Beverley
04/12	The Brook, Southampton
04/13	Alban Arena, St. Albans
04/14	Worcester Park, Surrey
04/17	City Varieties, Leeds
04/19	The Robin, Brierley Hill
04/20	The Standard, London
04/21	The Stables, Wavendon
04/23	Huntingdon Hall, Worcester
04/25	De Boerderij, Zoetermeer, Netherlands
04/26	Struve Party House, Sappemeer, Netherlands
04/27	ECR Building, Zolder, Belgium
07/14	Sint-Stevenskerk, Nijmegen, Netherlands
09/13	Waterside Theatre, Holbury
09/14	Rayners Hotel, Harrow
09/18	Whitaker Center, Harrisburg, Pennsylvania, USA
09/19	State Theatre, Falls Church, Virginia, USA
09/20	B.B. King's Blues Club & Grill, New York, New York, USA
09/21	Keswick Theatre, Glenside, Pennsylvania, USA (with Al Stewart)
09/23	The Tralf, Buffalo, New York, USA
09/24	Beachland Ballroom, Cleveland, Ohio, USA
09/26	Abbey Pub, Chicago, Illinois, USA
09/27	Miramar Theatre, Milwaukee, Wisconsin, USA
09/28	First Avenue, Minneapolis, Minnesota, USA

2003
01/23	Palethe Ontmoetingscentrum, Overpelt, Belgium
01/24	De Boerderij, Zoetermeer, Netherlands
01/25	Hotel de Giraf, Emmen, Netherlands
01/26	Hotel Igesz, Schagen, Netherlands
04/04	City Hall, Salisbury (with a string quartet)
04/09	Palace Theatre, Paignton (with a string quartet)
04/10	Arts Centre, Pontardawe, Wales (with a string quartet)
04/11-12	The Stables, Wavendon (with a string quartet; also with the band Argent)
04/17	The Brook, Southampton
04/18	Astor Theatre, Deal
04/22	Arts Centre, Swindon
04/26	Herringthorpe Centre, Rotherham

05/02	The Y Theatre, Leicester	04/07	Assembly Halls, Derby
05/09	The Robin 2, Bilston	04/08	Albert Halls, Bolton
06/06	Waterside Theatre, Holbury (with a string quartet)	04/09	Astor Theatre, Deal
06/07	Bloomsbury Theatre, London (with a string quartet; recorded for a live CD/DVD)	04/10	Marine Theatre, Lyme Regis
06/12	Huntingdon Hall, Worcester	04/30	Bloomsbury Theatre, London (with a string quartet)
06/13	MS1 Club, Cardiff, Wales	05/17	Backstage Club, Munich, Germany
06/14	Renfrewshire Ferry, Glasgow, Scotland	05/18	The Kanteen, Cologne, Germany
06/15	Memorial Hall, Sheffield	05/19	Downtown Blues Club, Hamburg, Germany
06/28	South Shields Amphitheatre, South Shields		
06/29	The Springhead Pub, Hull		US tour with Arthur Lee & Love (09/28/04 – 10/16/04):
08/07-08	Abbey Pub, Chicago, Illinois, USA		
08/10	Uptown Theater, Kansas City, Missouri, USA	09/28	Great American Music Hall, San Francisco, California, USA
08/13	Festival at Sandpoint, Sandpoint, Idaho, USA	09/29	Wilshire Ebell Theatre, Los Angeles, California, USA
08/14	Aladdin Theater, Portland, Oregon, USA	10/01	The Grove of Anaheim, Anaheim, California, USA
08/15	Crocodile Café, Seattle, Washington, USA	10/02	4th & B, San Diego, California, USA
08/17	Powerhouse Pub, Folsom, California, USA	10/07	First Avenue, Minneapolis, Minnesota, USA
08/19	Café du Nord, San Francisco, California, USA	10/08	Park West, Chicago, Illinois, USA
08/20	Earl Warren Showgrounds, Santa Barbara, California, USA	10/10	Royal Oak Music Theatre, Royal Oak, Michigan, USA
08/21	Knitting Factory, Los Angeles, California, USA	10/11	Beachland Ballroom and Tavern, Cleveland, Ohio, USA
08/22	The Coach House, San Juan Capistrano, California, USA	10/13	The Town Hall, New York, New York, USA
08/24	The Rock, Tucson, Arizona, USA	10/14	Scottish Rite Theatre, Collingswood, New Jersey, USA
08/29	Snow King Resort, Jackson Hole, Wyoming, USA	10/16	The State Theatre, Falls Church, Virginia, USA
08/30	Cannery Casino, Las Vegas, Nevada, USA		
11/17	Municipal Arts Centre, Pontypridd, Wales	11/02	De Tamboer, Hoogeveen, Netherlands
11/19	School Of Art And Design, Scarborough	11/03	Fortis Theater A/D/Schie, Schiedam, Netherlands
		11/04	Theater De Willem, Papendrecht, Netherlands
2004		11/05	De Boerderij, Zoetermeer, Netherlands
02/06	Palace Theatre, Stamford, Connecticut, USA	11/06	Schouwburg Cuijk, Cuijk, Netherlands
02/07	Trump Marina, Atlantic City, New Jersey, USA	11/09	Schowburg Agnietenhof, Tiel, Netherlands
02/08	The Downtown, Farmingdale, New York, USA	11/10	Stadsschouwburg Nijmegen, Nijmegen, Netherlands
02/11	B.B. King's Blues Club & Grill, New York, New York, USA	11/11	Theaters Nv Parkstad Limburg, Kerkrade, Netherlands
02/12	Rams Head On Stage, Annapolis, Maryland, USA	11/12	Patronaat, Haarlem, Netherlands
02/13	Amos Southend, Charlotte, North Carolina, USA	11/13	Theater Het Kruispunt, Barendrecht, Netherlands
02/14	The Dame, Lexington, Kentucky, USA	11/16	De Kom, Nieuwegein, Netherlands
02/15	The Masquerade, Atlanta, Georgia, USA	11/17	De Metropole, Almere, Netherlands
02/16	The Moon, Tallahassee, Florida, USA	11/18	De Meerse, Hoofddorp, Netherlands
02/18	B.B. King's Blues Club & Grill, Nashville, Tennessee, USA	11/19	Singer Theater, Laren, Netherlands
02/21	Engine Room, Houston, Texas, USA	11/20	De Kring, Roosendaal, Netherlands
02/22	Antone's, Austin, Texas, USA	11/21	Hotel Igesz, Schagen, Netherlands
02/25	Alice Cooper'stown, Phoenix, Arizona, USA	11/23	Rijswijkse Schouwburg, Rijswijk, Netherlands
02/26	Warner Grand Theatre, San Pedro, California, USA	11/24	Stadsschouwburg De Harmonie, Leeuwarden, Netherlands
02/27	Key Club, West Hollywood, California, USA	11/25	Schouwburg Arnhem, Arnhem, Netherlands
02/28	The Coach House, San Juan Capistrano, California, USA	11/26	Zaantheater, Zaandam, Netherlands
02/29	The Independent, San Francisco, California, USA	11/29	De Kleine Komedie, Amsterdam, Netherlands
03/04	Beaufort Theatre, Ebbw Vale, Wales	11/30	Schouwburg De Storm, Winterswijk, Netherlands
03/05	The Robin 2, Bilston	12/01	Stadsschouwburg Middelburg, Middelburg, Netherlands
03/07	Cavern Club, Liverpool	12/02	Chassé Theater, Breda, Netherlands
03/08	City Varieties, Leeds	12/03	Stadsgehoorzaal, Leiden, Netherlands
03/09	Opera House, Newcastle	12/04	Stadtgarten-Koln, Cologne, Germany
03/12	Martletts Hall, Burgess Hill		
03/16	Jagz At The Station, Ascot	**2005**	
03/18	The Stables, Wavendon (with a string quartet)	02/03	Lite Café, Manchester
03/19	Arts Centre, Norwich	02/04	Pacific Road Arts Centre, Birkenhead
03/20	Tivoli Theatre, Wimborne	02/05	Classic Rock Society, Herringthorpe Leisure Centre, Rotherham
03/21	The Brook, Southampton		
03/26	The Citadel, St. Helens	02/06	The Honiton Motel, Turks Head Corner, Honiton
03/27	The Y Theatre, Leicester	02/08	Jazz Café, London
03/30	Central Station, Wrexham	02/10	Park Hotel, Tynemouth
04/01	Renfrew Ferry, Glasgow, Scotland	02/11	Leisure Centre, Lochgelly, Scotland
04/02	Leisure Centre, Lochgelly, Scotland	02/12	Renfrew Ferry, Glasgow, Scotland
04/03	The Lemon Tree, Aberdeen, Scotland	02/13	City Varieties, Leeds
04/04	Memorial Hall, Sheffield	02/15	Arts Centre, Swindon
		02/16	The Brook, Southampton

Date	Venue
02/17	The Stables, Wavendon
02/18	Arts Centre, Norwich
02/20	Boom Boom Club, Sutton
02/21	The Toucan Club, Cardiff, Wales
02/23	Huntingdon Halls, Worcester
02/24	Princess Pavilion, Falmouth
02/25	The Robin 2, Bilston
02/26	Cheese And Grain, Frome, Somerset
02/27	Mick Jagger Centre, Dartford
04/24	All Tomorrow's Parties 2005, Pontins Camber Sands Holiday Park, Camber
05/25	Cabot Hall, London
05/27	Mr. Kyps, Poole
05/30	Coventry Jazz Festival, Coventry
06/01	Café de Paris, London
06/09	Sherborne Castle, Sherborne
06/10	Veendam Festival, Veendam, Netherlands
07/17	GuilFest 2005, Stoke Park, Guildford (with many other acts)
07/29-30	Casino Rama, Orillia, Ontario, Canada
07/31	Manitoba Summerfest, Grand Beach, Manitoba, Canada
08/02	B.B. King's Blues Club & Grill, New York, New York, USA ("A Tribute To Mike Smith": with Peter And Gordon, Billy J. Kramer, The Fab Faux, and bandleader Paul Shaffer – 2 shows: 7:30PM and 11:00PM)
08/03	Mohegan Sun Casino, Uncasville, Connecticut, USA
08/04	Palace Theatre, Manchester, New Hampshire, USA
08/06	Ohio State Fair, Celeste Center, Columbus, Ohio, USA
09/15	Concert For Africa, Alban Arena, St. Albans
10/22-23	The Bloomsbury Theatre, London
10/27	De Kade, Zaandam, Netherlands
10/28	De Boerderij, Zoetermeer, Netherlands
10/29	Hoogezand, Netherlands
10/30	Capitole, Ghent, Belgium
11/09	Waterside Arts Centre, Manchester
11/10	The Platform, Morecambe
11/11	Melton Theatre,, Melton Mowbray
11/12	Classic Rock Festival, Butlins, Bognor Regis
11/13	Martletts Hall, Burgess Hill
11/16	The Old Market, Hove
11/17	Broadway Theatre, Barking
11/18	Cox's Yard, Stratford-upon-Avon
11/23	Palace Theatre, Paignton
11/24	Gloucester Guildhall, Gloucester
11/25	The Robin 2, Bilton
12/07	Purple Weekend 2005, Estadio Hispánico, León, Spain (with The Chocolate Watch Band, Cooper, and Doctor Explosion)

2006

Date	Venue
02/10	Hard Rock Café, Manila, Philippines
02/13	Araneta Coliseum, Manila, Philippines
02/14	Ynares Coliseum, Antipoli, Philippines
03/06	Carpe Patque Almansa, San Javier (near Murcia), Spain
03/25	Porsche Oldie Night 2006, Hanns-Martin-Schleyer-Halle, Stuttgart, Germany
03/29-30	The Stables, Wavendon
03/31	Arts Centre, Norwich
04/02	Jazz Café, London
04/04	Huntingdon Hall, Worcester
04/07	Y Theatre, Leicester
04/08	Tivoli Theatre, Wimborne
04/09	Honiton Motel, Honiton
04/13	The Brook, Southampton
04/14	Astor Theatre, Deal
04/15	The Robin 2, Bilston
04/20	Quay Theatre, Sunderland
04/21	Albert Halls, Sterling
04/22	Leisure Centre, Lochgelly, Scotland
04/23	The Springhead, Hull
Aug.-Sept.	Canadian dates

US "Little Steven's Underground Garage" tour (with The Mooney Suzuki and various other bands that changed from night to night) (09/05/06 – 10/01/06):

Date	Venue
09/05	Belly Up Tavern, Solana Beach, California, USA
09/06	The Avalon/ Bardot Hollywood, Los Angeles, California, USA
09/07	12 Galaxies, San Francisco, California, USA
09/08	Musicfest NW Presents Project Pabst, Berbati's Pan, Portland, Oregon, USA (The Nice Boys were added)
09/09	El Corazon, Seattle, Washington, USA
09/14	Saint Andrew's Hall, Detroit, Michigan, USA
09/18	Axis, Boston, Massachusetts, USA
09/21	Irving Plaza, New York, New York, USA
09/23	The Theatre of Living Arts, Philadelphia, Pennsylvania, USA
09/28	Tampa, Florida, USA
10/01	Fort Lauderdale, Florida, USA
10/06	The Citadel, St. Helens
11/02	Schouwburg Amphion, Doetinchem, Netherlands
11/04	De Pul, Uden, Netherlands
11/11	Theater De Willem, Papendrecht, Netherlands
11/14	CC Het Spoor, Harlbeke, Belgium
11/15	Spirit Of 66, Verviers, Belgium

2007

Date	Venue
03/07	McPhillips Station Casino, Winnipeg, Manitoba, Canada
03/09	Century Casino Calgary, Calgary, Alberta, Canada
03/11	Richard's on Richards, Vancouver, British Columbia, Canada
03/12	The Triple Door, Seattle, Washington, USA
03/14	Raven Theater, Healdsburg, California, USA (with Ian Hunter and The Charms)
03/15	The Fillmore, San Francisco, California, USA (with Ian Hunter and The Charms)
03/16	Music Box at the Fonda Theatre, Los Angeles, California, USA (with The Charms)
03/17	The Grove of Anaheim, Anaheim, California, USA (with Ian Hunter)
04/21	North Sea Festival, Zaandam, Netherlands
05/04	Hall for Cornwall, Truro
05/10	The Brook, Southampton
05/13	Rescue Rooms, Nottingham
05/19	The Boardwalk, Sheffield
05/25	Swindon Arts Centre, Swindon
05/31	Jazz Café, London
06/09	BBC Radio 2 Studios, London

North American Tour: Hippiefest 2007 (with numerous acts) (07/25/07 – 08/21/07):

Date	Venue
07/25	Molson Amphitheatre, Toronto, Ontario, Canada
07/26	Seaside Park, Brooklyn, New York, USA
07/27	Chevrolet Theatre, Wallingford, Connecticut, USA
07/28	Vernon Downs, Vernon, New York, USA
07/29	Brookhaven Amphitheater, Farmingville, New York, USA

07/30	Filene Center at Wolf Trap, Vienna, Virginia, USA	05/30	Corn Exchange, Kings Lynn
08/02	Hard Rock Live, Hollywood, Florida, USA	05/31	Buxton Opera House, Buxton
08/03	Chastain Park Amphitheater, Atlanta, Georgia, USA	06/01	The Sage, Gateshead
08/04	Cessna Stadium, Wichita, Kansas, USA	06/04	Pavilion Theatre, Bournemouth
08/05	Nokia Live at Grand Prairie, Grand Prairie, Texas, USA	06/05	St. David's Hall, Cardiff, Wales
08/07	Cape Cod Melody Tent, Hyannis, Massachusetts, USA	06/06	Colston Hall, Bristol
08/08	South Shore Music Circus, Cohasset, Massachusetts, USA	06/07	Corn Exchange, Cambridge
08/09	The Mann Center for the Performing Arts, Philadelphia, Pennsylvania, USA	06/08	Swan Theatre, High Wycombe
		06/11	Preston Guildhall, Preston
08/10	Seven Springs Mountain Resort, Champion, Pennsylvania, USA	06/12	City Hall, Sheffield
		06/13	Nottingham Royal Concert Hall, Nottingham
08/11	Bethel Woods Center for the Arts, Bethel, New York, USA	06/14	Dome, Brighton
08/12	Meadowbrook Musical Arts Center, Gilford, New Hampshire, USA	06/15	Royal & Derngate, Northampton
		06/18	Liverpool Philharmonic Hall, Liverpool
08/16	Pechanga Theater, Temecula, California, USA	06/19	Assembly Hall Theatre, Tunbridge
08/17	Tachi Palace, Lemoore, California, USA	06/20	The Anvil, Basingstoke
08/18	Dodge Theatre, Phoenix, Arizona, USA	06/21	Alban Arena, St. Albans
08/20	The Mountain Winery, Saratoga, California, USA	06/22	Southend Cliffs Pavilion, Southend-on-Sea
08/21	Humphreys, San Diego, California, USA	06/25	City Hall, Salisbury
10/10	Queens Hall, Nuneaton	06/26	Warwick Arts Centre, Coventry
10/12	100 Club, London	06/27	Broadway, Peterborough
10/17	Spirit Of 66, Verviers, Belgium		
10/18	De Kade, Zaandam, Netherlands	07/03	Comerica CityFest 2008, New Center Park, Detroit, Michigan, USA
10/20	De Boerderij, Zoetermeer, Netherlands		
10/26	The Boom Boom Club, Sutton	07/05	Summerfest 2008, Henry W. Maier Festival Park, Milwaukee, Wisconsin, USA
10/27	The Y Theatre, Leicester		
10/30	Whelan's, Baile Átha Cliath, Ireland	07/06	Taste of Minnesota 2008, Harriet Island Regional Park, St. Paul, Minnesota, USA
11/02	Fabrikken, Oslo, Norway		
		07/10	Mohegan Sun, Uncasville, Connecticut, USA
2008		07/11	Fillmore at Irving Plaza, New York, New York, USA (with The Blues Magoos)
02/07	Amager Bio, Copenhagen, Denmark		
02/08	Rockefeller Music Hall, Oslo, Norway	07/12	Trump Marina, Atlantic City, New Jersey, USA
02/14	Whelan's, Baile Átha Cliath, Ireland	07/13	Westhampton Beach Performing Arts Center, Westhampton Beach, New York, USA
02/24	"I'd Like To Teach The World To Sing," Her Majesty's Theatre, Haymarket (a commemoration of Ian Adam's life)		
		07/15	The Birchmere, Alexandria, Virginia, USA
"Odessey And Oracle" 40th Anniversary tour (03/02/08 – 03/09/08):		07/17	The Grove of Anaheim, Anaheim, California, USA (with Jefferson Starship/ Marty Balin)
03/02-03	The Stables, Wavendon (warm-up gigs for the Shepherd's Bush concerts)	07/18	Cannery Hotel & Casino, North Las Vegas, Nevada, USA
		07/19	The Canyon, Agoura Hills, California
03/07-09	Shepherd's Bush Empire, London (03/08/08 concert filmed and recorded for release; with guitarist Keith Airey, keyboardist Darian Sahanaja, The Shotgun Horns [on "This Will Be Our Year"], Jim Rodford on backing vocals and percussion, Steve Rodford on percussion, and backing vocalist Vivienne Boucherat)	07/20	The Regency Ballroom, San Francisco, California (with Jefferson Starship/ Marty Balin)
		07/23	Wonder Ballroom, Portland, Oregon, USA (with The Sugarlumps)
		07/24	El Corazón, Seattle, Washington, USA (with Jon Auer and Guns & Rossetti)
		07/25	Cascades Casino – Summit Theatre, Langley, British Columbia, Canada
03/13	ChildLine Rocks 2008. indigO2, London (with Roger Daltrey, Glenn Hughes, Lulu, and Marillion; Russ Ballard joined The Zombies' performance of "Hold Your Head Up")	07/26	Deerfoot Inn & Casino, Calgary, Alberta, Canada
		07/27	Century Casino, Edmonton, Alberta, Canada
		07/29	Dakota Dunes Casino, Whitecap, Saskatchewan, Canada
		07/30	Casino Regina, Regina, Saskatchewan, Canada
UK tour with The Yardbirds (05/14/08 – 06/27/08):		07/31	Club Regent Event Centre, Winipeg, Manitoba, Canada
05/14	Bridgewater Hall, Manchester	08/23	Great British R&B Festival, The Muni Theatre, Colne (with The Yardbirds, Billy Boy Arnold, and many others)
05/15	Royal Concert Hall, Glasgow, Scotland		
05/16	The Sands Centre, Carlisle	08/31	Rhythm Festival 2008, Twinwood Arena, Bedford
05/18	Victoria Theatre, Halifax	09/12	DK NAU, Kiev, Ukraine
05/21	The Orchard, Dartford	09/26	Royal Garden Hotel, Trondheim, Norway (with Difference and The Shirrows)
05/22	De Montfort Hall, Leicester		
05/23	Hexagon Theatre, Reading (Jimmy Page attended!)	09/27	Parkteatret, Oslo, Norway
05/25	Symphony Hall, Birmingham	11/14	De Boerderij, Zoetermeer, Netherlands
05/28	Leas Cliff Hall, Folkstone	11/15	Florin, Utrecht, Netherlands
05/29	Fairfield Halls, Croydon	11/16	De Pul, Uden, Netherlands

2009

01/23	Whelan's, Baile Átha Cliath, Ireland
01/30	MO'FO 2009, Mains d'Œuvres, Saint-Ouen, France
01/31	Espace Vauban, Brest, France
03/05	Debaser Medis, Stockholm, Sweden
03/06	Katalin, Uppsala, Sweden
03/07	Trädgår'n, Gothenburg, Sweden
03/08	Kulturbolaget, Malmö, Sweden

"Odessey And Oracle And Beyond" tour (04/21/09 – 04/25/09):

04/21	O2 ABC, Glasgow, Scotland
04/23	Bristol Beacon, Bristol
04/24	The Bridgewater Hall, Manchester
04/25	HMV Hammersmith Apollo, London
05/15	Azkena Festival 2009, Recinto Mendizabala, Vitoria-Gasteiz, Spain (with many others)
06/04	Beatles Days, Piazza del Sole, Bellinzona, Switzerland
06/13	IOW Festival 2009, Seaclose Park, Newport, Isle of Wight (with many others)

US "Rock Royalty Live!" tour with The Yardbirds and The Spencer Davis Group (06/26/09 – 07/19/09):

06/26	Humphrey's Concerts by the Bay, San Diego, California, USA
06/27	The Wiltern, Los Angeles, California, USA
06/28	Napa Valley Performing Arts Center, Yountville, California, USA
06/30	Knitting Factory Concert House, Spokane, Washington, USA
07/02	Mount Baker Theatre, Bellingham, Washington, USA
07/08	Keswick Theatre, Glenside, Pennsylvania, USA
07/09	Capital One Bank Theatre, Westbury, New York, USA
07/10	Irving Plaza, New York, New York, USA
07/11	F.M. Kirby Center for the Performing Arts, Wilkes-Barre, Pennsylvania, USA
07/12	Pier Six Concert Pavilion, Baltimore, Maryland, USA
07/14	Cisco Systems Bluesfest 2009, LeBreton Flats Park, Ottawa, Ontario, Canada (with many others)
07/15	Mod Club Theatre, Toronto, Ontario, Canada (with Tim Bovaconti)
07/17	Club Regent Event Centre, Winnipeg, British Columbia, Canada (with John Kay & Steppenwolf, Blues Traveler, and Colin James)
07/19	Nakusp Music Festival, Nakusp, British Columbia, Canada (with Gregg Rolie and John Kay & Steppenwolf)
10/06-07	Jazz Café, London
10/21	The Duchess, York
10/23	The Ferry, Glasgow, Scotland
10/28	The Brewery Arts Centre, Kedal
10/29	The Robin 2, Bilston
10/30	The Assembly, Leamingston Spa
11/13	Cultuurcentrum Kortrijk, Kortrijk, Belgium
11/17	Schouwburg De Lawei, Drachten, Netherlands
11/20	Isala Theater, Capelle aan den IJssel, Netherlands
11/21	Muziekcentrum Schaaf, Leeuwarden, Netherlands
11/22	De Kade, Zaandam, Netherlands
11/26	De Boerderij, Zoetermeer, Netherlands
11/29	Mezz, Breda, Netherlands
11/30	De Kleine Komedie, Amsterdam, Netherlands (Keith Airey's last gig)

2010

04/22	Effenaar, Eindhovem North Brabant, Netherlands (Tom Toomey's first gig)
04/23	Central Studios, Utrecht, Netherlands
04/24	Poppodium Metropool, Hengelo, Netherlands
Apr.	Bahrain
05/12	Mr. Kyps, Poole
05/13	Du Maurier Festival, Fowey, Cornwall
05/14	Boom Boom Club, Sutton
05/15	Fort Purbrook, Portsmouth
05/16	Martlets Hall, Burgess Hill
05/27	The Robin 2, Bilston
05/28	Huntingdon Hall, Worcester
05/29	The Citadel, St. Helens
05/30	The Caves, Edinburgh, Scotland
05/31	Quays Theatre, Salford
06/10	Le Trabendo, Paris, France
06/12	Théâtre de Verdure du Pinsan, Eysines, France
09/03	Weyfest, The Rural Life Centre, Tilford, Farnham
09/10	Robert E. Parilla Performing Arts Center, Rockville, Maryland, USA
09/11	Wolf Den, Mohegan Sun, Uncasville, Connecticut, USA
09/12	Union County MusicFest 2010, Oak Ridge Park, Clark, New Jersey, USA
11/05	La [2] de Apolo, Barcelona, Spain
11/06	El Loco, Valencia, Spain
11/08	Aulario La Bomba, Cádiz, Spain
11/10	Sala Heineken, Madrid, Spain (with Imogen Heap)
11/11	Mondo Club Vigo, Vigo, Spain
11/12	Teatro Carrión, Valladolid, Spain
11/13	Kafe Antzokia, Bilbao, Spain
12/10	All Tomorrow's Parties 2010, Butlins, Minehead

2011

01/08	ITV Legends Live Concert Recording, Metropolis Studios, London
04/20	BBC Radio 6 Music Session, Salford
Apr.	Germany
05/05	Patras, Greece
05/06	Gagarin 205, Athens, Greece
05/07	Block33, Thessaloniki, Greece
05/18	Stanley Theatre, Liverpool
05/20	The Assembly, Leamington Spa
05/24	The Stables, Wavendon
05/27	O2 Shepherd's Bush Empire, London (Hugh Grundy and Chris White made a guest appearance)
07/01	RTV Rijnmond 93.4FM, Netherlands (radio appearance)
07/08	Shimokitazawa GARDEN, Tokyo, Japan
07/09	FEVER, Tokyo, Japan
07/10	Shimokitazawa GARDEN, Tokyo, Japan
07/12	Muse Hall, Osaka, Japan
07/30	Rheola Festival 2011, Rheola Estate, Neath, Wales
07/31	Boom Boom Club, Sutton
08/23	Reading 3, Tel Aviv, Israel
09/03	Café de la Danse, Paris, France (cancelled)

North American "50th Anniversary Tour" (09/09/11 – 10/13/11):

09/09	Casino Rama, Orillia, Ontario, Canada
09/10	The Bear's Den Showroom, Niagara Falls, New York, USA
09/11	Oneonta Theatre, Oneonta, New York, USA
09/13	Beachland Ballroom and Tavern, Cleveland, Ohio, USA
09/15	Musikfest Café, Bethlehem, Pennsylvania, USA (with The

	Strawbs through 10/13/11)
09/16	Cultural Arts Center at Takoma Park/ Silver Spring, Montgomery College, Silver Spring, Maryland, USA
09/17	Keswick Theatre, Glenside, Pennsylvania, USA
09/18	Tarrytown Music Hall, Tarrytown, New York, USA
09/19	Rams Head On Stage, Annapolis, Maryland, USA
09/21	Showcase Live, Foxborough, Massachusetts, USA
09/22	Tupelo Music Hall, Londonderry, New Hampshire, USA
09/23	Infinity Hall, Norfolk, Connecticut, USA
09/24	Wolf Den, Mohegan Sun, Uncasville, Connecticut, USA
09/26-27	City Winery, New York, New York, USA
09/28	The State Theatre, State College, Pennsylvania, USA
09/30	Celebrity Theatre, Phoenix, Arizona, USA
10/01	The Canyon, Agoura Hills, California, USA
10/02	The Coach House, San Juan Capistrano, California, USA
10/05	McPhillips Street Station Casino, Winnipeg, Manitoba, Canada
10/07	Casino Regina, Regina, Saskatchewan, Canada
10/09	Century Casino, Edmonton, Alberta, Canada
10/12	Kamloops Convention Centre, Kamloops, British Columbia, Canada
10/13	River Rock Casino, Richmond, British Columbia, Canada
11/02	Luxor Live, Arnhem, Netherlands
11/03	Iduna, Drachten, Netherlands
11/04	De Boerderij, Zoetermeer, Netherlands
11/06	De Pul, Uden, Netherlands
11/16	ARC, Stockton-on-Tees
11/17	Central Station & Yales, Wrexham
11/18	The Caves, Edinburgh, Scotland
11/19	The Ferry, Glasgow, Scotland
11/20	Backstage @ Green Hotel, Kinross, Scotland
11/23	Plinston, Letchworth
11/24	Tivoli Theatre, Wimborne
11/26	Grand Victorian Hotel, Worthing
11/27	Alban Arena, St. Albans
11/29	Stag Community Arts Centre, Sevenoaks
12/02	Gulbenkian Theatre, Canterbury

2012

03/27	Horsens Ny Teater, Horsens, Denmark (Keith Airey joins)
03/28	Debaser, Malmö, Sweden
03/29	Debaser Medis, Stockholm, Sweden
03/31	Kulttuuritehdas Korjaamo, Helsinki, Finland
05/07	The Garage, Swansea, Wales
05/10	The Robin 2, Bilston
05/12	Brudenell Social Club, Leeds
05/15	Stables Theatre, Wavendon
05/18	The Corn Exchange, Hertford
05/23	Jazz Café, London
05/25	Artrix, Bromsgrove
05/26	The Tunnels, Bristol
05/31	The Haunt, Brighton
06/07	Maddermarket Theatre, Norwich

US "The Zombies 2012" tour (07/27/12 – 08/09/12):

07/27	Largo Cultural Center, Largo, Florida, USA
07/28	Southern Ground Amphitheater, Fayetteville, Georgia, USA
07/29	Cat's Cradle, Carrboro, North Carolina, USA
07/31	Viper Alley, Lincolnshire, Illinois, USA
08/01	Mayne Stage, Chicago, Illinois, USA
08/02	Waterfest, Leach Amphitheater, Oshkosh, Washington, USA
08/04	At The Tabernacle, Mount Tabor, New Jersey, USA
08/05-06	Highline Ballroom, New York, New York, USA (with The Left Banke)
08/07	Mohegan Sun, Uncasville, Connecticut, USA
08/09	The Howard Theatre, Washington, District of Columbia, USA (with The Left Banke)
09/06	Zalen Schaaf, Leeuwarden, Netherlands
09/07	Oldenzaal Muzikaal 2012, Binnenstad, Oldenzaal, Netherlands
09/08	Manifesto, Hoorn, Netherlands
09/14	Hessle Town Hall, Hessle
09/21	Sub89, Reading
09/23	The Ferry, Glasgow, Scotland
09/26	Islington Assembly Hall, London
10/12	FEVER, Tokyo, Japan
10/13	Shimokitazawa GARDEN, Tokyo, Japan
10/14	AREA, Tokyo, Japan
10/17	Pacific Grand Ballroom, Waterfront Cebu City, Philippines
10/19	PICC Hall, Pasay City, Philippines

2013

02/28	Montréal en Lumière 2013, Metropolis, Montreal, Quebec, Canada
03/02	Molson Canadian Studio at Hamilton Place, Hamilton, Ontario, Canada
03/03	Sound Academy, Toronto, Ontario, Canada
03/04	The Empire Theatre, Belleville, Ontario, Canada (with Elephant Stone)
03/07	Hard Rock Live Biloxi, Biloxi, Mississippi, USA
03/09	Variety Playhouse, Atlanta, Georgia, USA (with Night Beats)
03/10	War Memorial Auditorium, Nashville, Tennessee, USA (with Night Beats and The Ettes)
03/13	The Kessler Theater, Dallas, Texas, USA (with Elephant Stone)
03/14	SXSW 2013, Kenny Dorham's Backyard, Austin, Texas, USA (with Et Tu Brucé)
03/15	SXSW 2013, The Stage on Sixth, Austin, Texas, USA
03/16	SXSW 2013, Brazos Hall, Austin, Texas, USA
03/16	SXSW 2013, Mellow Johnny's Bike Shop, Austin, Texas, USA (with Et Tu Brucé)
03/17	Fitzgerald's, Houston, Texas, USA (with Elephant Stone)
03/20-25	The Moody Blues Cruise, MSC Cruises – MSC Poesia, Fort Lauderdale, Florida, USA (with many others)
05/01	Palace Theatre, Southend-on-Sea
05/10	Open Air, Norwich
05/14	The Queen's Hall, Edinburgh, Scotland
05/15	Carnegie Hall, Dunfermline, Scotland
05/16	The Ryan Centre, Stranraer, Scotland
06/01	indigO2, London
06/02	Aylesbury Waterside Theatre, Aylesbury
06/08	Paradiso Grote Zaal, Amsterdam, Netherlands
06/13	Bergen Performing Arts Center, Englewood, New Jersey, USA (with Et Tu Brucé)
06/14	Wolf Den at Mohegan Sun, Uncasville, Connecticut, USA
06/15	Central Park SummerStage, New York, New York, USA (with Django Django)
06/16	Robert E. Parilla Performing Arts Center, Rockville, Maryland, USA (with Et Tu Brucé)
06/17	Rams Head On Stage, Annapolis, Maryland, USA (with Et Tu Brucé)
06/20	Penn's Peak, Jim Thorpe, Pennsylvania, USA (with Et Tu Brucé)
06/21	Keswick Theatre, Glenside, Pennsylvania, USA (with Et Tu Brucé and Al Kooper)

06/22	State Theatre Center for the Arts, Uniontown, Pennsylvania, USA (with Et Tu Brucé)	02/05	Assembly Hall Theatre, Tunbridge Wells
06/23	Tralf Music Hall, Buffalo, New York, USA (with Et Tu Brucé)	02/06	The Central Theatre, Chatham
06/26	Empire State Plaza, Albany, New York, USA (with Et Tu Brucé)	02/07	The Derngate, Northampton
06/28	Mayne Stage, Chicago, Illinois, USA (with Et Tu Brucé)	02/08	Marlowe Theatre, Canterbury
06/29	Summerfest, Henry Maier Festival Park, Milwaukee, Wisconsin, USA (with many others)	02/09	Cliffs Pavilion, Southend
06/30	Beachland Ballroom and Tavern, Cleveland, Ohio, USA (with Et Tu Brucé)	02/13	The Concert Hall, Perth, Scotland
07/03	Payomet Performing Arts Center, Truro, Massachusetts, USA (with Et Tu Brucé)	02/14	The Royal Concert Hall, Glasgow, Scotland
07/05	Town Center Park at Meadowbrook, Hamden, Connecticut, USA (with Et Tu Brucé)	02/15	The Music Hall, Aberdeen, Scotland
07/06	The Flying Monkey Movie House & Performance Center, Plymouth, New Hampshire, USA (with Et Tu Brucé)	02/19	The Bridgewater Hall, Manchester
07/07	Regent Theatre, Arlington, Massachusetts, USA (with Et Tu Brucé)	02/20	The City Hall, Salisbury
08/29	Aladdin Theater, Portland, Oregon, USA (with Et Tu Brucé)	02/21	Plymouth Pavilion, Plymouth
08/30	Pig Out In The Park, Riverfront Park, Spokane, Washington, USA (with Fruition, Lake Street Dive, and Et Tu Brucé)	02/22	The Lighthouse, Poole
09/01	Bumbershoot 2013, Seattle Center, Seattle, Washington, USA (with many others)	02/23	Theatre Royal Concert Hall, Nottingham
09/04	Yoshi's Oakland, Oakland, California, USA (with Et Tu Brucé)	02/25	Symphony Hall, Birmingham
09/05	The Addition, San Francisco, California, USA (with Et Tu Brucé)	02/26	Venue Cymru, Llandudno, Wales
09/06	Uptown Theatre Napa, Napa, California, USA (with Et Tu Brucé)	03/01	Philharmonic, Liverpool
09/07	South Shore Room at Harrah's Lake Tahoe, Stateline, Nevada, USA (with Et Tu Brucé)	03/02	Opera House, Blackpool
09/09	The Troubadour, West Hollywood, California, USA (with Et Tu Brucé)	03/04	The Sage, Gateshead
09/10	The Observatory, Santa Ana, California, USA (with Allah-Las and Mystic Braves)	03/07	De Montfort Hall, Leicester
09/12	McCabe's Guitar Shop, Santa Monica, California, USA (acoustic concert; with Et Tu Brucé)	04/02-06	Moody Blues Cruise 2014, MSC Cruises – MSC Divina. Miami, Florida, USA
09/13	The Satellite, Los Angeles, California, USA	04/08	Mardi Gras Casino, Hallandale Beach, Florida, USA
09/15	Fox Tucson Theatre, Tucson, Arizona, USA (with Et Tu Brucé)	04/11	The Plaza Theatre, Orlando, Florida, USA (with Pat Sansone)
09/16	Crescent Ballroom, Phoenix, Arizona, USA (with Et Tu Brucé)	04/12	Capitol Theatre, Clearwater, Florida, USA (with Pat Sansone)
09/19	The Cutting Room, New York, New York, USA	04/13	Ponte Vedra Concert Hall, Ponte Vedra Beach, Florida, USA (with Pat Sansone)
09/23	Kentucky Theatre, Lexington, Kentucky, USA (with Et Tu Brucé)	04/15	The Orange Peel, Asheville, North Carolina, USA (with Pat Sansone)
09/25	Pabst Theater, Milwaukee, Wisconsin, USA (with Et Tu Brucé)	04/16	Bijou Theatre, Knoxville, Tennessee, USA
09/27	Arcada Theate, St. Charles, Illinois, USA (with Burton Cummings and Et Tu Brucé)	04/17	Georgia Theatre, Athens, Georgia, USA (with Pat Sansone)
09/28	Maximum Ames Music Festival, DG's Tap House, Ames, Iowa, USA (with Murder By Death and Et Tu Brucé)	04/18	Cat's Cradle, Carrboro, North Carolina, USA (with Pat Sansone)
09/29	Ames City Auditorium, Ames, Iowa, USA	04/19	Jefferson Theater, Charlottesville, Virginia, USA (with Pat Sansone)

2014

UK "The Ultimate Rhythm And Blues" tour with The Yardbirds, The Animals And Friends, Maggie Bell, and Dave Berry (replacing Spencer Davis, who had a blood clot prior to the tour) (01/21/14 – 03/07/14):

		04/23	Iron City, Birmingham, Alabama, USA (with Hollis Brown)
		04/24	Hargray Capitol Theatre, Macon, Georgia, USA (with Hollis Brown)
		04/25	3rd & Lindsley Bar And Grill, Nashville, Tennessee, USA (with Hollis Brown)
		04/27	Hi-Tone Café, Memphis, Tennessee, USA (with Hollis Brown)
		04/30-05/01	The Kessler Theater, Dallas, Texas, USA (with Hollis Brown)
		05/02	Austin Psych Fest 2014, Carson Creek Ranch, Austin, Texas, USA (with many others)
		05/03	Cine El Rey Theatre, McAllen, Texas, USA (with Hollis Brown)
		05/04	The Big Barn at Dosey Doe, The Woodlands, Texas, USA (with Hollis Brown)
		07/26	Wickerman Festival, East Kirkcarswell Farm, Dundrennan, Scotland (with many others)
01/21	Boom Boom Club, Sutton		
01/23	Waterside Arts Centre, Manchester		
01/24	The Concert Hall, Stevenage		
01/25	The Great British Rock And Blues Festival, Skegness		
01/26	The Kings Theatre, Southsea		
01/29	Colston Hall, Bristol		
01/30	The Grand Theatre, Swansea, Wales		
01/31	St. David's Hall, Cardiff, Wales		
02/01	The New Theatre, Oxford		
02/02	The Regent, Ipswich		

US "Going Coastal Summer 2014" tour (08/06/14 – 09/23/14):

08/06	Narrows Center for the Arts, Fall River, Massachusetts, USA
08/07	Blue Ocean Music Hall, Salisbury, Massachusetts, USA
08/08	B.B. King's Blues Club & Grill, New York, New York, USA
08/09	Rams Head On Stage, Annapolis, Maryland, USA (with Carnivores)
08/10	The Newton Theatre, Newton, New Jersey, USA
08/13	John J. Burns Park, Massapequa, New York, USA (with Bruce Sudano)
08/14	The Birchmere, Alexandria, Virginia, USA (with Bruce Sudano)
08/15	Paramount Hudson Valley Theater, Peekskill, New York, USA

08/16	(with Bruce Sudano) Westampton Beach Performing Arts Center, Westhampton Beach, New York, USA (with Bruce Sudano)
08/17	Penn's Peak, Jim Thorpe, Pennsylvania, USA (with Hollis Brown)
08/20	House Of Blues, San Diego, California, USA
08/21	Santa Monica Pier, Santa Monica, California, USA (with Mystic Braves)
08/23	South Shore Room, Harrah's Lake Tahoe, Stateline, Nevada, USA
08/24	Stern Grove Festival 2014, Stern Grove, San Francisco, California, USA
09/22	ALL ATX: The British Invasion 2014, The Moody Theater, Austin, Texas, USA
09/23	The Belmont, Austin, Texas, USA
11/07	Bishop's Cleeve Tithe Barn, Cheltenham

2015

03/12	House Of Blues, New Orleans, Louisiana, USA
03/13-14	35 Denton Festival 2015, 35 Denton, Denton, Texas, USA
03/15	The Big Barn at Dosey Doe, The Woodlands, Texas, USA
03/19	SXSW 2015, Stubb's Bar-B-Q, Austin, Texas, USA
03/20	SXSW 2015, The Jackalope, Austin, Texas, USA
03/21	SXSW 2015, Whole Foods Market Lamar, Austin, Texas, USA
05/01	Union Chapel, London (acoustic concert)
05/15	The Alternative Escape 2015, The Black Lion, Brighton
05/16	Great Escape 2015, Horatio's Bar, Brighton
06/28	Glastonbury Festival 2015, Worthy Farm, Pilton (with many others)
07/10	Smart Araneta Coliseum, Quezon City, Philippines
07/12	Solaire Hotel & Casino, Manila, Philippines
07/14-15	duo Music Exchange, Tokyo, Japan

US "Odessey And Oracle Tour 2015" (09/30/15 – 10/30/15):

09/30	Majestic Theatre, Dallas, Texas, USA
10/01	Paramount Theatre, Austin, Texas, USA
10/03	Provincetown Town Hall, Provincetown, Massachusetts, USA
10/06	The Wilbur Theatre, Boston, Massachusetts, USA
10/08	Lincoln Theatre, Washington, District of Columbia, USA
10/09	The Society for Ethical Culture, New York, New York, USA
10/10	Park Theatre at RI Center for the Performing Arts, Cranston, Rhode Island, USA
10/11	Keswick Theatre, Glenside, Pennsylvania, USA
10/13	The Ridgefield Playhouse, Ridgefield, Connecticut, USA
10/14	Carnegie Music Hall of Homestead, Munhall, Pennsylvania, USA
10/15	Kent Stage, Kent, Ohio, USA
10/16	Star Plaza Theatre, Merrillville, Indiana, USA
10/17	South Milwaukee Performing Arts Center, South Milwaukee, Wisconsin, USA
10/19	Paramount Theatre, Denver, Colorado, USA
10/21	Benaroya Hall, Seattle, Washington, USA
10/22	Revolution Hall, Portland, Oregon, USA
10/24	Saban Theater, Beverly Hills, California, USA
10/25	Crest Theatre, Sacramento, California, USA
10/26	Cascade Theatre, Redding, California, USA
10/27	The Fillmore, San Francisco, California, USA
10/30	CBS Studios, New York, New York, USA (filming "Late Show With Stephen Colbert")

"Still Got That Hunger Tour 2015" (11/03/15 – 12/12/15):

11/03	BBC Maidstone Studios, Maidstone ("Later...With Jools Holland" filming)
11/10	O2 Forum Kentish Town, London
11/20	Bikini, Barcelona, Spain
11/21	Sala Arena, Madrid, Spain
11/22	Kafe Antzokia, Bilbao, Spain
11/24	Le Poste à Galène, Marseille, France
11/25	Centre culturel communal Charlie Chaplin, Vaulx-en-Velin, France
11/26	Seven Casino, Amnéville, France
11/27	La Maroquinerie, Paris, France
11/28	La Batterie, Guyancourt, France
12/01	The Haunt, Brighton
12/02	The Globe, Cardiff, Wales
12/03	Fleece, Bristol
12/04	O2 Institute2, Birmingham
12/05	OPEN Norwich, Norwich
12/07	Brudenell Social Club, Leeds
12/08	Òran Mór, Glasgow, Scotland
12/09	Club Academy, University of Manchester Students' Union, Manchester
12/10	Arts Club, Liverpool
12/12	Riverside, Newcastle

2016

01/05	Ottawa, Ontario, Canada (with Brian Wilson, Neil Sedaka, and Toto Cutugno)
02/02	Rough Trade East, London
02/24	The Plaza Theatre, Orlando, Florida, USA
02/25	Parker Playhouse, Fort Lauderdale, Florida, USA
02/26-03/01	Moody Blues Cruise 2016, Norwegian Cruise Line – Norwegian Pearl, Miami, Florida, USA
03/02	Capitol Theatre, Clearwater, Florida, USA (with The Pauses)
03/03	Ponte Vedra Concert Hall, Ponte Vedra Beach, Florida, USA
04/28	Cathedral Quarter Arts Festival 2016, Custom House Square, Belfast, Northern Ireland

"May Flowers Tour" (05/09/16 – 06/16/16):

05/09	Billboard Studios, New York, New York, USA
05/12	Rough Trade NYC, Brooklyn, New York, USA (private gig)
05/13	Wolf Den at Mohegan Sun, Uncasville, Connecticut, USA
05/14	Robert E. Parilla Performing Arts Center, Rockville, Maryland, USA (with Bruce Sudano)
05/15	Colonial Theatre, Phoenixville, Pennsylvania, USA (with Bruce Sudano)
05/16	Avalon Theatre, Easton, Maryland, USA (with Bruce Sudano)
05/18	Rams Head On Stage, Annapolis, Maryland, USA
05/19	NON-COMMvention 2016, World Café Live, Philadelphia, Pennsylvania, USA (with many others)
05/20	The Bear's Den Showroom, Niagara Falls, New York, USA
05/21	Wellmont Theater, Montclair, New Jersey, USA (with Felix Cavaliere's Rascals)
05/22	NYCB Theatre at Westbury, Westbury, New York, USA (with Felix Cavaliere's Rascals)
05/24	Count Basie Theatre, Red Bank, New Jersey, USA (with Felix Cavaliere's Rascals)
05/25	Harvester Performance Center, Rocky Mount, Virginia, USA
05/27	City Winery, Nashville, Tennessee, USA (with Bruce Sudano)
05/28	Abbey Road on the River 2016, Belvedere, Louisville, Kentucky, USA (with The Weeklings)

05/29	Arcada Theatre, St. Charles, Illinois, USA	03/25	The Town Hall, New York, New York, USA
06/04	Aberystwyth Arts Centre, Aberystwyth, Wales (with Fred Abbott)	03/28	The Wilbur Theatre, Boston, Massachusetts, USA
06/05	Lunar Festival 2016, Umberslade Estate, Solihull (with many others)	03/30	Ridgefield Playhouse, Ridgefield, Connecticut, USA
		03/31	Calvin Theatre, Northampton, Massachusetts, USA
06/16	Secret Solstice Fstival, Festival Grounds, Akureyri, Iceland (with many others)	04/01	Le National, Montreal, Quebec, Canada
		04/02	Danforth Music Hall, Toronto, Ontario, Canada
07/04	Cwmnewidion Isaf, Aberystwyth, Wales (with Fred Abbott)	04/04	Royal Oak Music Theatre, Royal Oak, Michigan, USA
07/07	The Coliseum, Aberdare, Wales (with Fred Abbott)	04/05	Lorain Palace Theatre, Lorain, Ohio, USA
07/09	The Brook, Southampton (with Fred Abbott)	04/07	Golden Nugget Biloxi Hotel & Casino, Biloxi, Mississippi, USA
07/10	Cornbury Music Festival 2016, Tew Park, Chipping Norton (with many others)	04/08	Variety Playhouse, Atlanta, Georgia, USA
		04/09	James K. Polk Theater at Tennessee Performing Arts Center, Nashville, Tennessee, USA
07/15	Hampton Pool Concert Series 2016, Hampton Pool, London (with The Pretty Things)	04/11	Sangamon Auditorium, Springfield, Illinois, USA
		04/13-14	Thalia Hall, Chicago, Illinois, USA
07/23	Ramblin' Man Fair 2016, Mote Park, Maidstone (with many others)	04/15	Barrymore Theatre, Madison, Wisconsin, USA
		04/17	First Avenue, Minneapolis, Minnesota, USA
07/26	The Water Rats, London	04/18	Club Regent Casino, Winnipeg, Manitoba, Canada
08/21	Vostertfeesten 2016, Festivalterrein Kluitshofweg, Bree, Belgium (with many others)	04/21	Commodore Ballroom, Vancouver, British Columbia, Canada
		04/22	Showbox, Seattle, Washington, USA
09/02	The Rose, Pasadena, California, USA (with Bruce Sudano)	04/23	Aladdin Theater, Portland, Oregon, USA
09/03	The Coach House, San Juan Capistrano, California, USA (with Bruce Sudano)	04/25	The UC Theatre Taube Family Music Hall, Berkeley, California, USA
09/04	Libbey Bowl, Ojai, California, USA (with Bruce Sudano)	04/27	Clive Davis Theater at the Grammy Museum, Los Angeles, California, USA
09/05	Sausalito Art Festival 2016, Marinship Park, Sausalito, California, USA (with many others)	04/28	Stagecoach 2017, Empire Polo Club, Indio, California, USA
		04/29	The Theatre at Ace Hotel, Los Angeles, California, USA
09/07	The Catalyst, Santa Cruz, California, USA (with Bruce Sudano)	05/01	Warner Bros. Studios, Burbank, California, USA
		05/04	The Heights Theater, Houston, Texas, USA
09/08	Belly Up Tavern, Solana Beach, California, USA (with Bruce Sudano)	05/06	aTrolla Music Festival, Reunion Tower, Dallas, Texas, USA (with many others)
09/09	The Showroom at Golden Nugget Casino, Las Vegas, Nevada, USA	05/08	The Ridgefield Playhouse, Ridgefield, Connecticut, USA
		05/09	The Wilbur Theatre, Boston, Massachusetts, USA
09/10	Rialto Theatre, Tucson, Arizona, USA	05/10	Calvin Theatre, Northampton, Massachusetts, USA
09/11	The Showroom at Talking Stick Resort, Scottsdale, Arizona, USA (with Felix Cavaliere's Rascals)	05/27	GetMAD! Festival 2017, But (sic), Madrid, Spain (with many others)
09/14	Boulder Theater, Boulder, Colorado, USA	05/29	Forum de Barcelona, Barcelona, Spain (cancelled)
09/16	McCabe's Guitar Shop, Santa Monica, California, USA	05/30	Zentral, Pamplona, Spain
10/21	St. Albans Cathedral, St. Albans	06/01	Primavera Sound 2017, Auditori Forum, Barcelona, Spain (with many others)
11/01	Aberystwyth Arts Centre, Aberystwyth, Wales (with Fred Abbott)	06/04	Stables Theatre, Wavendon
11/02	The Coliseum, Aberdare, Wales (with Fred Abbott)	06/05	BBC Wogan House Studios, London (recording for "Lauren Laverne" program)
11/03	Arlington Arts Centre, Newbury (with Fred Abbott)	06/29	Music In The Gardens, Sheffield Botanical Gardens, South Yorkshire
11/09	Komedia, Bath (with Fred Abbott)		
11/11	Thornden Hall, Eastleigh	07/06	Festival d'été de Québec 2017, Parc de la Francophonie, Quebec City, Quebec, Canada
11/18	Children in Need 2016, Maida Vale Studios, London	07/08	Casino Nova Scotia, Halifax, Nova Scotia, Canada
12/03	Electric Dreams 2016, Bultins Resort, Bognor Regis	07/11	RBC Royal Bank Bluesfest 2017, LeBreton Flats Park, Ottawa, Ontario, Canada (with many others)

2017

02/27-03/04	Flower Power Cruise 2017, Celebrity Cruises – Celebrity Constellation, Fort Lauderdale, Florida, USA	07/14	Bergen Performing Arts Center, Englewood, New Jersey, USA (with Don DiLego)

"Odessey And Oracle 50th Anniversary Tour" (03/10/17 – 09/29/17):

03/10	Scottish Rite Auditorium, Collingswood, New Jersey, USA	07/15	Infinity Music Hall & Bistro, Hartford, Connecticut, USA (with Don DiLego)
03/13	Rockefeller Center, New York, New York, USA	07/16	Great South Bay Music Festival 2017, Shorefront Park, Patchogue, New York, USA (with many others)
03/17	Keswick Theatre, Glenside, Pennsylvania, USA		
03/18	Penn's Peak, Jim Thorpe, Pennsylvania, USA	07/17	The Birchmere, Alexandria, Virginia, USA (with Don DiLego)
03/20	Carolina Theatre, Durham, North Carolina, USA	07/18	Quebec Summer Music Festival 2017, Quebec City, Quebec, Canada
03/21	Sandler Center for the Performing Arts, Virginia Beach, Virginia, USA	09/29	London Palladium, London
03/23	9:30 Club, Washington, District of Columbia, USA		
03/24	H. Ric Luhrs Performing Arts Center, Shippensburg, Pennsylvania, USA		

2018

"Odessey And Oracle 50th Anniversary Finale Tour" (01/02/18 – 01/14/18):

01/02-07	Moody Blues Cruise 2018, Celebrity Eclipse, Miami, Florida, USA (with many others)
01/08	Key West Theater, Key West, Florida, USA
01/09	The Parker Playhouse, Fort Lauderdale, Florida, USA
01/10	The Plaza Theatre, Orlando, Florida, USA
01/11	Capitol Theatre, Clearwater, Florida, USA
01/12	Ponte Vedra Concert Hall, Ponte Vedra Beach, Florida, USA
01/14	30A Songwriter's Festival 2018, Grand Boulevard Main Stage, Miramar Beach, Florida, USA (with many others)

"Edge Of The Rainbow" tour (02/27/18 – 10/27/18):

02/27-03/01	City Winery, New York, New York, USA (with Edward Rogers on 02/27, Bruce Sudano on 02/28, and Don DiLego on 03/01)
03/03-04	City Winery, Boston, Massachusetts, USA
03/07	The Music Of Led Zeppelin 2018, Isaac Stern Auditorium at Carnegie Hall, New York, New York, USA (they performed "Thank You")
03/08	Greenwich Odeum, East Greenwich, Rhode Island, USA (with Don DiLego)
03/09	Levon Helm Studios, Woodstock, New York, USA (with Don DiLego)
03/10	Scottish Rite Auditorium, Collingswood, New Jersey, USA (with Don DiLego)
03/11	Rams Head On Stage, Annapolis, Maryland, USA (with Edward Rogers)
03/13	The Birchmere, Alexandria, Virginia, USA (with Edward Rogers)
03/14	Rams Head On Stage, Annapolis, Maryland, USA (with Don DiLego)
03/16	City Winery, Atlanta, Georgia, USA
03/17	City Winery, Nashville, Tennessee, USA (with Don DiLego)
03/19-20	City Winery, Chicago, Illinois, USA (with Don DiLego)
03/23	The Avalon Ballroom Theatre, Niagara Falls, Ontario, Canada
03/24	Kent Stage, Kent, Ohio, USA (with Don DiLego)
03/25	The State Theatre, State College, Pennsylvania, USA (with Don DiLego)
06/02	Thornden Hall, Eastleigh
06/06	De La Warr Pavilion, Bexhill
06/08	Theatre Royal, Margate
06/09	The Sounds Of The 60's, South Woodham Ferrers Village Hall, Chelmsford
06/12	TramShed Cardiff, Cardiff, Wales
06/13	The Assembly, Royal Leamington Spa
06/14	O2 Shepherd's Bush Empire, London
06/16	The Queen's Hall, Edinburgh, Scotland
07/28	Stadstheater, Zoetermeer, Netherlands
07/29	Wassermusik 2018, Haus der Kulturen der Welt, Berlin, Germany
09/07	The Fillmore, San Francisco, California, USA (with Liz Brasher)
09/08	Mystic Theatre, Petaluma, California, USA
09/10-11	The Troubadour, West Hollywood, California, USA (with Liz Brasher)
09/13	Fremont Theater, San Luis Obispo, California, USA
09/14	KAABOO Festival 2018, Del Mar Fairgrounds, Del Mar, California, USA (with many others)
09/15	Lewis Family Playhouse, Rancho Cucamonga, California, USA
09/17	Revolution Hall, Portland, Oregon, USA
09/18	Neptune Theatre, Seattle, Washington, USA (with Liz Brasher)
09/20	The Greek Theatre, Los Angeles, California, USA (with Arcade Fire)
09/21	Ace Hotel & Swim Club, Palm Springs, California, USA
10/26	Druso, Ranica, Italy
10/27	Teatro Antoniano, Bologna, Italy

"2018 European Tour" (10/29/18 – 12/01/18):

10/29	Circus Krone, Munich, Germany
10/30	Liederhalle Hegelsaal, Stuttgart, Germany
10/31	Patronaat, Haarlem, Netherlands
11/02	Garage, Saarbrücken, Germany
11/03	Europahalle, Trier, Germany
11/04	Capitol, Offenbach am Main, Germany
11/06	Lichtburg, Essen, Germany
11/07	Magdalenazaal/ Salle de la Madeleine, Brussels, Belgium
11/09	Audimax, Regensburg, Germany
11/10	OberschwabenKlub, Ravensburg, Germany
11/12	Docks, Hamburg, Germany
11/13	Haus Auensee, Leipzig, Germany
11/14	Alter Schlachthof, Dresden, Germany
11/15	Capitol, Hanover, Germany
11/16	Admiralspalast, Berlin, Germany
11/18	Train, Aarhus, Denmark
11/20	Kulturhuset Viften, Rødovre, Denmark
11/21	Trädgår'n, Gothenburg, Sweden
11/22	USF Verftet, Bergen, Norway
11/23	Byscenen, Trondheim, Norway
11/24-25	Terminalen, Ålesund, Norway
11/27	Klubben/Fryshuset, Stockholm, Sweden
11/29	Kulttuuritalo, Helsinki, Finland
11/30	Seinäjoki Areena, Seinäjoki, Finland
12/01	Areena Oulu, Oulu, Finland

2019

01/20	Alban Arena, St. Albans (with Arc; a concert in honor of Jim Rodford)
02/09	Ruth Eckard Hall, Clearwater, Florida, USA
02/10-15	On The Blue Cruise 2019, Royal Caribbean Cruise Line - MS Mariner of the Seas, Miami, Florida, USA (with many others)
02/16	Southwest Florida Event Center, Bonita Springs, Florida, USA (with Liz Brasher)
02/17	Sunrise Theatre, Fort Pierce, Florida, USA (with Liz Brasher)
02/19	Capitol Theatre, Clearwater, Florida, USA (with Liz Brasher)
02/20	Ponte Vedra Concert Hall, Ponte Vedra Beach, Florida, USA (with Liz Brasher)
02/21	The Plaza Theatre, Orlando, Florida, USA (with Liz Brasher)
02/22	Amaturo Theater, Fort Lauderdale, Florida, USA (with Liz Brasher)
02/25	House of Blues, New Orleans, Louisiana, USA
02/27	The Heights Theater, Houston, Texas, USA (with Liz Brasher)
02/28	The Paper Tiger, San Antonio, Texas, USA
03/01	The Kessler Theater, Dallas, Texas, USA (with Liz Brasher)
03/02	Mohawk, Austin, Texas, USA
03/20-21	Boisdale of Canary Wharf, London
03/26	The Cutting Room, New York, New York, USA
03/30	The Fest For Beatles Fans 2019, Hyatt Regency Jersey City on the Hudson, Jersey City, New Jersey, USA
04/01	NBC Studios, New York, New York, USA (live appearance on "The Tonight Show Starring Jimmy Fallon")

04/15	Club Regent Casino, Winnipeg, Manitoba, Canada
04/18	Deerfoot Inn & Casino, Calgary, Alberta, Canada
05/24	Floral Pavilion Theatre, Wallasey
06/15	The Wyldes Lower Exe Farm, Bude
06/29	Rétro' C' Trop 2019, Château de Tilloloy, Tilloloy, France (with many others)
07/14	Rhythmtree Festival 2019, Three Gates Farm, Calbourne (with many others)
08/15	Waterfest 2019, Leach Amphitheater, Oshkosh, Wisconsin, USA
08/16	Woodstock 50, Watkins Glen, New York, USA (cancelled)
08/17	Rock & Roll Hall Of Fame, Cleveland, Ohio, USA
08/19-20	Ocean City Music Pier, Ocean City, New Jersey, USA (with Ninet Tayeb)
08/21	The Ridgefield Playhouse, Ridgefield, Connecticut, USA (with Ninet Tayeb)
08/23	The Cabot, Beverly, Massachusetts, USA
08/24	Tupelo Music Hall, Derry, New Hampshire, USA
08/25	Payomet Performing Arts Center, North Truro, Massachusetts, USA (with Ninet Tayeb)
08/27	Narrows Center for the Arts, Fall River, Massachusetts, USA (with Ninet Tayeb)
08/28	GRAMMY Museum Experience at The Prudential Center, Newark, New Jersey, USA
08/29	Bottle & Cork, Dewey Beach, Delaware, USA (with Ninet Tayeb)

US tour: Something Great From '68 (including all of "Odessey And Oracle") (with Brian Wilson, Al Jardine, and Blondie Chaplin) (08/31/18 – 09/29/19):

08/31	The Joint at Hard Rock Hotel, Las Vegas, Nevada, USA
09/01	Fantasy Springs Resort Casino, Indio, California, USA
09/06	Comerica Theatre, Phoenix, Arizona, USA
09/07	Starlight Theater, Pala, California, USA
09/08	Arlington Theatre, Santa Barbara, California, USA
09/12	Greek Theatre, Los Angeles, California, USA
09/13	Fox Theater, Oakland, California, USA
09/14	Ironstone Amphitheatre, Murphys, California, USA
09/16	Paramount Theatre, Seattle, Washington, USA
09/17	Arlene Schnitzer Concert Hall, Portland, Oregon, USA
09/19	Sandy Amphitheater, Sandy City, Utah, USA
09/20	Paramount Theatre, Denver, Colorado, USA
09/22	Riverside Theater, Milwaukee, Wisconsin, USA
09/23	Taft Theatre, Cincinnati, Ohio, USA
09/24	Royal Oak Music Theatre, Royal Oak, Michigan, USA
09/26	Beacon Theatre, New York, New York, USA
09/27	Palace Theater, Waterbury, Connecticut, USA
09/28	Tower Theatre, Upper Darby, Pennsylvania, USA
09/29	Robert E. Parilla Performing Arts Center, Rockville, Maryland, USA
12/13	Playa Club, Corunna, Spain
12/15	Independance Club (sic), Madrid, Spain
12/16	Sala BBK, Bilbao, Spain

2020
(all shows listed were cancelled due to COVID-19):

03/19	St. Albans Museum, St. Albans (museum exhibit and Q&A)
03/28-31	Flower Power Cruise, Miami, Florida, USA
04/01-08	On The Blue Cruise, Miami, Florida, USA (with Bruce Sudano)
04/09	Manship Theatre, Baton Rouge, Louisiana, USA (with Bruce Sudano)
04/10	Iron City, Birmingham, Alabama, USA
04/11	Hard Rock Live, Biloxi, Mississippi, USA
04/15	Club Regent Event Centre, Winnipeg, Manitoba, Canada
04/17	The Arden Theatre, St. Albert, Alberta, Canada
04/18	Deerfoot Inn & Casino, Calgrary, Alberta, Canada
04/20	Lougheed Performing Arts Centre, Camrose, Alberta, Canada
04/21	Esplanade Arts & Heritage Center, Medicine Hat, Alberta, Canada
04/22	Key City Theatre, Cranbrook, British Columbia, Canada
04/24	Commodore Ballroom, Vancouver, British Columbia, Canada
04/25	Alix Goolden Performance Hall, Victoria, British Columbia, Canada (cancelled on this date and its rescheduled date of 09/17/20, and rescheduled again to 07/13/22)
05/14-15	Harpenden Public Halls, Harpenden
05/16	High House Gardens, Congham
05/18	The Stables, Wavendon
05/19	The Tivoli Theatre, Dorset
05/27	Terminalen Byscene, Alesund, Norway
05/29	Byscenen, Trondheim, Norway
05/31	Ole Bull Scene, Bergen, Vestland, Norway
06/01	Folken Stavanger, Rogaland, Norway
06/02	Rockefeller Music Hall, Oslo, Norway
06/04	Råda Rum, Mölnlycke, Sweden
06/05	Kulturbolaget, Malmo, Sweden
09/16	Commodore Ballroom, Vancouver, British Columbia, Canada
09/17	Alix Goolden Performance Hall, Victoria, British Columbia, Canada
09/19	Deerfoot Inn & Casino, Calgary, Alberta, Canada
09/25	Club Regent Event Centre, Winnipeg, Alberta, Canada
10/09	Iron City, Birmingham, Alabama, USA
10/10	Hard Rock Café Biloxi, Biloxi, Mississippi, USA
10/11	Manship Theatre, Baton Rouge, Louisiana, USA (with Bruce Sudano)

2021
(all UK and Danish shows listed below were postponed due to COVID-19) – the original plan was to reschedule everything in early 2022, but these shows were moved until early 2023:

02/11-12	Harpenden Public Halls, Harpenden
02/13-14	Trading Boundaries, Fletching
02/16	The Stables, Wavendon
02/18	Oran Mor, Glasgow, Scotland
02/19	Sage Gateshead, Gateshead
02/20	Floral Pavilion, New Brighton, Wirral (Merseyside)
02/25	The Fleece, Bristol
02/26	Exmouth Pavilion, Exmouth, Devon
02/27	Ystradgynlais Welfare Hall, Ystradgynlais (near Swansea), Wales
02/28	Pontardawe Arts Centre, Pontardawe, Wales
03/04	Under The Bridge, London
03/05	The Tivoli Theatre, Wimborne Minster
03/06	The Brewhouse Theatre & Arts Centre, Taunton
06/05	Kun For Forrykte Festival, Stubbekøbing, Denmark (cancelled)

To create a "worldwide tour in one night," The Zombies created the following event:

09/18	Studio 2, Abbey Road Studios, London (livestream concert billed as "The Zombies: Live From Studio Two – A Worldwide Streaming Event From Abbey Road")

Set list: Moving On; I Want You Back Again; Edge Of The Rainbow; I Love You; Say You Don't Mind; Different Game (live debut; with string quartet); You Could Be My Love (live debut; with string quartet); I Want To Fly (with string quartet); Tell Her No; Care Of Cell 44; This Will Be Our Year; I Want Her She Wants Me; Time Of The Season; Merry Go Round; Runaway; Hold Your Head Up; She's Not There; Encore: The Way I Feel Inside

2022

03/28-30	Flower Power Cruise, Celebrity Cruises – Celebrity Summit, Miami, Florida, USA (the band then got off the ship, and the cruise went until 04/04/22)

"Life Is A Merry-Go-Round" tour (04/01/22 – 10/04/22):

04/01	The Plaza Theatre, Orlando, Florida, USA (with Bruce Sudano)
04/02	Sunrise Theatre, Fort Pierce, Florida, USA (with Bruce Sudano)
04/03	Lillian S. Wells Hall at The Parker, Fort Lauderdale, Florida, USA (with Bruce Sudano)
04/05	The Nancy and David Bilheimer Capitol Theatre, Clearwater, Florida, USA (with Bruce Sudano)
04/06	Ponte Vedra Concert Hall, Ponde Vedra Beach, Florida, USA (with Bruce Sudano)
04/07	Center Stage, Atlanta, Georgia, USA (with Bruce Sudano)
04/09	Manship Theatre, Baton Rouge, Louisiana, USA (with Bruce Sudano)
04/10	Iron City, Birmingham, Alabama, USA (with Bruce Sudano)
04/13	Ryman Auditorium, Nashville, Tennessee, USA (with Bruce Sudano)
04/14	Bijou Theatre, Knoxville, Tennessee, USA
04/16	Webster Hall, New York, New York, USA
04/18	The Birchmere, Alexandria, Virginia, USA (with Jesse Lynn Madera)
04/19	Maryland Hall for the Creative Arts, Annapolis, Maryland, USA
04/20	Colonial Theatre, Phoenixville, Pennsylvania, USA
04/22	Tarrytown Music Hall, Tarrytown, New York, USA
04/23	The Music Box at The Borgata, Atlantic City, New Jersey, USA
04/24	Suffolk Theater, Riverhead, New York, USA
04/26	Academy of Music Theatre, Northampton, Massachusetts, USA
04/27	The Capitol Center for the Arts, Concord, New Hampshire, USA
04/29	The Cabot, Beverly, Massachusetts, USA (with Jesse Lynn Madera)
04/30	Ridgefield Playhouse, Ridgefield, Connecticut, USA
05/01	Narrows Center for the Arts, Fall River, Massachusetts, USA

At the end of May 2022, Colin Blunstone and Rod Argent tested positive for COVID-19. Some dates were cancelled and/or postponed. The tour resumed on 06/24/22.

06/19	The Chapel, San Francisco, California, USA (cancelled due to COVID-19)
06/21	Empire Theatre, Belleville, Ontario, Canada (cancelled due to COVID-19; with Altameda)
06/22	Living Arts Centre, Mississauga, Ontario, Canada (cancelled due to COVID-19; with Altameda)
06/24	Penn's Peak, Jim Thorpe, Pennsylvania, USA (tour resumed; with Altameda)
06/25	Point of the Bluff Vineyards, Hammondsport, New York, USA (with Altameda)
06/26	Carnegie Music Hall of Homestead, Munhall, Pennsylvania, USA (with Altameda)
06/28	Kent Stage, Kent, Ohio, USA (with Altameda)
06/30	Ludlow Garage Cincinnati, Cincinnati, Ohio, USA (with Altameda)
07/01	Old Town School of Folk Music, Chicago, Illinois, USA (with Altameda)
07/02	Codfish Hollow Barnstormers, Maquoketa, Iowa, USA (with Altameda)
07/03	Barrymore Theatre, Madison, Wisconsin, USA (with Altameda)
07/05	First Avenue, Minneapolis, Minnesota, USA (with Altameda)
07/07	Club Regent Casino, Winnipeg, Manitoba, Canada
07/09	Deerfoot Inn & Casino, Calgary, Alberta, Canada
07/11	The Arden Theatre, St. Albert, Alberta, Canada
07/13	Alix Goolden Performance Hall, Victoria, British Columbia, Canada (rescheduled from 04/25/20)
07/14	Commodore Ballroom, Vancouver, British Columbia, Canada (with Altameda)
07/15	The Historic Everett Theatre, Everett, Washington, USA
07/16	Aladdin Theater, Portland, Oregon, USA
07/18-19	The Chapel. San Francisco, California, USA
07/21	Pappy & Harriet's Pioneertown Palace, Pioneertown, California, USA (livestream concert; with Rooney)
07/22	Libbey Bowl, Ojai, California, USA
07/23	The Fonda Theatre, Los Angeles, California, USA
07/24	Belly Up Tavern, Solana Beach, California, USA
07/26	Rialto Theatre, Tucson, Arizona, USA
07/28-30	The Egyptian Theatre, Park City, Utah, USA
09/02	Kulturbolaget, Malmo, Sweden
09/03	Rada Rum, Mölnlycke, Sweden
09/04	Nalen, Stockholm, Stockholm, Sweden
09/06	Rockefeller Music Hall, Oslo, Oslo, Norway
09/07	Byscenen, Trondheim, Trøndelag, Norway
09/08	Terminalen Byscene, Alesund, Norway
09/10	USF Verftet, Bergen, Vestland, Norway
09/11	Folken Stavanger, Rogaland, Norway
09/13	Kulturvaerftet, Helsingor, Denmark
09/14	Fabrik, Worbis, Germany
09/16	Passionskirche, Berlin, Germany
09/17	Kulturkirche, Neuruppin, Germany
09/18	Harmonie, Bonn, North Rhine-Westphalia, Germany
09/20	Posthof, Linz, Upper Austria, Austria
09/22	Airport Obertraubling, Regensburg, Bavaria, Germany
09/23	Colos-Saal, A-Burg, Bavaria, Germany
09/24	Capitol Offenbach, Hesse, Germany
09/25	Theater Heerlen, Heerlen, Limburg, Netherlands
09/27	Concertgebouw Amsterdam, North Holland, Netherlands
09/28	013, Tilburg, North Brabant, Netherlands
09/29	Stadsschouwburg de Harmonie, Leeuwarden, Friesland, Netherlands
09/30	CCXL Theater, Vlissingen, Netherlands
10/02	Grote Zaal, Utrecht, Utrecht, Netherlands
10/03	AMARE, The Hague, Netherlands
10/04	Theater de Spiegel, Zwolle, Overijssel, Netherlands

2023

"The Invaders Return Tour" (04/05/23 – 05/06/23):

04/05	Tivoli Theatre, Wimborne (with Bruce Sudano)
04/06	Exmouth Pavilion, Exmouth (with Bruce Sudano)
04/07-09	Trading Boundaries, Fletching (with Bruce Sudano)

04/12	Pontardawe Art, Pontardawe, Wales
04/13	The Fleece, Bristol
04/14	Under The Bridge, London
04/15	The Apex, Bury St. Edmunds (with Rogers & Butler)
04/18	Studio 3 at Epic Studios, Norwich
04/19	Spa Pavilion Theatre, Felixstowe (with Bruce Sudano)
04/20-21	The Eric Morecambe Centre, Harpenden (with Rogers & Butler)
04/23-24	Backstage @ The Green Hotel, Kinross, Scotland
04/26	Òran Mór, Glasgow, Scotland (with Bruce Sudano)
04/27	Picturedrome, Holmfirth (with Bruce Sudano)
04/28	The Met Arts Centre, Bury (with Rogers & Butler)
04/29	Brewhouse Theatre, Taunton (with Rogers & Butler)
05/03	ARC, Stockton-on-Tees (with Bruce Sudano)
05/04	Old Fire Station, Cumbria (with Bruce Sudano)
05/05	Floral Pavilion Theatre & Blue Lounge, New Brighton (rescheduled from 02/26/22)
05/06	The Stables, Wavendon (a charity performance; with Rogers & Butler)

ZOMBIES GET 1ST GOLD DISK

NEW YORK—The Zombies have been awarded their first gold record for their Date single "Time of the Season." The single is a cut from the Zombies' Date LP, "Time of the Season"/"Odyssey and Oracle." The gold record award signifies that the single has sold over one million copies as certified by the Record Industry Assn. of America.

time of the season

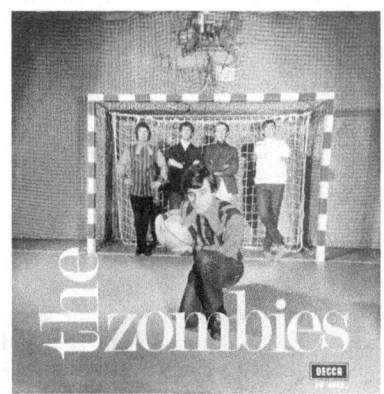